B"H

Compliments of
Valley Chabad

In appreciation for your
generous partnership
Thank You!

Wishing you a good and sweet year

Rabbi Dov & Hindy Drizin
Rosh Hashanah 2018 - 5779

Daily Wisdom

DAILY WISDOM

Inspiring Insights on the Torah Portion
from the Lubavitcher Rebbe

Rabbi Menachem M. Schneerson

זצוקללה"ה נבג"מ זי"ע

TRANSLATED AND ADAPTED BY
Rabbi Moshe Wisnefsky

KEHOT PUBLICATION SOCIETY
770 Eastern Parkway, Brooklyn, NY 11213

CHABAD HOUSE
PUBLICATIONS

DAILY WISDOM
Inspiring Insights on the Torah Portion
from the Lubavitcher Rebbe

Copyright © 2014–2017 by
CHABAD HOUSE PUBLICATIONS
Los Angeles, CA 90024
info@chabadhousepublications.org
www.chabadhousepublications.org

1st standard edition, June 2014 (reprinted August 2014, July 2015, September 2017)
1st compact edition, November 2014 (reprinted January 2015,
March 2015, July 2015, March 2016, September 2017)

Hebrew translation (להחיות את היום) – 1st edition, June 2014

French translation (*Sagesse au Quotidien*) – 1st compact
edition, December 2015 (reprinted April 2016)

Spanish translation (*Sabiduría Diaria*) – 1st standard edition, February 2017;
1st compact edition, March 2016 (reprinted April 2016, June 2016)

Russian translation (Мудрость на каждый день) – 1st compact edition, August 2016

Published by
KEHOT PUBLICATION SOCIETY
770 Eastern Parkway, Brooklyn, NY 11213
+1-718-774-4000 / Fax +1-718-774-2718
editor@kehot.com

ORDER DEPARTMENT:
291 Kingston Avenue, Brooklyn, NY 11213
+1-718-778-0226 / Fax +1-718-778-4148
www.kehot.com

Typesetting by Raphaël Freeman, Renana Typesetting

ISBN: 978-0-8266-0095-0

Manufactured in the United States of America

A PROJECT OF Chabad House Publications

DIRECTOR & GENERAL EDITOR Rabbi Chaim Nochum Cunin

EDITOR IN CHIEF Rabbi Moshe Yaakov Wisnefsky

RABBINIC CONSULTANTS
Rabbi Yosef Friedman
Rabbi Dovid Olidort
Rabbi Aaron Leib Raskin
Rabbi Asi Spiegel
Rabbi Avraham D. Vaisfiche

CHIEF COPY EDITOR Richard (Reuven) Macales

PROOFREADING Sheina Malka Tannenbaum

COVER ART Yossi Belkin

DESIGN & LAYOUT Raphaël Freeman, Renana Typesetting

SPECIAL THANKS TO Rabbi Boruch Shlomo Eliyohu Cunin,
Rabbi Yehuda Krinsky, Rabbis Avraham Tsvi
Beuthner, Danny Cohen, Levi Yitzchak Cunin, Yosef
Cunin, Zushe Cunin, Menachem Even-Israel, Michoel
Goldman, Yankel Kagan, Baruch Kaplan, Betzalel
Lifshitz, Shalom Lipskar, Zalman Lipskar, Chaim Marcus,
Yosef Marcus, Abi Michaan, Yitzchak Michaan, Moshe
Pinson, Ezzy Rappaport, Leizer Shemtov, Moshe Shilat,
Dov Wagner, and Aryeh Wuensch;

Asher David Milstein, Tova Cunin, Matti Leshem,
Nir Menusi, David Suissa, and the dedicated staff of
Kehot Publication Society.

Preface

WITH GRATITUDE TO G-D, IN CONNECTION WITH THE 20TH *yahrtzeit* since the passing of the Lubavitcher Rebbe, Rabbi Menachem M. Schneerson, of righteous memory, we are pleased to present to the public the present anthology of the Rebbe's teachings on each day's section of the weekly Torah reading. By studying the appropriate selection each day, the reader can follow the daily course of Torah-study and be inspired by the Rebbe's teachings on a daily basis.

The Rebbe stresses in his teachings that the world as we know it today is incomplete and broken; that our mission is to correct and refine this world, thereby hastening the coming of Mashiach, who will usher in the final Redemption. The inner meaning of these concepts and how they are rooted in the Torah is to be found in the teachings presented in this book.

It is our hope that through studying the Rebbe's teachings, we will very soon merit the fulfillment of our ultimate goal, the arrival of the immediate redemption.

CHABAD HOUSE PUBLICATIONS

3 TAMUZ 5774

Contents

Preface   ix

Introduction   xv

GENESIS

Bereishit: Creation, Adam and Eve, and Humanity's Early
    History   3

Noach: Noah, the Flood, and Beyond   11

Lech Lecha: Abraham's Calling   19

Vayeira: Founder of the Faith   27

Chayei Sarah: The Burial of Sarah and the Marriage of
    Isaac and Rebecca   35

Toledot: Isaac, Jacob, and Esau   43

Vayeitzei: Jacob in Aram   51

Vayishlach: Jacob in Canaan   59

Vayeishev: Joseph in Egypt   67

Mikeitz: Joseph the Viceroy   75

Vayigash: Jacob and Joseph Reunited   83

Vaichi: The Close of the Patriarchal Era   91

EXODUS

Shemot: Slavery   101

Va'eira: The First Seven Plagues   109

Bo: The Last Three Plagues; The Exodus   117

Beshalach: The Splitting of the Sea   125

Yitro: The Giving of the Torah   133

Mishpatim: Laws   141

Terumah: The Tabernacle   149

Tetzaveh: The Priests   157

Tisa: The Golden Calf   165

Vayakheil: Constructing the Tabernacle   173

Pekudei: Erecting the Tabernacle   181

LEVITICUS

Vayikra: Sacrifices   191

Tzav: Details of the Sacrifices; The Installation Rites   199

Shemini: The Conclusion of the Installation Rites; Kashrut 207

Tazri'a: Tzara'at   215

Metzora: Purification from *Tzara'at*   223

Acharei: Yom Kippur   231

Kedoshim: Holiness   239

Emor: The Priesthood; The Festivals   247

Behar: The Sabbatical and Jubilee Years   255

Bechukotai: Reward and Corrective Punishment; Donations 263

NUMBERS

Bemidbar: The Jewish Army   273

Naso: Preparations for the Journey   281

Beha'alotecha: The Journey Begins   289

Shelach: Scouting Out the Land   297

Korach: Mutiny   305

Chukat: Final Journeys in the Desert   313

Balak: Curses into Blessings   321

Pinechas: Preparing for Conquest   329

Matot: Facing Challenges   337

Mas'ei: Journeys   345

DEUTERONOMY

Devarim: Constructive Rebuke   355

Va'etchanan: The Foundations of Judaism   363

Eikev: Appreciation and Love   371

Re'eih: Devotion to G-d   379

Shofetim: Leaders   387

Teitzei: Expanding Divine Consciousness   395

Tavo: Entering the Covenant   403

Nitzavim: Sealing the Covenant   411

Vayeilech: Recording and Sealing the Covenant   419

Ha'azinu: The Poem of Testimony   427

Vezot Haberachah: The Final Blessing   435

Appendix: The Jewish Calendar   443

Annual Torah Study Calendar   444

Bibliography   447

Index   449

Introduction

JEWISH TRADITION, OVER 3,000 YEARS OLD, INFORMS US THAT G-d not only created the universe but taught His creatures how to live in it. This Divine teaching is the Torah, G-d's "user's manual" for the world.

The word *Torah* in Hebrew means "instruction." In its broadest sense, it refers to either the totality or any part of G-d's teachings. Specifically, however, it refers to the teachings that G-d communicated to humanity through Moses. These teachings took the form of a written document (the "Five Books of Moses": Genesis, Exodus, Leviticus, Numbers, and Deuteronomy) and its interpretation (the "Oral Torah").[1]

After Moses' death, the Jewish people's successes and failures in fulfilling the teachings of the Torah in their land resulted in the expansion of the Written Torah to include books of the Prophets[2]

1. The Oral Torah was also eventually written down, and is preserved principally in the Talmud and Midrashim. The *Talmud* ("learning") consists of the *Mishnah* ("repetition"), the basic compendium of Jewish law and lore, recorded by Rabbi Yehudah the Prince in the second century CE, and the *Gemara* ("completion"), which elucidates the Mishnah with the help of the extra-mishnaic material Rabbi Yehudah did not include in the Mishnah, and which includes many more teachings. The process of elucidating the Mishnah took place both in the academies of the Land of Israel and those of Babylonia, and thus there are two Talmuds: the Jerusalem Talmud and the Babylonian Talmud. A *Midrash* ("exegesis") is a compilation of teachings derived by comparing and contrasting Scriptural passages. There are both legal and homiletic Midrashim. The Babylonian Talmud includes much midrashic material, while the midrashic teachings of the academies of the Land of Israel are recorded separately, in the *Midrash Rabbah* series.

2. Comprising the books of Joshua, Judges, Samuel, Kings, Isaiah, Jeremiah, Ezekiel, Hosea, Joel, Amos, Obadiah, Jonah, Micah, Nahum, Habakkuk, Zephaniah, Haggai, Zechariah, and Malachi.

(*Nevi'im*) and the Writings (*Ketuvvim*).³ Nonetheless, the Five Books of Moses remain the primary repository of G-d's teachings. They are complete by themselves, containing all the legal and homiletical material necessary for humanity to live as G-d intends. The Prophets and Writings form an essential complement to the Five Books, but add no *new* legal or philosophical content.⁴

INASMUCH AS THE TORAH EMBODIES G-D'S INSTRUCTIONS concerning how we are to live our lives, it is essential for everyone to be conversant in the Torah's text and teachings. Moses instituted the practice of reading publicly from a Torah scroll on Sabbath and Festival mornings as well as on Monday and Thursday mornings.⁵ In order to complete the reading of the whole Torah in a year, the Torah is divided into 54 sections. Since the Jewish calendar comprises both regular years (of 12 months) and leap years (of 13 months), two sections are sometimes read on the same Sabbath. Moses further instituted that the Torah reading on the Sabbath be divided among seven people. For this purpose, each of the 54 sections were divided into seven sub-sections.

THE TEACHINGS OF THE CHASIDIC MOVEMENT, FOUNDED BY Rabbi Yisrael Ba'al Shem Tov (1698–1760), revealed how the Torah describes the connection between G-d and creation in general and each individual in particular. In this spirit, the founder of the Chabad branch of Chasidism, Rabbi Shneur Zalman of Lyadi (1745–1812) once told his followers to "live with the times," by which he meant to live throughout the year with the section

---

3. Comprising the books of Psalms, Proverbs, Job, The Song of Songs, Ruth, Lamentations, Ecclesiastes, Esther, Daniel, Ezra-Nehemiah, and Chronicles.

4. See *Torah Or* 60a–d. It is therefore taught that "had the Jewish people never sinned, there would have been no need for any books other than the Five Books of Moses and the Book of Joshua" (*Nedarim* 22b).

5. *Soferim* 10:1–2; *Megilah* 3:6; *Bava Kama* 82a; *Megilah* 31b; *Yerushalmi Megilah* 4:5; *Mishneh Torah, Tefilah* 12:1; *Kesef Mishneh ad loc.* The custom of reading the beginning of the following Sabbath morning's reading on the Sabbath afternoon was instituted by Ezra (ibid.).

of the Torah that is studied at the time.[6] Thus, the law and lore of the Torah is studied not only as legal and historical information, but also personally, as if we are experiencing the spiritual growth processes implicit in them. In this way, the Torah becomes our own personal story; the chronicle of our developing relationship with G-d. Rabbi Shneur Zalman also instituted the practice of studying each day the corresponding sub-section of the weekly Torah section.[7] In this context, Rabbi Shneur Zalman's exhortation to "live with the times" came to mean not only living with the Torah-section of the week but with the sub-section of the day.

In addition to continuing to develop the teachings of his predecessors, the seventh Lubavitcher Rebbe,[8] Rabbi Menachem Mendel Schneerson, devoted considerable time to elucidating both the basic meaning of the Torah's text and the Torah's inner lessons. In his public discourses, his private audiences, and his voluminous correspondence, spread over the 44 years of his public leadership, the Rebbe demonstrated how the Torah's teachings are eternally relevant and applicable to every aspect of life, even those that have come to existence only in modern times.

THIS BOOK CONTAINS A CONCISE INSIGHT FROM TEACHINGS of the Rebbe or his predecessors for each of the seven sub-sections of the 54 sections of the Torah – one for each day of the week, for the full year of Torah study. Of course, in order to know which insight to read for any given day, the reader will need know what section of the Torah is being studied that week. We have provided a calendar for this purpose on p. 444; in addition, any Jewish calendar, as well as numerous online resources, can provide this information.

Thus, the impact of the insights presented in this book will be felt to the greatest extent when the reader reads each insight on

---

6. *Sefer HaSichot 5702*, pp. 29–30; *HaYom Yom*, 2 Cheshvan.
7. *Sefer HaSichot 5702*, p. 27; *HaYom Yom*, 19 Tevet.
8. Lubavitch is the name of the town in White Russia where the Chabad movement flourished. The various branches of the Chasidic movement are usually known by the name of the locale in which they developed.

the day it is meant to be read, rather than by reading the book, say, cover to cover, or by browsing through it. Since the Rebbe emphasized certain key lessons repeatedly, seeing them alluded to over and over again in the Torah, these lessons are also highlighted numerous times throughout this book.

We have prefaced each weekly section with a short summary of the entire section, and each daily sub-section with a synopsis of the content of the Torah's narrative leading up to the verse being expounded. For the chronology provided in these synopses, we have used the traditional Jewish reckoning of time, i.e., from the creation of the world, and the Jewish months. A table of these months and their approximate correspondence to Gregorian months is given in the appendix.

We have given the sources for each insight in published Chasidic texts. We should point out, however, that in many cases we have fleshed out the original sources with material culled from other sources in the Rebbe's teachings.[9] Also, we have presented the Rebbe's or his predecessors' teachings often in a somewhat "digested" form, i.e., the way the teachings have spoken to us and how we think they could speak to the reader. Whenever anyone attempts to convey another person's thoughts in his own words, he runs the risk of inadvertently distorting them; we hope this has been minimal in our case.

Our goal of providing insights that would be accessible to the widest possible readership has precluded many of the Rebbe's profound insights, simply because doing them justice would have required more space. We hope that the glimpse that this work provides will inspire the reader to seek further and deeper knowledge of the Rebbe's empowering teachings.

We further hope that this work inspires its readers to live with

---

9. In accordance with the Talmudic sages' statement that "the teachings of the Torah are poor in their place but enriched in another place" (*Yerushalmi Rosh HaShanah* 3:5).

the Torah's ultimate message, as highlighted by the Rebbe: to actualize the Messianic imperative to make this world into G-d's ultimate home.

THE EDITORIAL STAFF

GENESIS

Bereishit

Creation, Adam and Eve, and Humanity's Early History
Genesis 1:1–6:8

THE NAME OF THE FIRST SECTION OF THE BOOK OF GENESIS
is taken from its first words, "In the beginning" (*Bereishit*, in
Hebrew), and opens with G-d's creation of the world. Humanity
was created with the ability to choose between good and evil,
but the first humans, Adam and Eve, misused this gift, launching
humanity onto a path of increasing moral degeneration. Eventually, it became necessary to establish a new order and give the
world a fresh start.

FIRST READING
Genesis 1:1–2:3

The Torah begins with its account of how G-d created the world in six days.

The Purpose of Creation

בְּרֵאשִׁית בָּרָא אֱלֹקִים אֵת הַשָּׁמַיִם וְאֵת הָאָרֶץ: (בראשית א, א)

In the beginning of G-d's creation of heaven and earth...

We are taught in the Midrash that G-d created the world as a "lower realm" – i.e., a realm initially devoid of Divine consciousness, and even opposed to it – intending that humanity fill the world with Divine consciousness. The tool that G-d gave humanity in order to enable it to perform this feat is the Torah. The drama of creation thus required three elements: the world, the human race, and the Torah, serving respectively as the setting, the actors, and the script.

G-d gave humanity the free choice to ignore Him and His intentions for the world, and this is exactly what the early generations did. In keeping with His decision to grant free choice, G-d obliged, so to speak, by removing His revelation from the world, hiding progressively further behind the façade of nature.

In response to most of humanity's choice to ignore Him, G-d implemented His "contingency plan": He took the one family that continued to nurture the original ideal of Divine consciousness and forged them into a nation – the Jewish people – with whom He then entrusted the mission of fulfilling His original purpose for creation. The Jewish people would both serve as an inspiration and example for the rest of humanity and encourage them to play their role in His scheme for transforming the world into His home. The Book of Genesis is the chronicle of how the creation of the Jewish people became necessary and how it came to be.[1]

1. *Likutei Sichot*, vol. 5, pp. 1–15; vol. 10, pp. 3–6; *Yom Tov shel Rosh HaShanah 5666*, pp. 1–9.

SECOND READING

Genesis 2:4–2:19

On the first day, the world was created as a core of solid matter submerged entirely in water. Light was created later on the first day, and the atmosphere on the second day. On the third day, the dry land rose above sea level. The heavenly bodies were placed in outer space on the fourth day, the sea animals populated the oceans on the fifth day, and the land animals and first humans populated the dry land on the sixth day. On the seventh day, G-d "rested" from creating. Unlike the way He created the other creatures, G-d created the first human in two stages: He first made a lifeless body, into which He then "blew" the human soul.

The Divine Soul

וַיִּיצֶר ה' אֱלֹקִים אֶת הָאָדָם עָפָר מִן הָאֲדָמָה וַיִּפַּח
בְּאַפָּיו נִשְׁמַת חַיִּים וְגוֹ': (בראשית ב, ז)

**G-d formed the human out of the dust of the
ground and blew into his nostrils a soul of life.**

By "blowing" the soul into the body, G-d indicated that our soul originates deeper "within" Him than does the rest of creation. This emphasizes the fact that we are the primary purpose of Creation, whereas everything else is secondary.

Our Divine soul is a spark of G-d. Therefore, the soul can never lose its intrinsic connection with G-d. Our challenge is to ensure that this connection remain manifested within our physical being. Just as when one blows, the air can reach its destination only if there are no physical obstructions, so too, the more we free our lives of spiritual "sludge" – harmful or negative thoughts, words, or deeds – the more our G-dly souls can shine freely.[2]

2. *Tanya*, chapter 2; *Igeret HaTeshuvah*, chapters 4–5.

THIRD READING
Genesis 2:20–3:21

The first human couple lived in the Garden of Eden, where they were meant to enjoy G-d's creation – including their own sensuality – innocently, as a means toward enhancing their awareness of G-d and His goodness. However, they succumbed to the temptation to increase their self-awareness (as personified by the primordial snake) by eating the forbidden fruit of the Tree of Knowledge, and thereby lost their native innocence.

Modesty and Innocence

וַיִּהְיוּ שְׁנֵיהֶם עֲרוּמִּים הָאָדָם וְאִשְׁתּוֹ וְלֹא יִתְבֹּשָׁשׁוּ: (בראשית ב, כה)

**The two of them were naked – the man
and his wife – and felt no shame.**

Adam and Eve did not possess any sense of self-centeredness before they ate the forbidden fruit. They therefore ate, for example, not in order to satisfy any lust for the taste of the food but to satisfy their hunger and enjoy the goodness G-d had given them. Similarly, they engaged in marital relations not to satisfy any egocentric lust for sensual delight but to unite with each other, to enjoy the goodness G-d had given them, and to have children.

It was only when they acquired the subjective knowledge of good and evil and its accompanying sense of self-centeredness – by eating the forbidden fruit – that they realized that sensuality could be something pursued for personal pleasure. Therefore, of all their naked limbs, they became ashamed first and foremost of their reproductive organs, and tried to lessen their power over human consciousness by keeping them covered.

It is thus through modesty in attire and behavior that we can regain our innate human innocence and elevate our sensual drives to the pristine purity of Adam and Eve's in the Garden of Eden.[3]

3. *Likutei Sichot*, vol. 3, p. 893.

FOURTH READING

Genesis 3:22–4:18

Had they repented properly, Adam and Eve would have been forgiven and been allowed to remain in the Garden of Eden. But since they did not rise to the occasion, they were banished from it. Their firstborn child, Cain, was presented with a similar opportunity after killing his brother Abel when G-d accepted Abel's offering but not Cain's.

Learning from Failures

הֲלוֹא אִם תֵּיטִיב שְׂאֵת וגו' (בראשית ד, ז)

[G-d told Cain,] "If you improve, you will be forgiven."

Cain's true failure was that he did not learn from G-d's positive response to Abel, who had offered up the choicest of his animals. Had Cain presented a second offering, this time from the choicest of his crop, G-d would have forgiven him and accepted it. G-d here tried to teach him that if an individual learns from his errors, his slate can be wiped clean. However, Cain refused to admit his error. Convinced of the rightness of his action, he felt that if Abel were eliminated, his own view would necessarily prevail.

Our challenge, as well, is to learn from our failures, rather than to stubbornly refuse to admit them and even rationalize them. By learning from our failures, we can transform every one of them into an impetus for further spiritual growth.[4]

4. *Likutei Sichot*, vol. 15, p. 22.

FIFTH READING

Genesis 4:19–22

Although he did not mend his ways completely, Cain did express some degree of remorse for having killed his brother Abel. G-d therefore postponed Cain's punishment for seven generations in order to give his descendants further opportunity to repent. Yet again, this opportunity was spurned, as demonstrated by the behavior of Cain's descendant Lemech.

Femininity

וַיִּקַּח לוֹ לֶמֶךְ שְׁתֵּי נָשִׁים וגו': (בראשית ד, יט)

Lemech married two women.

By Lemech's time, society had morally degenerated to the point that men were objectifying female beauty and depersonalizing women. It became customary for men to marry one woman for her beauty and a second woman for the purpose of procreation. The first wife would be given a contraceptive so that pregnancy and childbirth not mar her appearance. The husband would spend his time chiefly with her, ignoring his second wife.

Needless to say, this objectification of women goes against G-d's intention. G-d created the world in such a way that all relationships consist of someone or something acting as a giver and someone or something else acting as the receiver. Both have to take the other into consideration. This is possible only because there is no absolute separation between the "giver" (male) and "receiver" (female) aspects of the relationship: Men have their female aspects and women have their male aspects. As such, each of us can and should appreciate how our spouse complements us, realizing that we have to combine our particular strengths in order to fulfill G-d's purpose, cherishing the contributions we each can make toward our common purpose.[5]

5. *Torah Or* 5a–b.

SIXTH READING
Genesis 4:23–5:24

In addition to his sons Cain and Abel, Adam and Eve had a third son, Seth. One of Seth's fifth-generation descendants was Enoch, who resisted the degeneration into which the rest of humanity was sinking, and lived a righteous life.

The Largeness of Small Things

וַיִּתְהַלֵּךְ חֲנוֹךְ אֶת הָאֱלֹקִים וְגו': (בראשית ה, כב)

Enoch walked with G-d.

Enoch was a shoemaker, yet, because of his holiness, his mundane occupation did not distract him from his service of G-d. On the contrary, we are taught that with every stitch he brought about a further degree of harmony within the spiritual spheres.

We, too, on our own level, can follow in Enoch's footsteps: We can so infuse our earthly activities with holy intentions that can positively influence the heavens.[6]

SEVENTH READING
Genesis 5:25–6:8

Despite Enoch's positive example, humanity continued in its downward spiral of moral degeneration. Eventually, G-d saw that the only remedy was to give humanity a fresh start.

The Power of Speech

וַיַּרְא ה' כִּי רַבָּה רָעַת הָאָדָם וגו': (בראשית ו, ה)

G-d saw how great was humanity's wickedness.

When G-d saw humanity's moral state, He did not at first express His decision to wipe out the world with a flood. Only after He formulated a way for humanity to survive (i.e., through Noah) did He pronounce His decision. This was because once an idea descends from thought into speech, its reality becomes more concrete and therefore it becomes harder to revoke.

Similarly, we should always be aware of the awesome power of speech: By articulating a negative assessment of someone – even if they are unaware that we have done so! – we have unwittingly reinforced their negative traits and made it harder for them to rid themselves of them.

We should therefore think twice before uttering a negative judgment about anyone; on the contrary, we should always seek to make positive, constructive comments about others. Doing so reinforces their positive traits and raises them to greater spiritual heights.[7]

---

7. *Likutei Sichot*, vol. 15, p. 29 ff.

Noach

Noah, the Flood, and Beyond

Genesis 6:9–11:32

THE SECOND SECTION OF THE BOOK OF GENESIS IS NAMED after its central character, Noah (*Noach* in Hebrew), and begins with the account of the great Flood that washed the world clean of the depravity and degeneration into which humanity had sunk since the creation of the world. This is followed by the account of how the world was divided up between Noah's sons, the dispersion of humanity brought about by the incident of the Tower of Babel, and the prelude to the upcoming sections' account of humanity's next great hero, Abraham.

FIRST READING

Genesis 6:9–22

Noah, in contrast to the degeneration that characterized his times, remained faithful to the traditions of morality that had been inherited from the first human beings. G-d therefore chose Noah to survive the flood and repopulate the world in its aftermath.

It's Never too Late

וַיֹּאמֶר אֱלֹקִים לְנֹחַ קֵץ כָּל בָּשָׂר בָּא לְפָנַי וגו': (בראשית ו, יג)

G-d said to Noah, "I have decided to put an end to all flesh."

G-d did not bring on the Flood because He suddenly realized that He had made a mistake by creating the world. Rather, the pre-Flood and post-Flood realities were necessary stages in the world's development, stages that are reflected in every individual's life.

Before the Flood, reality was locked into the irresistible forces of cause and effect. Every good choice reinforced goodness permanently; every bad choice reinforced evil permanently.

The Flood softened reality by introducing the opportunity of repentance. Thus, when Noah emerged from the ark, what he beheld was not a ruined, post-apocalyptic devastation, but a new, fresh, world, full of promise and free from the shackles of the past.

In our own lives, too, we can mistakenly think that we are inescapably locked into a destiny dictated to us by our heredity, our upbringing, or our own prior errors. Because of the Flood, the exact opposite is true: it is never too late. G-d is always waiting to welcome us back with open arms to begin anew. Repentance, like the Flood, enables us to transform any challenging situation or turbulent phase of our lives into a means to cleanse us, refine us, and prepare us to carry on with greater faith and strength.[1]

1. *Likutei Sichot*, vol. 20, pp. 285–287.

SECOND READING
Genesis 7:1–16

G-d told Noah to build an ark in order that he, his family, and representatives of all forms of animal life survive the Flood.

Respite and Regeneration

וַיֹּאמֶר ה' לְנֹחַ בֹּא... אֶל הַתֵּבָה וגו': (בראשית ז, א)

G-d said to Noah, "Come into the ark."

Metaphorically, our personal "arks" are our periods of Torah study and prayer. Just as Noah and his family were protected by the ark from the flood that raged outside it, we can "enter" the worlds of Torah study and prayer in order to be protected from the "flood" of worldly concerns that threatens to inundate us.

It is particularly helpful to immerse ourselves in prayer first thing in the morning. When we confront the world anew each morning, it and everything in it can seem to exist self-sufficiently, as if in no need of G-d. The morning prayers help us recognize that the world could not exist on its own, and that its purpose is to be made into G-d's natural home.

Beginning our day this way helps us to consciously avoid activities that do not further this goal, taking care instead to use every moment as an opportunity to fulfill it. Thus prepared, we can engage in worldly pursuits without fear that they will turn into "raging waters" that overwhelm us with anxiety, stress, and distractions.[2]

2. *Likutei Sichot*, vol. 1, pp. 6–8.

THIRD READING
Genesis 7:17–8:14

The rain lasted 40 days, after which the earth remained submerged for 150 additional days until the water began to subside. Sixty days after the water began to subside, Noah sent out a raven and then a dove in order to see if the water had receded completely.

Not Waiting for G-d

וַיִּפְתַּח נֹחַ אֶת חַלּוֹן הַתֵּבָה אֲשֶׁר עָשָׂה: וַיְשַׁלַּח אֶת הָעֹרֵב וגו': (בראשית ח, ו-ז)

**Noah opened the window he had made
in the ark and sent out the raven.**

As the Torah will recount, Noah did not leave the ark until G-d told him to do so. So what was the purpose of seeing if the land was dry by sending out these birds?

The answer is that since G-d had entrusted him with the survival of life, Noah felt responsible to take whatever natural steps would encourage G-d to hasten the renewal of life on earth.

The pain of exile is compared to the raging waters of the Flood. Like the Flood, only G-d can end the exile. But, like Noah, we can hasten the redemption by actively yearning for it and doing all in our power to hasten its arrival.[3]

3. *Hitva'aduyot 5745*, vol. 4, pp. 2407–2409.

FOURTH READING

Genesis 8:15–9:7

Exactly one year after the Flood began, the earth was dry enough to be habitable. But Noah was reluctant to leave the ark, for he and the animals had lived in peace and harmony within it. Noah knew that once the animals would leave the ark, they would revert to their naturally aggressive behavior.

Accepting the Challenge

וַיְדַבֵּר אֱלֹקִים אֶל נֹחַ לֵאמֹר: צֵא מִן הַתֵּבָה וגו': (בראשית ח, טו-טז)

G-d spoke to Noah, saying "Leave the ark!"

As we have seen, "entering the ark" is a metaphor for the need to immerse ourselves in Torah study and prayer. However, the true purpose of entering the ark is to leave it. G-d command us – as He commanded Noah – not to remain in the protective spiritual environment of Torah study and prayer, but to emerge from it, enter the world, and transform the world into G-d's home.[4]

---

4. *Likutei Sichot*, vol. 1, pp. 9–10.

FIFTH READING
Genesis 9:8–17

Although Noah left the ark, he was hesitant to fulfill G-d's command to procreate and repopulate the earth, fearing that his descendants might one day be wiped away in another Flood. G-d therefore swore to Noah that there would be no future Flood.

Elevating Earthiness

וַהֲקִמֹתִי אֶת בְּרִיתִי אִתְּכֶם וְלֹא יִכָּרֵת כָּל בָּשָׂר עוֹד מִמֵּי
הַמַּבּוּל וְלֹא יִהְיֶה עוֹד מַבּוּל לְשַׁחֵת הָאָרֶץ: (בראשית ט, יא)

[G-d said,] "Never again will there be
a flood to destroy the earth."

When the Torah says that G-d "destroyed the earth," it means that He destroyed "earthiness" – i.e., the mistaken belief that the world exists independent of G-d. The Flood completely submerged the world in Divine awareness, and thus purified it from its moral degeneration and made it permanently receptive to Divine consciousness. Thus, no further Flood would ever be necessary.

Now, thanks to the Flood, we can bring Divine consciousness even into our "earthly" lives. First, we must periodically immerse ourselves in Divinity – in daily prayer and Torah study, the weekly observance of the Sabbath, and the annual Jewish holidays. Then, we must bring this Divine awareness into every facet of our daily lives. These efforts will hasten the world's attainment of complete Divine consciousness in the Messianic Era.[5]

5. *Likutei Sichot*, vol. 30, pp. 21–23.

SIXTH READING
Genesis 9:18–10:32

Noah realized that, as the father of all future humanity, he was playing the role of Adam in the new, post-Flood world. He therefore tried to rectify Adam and Eve's mistake. Whereas they had misused wine (the fruit of the Tree of Knowledge) to achieve self-awareness, he tried to use it to lose himself in Divine joy, by becoming intoxicated. But because this selflessness was artificial, it backfired, and Noah instead exposed himself indecently. Hearing of this, Noah's sons covered him up, but whereas his youngest son, Ham, focused on his indecency, his older sons, Shem and Japheth, focused on the task of restoring their father's modesty.

Human Mirrors

וַיֵּלְכוּ אֲחֹרַנִּית וַיְכַסּוּ אֵת עֶרְוַת אֲבִיהֶם וגו': (בראשית ט, כג)

**[Shem and Japheth] walked backwards and
covered their father's nakedness.**

The Ba'al Shem Tov taught that the people we encounter in our lives are our mirrors: If we see evil in them, we are really seeing a reflection of the evil within us. Since we are generally blind to our own faults, G-d arranges for us to notice them in someone else, expecting us to take the cue and recognize that we possess these same faults so we can correct them in ourselves.

Thus, since Shem and Japheth did not share their father Noah's weakness, they did not focus on it; instead, they focused on how they could help him. In contrast, Ham did share his father's weakness; therefore, he focused on his father's shame rather than how he could be of help.[6]

6. *Likutei Sichot*, vol. 10, pp. 24–29.

SEVENTH READING
Genesis 11:1–32

Instead of obeying G-d's command to disperse and populate the world, the survivors of the Flood congregated under the leadership of Ham's great-grandson Nimrod. Nimrod convinced them that in order to prevent another Flood, they should build an enormous tower so they could take measures to control the rainfall, if necessary. In order to teach them that unity serves no purpose if it leads to rebellion against Him, G-d made each clan suddenly speak its own language; thus humanity dispersed from the Tower of Babel, in accordance with G-d's original intentions.

The Purpose of Civilization

וַיֹּאמְרוּ הָבָה נִבְנֶה לָּנוּ עִיר וּמִגְדָּל וְגו': (בראשית יא, ד)

They said, "Come, let us build ourselves a city and a tower."

The survivors of the Flood overlooked the Flood's lesson that we should look to G-d as the source of our well-being.

We, the survivors of a "flood" that killed 6,000,000 Jews, should learn from the mistake of the survivors of Noah's Flood. Rebuilding the infrastructure of Jewish civilization is praiseworthy and noble, but it is not an end in itself.

Our "city and tower" must possess a deeper, spiritual purpose, which means that our houses of prayer and Torah study should be the most prominent and cherished buildings in our cities.

Similarly, our careers, homes, lives, and families should express our desire to fulfill G-d's will rather than just empty self-pride. Their Jewish trappings – *mezuzot, tefilin,* Sabbath candles, etc. – should be of the highest ritual quality; our collection of Torah books should be well-stocked, prominently displayed, and well-read; the music and conversation heard within our homes should befit a Jewish home; and so on.[7]

---

7. *Likutei Sichot,* vol. 3, pp. 751–753.

Lech Lecha

Abraham's Calling

Genesis 12:1–17:27

THE THIRD SECTION OF THE BOOK OF GENESIS BEGINS THE chronicle of Abraham, who was selected by G-d to found the Jewish people, through whom the process of moral degeneration that humanity had been locked into since their expulsion from the Garden of Eden would be reversed. The name of this section (*Lech Lecha*) is taken from G-d's first words to Abraham: "Go...," in which He told him to leave his native Mesopotamia (modern-day Iraq) and settle in the Promised Land. Throughout his journeys, Abraham challenged paganism, spreading awareness of all reality's source and continuous dependence on the one G-d.

FIRST READING
Genesis 12:1–13

After humanity's dispersion from the Tower of Babel, the original traditions of morality and monotheism were only preserved by select individuals. Responding to Abraham's efforts to restore the world's monotheism, G-d informs him that he has been selected to found the chosen people and instructs him to settle in the Promised Land.

Reaching the True Self

וַיֹּאמֶר ה' אֶל אַבְרָם לֶךְ לְךָ וגו': (בראשית יב, א)

G-d said [to Abraham], "Go."

Although Abraham's accomplishments in spreading Divine consciousness so far had been impressive, they had been limited by the fact that he was speaking only from his personal convictions and reasoning.

All this changed when G-d spoke to Abraham. His first words to him were literally "Go, to you," meaning "Go to your true, higher self, the self you could never reach on your own." Through these words, G-d made Abraham into a person who could progress beyond his own abilities.

As we saw, the Flood introduced into the world the possibility to correct wrongdoing and remake our lives even after committing what would otherwise appear to be fatal mistakes. Now, when G-d told Abraham to "go, to you," He made it possible for us not only to return to our original selves but to "return" to our authentic, fundamental selves – the selves we never even knew existed, constantly uncovering new and infinitely higher vistas of our innate Divine personality and connection with G-d.[1]

---

1. *Likutei Sichot*, vol. 20, pp. 58–60, 301–308.

SECOND READING

Genesis 12:14–13:4

The first challenge Abraham faced in the Promised Land was the famine that set in immediately upon his arrival, forcing him to temporarily relocate to neighboring Egypt.

Transforming Descent into Ascent

וַיְהִי כְּבוֹא אַבְרָם מִצְרָיְמָה וגו': (בראשית יב, יד)

When Abraham came to Egypt . . .

Instead of being allowed to pursue his monotheistic revival in G-d's Promised Land, Abraham was thrust into the world's most prominent bastion of paganism. How ironic it must have seemed to witness this ambitious monotheist suddenly reduced to seeking the mercy of a cultural environment that mocked his every ideal!

Yet, in a miraculous reversal of fortune, Abraham soon had the Egyptians begging *him* for mercy, and shortly thereafter returned to the Land of Israel with greater wealth, with a greater reputation, and accompanied by Hagar, the Egyptian princess who would, in time, become the mother of Ishmael, his first child. It thus became retroactively clear that this apparent regression was actually a further stage in Abraham's progression toward his goals.

Similarly, we must never be intimidated by the world – neither by the world outside us nor by the "world" of personal desires, fears, or preconceived notions within us. Once we answer G-d's call to "go, to yourself," we are no longer bound by the limits of our own capabilities; even apparent regressions will ultimately prove to be an integral part of the process leading to ever-higher realizations of our Divine purpose in life.[2]

2. *Likutei Sichot*, vol. 5, pp. 58–63.

THIRD READING
Genesis 13:5–18

In the course of his travels throughout the Promised Land, Abraham built altars to G-d in three different locations.

The Ladder of Divine Consciousness

וַיִּבֶן שָׁם מִזְבֵּחַ לַה': (בראשית יג, יח)

He built an altar to G-d.

The three altars that Abraham built express the three levels through which we can ascend in our relationship with G-d. Abraham built his first altar to thank G-d for the promise of sustenance, children, and a land in which they could live. This corresponds to observing G-d's commandments, which gives life to the soul and sustains its connection to the body.

Abraham built his second altar to acknowledge the Divine gift of repentance. This altar expresses how we deepen our relationship with G-d in order to restore it after having sinned.

Abraham built his third altar purely for the sake of glorifying G-d. This altar expresses our ability to abandon our sense of independent selfhood and fuse with Him. All reality will fully attain this level of Divine consciousness only in the Messianic Era, but our awareness of this fact fuels our yearning for the Messianic Era, and G-d will hasten its arrival commensurate with our yearning for it.[3]

3. *Likutei Sichot*, vol. 30, pp. 40–43.

FOURTH READING

Genesis 14:1–20

Abraham's nephew Lot had accompanied him to the Promised Land. Abraham was too idealistic for Lot, so Lot left him, settling near the Dead Sea. When the Land of Israel was later invaded by a coalition of nations who captured Lot, Abraham pursued them in his defense. After Abraham miraculously defeated the invaders, he gave a tenth of the spoils of war to his ancestor, Noah's son Shem, who was then known as Malki-tzedek, king of Salem.

Tithing for Spiritual Growth

וַיִּתֶּן לוֹ מַעֲשֵׂר מִכֹּל: (בראשית יד, כ)

He gave him a tenth of everything.

Tithing our wealth expresses our awareness that everything we possess really belongs to G-d and must therefore be used for holy purposes. Generally, we amass wealth in order to improve our lives and the lives of our loved ones; the more we internalize the Torah's values, the more these motives fuse with our desire to make the world more G-dly.

However, when unearned wealth comes our way, it might not occur to us to relate to it in the same way. By tithing the spoils of war, which he received miraculously, Abraham demonstrated that not only the wealth that we have produced ourselves belongs to G-d, but all our wealth.

G-d promises to pay us back many times over for giving Him our tithes, and in fact implores us to test Him in this. By following Abraham's example even with our unearned wealth, our lives will demonstrate how G-d rewards those who fulfill His will. In this way, we, like Abraham, will disseminate the knowledge of G-d's goodness and kindness throughout the world.[4]

4. *Likutei Sichot*, vol. 5, pp. 68–76.

FIFTH READING
Genesis 14:21–15:6

After his victory over the invading coalition, Abraham was concerned that his miraculous victory in battle was his full compensation for his accrued merits, thereby supplanting the other rewards G-d previously promised him, namely: offspring and the Land of Israel. G-d thereupon reiterated His promises to Abraham.

To Shine Like the Stars

הַבֶּט נָא הַשָּׁמַיְמָה וּסְפֹר הַכּוֹכָבִים אִם תּוּכַל לִסְפֹּר

אֹתָם וַיֹּאמֶר לוֹ כֹּה יִהְיֶה זַרְעֶךָ: (בראשית טו, ה)

**[G-d told Abraham,] "Look toward heaven
and count the stars – if you can count them!
That is how your descendants will be."**

Although the plain meaning of this statement is that the Jewish people will eventually be as numerous as the stars, its metaphorical meaning is that they will sparkle like the stars; their light is so bright that even those walking in the thick of night will not stumble.

We are all Abraham's "shining stars," possessing sufficient moral and spiritual fortitude to prevent those around us from stumbling and to exert a positive influence on them.[5]

---

5. *HaYom Yom,* 5 Marcheshvan.

SIXTH READING
Genesis 15:7–17:6

G-d also promised Abraham the Land of Israel.

Asserting our Inheritance

לְזַרְעֲךָ נָתַתִּי אֶת הָאָרֶץ הַזֹּאת וגו': (בראשית טו, יח)

**[G-d said to Abraham,] "I have given
this land to your descendants."**

When G-d promised the Land of Israel to Abraham's descendants, the land in its entirety became – and remains to this day – the inheritance of every Jew, not subject to negotiation or trade. It is solely G-d's promise to Abraham that constitutes our connection to our land. When we articulate this confidently and unapologetically, the community of nations will acknowledge its truth. In contrast, basing our claims to the Promised Land on treaties, military victories, or diplomatic machinations will undermine other nations' respect for our inheritance. By asserting our inviolable connection to the Land of Israel, we hasten the Messianic Redemption, when G-d will grant us its full possession peacefully.[6]

6. *Likutei Sichot*, vol. 15, pp. 100–109.

SHABBAT

SEVENTH READING
Genesis 17:7–27

Despite G-d's promise, Abraham and his wife Sarah had not yet had any children. Sarah therefore asked her Egyptian bond-woman, Hagar, to bear a child by Abraham, hoping that in this merit she would also conceive. Hagar indeed quickly conceived. Concluding from this that her spiritual merits were greater than her mistress's, Hagar mocked Sarah, who then told Abraham to send her away. Hagar gave birth to Abraham's first son, Ishmael. Thirteen years later, G-d told Abraham that the time had arrived for him to have a son with Sarah, and in preparation for this, he should circumcise himself.

Circumcising Negativity

בְּעֶצֶם הַיּוֹם הַזֶּה נִמּוֹל אַבְרָהָם וגו': (בראשית יז, כו)

On that day, Abraham was circumcised.

Spiritually, circumcision is the removal of the "foreskin of the heart," the layer of apathy and haughtiness that obstructs our true connection with G-d. In order to spiritually circumcise ourselves, we must wean ourselves of our attachment to self-indulgence. It is usually not so difficult to renounce obvious or coarse material gratifications. It is harder to wean ourselves of more subtle attachments, whose negative effect on us might not be so apparent. Therefore, G-d has promised to complete the process of spiritual circumcision for us. This latter aspect of circumcision will occur in its fullest sense only in the Messianic Era.

Circumcision is the only commandment that is sealed in our physical flesh. Through it, every Jew is connected physically and irrevocably to G-d, and thus we are given the power to transcend our material drives in order to manifest our true G-dly natures.[7]

---

7. *Torah Or* 13ab; *Igeret HaKodesh* 4 (105b–106a).

Vayeira

Founder of the Faith
Genesis 18:1–22:24

THE FOURTH SECTION OF THE BOOK OF GENESIS CONTINUES the chronicle of Abraham. The name of this section (*Vayeira*, "He appeared") is its first word, describing G-d's revelation to Abraham after his circumcision. This revelation is followed by the visit of three angels, who inform Abraham of his son Isaac's imminent birth. We then follow Abraham as he argues with G-d over the destruction of Sodom and Gomorrah, migrates to Philistia, banishes Hagar and Ishmael after Isaac is born, and is finally tested by G-d's directive to sacrifice Isaac.

FIRST READING

Genesis 18:1–14

On the third day of Abraham's recovery after his circumcision, G-d appeared to him, paying a visit to the sick.

Spiritual Transparency

וַיֵּרָא אֵלָיו ה' וגו': (בראשית יח, א)

G-d appeared to [Abraham].

G-d's self-revelation here to Abraham was on a fundamentally higher plane than His previous appearances to him. By circumcising himself in response to G-d's command, Abraham became the first human being to surrender his selfhood entirely to G-d. Abraham could now experience G-d directly, without his ego getting in the way. Thus, Abraham's circumcision paved the way for the Giving of the Torah, through which this direct experience of G-d became the hallmark of Jewish existence.

This means that by accepting the Torah from G-d and committing ourselves to living according to His vision for us, we can remove all barriers between G-d and ourselves. This, in turn, enables G-d to reveal Himself in our lives in increasingly tangible ways.[1]

1. *Likutei Sichot,* vol. 10, pp. 49–54.

SECOND READING

Genesis 18:15–33

The kindness and hospitality practiced by Abraham in Hebron stood in stark contrast to the wickedness and inhospitality of the nearby cities of Sodom, Gomorrah, and their neighbors. After the three angels visited Abraham, G-d informed Abraham that He was going to eliminate these cities, but Abraham pleaded with G-d on their behalf.

Transcending Our Selves

וַיִּגַּשׁ אַבְרָהָם וַיֹּאמַר הַאַף תִּסְפֶּה צַדִּיק עִם רָשָׁע: (בראשית יח, כג)

[Abraham] came forward and said [to G-d], "Would you obliterate the righteous along with the wicked?!"

When Abraham saw that the angels were already headed toward Sodom in order to annihilate it, he realized that he had to go against his naturally kind disposition and that he could not mince words. He had to argue vehemently and demand of G-d that He annul His decree.

From Abraham's example we learn that when we are presented with the opportunity to save another person, either physically or spiritually, we must not hesitate. We should immediately do all in our power to come to the person's aid, even if that means acting in direct opposition to our natural dispositions.[2]

2. *Likutei Sichot*, vol. 10, pp. 58–59.

THIRD READING
Genesis 19:1–20

Despite Abraham's pleas, the wickedness of Sodom and its neighbors was so great that it could not be overlooked. The angels arrived at Lot's house in order to rescue him from the impending destruction.

Misguided Piety

כִּי מַשְׁחִתִים אֲנַחְנוּ אֶת הַמָּקוֹם הַזֶּה כִּי גָדְלָה צַעֲקָתָם
אֶת פְּנֵי ה' וַיְשַׁלְּחֵנוּ ה' לְשַׁחֲתָהּ: (בראשית יט, יג)

[The angels said,] "...because we are about to destroy this place, for the outcry before G-d has increased, and G-d has sent us to destroy it."

The wickedness of Sodom and its neighbors was a misguided overreaction to Noah's Flood. The generation of the Flood had been wiped out chiefly because they practiced and condoned robbery – the forceful and unjust taking of one person's property by another. The residents of Sodom, aware of this, declared private property rights absolute, outlawing charity and hospitality as unjust uses of another person's possessions.

In their zeal, the people of Sodom did not realize that this opposite extreme was just as destructive as condoning robbery. So, since the world cannot fulfill its purpose of being G-d's true home if we human beings cannot get along with each other, Sodom and its neighbors had to be eliminated, just like the generation of the Flood. Nonetheless, since their intentions, however warped, stemmed from a desire to do the right thing, we are told that these cities will be restored in the Messianic Era.[3]

We can learn from this that our challenge is to find proper balance rather than live a life of extremes.[4]

---

3. Ezekiel 16:53.
4. *Likutei Sichot*, vol. 35, p. 74.

FOURTH READING

Genesis 19:21–21:4

The angel sent to overthrow Sodom told Lot that *he* was about to destroy it, as if to say that he had the power to do so himself.

Words that Matter

מַהֵר הִמָּלֵט שָׁמָּה כִּי לֹא אוּכַל לַעֲשׂוֹת דָּבָר
עַד בֹּאֲךָ שָׁמָּה וְגו': (בראשית יט, כב)

**[The angel said to Lot,] "Hurry! Escape [to the nearby
city], for I can do nothing until you arrive there."**

Angels possess no intrinsic identity; they are simply personifications of G-d's missions. Therefore, when the angels previously declared, "We are going to destroy the city," they meant that G-d was going to destroy the city through them, since they did not perceive themselves as separate from G-d.

Lot, however, misunderstood their words to mean that they did have independent powers outside of G-d's. Therefore, the angel appointed to rescue Lot was compelled to say "I can do nothing until you arrive there," stating clearly that their power came from G-d.

When speaking with others, we too must take into account how they will interpret our words, ensuring that our intentions not be misinterpreted.[5]

5. *Sichot Kodesh 5733*, vol. 1, pp. 251–252.

FIFTH READING
Genesis 21:5–21

Abraham moved from Hebron to Philistia, and when he was 100 years old and his wife Sarah was 90, their son Isaac was born. In the meantime, Hagar's son Ishmael was showing himself unreceptive to the moral education he was receiving from Abraham. In order to prevent him from being a negative influence on Isaac, Sarah insisted that Abraham banish Hagar and Ishmael. Abraham was reluctant to do so, but G-d validated Sarah's judgment.

Feminine Power

וַיֹּאמֶר אֱלֹקִים אֶל אַבְרָהָם . . . כֹּל אֲשֶׁר תֹּאמַר אֵלֶיךָ
שָׂרָה שְׁמַע בְּקֹלָה וְגו': (בראשית כא, יב)

**G-d said to Abraham, "...Whatever
Sarah tells you, heed her voice."**

The more attuned a prophet is to the affairs of this world, the greater his or her degree of prophecy. Since Abraham was somewhat detached from worldly matters, he could not perceive Ishmael's true negativity. Sarah, in contrast, was more involved in worldly matters, so she readily was able to perceive Ishmael's evil. Her prophetic vision was therefore superior to Abraham's.

Furthermore, we are taught that in the Messianic Era, the feminine aspect of creation will rise above the masculine. Abraham's and Sarah's spiritual refinement was so lofty that it enabled them to experience a foretaste of the Messianic Era. For this reason, too, Sarah's prophetic vision was superior to Abraham's.

Nowadays, as we approach the Messianic Era, all of us can welcome the flowering of feminine power in the world, acknowledging that women's more intense experience of physical life grants them a higher level of spiritual insight than that given to men.[6]

6. *Likutei Sichot*, vol. 1, p. 31.

SIXTH READING

Genesis 21:22–34

After the birth of Isaac, Abraham concluded a treaty with the local Philistine king and opened an inn in Beersheba, where he taught wayfarers about monotheism.

Being a Positive Influence

וַיִּטַּע אֶשֶׁל בִּבְאֵר שָׁבַע וַיִּקְרָא שָׁם בְּשֵׁם ה' אֵל עוֹלָם: (בראשית כא, לג)

[Abraham] planted an orchard [and opened an inn] in Beersheba. There he proclaimed the name of G-d.

Abraham's inn was the first public institution devoted to the dissemination of the belief in monotheism and to the ethical behavior that follows from this belief. By establishing a public institution that challenged the world's hallowed tenets, Abraham promoted the awareness of monotheism even among people who never actually visited his inn. As its renown spread, Abraham's inn wielded increasingly profound and broad influence.

Likewise today, the very existence of synagogues and institutions of Torah study exert great positive influence upon a city simply by the mere virtue of their presence, over and above the intrinsic value of the study and prayer that take place within their walls.[7]

---

7. *Sefer HaMa'amarim 5686*, p. 82.

SEVENTH READING

Genesis 22:1–22:24

Abraham's greatest challenge came 37 years after his son Isaac was born. G-d commanded him to sacrifice Isaac.

Tests

וַיֹּאמֶר קַח נָא אֶת בִּנְךָ אֶת יְחִידְךָ אֲשֶׁר אָהַבְתָּ אֶת יִצְחָק וְלֶךְ לְךָ אֶל אֶרֶץ הַמֹּרִיָּה וְהַעֲלֵהוּ שָׁם לְעֹלָה עַל אַחַד הֶהָרִים אֲשֶׁר אֹמַר אֵלֶיךָ: (בראשית כב, ב)

[G-d] said [to Abraham], "Please Take your son, your only one, the one you love, Isaac, and go to the land of Moriah. Take him up there as an ascent-offering, on one of the mountains that I will designate to you."

The primary aspect of this test was not the self-sacrifice it entailed but the challenge it posed to Abraham's implicit faith in G-d: G-d had promised Abraham that Isaac would be the one to perpetuate his legacy; now G-d was commanding Abraham to sacrifice Isaac, in seeming contradiction to His very own word. Yet Abraham unquestioningly carried out G-d's command.

G-d tests us in order to bring our hidden soul-powers to the fore. In fact, life in general is such a test. Before it descended into this world, the soul related to G-d within the limits of reason; the soul never experienced a love for Him that transcends reason. But once the soul is encased in a physical body, which is by nature antagonistic to spirituality, it must summon its innermost strength to remain faithful to G-d despite life's daily trials and tribulations. With this newfound strength, the soul comes to understand and appreciate G-d in a much more profound and intimate way than it ever could have before descending into this world.[8]

8. *Sefer HaMa'amarim 5700*, p. 37.

Chayei Sarah

The Burial of Sarah and the Marriage of Isaac and Rebecca

Genesis 23:1–25:18

THE NAME OF FIFTH SECTION OF THE BOOK OF GENESIS IS
taken from its first words, "The Life of Sarah" (*Chayei Sarah* in
Hebrew), and begins with Sarah's death and burial. We then follow
Abraham's servant, Eliezer, as he betroths Abraham's grandniece
Rebecca to Abraham's son Isaac. This account is followed by that
of Isaac and Rebecca's marriage and the closing phases of Abraham's life: his remarriage to Hagar, his death, and his son Ishmael's
departure from his family and its Divine mission.

FIRST READING
Genesis 23:1–16

When the news reached Sarah that Isaac was nearly sacrificed, the shock of his near loss coupled with the relief of his life being spared was too much for her to bear, and she died. Abraham purchased the Machpeilah Cave and the surrounding field from the local Hittites for her burial grounds in Hebron.

Jewish Destiny

תְּנוּ לִי אֲחֻזַּת קֶבֶר עִמָּכֶם וְגוֹ': (בראשית כג, ד)

**[Abraham said to the Hittites,] "Allow me
[to buy] a burial ground among you."**

The Machpeilah Cave is the burial site of Adam and Eve, the first human beings; as such, it originally belonged to all humanity. In purchasing it, Abraham articulated G-d's intention that the mission originally given to humanity as a whole now be passed on to the Jewish people. By accepting this task, the Jewish people were fundamentally separating themselves from the rest of humanity and assuming the role of its mentors. It is our challenge to recognize this destiny today, as well.[1]

---

1. *Likutei Sichot*, vol. 15, pp. 145–154; vol. 5, pp. 338–344; *Sefer HaSichot 5748*, vol. 1, pp. 85–89.

SECOND READING
Genesis 23:17–24:9

After burying Sarah, Abraham sent his servant, Eliezer, to his brother's household in Aram to select a suitable wife for Isaac.

G-d's Estranged Wives

כִּי אֶל אַרְצִי וְאֶל מוֹלַדְתִּי תֵּלֵךְ וְלָקַחְתָּ אִשָּׁה לִבְנִי לְיִצְחָק: (בראשית כד, ד)

**[Abraham told Eliezer,] "You must go to my land, to
my family, and take a wife for my son, Isaac."**

The prophets often describe the relationship between G-d and the Jewish people as that of husband and wife. In this sense, we are all entrusted with a mission comparable to the one that Abraham gave Eliezer – to go out and find those souls that have drifted away and bring them back to G-d, their "husband."[2]

2. *Likutei Sichot*, vol. 25, pp. 104–105.

THIRD READING

Genesis 24:10–26

Eliezer and his caravan set out for Aram. They arrived at the well outside Haran, the city of Abraham's brother, Nachor, when the women of the city were drawing water. Eliezer prayed to G-d to guide him toward Isaac's proper match by having her respond generously to his request that she draw water for him and his entourage.

Benevolence

וְהָיָה הַנַּעֲרָ אֲשֶׁר אֹמַר אֵלֶיהָ הַטִּי נָא כַדֵּךְ וְאֶשְׁתֶּה וְאָמְרָה
שְׁתֵה וְגַם גְּמַלֶּיךָ אַשְׁקֶה אֹתָהּ הֹכַחְתָּ לְעַבְדְּךָ לְיִצְחָק
וּבָהּ אֵדַע כִּי עָשִׂיתָ חֶסֶד עִם אֲדֹנִי: (בראשית כד, יד)

[Eliezer prayed,] "Let it be that the maiden to whom I will say, 'Please tilt your pitcher so that I may drink,' and she replies, 'Drink, and I will also give water to your camels,' will be the one whom You have designated for Your servant Isaac."

Since G-d lacks nothing, generosity is the primary way in which He relates to the world. For the same reason, generosity is the natural hallmark of people who feel closely connected to G-d. In contrast, the hallmark of evil is selfishness. No matter how much an evil person possesses, he remains unsatisfied, so he seeks only to take and never to give.

Eliezer therefore sought a woman for Isaac who would display kindness. When Rebecca went beyond fulfilling Eliezer's specific request by offering to also water his camels, he understood that she was a G-dly person and thus a fitting match for the son of Abraham.

By demonstrating kindness to others, we too are "matched" with the most worthy partners – whether soul-mates, friends, business partners, or callings in life.[3]

3. *Sidur im Dach* 92b.

FOURTH READING

Genesis 24:27–52

The girl who gave water to Eliezer and his caravan was indeed Rebecca, Abraham's grandniece. After having betrothed Rebecca to Isaac, Eliezer met Rebecca's family and told them the details of his mission.

G-d Spares Nothing

וַתֵּלֶד שָׂרָה אֵשֶׁת אֲדֹנִי בֵן לַאדֹנִי אַחֲרֵי זִקְנָתָהּ
וַיִּתֶּן לוֹ אֶת כָּל אֲשֶׁר לוֹ: (בראשית כד, לו)

**[Eliezer said to Rebecca's family,] "My master's wife
Sarah bore my master a son after she had grown old,
and he gave [his son, Isaac,] all that he owned."**

Abraham was willing to give up his entire fortune in order to ensure that Isaac marry Rebecca. So, too, G-d is willing to give up "all His bounty" to help each and every one of us fulfill our mission of bringing about the "marriage" of the physical and the spiritual dimensions of reality by transforming the world into G-d's home through our good deeds.[4]

---

4. *Sefer HaSichot 5752*, vol. 1, p. 109.

FIFTH READING

Genesis 24:53–67

Eliezer set out with Rebecca back to Canaan to meet Isaac. After Isaac and Rebecca married, Rebecca assumed Sarah's place as the family matriarch.

Lighting Up the World

וַיְבִאֶהָ יִצְחָק הָאֹהֱלָה שָׂרָה אִמּוֹ וגו': (בראשית כד, סז)

Isaac brought Rebecca into the tent of his mother Sarah.

Although Abraham lit the Sabbath candles after Sarah's passing (for he observed all the Torah's commandments), his candles did not remain lit throughout the week, as Sarah's had. But when Rebecca began kindling the Sabbath lights, her candles continued to burn miraculously the whole week.

This demonstrates the unique ability of Jewish women and girls – who are all "daughters" of Sarah and Rebecca – to influence the spiritual character of the home, illuminating it with the holiness of the Sabbath throughout the ensuing mundane week. Although the illumination provided by their candles might be physically visible for only a limited time, their spiritual illumination continues throughout the entire week.[5]

5. *Likutei Sichot*, vol. 11, pp. 283–284, vol. 15, pp. 171–173

SIXTH READING

Genesis 25:1–11

Shortly after Isaac married Rebecca, Abraham remarried Hagar, and had six more sons through her. Years later, when he was 175 years old, Abraham died.

The Reward of Discipline

וַיִּקְבְּרוּ אֹתוֹ יִצְחָק וְיִשְׁמָעֵאל בָּנָיו אֶל מְעָרַת הַמַּכְפֵּלָה וגו': (בראשית כה, ט)

[Abraham's] sons – Isaac and Ishmael –
buried him in the Machpeilah Cave.

Isaac is mentioned first, indicating that although Ishmael was the elder son, he allowed Isaac to lead the funeral. Ishmael thus demonstrated that he had truly repented: His primary sin had been his claim to Isaac's inheritance; it was only after Abraham died that Ishmael could have made this claim, yet he did not.

Sarah deserves the credit for Ishmael's improvement of character. Her insistence on directing Ishmael properly eventually led him to repent enough to recognize the truth of Isaac's primacy. Following Sarah's example, we too should not give up or shy away from correcting and assisting those who truly need our help in the ongoing challenge of self-refinement.[6]

6. *Likutei Sichot*, vol. 15, pp. 149–150.

SEVENTH READING

Genesis 25:12–18

After chronicling Abraham's death, the Torah lists the descendants of Ishmael before continuing with the chronicle of Isaac in the next section.

True Love

עַל פְּנֵי כָל אֶחָיו נָפָל: (בראשית כה, יח)

**[Ishmael] dwelled throughout the area
[settled by] all his descendants.**

Literally, the Hebrew original reads: "He *fell* throughout the area...." Ishmael was the "fallen" version of Abraham. Abraham personified holy love – love for G-d and kindness to others. Ishmael personified love in its "fallen" version, an obsessive desire for physicality and sensuality.

In our own lives, it is our task to transform our love and passion for material things – the fallen love of Ishmael – into a holy love for G-d.[7]

---

7. *Sefer HaMa'amarim 5648*, p. 196.

Toledot

Isaac, Jacob, and Esau

Genesis 25:19–28:9

THE SIXTH SECTION OF THE BOOK OF GENESIS DESCRIBES the history (*Toledot*, in Hebrew) of Isaac and his sons, the righteous Jacob and wicked Esau. It first chronicles their birth, which foretells their future conflict. Esau, the firstborn, sells his birthright to Jacob. The narrative then follows Isaac to Philistia, focusing on his curious project of digging wells. We then see Esau marry. Shortly afterward, Rebecca tricks Isaac into conferring his blessings – and thus the future leadership of the Jewish people – to Jacob rather than to his actual firstborn, Esau. After realizing that Rebecca was correct, Isaac sends Jacob to Aram to marry a daughter of one of his kinsmen.

FIRST READING

Genesis 25:19–26:5

Isaac and Rebecca had no children for the first 20 years of their marriage. When their prayers were finally answered and Rebecca conceived, she suffered intense pregnancy pain. G-d informed her that she was pregnant with twins who would be opposite – not only physically, but morally, as well – and that each one's success in pursuing his path in life would be at the expense of the other's.

Double Identity

וַיֹּאמֶר ה' לָהּ שְׁנֵי גוֹיִם בְּבִטְנֵךְ וּשְׁנֵי לְאֻמִּים מִמֵּעַיִךְ

יִפָּרֵדוּ וּלְאֹם מִלְאֹם יֶאֱמָץ וגו': (בראשית כה, כג)

G-d told her, "Two nations are in your womb; two powers will diverge from within you. The upper hand will pass from one power to the other."

Metaphorically, Jacob and Esau represent the two souls (and their opposing drives) that exist within each of us. We each possess an inner Jacob – i.e., our Divine soul with its G-dly drives, and also an inner Esau – i.e., our animating soul with its selfish drives. When our Divine soul asserts itself, it weakens the materialistic tendencies of the animating soul.

The Divine soul overcomes the animating soul in the same way that light overcomes darkness. Light does not have to actively exert itself to dispel darkness – darkness simply ceases to exist in the presence of light. Similarly, as soon as we let the holiness and goodness of our Divine souls shine by studying the Torah and observing the commandments, the selfishness of the animating soul disappears.[1]

---

1. *Sefer HaMa'amarim 5691*, p. 328.

SECOND READING
Genesis 26:6–12

When Rebecca gave birth, the first twin to emerge was Esau, although Jacob was actually conceived first. Already as young boys, Esau was drawn toward sensual thrills while Jacob was drawn toward absorbing the wisdom and traditions transmitted by Abraham and Isaac. Understanding that he would be the more faithful steward of the family's ideals, Jacob offered to trade the right of leadership from Esau for a hot meal, to which Esau readily agreed. After this, when Canaan was plagued by famine, Isaac relocated his family to Philistia, where Rebecca was almost abducted by the Philistine king. Isaac's righteousness was made evident to everyone when the yield of his crop was miraculously out of proportion to the amount he planted.

The Purpose of Wealth

וַיִּזְרַע יִצְחָק בָּאָרֶץ הַהִוא וַיִּמְצָא בַּשָּׁנָה הַהִוא
מֵאָה שְׁעָרִים וַיְבָרֲכֵהוּ ה': (בראשית כו, יב)

Isaac sowed grain in that region that year. He reaped a hundredfold, for G-d had blessed him.

It is clear from a close reading of the Torah's narrative that the patriarchs were astute businessmen. Nonetheless, it is also clear that they engaged in material pursuits solely with the objective of fulfilling G-d's will. In this case, Isaac's true goal in sowing grain was to be able to give charity to the poor, which the Torah stipulates can only be performed with one's own produce. Like our patriarchs, when our involvement in the pursuit of a livelihood and wealth is similarly motivated, we are blessed with overwhelming success.[2]

2. *Mishneh Torah, Ma'aser* 2:2. *Likutei Sichot*, vol. 5, p. 74, based on *Pirkei d'Rabbi Eliezer* 33.

THIRD READING
Genesis 26:13–22

The king of Philistia, fearful of Isaac's growing economic influence, asked him to leave. Isaac settled nearby, and then began his life project: digging wells to provide sources of water for new towns and villages.

Uncovering Hidden Potentials

וַיַּחְפְּרוּ עַבְדֵי יִצְחָק בַּנָּחַל וַיִּמְצְאוּ שָׁם בְּאֵר מַיִם חַיִּים: (בראשית כו, יט)

**Isaac's servants dug in the valley and found
a well of fresh spring water there.**

Although digging wells certainly served to further the advance of civilization wherever they were dug, they more importantly exemplified Isaac's message to the world. As opposed to filling a pit with water brought from elsewhere, digging a well reveals an already-existing source of water concealed beneath layers of earth. Thus, whereas Abraham's message to the world was: "Let me revive you with the refreshing water of Divine consciousness," Isaac's message was: "Now that you have been revived, look for your inner source of water. Dig away all the dirt encumbering your life, and you will reveal within yourself a wellspring of Divine awareness. This awareness will quench your spiritual thirst throughout your whole life."

Isaac's well-digging teaches us that our flashes of insight or inspiration must be followed up with self-improvement and self-refinement in order for them to make lasting changes.[3]

---

3. *Torah Or* 17c; *Likutei Sichot*, vol. 1, pp. 27–29, vol. 5, pp. 71–72, vol. 15, pp. 194–195, vol. 25, pp. 123–130.

FOURTH READING

Genesis 26:23–29

Eventually, Isaac settled in Beersheba. The king of the Philistines then asked Isaac to forge an alliance with him, acknowledging that Isaac was blessed with Divine favor and success.

The Reward of Perseverance

וַיֹּאמְרוּ רָאוֹ רָאִינוּ כִּי הָיָה ה' עִמָּךְ וַנֹּאמֶר תְּהִי נָא אָלָה
בֵּינוֹתֵינוּ בֵּינֵינוּ וּבֵינֶךָ וְנִכְרְתָה בְרִית עִמָּךְ: (בראשית כו, כח)

**[The king of Philistia and his entourage] said [to
Isaac], "We have seen that G-d has been with you, so
we said: Let there now be a solemn oath between
us, and let us make a covenant with you."**

At first, the Philistines seized the wells that Isaac dug, but in the end they actively sought him out to make peace with him. Similarly, even our most well-intentioned efforts or spiritual labors can sometimes boomerang, actually strengthening the forces that oppose holiness. However, we learn from Isaac to not be discouraged in the face of such unexpected setbacks. Rather, we should continue our endeavors, which are certain to eventually succeed.[4]

4. *Likutei Sichot*, vol. 1, pp. 29–31.

FIFTH READING

Genesis 26:30–27:27

When Esau turned 40, he married two Canaanite women. Sometime after this, Isaac, who by then had gone blind, felt that it was time to officially pass on the mantle of leadership, so he told Esau to prepare to receive his blessings.

Qualifications for Leadership

וַעֲשֵׂה...בַּעֲבוּר תְּבָרֶכְךָ נַפְשִׁי בְּטֶרֶם אָמוּת: (בראשית כז, ד)

**[Isaac said to Esau,] "Prepare . . . so that I may
grant you my soul's blessing before I die."**

Isaac wanted to name Esau his successor because he recognized Esau's potential to become a fearless, G-dly warrior, dedicated to combating evil. Although Isaac had seen Esau give in to the very temptations he should have battled, Isaac felt that if he would bless Esau, Esau would take up the cause of goodness and righteousness. With his superior power, sophistication, and skill, Esau would then be able to accomplish G-d's purposes on earth far better than Jacob could.

Rebecca realized Isaac's error. It was true that Jacob was not the cunning, wild warrior that Esau was. But the keen perception that Jacob had developed by devoting himself to the study of the Torah could well provide him with the cunning necessary to overcome evil when confronted with it. Moreover, Jacob's devotion to the Torah gave him a much stronger drive to make the world into G-d's home than Esau could ever have.

From Rebecca's wisdom, we learn that possessing skill and power cannot on its own make us reliable leaders. We can best develop our own leadership qualities by studying the Torah devotedly, and we should consider scholars of the Torah the ones whom we look to for leadership.[5]

---

5. *Likutei Sichot*, vol. 20, p. 114.

SIXTH READING
Genesis 27:28–28:4

Rebecca immediately disguised Jacob as Esau and had him impersonate Esau before Isaac in order that Jacob be given the blessings. When Esau later returned in order to receive the blessings, Isaac realized what had happened, and acknowledged that Jacob was in fact the more appropriate choice.

The Use of Trickery

וַיֹּאמֶר בָּא אָחִיךָ בְּמִרְמָה וַיִּקַּח בִּרְכָתֶךָ: (בראשית כז, לה)

**[Isaac told Esau,] "Your brother came
with guile and took your blessing."**

The blessings Isaac bestowed upon Jacob were for material prosperity. The fact that Jacob obtained these blessings through cleverness teaches us how we should engage in our own material pursuits. When eating or conducting business, for example, we can appear to be merely tending to our physical needs, similar to the materialistic Esau. But behind this façade, we should really be thinking like Jacob: our true purposes should be spiritual: We should eat in order to have the strength to do good deeds, study the Torah, and observe G-d's commandments. We should earn our livelihood in order to have the financial means with which to do all these things, and so on. This is the sort of "duplicity" that we are meant to employ in our interactions with the material world.[6]

---

6. *Likutei Sichot*, vol. 3, p. 796.

SEVENTH READING

Genesis 28:5–9

Esau hated Jacob for receiving Isaac's blessings instead of him, and resolved to murder him as soon as Isaac would die. Prophetically sensing this, Rebecca convinced Isaac to send Jacob to Aram in order to find a wife. When Esau saw that his parents disapproved of Canaanite wives, he married one of the daughters of his uncle Ishmael.

Showing Respect Respectfully

וַיֵּלֶךְ עֵשָׂו אֶל יִשְׁמָעֵאל וַיִּקַּח אֶת מַחֲלַת בַּת יִשְׁמָעֵאל
בֶּן אַבְרָהָם... לוֹ לְאִשָּׁה: (בראשית כח, ט)

Esau went to Ishmael and married Machalat, the daughter of Abraham's son Ishmael.

Esau's respect for his father was exemplary. He waited on his father dressed in special garments. When he decided to kill Jacob, he refrained from doing so despite his raging anger in order not to pain his father. As soon as he heard that his Canaanite wives displeased his parents, he lost no time in marrying his cousin.

Nevertheless, Esau's reverence for his father did not prevent him from speaking to Isaac disrespectfully, saying, "My father, arise." In contrast, his brother Jacob courteously asked Isaac to "Please arise." Similarly, Esau later referred to his father's death harshly, saying, "The days of mourning for my father will soon be here."

We can learn from Esau's coarse behavior that an essential facet of doing what is right is doing it in a kind and considerate way. For example, the words we speak should not only be meaningful and free of any prohibited types of talk (falsehood, gossip, slander, etc.); they should also be refined and delicate, as were Jacob's.[7]

---

7. *Sefer HaMa'amarim 5697*, p. 232.

Vayeitzei

Jacob in Aram

Genesis 28:10–32:3

THE SEVENTH SECTION OF THE BOOK OF GENESIS BEGINS THE chronicle of the third patriarch, Jacob. It opens as he leaves (*Vayeitzei*, "he left" in Hebrew) Canaan to find a wife from among his kinsmen in Aram. He in fact marries four wives there and fathers a large family, as well as amassing a considerable fortune with Divine help. After 20 years, he secretly flees Aram, fearful that his possessive father-in-law Laban will try to prevent him from leaving. But after Laban overtakes him, they make peace.

FIRST READING
Genesis 28:10–22

On the way to Aram, Jacob spent the night on Mount Moriah (known today as the Temple Mount in Jerusalem), and in his dream saw a vision of angels ascending and descending a ladder to heaven. When he awoke, realizing the intrinsic holiness of this site, he vowed that if G-d would protect him, provide for him throughout his stay in Aram, and enable him to return both physically and spiritually unharmed, he would consecrate this place as the site of the future Temple.

Feeding and Clothing the Soul

וַיִּדַּר יַעֲקֹב נֶדֶר לֵאמֹר אִם יִהְיֶה אֱלֹקִים עִמָּדִי וּשְׁמָרַנִי בַּדֶּרֶךְ
הַזֶּה אֲשֶׁר אָנֹכִי הוֹלֵךְ וְנָתַן לִי לֶחֶם לֶאֱכֹל וּבֶגֶד לִלְבֹּשׁ:
וְשַׁבְתִּי בְשָׁלוֹם אֶל בֵּית אָבִי וְגוֹ': (בראשית כח, כ-כא)

Jacob vowed, "If G-d will be with me and protect me on this journey that I am undertaking, and will provide me with bread to eat and clothing to wear, returning me to my father's house untainted."

Bread and clothing refer allegorically to the study of the Torah and to the performance of G-d's commandments, respectively. When we study the Torah, G-d's wisdom becomes part of us, just as the food we eat becomes part of us. When we perform a commandment, we are enveloped by an external, transcendent feeling of inspiration, much as a garment surrounds and warms us.

In this context, "returning to my father's house untainted" alludes to our return to the domain of holiness after venturing out temporarily into the mundane world in order to refine and elevate it to holiness.[1]

---

1. *Sefer HaMa'amarim Melukat*, vol. 2, pp. 162–163.

SECOND READING

Genesis 29:1–17

Thus confident of G-d's protection, Jacob set out for Aram.

The Source of Confidence and Joy

וַיִּשָּׂא יַעֲקֹב רַגְלָיו וַיֵּלֶךְ אַרְצָה בְנֵי־קֶדֶם: (בראשית כט, א)

**Light of foot, Jacob set out for the land of
the people who lived to the east.**

Even though Jacob was on his way to enter a spiritually dangerous environment, his joy in fulfilling his Divine mission and trust in G-d's protection permeated his entire being, down to his feet, making him lightfooted.[2]

Following Jacob's example, we can adopt the same joyful and confident attitude when we set out to tackle life's numerous daily, mundane activities, even though they may not seem as spiritual. The key is to make sure beforehand that, like Jacob, we are properly nourished (by studying the Torah), properly clothed (by observing G-d's commandments), and properly focused on our goal (of making the world into G-d's home).[3]

---

2. *Hitva'aduyot 5745*, vol. 5, p. 3100.
3. *Sichot Kodesh 5731*, vol. 1, p. 178; *Hitva'aduyot 5719*, vol. 1, pp. 233–234.

THIRD READING
Genesis 29:18–30:13

Arriving in Aram, Jacob met Laban's daughter Rachel shepherding her father's flocks at the well outside the city. Rachel introduced him to Laban, who put him in charge of his flocks. Jacob asked to marry Rachel in return for working for Laban for seven years. Laban agreed, but at the last minute forced Jacob to marry Rachel's older sister Leah. Laban then allowed Jacob to marry Rachel as well, on condition that he work for another seven years afterward. Leah gave birth to four sons in succession, while Rachel remained childless.

The Proper Use of Jealousy

וַתֵּרֶא רָחֵל כִּי לֹא יָלְדָה לְיַעֲקֹב וַתְּקַנֵּא רָחֵל בַּאֲחֹתָהּ וְגו': (בראשית ל, א)

Rachel saw that she had not borne Jacob any children; Rachel was jealous of her sister [Leah].

Destructive, petty jealousy is born of the fear that the other person's successes will lessen our own self-worth. In contrast, Rachel attributed Leah's fertility to her righteousness, and was therefore jealous of her sister's good deeds. This sort of jealousy is constructive, since it spurs us on to improve ourselves. Our sages similarly state that jealousy among Torah scholars increases wisdom, for it stimulates study. Jealousy can be a positive force in our lives when we learn to apply it correctly.[4]

4. *Bava Batra* 21a. *Hitva'aduyot 5745*, vol. 2, p. 870, citing *Or HaTorah, Bereishit*, vol. 1, 218a ff.

FOURTH READING
Genesis 30:14–27

Like Sarah before her, Rachel had her bondwoman, Bilhah (who was also her half-sister), marry her husband, hoping that in this merit she would also be blessed with children. After Bilhah had two sons, Leah – who had stopped bearing children by then – had her bondwoman, Zilpah (who was Leah's and Rachel's other half-sister), marry Jacob, with the same hope. Zilpah also had two sons; after this, Leah's fertility was indeed restored, and she had two more sons and a daughter. Rachel then finally conceived and bore her first son, whom she named Joseph.

Bringing Home the Estranged

וַתִּקְרָא אֶת שְׁמוֹ יוֹסֵף לֵאמֹר יֹסֵף ה' לִי בֵּן אַחֵר: (בראשית ל, כד)

[Rachel] named him Joseph ["May He add" in Hebrew], saying, "May G-d add another son for me."

Rachel's prayer sums up Joseph's spiritual mission in life – to turn "an other," i.e., a seeming stranger, into a "son." This mission expresses itself in three ways: First, in making the mundane world – which appears to be separate from G-d – acknowledge and celebrate its Divine source. Second, in personal repentance, through which we transform ourselves from estranged "others" into "sons" who belong to G-d. Third, in reaching out to those who seem estranged from G-d, revealing to them that they are G-d's precious children, for whom living life according to G-d's plan is simply natural.[5]

Let us not feel inadequate or incapable of effecting such transformations, for we do not work unaided. Rachel said, "May *G-d* add for me another son" – we are merely G-d's instruments, and it is really He who lovingly welcomes His estranged children home.[6]

---

5. *Hitva'aduyot 5743*, vol. 2, p. 783.
6. *Hitva'aduyot 5745*, vol. 2, p. 1112.

FIFTH READING
Genesis 30:28–31:16

After having served Laban faithfully for 14 years, Jacob worked for him for another six years in order to build up his personal wealth.

True Wealth

וַיִּפְרֹץ הָאִישׁ מְאֹד מְאֹד וְגו': (בראשית ל, מג)

The man thus became exceedingly prosperous.

Aside from his material wealth, Jacob also attained true, spiritual wealth: he succeeded in raising all of his children to follow in the righteous ways of Abraham and Isaac, and did not produce a single wicked son (of the likes of Esau or Ishmael, who were born to his forbears Abraham and Isaac).

Jacob was able to do this because he synthesized the inspirational approach of Abraham and the self-disciplining approach of Isaac. By relating to G-d with simple sincerity, Jacob both transcended the differences between the opposite approaches of his forebears and was able to relate equally well to each of his children's different personalities. It was also because of his simple sincerity that Jacob was able to outwit the crafty, scheming Laban.

Jacob's example teaches us that while logic and reason have their place, the foundation of our relationship with G-d is simple, sincerity. This sincerity then enables us to relate effectively to others no matter how different they may be from us.[7]

---

7. *Likutei Sichot*, vol. 1, pp. 63–65; *Sichot Kodesh 5740*, vol. 1, pp. 448–451.

SIXTH READING
Genesis 31:17–42

Jacob fled Aram with his family and flock in secret, fearful that his possessive father-in-law would try to prevent him. Laban indeed pursued him, and when he overtook him, he accused Jacob of spiriting his daughters and grandchildren away before he could say goodbye properly.

Longing for Home

וְעַתָּה הָלֹךְ הָלַכְתָּ כִּי נִכְסֹף נִכְסַפְתָּה לְבֵית אָבִיךְ וְגוֹ': (בראשית לא, ל)

[Laban said to Jacob,] "You departed now because you longed continuously for your father's house."

Jacob's stay with Laban foretold our own sojourn in exile. Just as Jacob was far away from his physical home and immersed in an environment that opposed spirituality, our exile comprises both a physical Diaspora and – more importantly – the spiritual darkness of the unredeemed world. And just as Jacob was never comfortable in his place of exile and constantly yearned to return to his father's home, so must we constantly yearn to return to our Father's "home." No matter how successful we are in fulfilling our Divine mission in exile, we must never feel "at home" in it.

When we consider how long the exile has continued, we might erroneously feel that our longing has not born any fruit. The truth is, however, that the more we realize the significance of our spiritual exile, the more our longing for the Messianic Redemption is intensified, which in turn hastens the Redemption.[8]

8. *Hitva'aduyot 5746*, vol. 1, pp. 655–656, 664–665.

SEVENTH READING
Genesis 31:43–32:3

When Jacob rebuked Laban for mistreating him and his family, Laban relented and the two made a pact. Jacob erected a stone mound as a monument to their agreement to pass it only to do business, not for hostile purposes.

Respect for Boundaries

אִם אָנִי לֹא אֶעֱבֹר אֵלֶיךָ אֶת הַגַּל הַזֶּה וְאִם אַתָּה לֹא תַעֲבֹר אֵלַי

אֶת הַגַּל הַזֶּה וְאֶת הַמַּצֵּבָה הַזֹּאת לְרָעָה: (בראשית לא, נב)

[Laban said to Jacob,] "I will not cross over to you beyond this mound, and you will not cross over to me beyond this mound and this monument."

As opposed to a solid wall, a mound is a collection of unconnected stones, signifying that the separation between Laban and Jacob would not be absolute.[9] Spiritually, this means that Jacob was not erecting an impenetrable barrier between himself and the realm of Laban. He would continue to enter Laban's realm for the "business" of harnessing the sparks of holiness that reside there, but he would do so while remaining detached from the negative influences of Laban's philosophy of life.

Similarly, the conceptual "mound" that we must erect to distinguish between ourselves and the mundane world around us must be left semi-permeable. Although we must cross that mound in order to conduct our business of sanctifying the material world, we at the same time must remain immune to its negative aspects.[10]

---

9. *Likutei Sichot*, vol. 5, p. 129.
10. *Likutei Sichot*, vol. 3, p. 794.

Vayishlach

Jacob in Canaan

Genesis 32:4–36:43

THE EIGHTH SECTION OF THE BOOK OF GENESIS CHRONICLES
the patriarch Jacob's challenges as he returns to the Land of Israel
after concluding his stay in Aram. It opens as he hears that his
grudge-bearing brother Esau is on his way to confront him. Jacob
sends (*Vayishlach*, "he sent" in Hebrew) a diplomatic entourage
to meet Esau. After neutralizing the threat from Esau, Jacob has
to respond to his daughter Dinah's abduction and violation by
the local populace. After this, his wife Rachel dies in childbirth.
The narrative then concludes its account of Jacob's father Isaac
and his brother Esau, preparing to continue with the chronicle
of Jacob in the next section.

FIRST READING
Genesis 32:4–13

Jacob sent messengers to Esau to inform him that he was returning to Canaan and wanted to make peace with him. The messengers returned to Jacob with the news that Esau was preparing to meet him with a battalion of warriors. Jacob adopted a three-pronged response to this news: he sent Esau a generous gift to try to appease him, he prayed to G-d, and he prepared for war if it would prove necessary.

Selfless Prayer

קָטֹנְתִּי מִכֹּל הַחֲסָדִים וּמִכָּל הָאֱמֶת אֲשֶׁר עָשִׂיתָ אֶת עַבְדֶּךָ וְגוֹ': (בראשית לב, יא)

**[Jacob began his prayer], "I am no longer worthy,
due to all the acts of kindness and trustworthiness
that You have done for me, Your servant."**

Although Jacob was certainly aware of his many merits, he was also able to rise above natural human shortsightedness and realize how infinitely indebted we are all to G-d. With this perspective, Jacob humbly assumed that his merits were insufficient to deserve G-d's protection. Therefore, he petitioned G-d to save him and his family not on account of his own merits – although he was indeed worthy – but out of His pure kindness.

Following Jacob's example, whenever we ask something of G-d, we too should appeal solely to His kindness and compassion. If we ask for assistance based on our worthiness – and we all certainly possess many merits – G-d's response will be limited to the extent of our worthiness. But when we humbly disregard our worthiness, demonstrating that we, like Jacob, have risen above our natural shortsightedness, G-d will respond with blessings that transcend the natural order.[1]

---

1. *Likutei Sichot*, vol. 15, pp. 277–280.

SECOND READING

Genesis 32:14–30

That night, Esau's guardian angel wrestled with Jacob; Jacob prevailed, although the angel did succeed in dislocating his thigh. Jacob demanded that the angel bless him; so the angel informed him that G-d was going to give him the additional name of Israel, which means "He who has wrestled with G-d [and prevailed]."

Elevating the Material World

וַיֹּאמֶר לֹא יַעֲקֹב יֵאָמֵר עוֹד שִׁמְךָ כִּי אִם יִשְׂרָאֵל וגו': (בראשית לב, כט)

**[The angel said to Jacob,] "No longer will it be
said that your name is Jacob, but Israel."**

The name "Israel" did not replace Jacob's original name but complemented it. It expressed a new, loftier status that he was now granted. Whereas "Jacob" had to struggle with Esau to secure Isaac's blessings, these blessings were now granted to "Israel" openly by Esau's guardian angel.

Jacob's two names represent the two ways in which we interact with the world. Sometimes the material world or our own materialistic tendencies can get in the way of our Divine consciousness or mission in life; we must then, like "Jacob," struggle to reveal the Divinity that underlies the material world. At other times, the world can be used as a means to enhance Divine consciousness or fulfill our Divine mission; at such times, our challenge, like "Israel," is to use these opportunities both to bring the world to a higher level of Divine consciousness and to promote our own spiritual growth.[2]

2. *Likutei Sichot*, vol. 3, pp. 795–798.

THIRD READING
Genesis 32:31–33:5

As Esau approached, Jacob presented his family and then bowed down to Esau himself. Esau was overcome by Jacob's gift and display of brotherly sentiments, and kissed him.

The Rectification of Esau

וַיִּשְׁתַּחוּ אַרְצָה שֶׁבַע פְּעָמִים עַד גִּשְׁתּוֹ עַד אָחִיו: (בראשית לג, ג)

**[Jacob] prostrated himself seven times
as he approached his brother.**

Jacob acknowledged those qualities of Esau's that were superior to his own, and understood that in order to bring the world to its ultimate destiny, it was necessary to combine Esau's strengths with his own. At the same time, Jacob understood that he – and not Esau – would have to be the one to oversee this synthesis in order for it to work. Due to his faithful devotion to the study of the Torah, Jacob was the one who possessed the breadth of vision and knowledge of G-d's will necessary to harness the raw, untamed power of Esau. Jacob hoped that he could impress Esau enough to submit to his leadership if he would appease him with a lavish gift, acknowledging his superior strengths, and inform him that he had proven himself capable of raising a righteous family, outwitting the crafty Laban, and amassing a sizeable fortune.

When it became clear that Esau was not ready to cooperate, Jacob understood that harnessing Esau's strengths would be a long and difficult process. This union of Esau's superior strength and Jacob's wisdom will be the defining characteristic of the Messianic future, and is therefore the key to ushering it in. Indeed, our undying devotion to the Torah and its commandments ever since Jacob's time has largely refined the power of Esau, and we are now at the threshold of the final, Messianic Redemption.[3]

3. *Torah Or*, pp. 24–26; *Sefer HaSichot 5748*, vol. 1, pp. 138–144; *Hitva'aduyot 5743*, vol. 1, pp. 571–572.

FOURTH READING

Genesis 33:6–20

Esau offered to escort Jacob and his family into Canaan, but Jacob declined the favor, promising to visit Esau at his home on Mount Sei'ir.

Maintaining Focus

יַעֲבָר נָא אֲדֹנִי לִפְנֵי עַבְדּוֹ . . . עַד אֲשֶׁר אָבֹא אֶל אֲדֹנִי שֵׂעִירָה: (בראשית לג, יד)

**[Jacob said to Esau,] "Let my master please go
on ahead of [me,] his servant . . . [and wait there]
until I reach [you,] my master, at Sei'ir."**

Jacob alludes here to Esau's future transformation in the Messianic Era – "until I reach my master [Esau] at Sei'ir." Jacob's approach to Esau teaches us how to neutralize the potential hostility of the "Esaus" we encounter during our exile.

If we fall prey to the external comforts of exile and feel subservient to the rulership of "Esau," our attitude becomes a self-fulfilling prophecy – our exile starts to truly rules us. To neutralize Esau's power, we must see past the façade of exile to its inner purpose, which is to enable us to prepare the world for the Messianic Era. At that time, "Esau" will be subdued and transformed. By viewing the long adventure of exile as a journey toward Sei'ir, focusing on our ultimate goal, "Esau" is rendered harmless even during the exile.[4]

---

4. *Likutei Sichot*, vol. 20, p. 164.

FIFTH READING
Genesis 34:1–35:11

Jacob and his family proceeded to the city of Shechem. Jacob's daughter Dinah went out to meet the women of Shechem and was abducted and violated by the king of Shechem's son, who then offered to pay any dowry that Jacob would demand in order to marry her. He suggested further that his and Jacob's clans intermarry. Jacob's sons replied that the citizens of Shechem would first have to circumcise themselves, to which they readily agreed. When they were recovering from their circumcision, Jacob's sons Simeon and Levi raided the city, killed all the males, and rescued Dinah.

Modest Exposure

וַתֵּצֵא דִינָה . . . לִרְאוֹת בִּבְנוֹת הָאָרֶץ: (בראשית לד, א)

Dinah went out to observe the girls of the region.

Dinah's intention was to convince the women of Shechem to adopt the righteous ways of Jacob's family. Although it appears that she was hardly successful, her efforts were not entirely in vain. Although having the men of Shechem circumcise themselves was partly a ruse to weaken them, their assent indicated that they agreed to be spiritually refined to a certain degree. Refining themselves this way refined their society in general, including the women. And indeed, the women and children were taken captive, most of them becoming servants in Jacob's household and thereby absorbing Jacob's values and morals.

Dinah's behavior teaches us that women who are blessed with unique talents that enable them to influence others should utilize those talents not just to build their home and family; they should also use them to draw the hearts of their fellow women to the Torah and its ways of goodness and kindness.[5]

---

5. *Likutei Sichot*, vol. 35, pp. 154–155. See *Sefer HaSichot 5751*, vol. 1, pp. 83 ff.

SIXTH READING

Genesis 35:12–36:19

Fulfilling his earlier vow, Jacob returned to the site where he had dreamt of the ladder ascending to heaven and built an altar there. G-d then gave him the additional name of Israel, as the angel had informed him. As Jacob's clan moved further south and approached Bethlehem, Rachel went into labor and died while delivering her second son, whom Jacob named Benjamin.

The Power of Altruism

וַתָּמָת רָחֵל וַתִּקָּבֵר בְּדֶרֶךְ אֶפְרָתָה הִוא בֵּית לָחֶם: (בראשית לה, יט)

**Rachel died and was buried on the road leading
to Efrat. Efrat is also known as Bethlehem.**

We are taught that Rachel chose to be buried in Bethlehem, rather than in Hebron with the other patriarchs and matriarchs. She foresaw that the Jewish people would pass by Bethlehem many centuries later when they were driven out of the Land of Israel following the destruction of the first Temple. At that time, after the patriarchs tried but failed to appease G-d, Rachel argued that just as she had not been jealous of her sister Leah when she became Jacob's wife, G-d should not be "jealous" of the idols the Jews had worshiped. G-d accepted her argument, and proclaimed: "Because of you, Rachel, I will return the Jewish people to their homeland."

It is Rachel's self-sacrifice and devotion that evoke G-d's promise to redeem us, despite our misdeeds and shortcomings.[6]

---

6. Rashi and Radak on Jeremiah 31:14, based on *Eichah Rabbah, Petichta* 24. *Hitva'aduyot 5711*, vol. 2, pp. 59–61; *Likutei Sichot*, vol. 30, p. 238.

SEVENTH READING
Genesis 36:20–43

Jacob finally rejoined his father Isaac in Hebron. The Torah then records the death of Isaac, and then lists the descendants of Esau. After Esau's death, his descendants could not establish a stable monarchy, but had to appoint foreigners as kings, in order to keep order among their separate clans.

The Cosmic Drama of Free Choice

וְאֵלֶּה הַמְּלָכִים אֲשֶׁר מָלְכוּ בְּאֶרֶץ אֱדוֹם וגו': (בראשית לו, לא)

These are the kings who reigned in Edom.

The account of these kings alludes to the creation and subsequent collapse of the spiritual world of "Chaos" (*Tohu*), which preceded the spiritual world of "Rectification" (*Tikun*). Our physical universe is derived from the world of "Rectification" but also contains residual elements from the world of "Chaos."

The world of "Chaos" was known by this name because the energies within it were too self-centered to cooperate with each other, just as an immature child cannot reconcile his conflicting emotions. And just as a child's childishness must be shattered by the crisis of adolescence in order for him to pass into mature adulthood, the world of "Chaos" had to shatter in order for the world of "Rectification" to be created on its ruins.

Self-centeredness is thus embedded within our world as the remnants of this shattered world. These sparks of the world of "Chaos" are necessary, for in order for there to be free choice, there must be an element of "evil," i.e., egocentricity, available as an alternative to selflessness and goodness.

The task of Jacob and his descendants throughout history is to elevate Esau's spiritual descendants – the fallen sparks of the world of "Chaos" – through sanctifying the material world.[7]

7. *Likutei Torah* (Arizal); *Ma'amarei Admur HaZaken 5568*, vol. 1, pp. 1ff, *et al.*

Vayeishev

Joseph in Egypt

Genesis 37:1–40:23

THE NINTH SECTION OF THE BOOK OF GENESIS BEGINS THE chronicle of Jacob's son Joseph, after Jacob settles (*Vayeishev*, "he settled" in Hebrew) in Hebron. Joseph shares his dreams, in which he envisions himself as the future leader of Jacob's family, with his brothers. This convinces his brothers that he is a threat to the family's Divine mission, so they decide to eliminate him. He is sold to Egypt as a slave, where he first rises to a position of responsibility in his master's household, after which he is placed in prison as a result of slanderous accusations. Interrupting this narrative is the account of how Jacob's son Judah is ostracized by his family and later deceived into fathering children by his widowed daughter-in-law, Tamar.

FIRST READING

Genesis 37:1–11

Having arrived safely at Hebron, Jacob assumed the mantle of leadership. Joseph shared his two dreams with the family, one in which his brother's sheaves bowed down to his, and a second in which the sun and moon and eleven stars bowed down to him. Joseph's brothers took this brazen display of conceit as evidence that Joseph was in fact the self-centered Esau's spiritual heir more than Jacob's. Jacob, however, approved of Joseph's dreams, since he himself already envisioned Joseph as his successor.

The Need for Spiritual Mentors

וַיֹּאמֶר אֲלֵיהֶם שִׁמְעוּ נָא הַחֲלוֹם הַזֶּה אֲשֶׁר חָלָמְתִּי: (בראשית לז, ו)

[Joseph] said to [his brothers], "Please listen to this dream I had."

Joseph's two dreams seem to convey the same idea. The reason for the apparent repetition is that they symbolize two distinct stages in the relationship between each generation and its leaders.

Sheaves of grain are made up of individual stalks, which grow discretely from one another, each in its own groove. Binding them into sheaves symbolizes our first task in life: gathering together all of our capacities and talents and uniting them in the work of holiness. Once we have become a "sheaf," we need to seek guidance and inspiration from a "Joseph," a spiritual leader.

As we mature spiritually, we reach a higher level: having risen above earthly consciousness, we regain our soul's original heavenly consciousness and shine like a "star." Yet even on this level, we should not rely on our own achievements for inspiration, for this can lead to stagnation and complacency. Rather, we must still continue to turn to our "Joseph" – i.e., our spiritual mentor – for further insight and inspiration.[1]

---

1. *Likutei Sichot*, vol. 3, pp. 805–810. See also *Hitva'aduyot 5744*, vol. 2, p. 715; *Likutei Sichot*, vol. 15, p. 345, sub-note *.

SECOND READING

Genesis 37:12–22

While pasturing their flocks, Joseph's brothers plotted how best to eliminate him and the threat they believed he posed. Jacob sent Joseph after them.

Relying on Divine Providence

וּבְטֶרֶם יִקְרַב אֲלֵיהֶם וַיִּתְנַכְּלוּ אֹתוֹ וגו': (בראשית לז, יח)

**Before [Joseph] reached [his brothers],
they conspired against him.**

Although they neither intended it nor foresaw it, the brothers' actions led to Joseph's eventual rise to power and the survival of Jacob's entire family. Joseph's experience vividly demonstrates that whether we realize it or not, everything that happens to us is orchestrated by G-d for our benefit.

It is therefore foolish and unproductive to be angry with those who appear to be harming us. Although they may indeed be guilty for their actions, they cannot do anything to us that G-d does not will. Rather, we should learn from Joseph, who repaid his brothers' evil with kindness, continuing to love them despite their hatred toward him.[2]

2. See *Tanya*, chapter 12, end. *Likutei Sichot*, vol. 20, pp. 187–191.

TUESDAY

THIRD READING
Genesis 37:23–36

Joseph's brothers Simeon and Levi suggested killing Joseph outright, but Reuben, the eldest brother, suggested that he be thrown into a pit, leaving his fate to Divine providence. The pit they chose was dry, and filled with snakes and scorpions.

Avoiding Negativity

וְהַבּוֹר רֵק אֵין בּוֹ מָיִם: (בראשית לז, כד)

The pit was empty of water.

Allegorically, the pit represents the human mind and water represents the Torah. This incident thus tells us that the surest way to keep our mind free of "snakes and scorpions" – negative and destructive notions – is to ensure that it is always full of Torah-related content, for "G-d's Torah is wholesome, restoring the soul."[3]

---

3. Psalms 19:8. *Likutei Sichot*, vol. 15, pp. 324–325, based on *Bereishit Rabbah* 84:16 and *Tzava'at HaRibash* (ed. Kehot) 76.

FOURTH READING

Genesis 38:1–30

Judah convinced his brothers to sell Joseph as a slave. They then sent Joseph's robe, smeared with goat blood, to Jacob. Jacob mourned for Joseph inconsolably. The brothers then shunned Judah for not insisting that they return Joseph to Jacob. Judah left Hebron, married, and had three sons. He married off his eldest to Tamar, who was anxious to bear Judah's descendants. When Judah's eldest died, he married his second son to her; when the second son also died, Judah was afraid to marry his third son to her. Tamar disguised herself as a prostitute in order to trick Judah into having children by her.

The Purpose of Evil

וַיִּקְרָא שְׁמוֹ פָּרֶץ: (בראשית לח, כט)

[Judah] named [Tamar's firstborn] Peretz.

The Messiah is descended from Judah through his and Tamar's son Peretz. In order to understand why it was necessary for the Messiah to enter the world in such a seemingly scandalous way, we need to recall that G-d only created evil in order for there to be free choice. In order for free choice to exist, the forces of evil and the forces of good have to be perfectly balanced.

When the messianic line was about to enter the world, the forces of evil "argued" that the balance was about to be tipped against them. Therefore, the union that would bear the ancestor of the Messiah had to occur in a way that the forces of evil would consider beneficial to them. Just as in military strategy, an army sometimes pretends to retreat in order to draw the enemy into a vulnerable position, the forces of holiness here yielded a seeming victory to the forces of evil in the form of this seemingly sinful act, in order to gain the upper hand.[4]

4. *Derech Mitzvotecha* 32a–32b; *Or HaTorah, Bereishit*, vol. 6, 1096b–1097a.

FIFTH READING
Genesis 39:1–6

In the meantime, Joseph had been sold as a slave to the Egyptian Potiphar, chief of the Pharaoh's butchers. Recognizing Joseph's intelligence, integrity, piety, and regal bearing, Potiphar appointed him over his household affairs.

Caring for Our Inner Beauty

וַיְהִי יוֹסֵף יְפֵה תֹאַר וִיפֵה מַרְאֶה: (בראשית לט, ו)

Joseph was beautiful in form and complexion.

Joseph's physical beauty was a reflection of his inner, spiritual beauty – his uncompromising dedication to the ideals of the Torah. By virtue of his own spiritual perfection, Joseph was able to fulfill his Divine mission: bringing others closer to G-d.

Like Joseph, we are all called upon to bring others closer to G-d. In order to succeed as Joseph did, we must try to be, like him, spiritually "beautiful in form and complexion."

This does not mean we should wait until we achieve spiritual perfection before reaching out to others; perfection is relative, and compared to those who know less than we, we are "beautiful" enough to inspire them. Nevertheless, we must also remember that if we neglect our own spiritual growth, others will take note, and as a result be less inclined to take our words to heart.[5]

5. *Likutei Sichot,* vol. 1, p. 79.

SIXTH READING
Genesis 39:7–23

Potiphar's wife saw through astrological means that she was destined to be the ancestress of Joseph's descendants. Not knowing that this would happen through her daughter, she sought to seduce Joseph.

Facing Temptation

וְאֵיךְ אֶעֱשֶׂה הָרָעָה הַגְּדֹלָה הַזֹּאת וְחָטָאתִי לֵאלֹקִים: (בראשית לט, ט)

[Joseph told Potiphar's wife,] "How could I commit such a great wrong and also sin before G-d?"

Being a servant, Joseph was obviously at the mercy of his master's wife. Potiphar's wife intimidated Joseph with all sorts of threats, including death, if he would not acquiesce to her seduction.[6] But then Joseph saw an image of his father Jacob's face in front of him, from which he understood he was obligated to resist her temptations. Jacob's face reminded Joseph that our individual sins are not only our own personal matters, for which there might be mitigating rationalizations; they affect the moral balance of all reality.

When confronted with temptation, it is tempting to convince ourselves that nobody will know about it, that it is technically justified, that succumbing to it is only a temporary setback and that we can later repent, and so on. In such moments, we too must "envision the image of Jacob," that is, remember that our actions are not merely the isolated deeds of individuals in isolated times and places. Our deeds have cosmic ramifications; they can harm or heal the entire world.[7]

6. See *Yoma* 35b; *Bemidbar Rabbah* 14:18.
7. *Hitva'aduyot 5721*, vol. 1, pp. 262–265.

SEVENTH READING

Genesis 40:1–23

Frustrated by her failure to seduce Joseph, Potiphar's wife slandered him and Potiphar threw him into prison. Here too, Joseph rapidly rose to a position of responsibility. Shortly after his imprisonment, Pharaoh's chief cupbearer and chief baker were also put in prison. The morning after they both had disturbing dreams, Joseph noticed their anxiety and offered to help. They told him their dreams, which he correctly interpreted as meaning that in three days the cupbearer would be restored to his position and the baker would be executed. Joseph asked the cupbearer to speak to Pharaoh on Joseph's behalf after his release, but the cupbearer forgot about Joseph.

The Power of the Deed

וַיִּשְׁאַל אֶת סְרִיסֵי פַרְעֹה . . . לֵאמֹר מַדּוּעַ פְּנֵיכֶם רָעִים הַיּוֹם: (בראשית מ, ז)

**[Joseph] asked Pharaoh's servants, "Why
are your faces so downcast today?"**

Joseph had suffered horrible humiliations. It would have been logical for him to become absorbed in his own pain, angry at the world. But Joseph did not become bitter. He remained sensitive to others and to his Divine mission in life. Not only did he perceive the anguish of Pharaoh's servants, he reached out to help them. To Joseph, the fact that G-d had arranged for him to notice someone in need indicated that it was his duty to help.

As the result of this one, seemingly minor good deed, Joseph became the viceroy of Egypt, and was able to save the civilized world from famine. We see here, once again, the unimaginably far-reaching results that can come from one small good deed.[8]

---

8. *Mishneh Torah, Teshuvah* 3:4; *Sichot Kodesh 5734*, vol. 1, pp. 208–213.

Mikeitz

Joseph the Viceroy

Genesis 41:1–44:17

THE TENTH SECTION OF THE BOOK OF GENESIS CONTINUES the chronicle of Joseph. It begins two years after (*Mikeitz*, "at the end of" in Hebrew) Joseph asked Pharoah's cupbearer to intercede for him. This time it is Pharaoh who dreams – twice – and seeks a qualified interpreter. Joseph interprets Pharaoh's dreams convincingly as referring to seven coming years of plenty followed by seven years of famine, and this leads Pharaoh to appoint Joseph as viceroy of Egypt. The onset of famine brings Joseph's brothers to Egypt to buy food that Joseph stored up during the years of plenty. When Joseph sees them, he devises a way to determine if they have abandoned their former hatred of him and are ready to join him in moving the family forward in its Divine mission.

FIRST READING

Genesis 41:1–14

In his first dream, Pharaoh saw seven robust cows emerge from the Nile River, followed by seven lean cows that devoured the seven robust ones. In his second dream, he saw seven healthy ears of grain devoured by seven scrawny ones.

The Price of a Free Lunch

וַיִּיקַץ פַּרְעֹה וְהִנֵּה חֲלוֹם: (בראשית מא, ז)

Pharaoh awoke, and perceived that [what he had seen] was a dream.

The content of Pharaoh's dreams differed profoundly from that of Joseph's. Pharaoh dreamed of animals and produce but not of work. Joseph's dreams, in contrast, began with the image of work – the brothers gathering sheaves in the field.

This reflects the difference between how G-d provides sustenance for holy and less holy people. G-d sustains holy people directly, in deserved reward for their earnest work in aligning themselves with His will. In contrast, less holy people balk at the idea of self-discipline and work; G-d therefore only sustains them because He has to in order for them to continue to exist. Moreover, sustenance received without effort is flawed goodness, since human nature is such that we do not truly appreciate something gained without effort.

Similarly, when we are tempted to think that we can get by without hard work, we must realize that such notions stem from our less holy side. Likewise, anything we receive "for free" is either flawed or will not endure.[1]

---

1. *Likutei Sichot*, vol. 3, pp. 805–810, 820–822.

SECOND READING
Genesis 41:15–38

Although it was obvious that Pharaoh's dreams had something to say about Egypt's economy, none of Pharaoh's advisors could explain how the robust cows or grain could exist at the same time as the scrawny ones. At that point, Pharaoh's cupbearer recalled how Joseph had correctly interpreted his dream in prison, and mentioned this to Pharaoh, who then summoned Joseph. Joseph interpreted the simultaneous existence of robust and scrawny years to mean that grain should be stored away during the plentiful years for use during the famine years.

Hypocrisy is a Dream

וַיֹּאמֶר פַּרְעֹה אֶל יוֹסֵף חֲלוֹם חָלַמְתִּי וּפֹתֵר אֵין אֹתוֹ וְגו': (בראשית מא, טו)

Pharaoh said to Joseph, "I had a dream, but there is no one who can interpret it."

The dreams of Joseph and Pharaoh led to the Jewish people's exile in Egypt. Exile was caused by dreams because exile itself is like a dream. In dreams, conflicting and contradictory situations can coexist. Similarly, our behavior in exile seems hypocritical: selflessness and selfishness coexist almost simultaneously.

Living this spiritually inconsistent life is potentially frustrating. We may think that we are being dishonest with ourselves. Considering all our faults, we may feel that our connection to G-d is not real, that our efforts to advance spiritually are ultimately futile.

The connection between exile and dreams teaches us that although our actions may seem hypocritical at times, we should not become disheartened. We must strive to live as consistently as possible, not giving up because of momentary lapses. The effects of misdeeds last only until we repair their damage through repentance. The effects of our good deeds, in contrast, last forever.[2]

2. *Likutei Sichot*, vol.1, pp. 85–87.

THIRD READING

Genesis 41:39–52

Pharaoh was so impressed with Joseph's skillful interpretation of his dream that he appointed him viceroy of Egypt in order to enable him to implement his plan. After he was made viceroy, Joseph's former master, Potiphar, gave him his daughter in marriage. During the seven years of plenty, Joseph had two sons: Manasseh and Ephraim.

Remembering in order to Progress

וַיִּקְרָא יוֹסֵף אֶת שֵׁם הַבְּכוֹר מְנַשֶּׁה...וְאֵת שֵׁם הַשֵּׁנִי קָרָא אֶפְרָיִם וְגו': (בראשית מא, נא-נב)

Joseph named his firstborn Manasseh...he named his second son Ephraim.

Living in exile requires us to use two apparently contradictory approaches toward the world at large: On the one hand, we must be constantly on guard against harmful influences; on the other hand, we must engage the outside world in order to influence it positively.

Clearly, influencing our environment is a greater accomplishment than merely maintaining our values. Nonetheless, maintaining our values must be taken care of first, for if we forget our roots we will no longer have anything to contribute to the world.

The two sons of Joseph, born and raised in Egypt, personified these two aspects of life in exile. Joseph named his firstborn Manasseh (meaning "[Exile] causes one to forget") in order not to forget his family and heritage. Joseph named his second son Ephraim ("he will be fruitful") in order to emphasize that our purpose in the world is to influence it positively.[3]

---

3. *Likutei Sichot*, vol. 15, pp. 432 ff. See below on 44:14, above on 38:28.

FOURTH READING
Genesis 41:53–42:18

Although the Egyptians stored up grain during the seven years of plenty, as Joseph directed them to, as soon as the seven years of famine began, everyone's grain except for Joseph's rotted. The populace of Egypt thus found themselves dependent upon Joseph for food. Joseph agreed to give them grain on the condition that they circumcise themselves first.

Refining the World

וַיֹּאמֶר פַּרְעֹה לְכָל מִצְרַיִם לְכוּ אֶל יוֹסֵף אֲשֶׁר
יֹאמַר לָכֶם תַּעֲשׂוּ: (בראשית מא, נה)

**Pharaoh said to all Egypt, "Go to Joseph
and do whatever he tells you to."**

Egyptian society was steeped in the pursuit of self-serving carnal pleasure, which is reduced by circumcision. Thus, by having the Egyptians circumcised, Joseph subdued their obsession with carnal indulgence. Pharaoh himself instructed them to go along with Joseph's condition; thus, even the living symbol of Egyptian corruption was willing to be refined, at least somewhat.

We follow Joseph's example by remaining spiritually uncontaminated by our materialistic environment and even refining it. By strengthening our own commitment to Judaism, we influence our fellow Jews to strengthen theirs. Moreover, we influence the broader community of non-Jews to keep the Torah's laws that apply to them (the "Noahide" laws). Thus, we will ultimately transform the entire world into G-d's home.[4]

4. *Likutei Sichot*, vol. 10, p. 141.

FIFTH READING
Genesis 42:19–43:15

Jacob sent his sons – except Benjamin – to Egypt to buy grain.
Joseph recognized them, but they did not recognize him. He
devised a plan to see if they were ready to accept him as Jacob's
successor: He threatened not to receive them next time without
Benjamin. Once Benjamin would be in Egypt, Joseph would
invent an excuse to keep him there. If the brothers would be
prepared to fight for Benjamin, it would mean that they had
overcome their jealousy of Rachel's sons. Jacob was reluctant to
send Benjamin, but his other sons convinced Jacob that they had
no choice. So Jacob agreed, but first prayed for their success.

Natural Miracles

וְאֵל שַׁדַּי יִתֵּן לָכֶם רַחֲמִים לִפְנֵי הָאִישׁ וגו': (בראשית מג, יד)

**[After preparing a gift to send to Joseph, Jacob prayed,]
"May G-d Almighty grant that the man be merciful to you."**

Conventional wisdom has it that prayer is necessary only in desperate situations. Thus, Jacob's sons assumed that since Joseph
was detaining their brother because he suspected them of being
thieves or spies, it would be enough to pacify him with a gift.

From Jacob's words to his children, however, we learn that even
when a favorable outcome seems perfectly natural, we should
never assume that we can reach it without Divine assistance. We
must always pray – and not as a secondary measure, but as the
primary measure.

Although we must create natural channels to facilitate G-d's
blessings, we should realize that G-d, who is beyond nature, con-
trols every aspect of our lives. When we realize this fully, we will
indeed perceive that the "natural" occurrences of our lives are all
in fact miracles garbed in nature.[5]

5. *Likutei Sichot*, vol. 25, pp. 227–234.

SIXTH READING
Genesis 43:16–29

Along with speaking harshly to his brothers, Joseph also occasionally treated them kindly, in order to gradually prepare them for when he would reveal his identity to them. Thus, when they all returned, with Benjamin, he prepared a fine meal for them.

Hospitality vs. Austerity

וַיֹּאמֶר לַאֲשֶׁר עַל בֵּיתוֹ... וּטְבֹחַ טֶבַח וְהָכֵן כִּי אִתִּי

יֹאכְלוּ הָאֲנָשִׁים בַּצָּהֳרָיִם: (בראשית מג, טז)

[Joseph] said to the overseer of his household, "Have animals slaughtered and prepared, for these men will dine with me."

Hospitality requires that hosts try their best to care for all their guests' needs. Even if they are not sure that the guests will partake of what is prepared for them, the hosts should nevertheless provide abundantly for them.

Similarly, although living frugally is a value found in the Torah, it is one we should impose on ourselves, not on others. When we think about providing for a poor family, for example, we should not provide them with only their bare necessities, but with enough to allow them to live according to a dignified standard of living.[6]

---

6. *Sichot Kodesh 5728*, vol. 1, p. 322.

SEVENTH READING
Genesis 43:30–44:17

After the meal, Joseph sent the brothers off. Unbeknown to them, however, Joseph had instructed his servant to hide his silver goblet in Benjamin's pack. Joseph sent his servant to pursue his brothers and the goblet was discovered. By framing Benjamin, Joseph was creating a situation where his brothers could atone for having sold him. When the brothers would put their own lives at risk to save Benjamin, it would be as if they were doing so to save Joseph; thus, they would "undo" their crime against Joseph by doing the exact opposite. The brothers returned to Joseph, who informed them that they were all free to return home except for Benjamin.

The Gift of Love

וְאֶת גְּבִיעִי גְּבִיעַ הַכֶּסֶף תָּשִׂים בְּפִי אַמְתַּחַת הַקָּטֹן וְגו': (בראשית מד, ב)

[Joseph said,] "Put my goblet – the silver goblet – at the top of the pack of [Benjamin], the youngest one."

Joseph knew that the Jewish people would be in exile for a long time, and that not all of them would possess the same level of Divine consciousness that enabled him to thrive in Egypt. Joseph therefore sought a way of protecting them from Egyptian depravity, ensuring that they would eventually leave Egypt and receive the Torah. Joseph realized that what they needed was a love for G-d powerful enough to overcome the materialism of Egypt. Joseph's silver goblet alludes to this love, for the word for "silver" (*kesef*) is related to the word for "yearning" (*kisuf*). Joseph further knew that not-yet-fully-righteous people cannot spark such a love by themselves, so he implanted this love in them by "implanting" it within Benjamin.[7]

7. *Likutei Torah* 3:90bc; *Ma'amarei Admur HaEmtzai, Bereishit*, pp. 291 ff; *Or HaTorah, Bereishit*, vol. 2, 341a ff; ibid., vol. 6, 1103b ff.

Vayigash

Jacob and Joseph Reunited

Genesis 44:18–47:27

IN THE ELEVENTH SECTION OF THE BOOK OF GENESIS, WE reach the dramatic climax of the chronicle of Joseph. It begins as Judah approaches (*Vayigash*, "and he approached" in Hebrew) Joseph in defense of Benjamin. Judah's willingness to save Benjamin convinces Joseph that the brothers have repented and risen above their previous jealousy, so he ends the masquerade and reveals his true identity to them. Joseph then immediately sends all the brothers to bring their father Jacob to Egypt, where the family will settle in order to live through the famine. Ironically, the famine ends as soon as Jacob arrives, but the family stays in Egypt in fulfillment of G-d's plan as originally promised to Abraham.

FIRST READING
Genesis 44:18–30

Hearing that Joseph intended to retain Benjamin as his slave, Judah stepped forward to argue with Joseph. Although he spoke respectfully, he told Joseph that he would not tolerate this injustice to his brother – as well as to his father Jacob, who would not survive the loss of the only remaining son of his wife Rachel.

Crisis Mode

וַיִּגַּשׁ אֵלָיו יְהוּדָה וְגוֹ': (בראשית מד, יח)

Judah then approached [Joseph].

Judah did not shy away from speaking harshly with Joseph; moreover, he *began* his appeal harshly. He knew that when someone's life is at stake, we must not be diplomatic; our listeners must sense that we are not involved because of ulterior motives, such as political or financial interests. When it is clear that the cause for which we are fighting cuts to the core of our being, it will evoke an honorable and compassionate response.

Today's "Benjamins," our Jewish children, are threatened by a different sort of "Egypt" – that of assimilation. To save these Benjamins, we cannot wait for someone to appoint committees that will conduct lengthy research and then deliberate over what should be done and how much it will cost, etc. When lives are at stake, we must do whatever we can to save them, immediately.

Judah's efforts proved unexpectedly fruitful: his presumed enemy proved to be his greatest ally, and even Pharaoh himself provided the greatest possible means for securing the uncompromised continuity of Jewish tradition. So it will be when we follow Judah's example, selflessly and vigorously exerting ourselves on behalf of our children.[1]

1. *Likutei Sichot*, vol. 20, pp. 216–217.

SECOND READING

Genesis 44:31–45:7

Judah's display of self-sacrifice for Benjamin convinced Joseph that his brothers had truly repented of their former animosity toward him. He therefore revealed his true identity to them. They were understandably afraid that he would take revenge on them, but Joseph assured them that he viewed the entire episode as Divine providence and did not hold them responsible.

Transcending and Transforming

וַיִּשְׁלָחֵנִי אֱלֹקִים לִפְנֵיכֶם לָשׂוּם לָכֶם שְׁאֵרִית בָּאָרֶץ וְגוֹ': (בראשית מה, ז)

[Joseph told his brothers,] "G-d sent me ahead of you to ensure that you survive in [this] land."

It was impressive that Joseph maintained his holiness in exile, but his primary achievement was that he increased holiness in the world, by teaching the Egyptians about G-d. Joseph's example gives us the strength to follow in his footsteps, by first remaining immune to the negativity of exile and then by transforming it into holiness.[2]

---

2. See *Mishneh Torah, Melachim* 8, end. *Likutei Sichot*, vol. 30, pp. 224–228.

THIRD READING

Genesis 45:8–27

Joseph then told his brothers to return to the Land of Israel and bring their father Jacob to Egypt. He arranged for the family to settle in the luxurious province of Goshen, which was also removed from the negative spiritual influence of the idolatrous Egyptians.

Manifest Destiny

שָׂמַנִי אֱלֹקִים לְאָדוֹן לְכָל מִצְרָיִם רְדָה אֵלַי אַל תַּעֲמֹד: (בראשית מה, ט)

[Joseph told his brothers to tell their father,] "G-d has made me master of all Egypt; Come down to me; do not delay."

The primary purpose of the Egyptian exile was for the Jewish people to liberate the sparks of holiness that were trapped in Egypt. Since Egypt was the economic superpower of that era, the wealth of the whole civilized world was tied to that of Egypt. Thus, when the Jewish people took the wealth of Egypt with them when they later left, they were not only elevating the wealth of Egypt but that of all the nations of the world. This is why Joseph told his father that he was the master of Egypt: He was saying, "Now that I have become ruler over Egypt and gathered the world's wealth, the Egyptian exile can begin, since the fulfillment of its purpose is now possible."

Similarly, the purpose of our present exile is to elevate the physical world by revealing the G-dliness inherent in it.[3]

3. *Likutei Sichot*, vol. 3, pp. 823 ff.

FOURTH READING

Genesis 45:28–46:7

Jacob was overjoyed to hear that Joseph was still alive and that he had remained true to Jacob's ideals. Although he looked forward to joining Joseph, he regretted having to leave the land promised to his forebears. G-d therefore appeared to him and assured him that his family would grow into a nation while in Egypt.

Healthy Regret

אַל תִּירָא מֵרְדָה מִצְרַיְמָה כִּי לְגוֹי גָּדוֹל אֲשִׂימְךָ שָׁם: (בראשית מו, ג)

[G-d said to Jacob,] "Do not be afraid to go down to Egypt, for it is there that I will make you into a great nation."

G-d was not trying to soothe Jacob's regret over leaving the Promised Land, for a Jew *should* regret not living in the Land of Israel. Rather, G-d was telling Jacob that his regret over going into exile was the key to not becoming intimidated by it, and therefore, the key to overcoming it.

Since G-d put us in exile, it follows that He has given us all the strength we need to overcome its challenges. As long as the exile continues, it is the optimal setting for our individual and collective growth and development. Here, however, lurks a great danger. When we realize that we have no reason to be intimidated by exile and that we benefit so greatly from it, we can fall into the trap of becoming habituated to it. As a consequence, we can become vulnerable to exile's negative effects on us, and it goes without saying that we can no longer elevate it properly.

Therefore, like Jacob, we should always cultivate regret over the fact that we are not in our proper environment, the Land of Israel in the Messianic Redemption. As long as we remember who we really are and the lives we are really meant to lead, we need not fear exile; we will overcome it.[4]

4. *Likutei Sichot*, vol. 30, pp. 234–235.

FIFTH READING
Genesis 46:8–27

The Torah then lists and counts Jacob's family – children and grandchildren – noting that they totaled 70 people. The 70th and youngest in this census was Levi's daughter Yocheved, whom we will meet later as the mother of Moses.

Feminine Power

כָּל הַנֶּפֶשׁ לְבֵית יַעֲקֹב הַבָּאָה מִצְרַיְמָה שִׁבְעִים: (בראשית מו, כז)

**The total of Jacob's household who
came to Egypt was 70 persons.**

By descending into the Egyptian exile, the Jewish people began the process of elevating and transforming the 70 nations of the world. Yocheved's birth just before Jacob's family entered Egypt brought their number to 70, thus enabling Jacob to begin the mission of refining the 70 nations.

The process of transforming the world is twofold: first, we must cure the world of its opposition to holiness, and then, we must transform it into holiness. The former is the "masculine," assertive approach, whereas the latter is the "feminine," nurturing approach.

Thus, the commandments entrusted to women – ensuring that the family is nourished in accordance with the Torah's laws, ensuring the safety and spiritual warmth of the home (as exemplified by kindling the Sabbath candles), and sanctifying marital life (as exemplified by observing the laws of "Family Purity") – are all ways of transforming the mundane aspects of ordinary human life into expressions of holiness.[5]

---

5. *Likutei Sichot*, vol. 20, pp. 218 ff.

SIXTH READING
Genesis 46:28–47:10

In advance of his arrival in Egypt, Jacob sent Judah to prepare
a *yeshiva* – a place where he and his descendants could devote
themselves to constant study of the Torah.

Undistracted Attention to Spiritual Growth

וְאֶת יְהוּדָה שָׁלַח לְפָנָיו אֶל יוֹסֵף לְהוֹרֹת לְפָנָיו גֹּשְׁנָה וגו': (בראשית מו, כח)

**[Jacob] sent Judah ahead of him to Joseph, to
make advance preparations in Goshen.**

Jacob sent Judah to start a school rather than asking Joseph to
do so, recognizing that a Torah academy must be headed by a
person who is completely removed from mundane affairs and is
fully immersed in the study of the Torah. Since Joseph's Divine
mission required that he run the mundane affairs of Egypt, he
could not also head Jacob's school of Torah, notwithstanding his
undisputed righteousness.

Likewise, those who wish to adopt the vocation of the Torah
scholar or teacher must be both allowed and required to be completely separated from worldly affairs, in order to be able to focus
on educating our children without any distractions.[6]

---

6. *Likutei Sichot*, vol. 3, pp. 827–830. See *Eiruvin* 65a.

SEVENTH READING

Genesis 47:11–27

When Jacob arrived in Egypt, Joseph presented him to Pharaoh. Jacob blessed Pharaoh that the Nile River should miraculously overflow when he approached it. As a result of this blessing, the predicted seven years of famine ended after only two years. As he promised, Joseph settled his family in the province of Goshen.

Forgiveness

וַיְכַלְכֵּל יוֹסֵף אֶת אָבִיו וְאֶת אֶחָיו וְאֵת כָּל בֵּית
אָבִיו לֶחֶם לְפִי הַטָּף: (בראשית מז, יב)

**Joseph provided for his father and his brothers
and his father's entire household.**

Joseph taught us to repay evil with goodness, just as he did with his brothers, sustaining them for the rest of his life. He was able to forgive his brothers not only because he was a master of self-control, but chiefly because he understood the nature of human evil. As we have seen, the brothers' evil act of selling him into slavery served G-d's plan that Joseph eventually become viceroy of Egypt. Joseph focused on the positive outcome of his brothers' acts rather than on their evil essence.

Similarly, we ask G-d to treat us like Joseph treated his brothers, perceiving our misdeeds as being ultimately for the good and responding to them with kindness. In order to "inspire" G-d to see our misdeeds as being ultimately for the good, we must first do the same ourselves, by utilizing our misdeeds as motivation for self-improvement. The misdeed that fuels this transformation thus becomes a merit, retroactively serving a good purpose.

We can further enhance our ability to transform our own misdeeds into merits by training ourselves to see other people's offenses as potential merits, as well.[7]

---

7. *Likutei Sichot*, vol. 5, pp. 241 ff.

Vaichi

The Close of the Patriarchal Era

Genesis 47:28–50:26

THE TWELFTH AND FINAL SECTION OF THE BOOK OF GENESIS
chronicles the last period in the life of Jacob and the succession of
his son Joseph. Jacob lived (*Vaichi*, "and he lived" in Hebrew) the
last 17 years of his life in Egypt. Besides devoting himself to the
ongoing moral education of his descendants, Jacob organized his
family into tribes in order to prepare it for its spiritual destiny, and
then bequeathed to each tribe its unique spiritual characteristics.
After his death, Jacob's sons bury him in the family burial plot in
Hebron. The section closes with the subsequent death of Joseph
and his promise that G-d would eventually take them back to
the Promised Land.

FIRST READING

Genesis 47:28–48:9

Jacob's final years, spent in Egypt with his reunited family, were the best in his life.

True Joy

וַיְחִי יַעֲקֹב בְּאֶרֶץ מִצְרַיִם שְׁבַע עֶשְׂרֵה שָׁנָה וגו': (בראשית מז, כח)

Jacob lived 17 years in Egypt.

Notwithstanding Jacob's joy in seeing his family reunited and faithful to their traditions, it is still hard to imagine how the years he spent in the idolatrous environment of Egypt could be the best of his life. The answer to this puzzle is that, as mentioned previously, Jacob had sent Judah to set up an academy for the study of the Torah in Egypt. Jacob thereby ensured that he and his descendants would remain immune to the negative influences of Egypt's corrupt society.

Furthermore, by resisting the enticements of Egypt, Jacob's children grew in a way that is only possible when we are faced with challenges. This is why Jacob's *best* years were those that he spent in Egypt, for it was only there that he could see that his children had fully absorbed his moral instruction and guidance. He now knew that the Divine mission begun by his grandfather, Abraham, would continue.

Similarly, we often find ourselves in "Egypt," in places of spiritual darkness. Like Jacob and his family, through studying the Torah we remain safe from the darkness of "Egypt" and reveal G-dliness even there.[1]

1. *Likutei Sichot*, vol. 10, pp. 160–166.

SECOND READING

Genesis 48:10–16

When Jacob sensed that he was about to die, he sent for Joseph. Jacob instructed Joseph not to bury him in Egypt, fearing that the Egyptians might turn his grave into an object of worship since it was his blessing that had ended the years of famine. Instead, Jacob instructed Joseph to bury him in the family tomb in Hebron. Some time later, when Jacob became ill, Joseph took his two sons, Manasseh and Ephraim, to Jacob in order for them to receive his final blessing. Jacob surprised Joseph by informing him that he was making Joseph's sons the heads of two separate tribes, on an equal footing with Jacob's own sons.

The Reward of Loyalty

וַיֹּאמֶר . . . אֶל יוֹסֵף רְאֹה פָנֶיךָ לֹא פִלָּלְתִּי וְהִנֵּה הֶרְאָה

אֹתִי אֱלֹקִים גַּם אֶת זַרְעֶךָ: (בראשית מח, יא)

[Jacob] said to Joseph, "I dared not even hope to see your face, yet now G-d has even shown me your children."

Jacob intimated why he considered Ephraim and Manasseh his own sons by referring to them as "your two sons who were born to you in Egypt before I came to you." Even though Ephraim and Manasseh were born and raised in Egypt before Jacob's arrival, they grew up true to their grandfather's ideals. Therefore, Jacob considered them as loyal to him and his ideals as his own children.[2]

2. *Likutei Sichot*, vol. 15, p. 435.

THIRD READING

Genesis 48:17–22

Jacob then surprised Joseph further by giving Ephraim precedence over Manasseh, even though Manasseh was older.

Immunization vs. Influence

וְאוּלָם אָחִיו הַקָּטֹן יִגְדַּל מִמֶּנּוּ וְגוֹ': (בראשית מח, יט)

[Jacob told Joseph,] "But his younger brother will become greater than he."

As we have seen, Manasseh represents our obligation to protect ourselves from the negative influences of our surroundings. Ephraim, in contrast, represents our obligation to influence our surroundings, to redeem ourselves and the world from exile. Since before influencing the world we must ensure that we are protected from its temptations, Joseph named his firstborn Manasseh, and wished to give him precedence in receiving Jacob's blessing, as well.

In granting his blessing, however, Jacob focused on the *purpose* of our descent into exile: not mere spiritual survival, but the spiritual growth that results from our successful encounter with exile. Jacob therefore gave precedence to Ephraim.

Likewise, in our exile: although – just like Manasseh is the firstborn – securing our Jewish identity is the first step, our main purpose is to be an Ephraim, to positively influence the world around us.[3]

---

3. *Likutei Sichot*, vol. 15, pp. 432–434, vol. 5, pp. 459 ff. See Rashi on 25:26, above. See *Likutei Sichot*, vol. 20, pp. 241–242.

FOURTH READING

Genesis 49:1–18

Jacob then summoned the rest of his sons and blessed each one in accordance with his unique contribution to the overall Divine mission of the Jewish people. These individual emphases became the defining characteristics of the 12 tribes that descended from them. In his blessing to Judah, Jacob said that Judah's portion of the Land of Israel will be so suited to growing grapes that he will be able to wash his clothes in wine.

The Torah's Inner Dimension

כִּבֶּס בַּיַּיִן לְבֻשׁוֹ וגו': (בראשית מט, יא)

He will launder his clothes in wine.

Every time we observe a commandment, we create a spiritual "garment" for our souls. These garments, however, must be "laundered in wine" – our fulfillment of the commandments must be imbued with joy.

The way to achieve this joy is by studying the inner dimension of the Torah – the teachings of Jewish mysticism (Kabbalah and Chassidism) – for this dimension of the Torah inspires us to love G-d and cleave to Him through observance of His commandments. It is for this reason that this aspect of the Torah is referred to as "the wine of Torah."[4]

---

4. *Sefer HaMa'amarim 5699*, pp. 58–59; see *Torah Or* 46c–d.

FIFTH READING

Genesis 49:19–26

In his blessing to his son Naphtali, Jacob said that his portion of the Promised Land would be swift to ripen its fruits, comparing this swiftness to that of a deer.

Escapism and Devotion

נַפְתָּלִי אַיָּלָה שְׁלֻחָה וגו': (בראשית מט, כא)

Naphtali is a deer let loose.

In his blessings, Jacob compares some of the tribes to wild beasts (e.g., Judah to a lion, Benjamin to a wolf) and others to domestic animals (e.g., Issachar to a donkey, Joseph to an ox). The tribes compared to wild animals are characterized by a passionate love for G-d and a yearning to escape material existence to cleave to Him. The tribes compared to domestic animals – whose nature is to dutifully accept the work given to them – are characterized by submission to the task of revealing G-dliness within material existence.

Jacob concludes by blessing all the tribes with the characteristics unique to each tribe individually. Thus, although each tribe preserves its particular emphasis on the Jewish people's Divine mission, it also can and should incorporate the other tribes' paths within its own. Therefore, we all embody these two ways of relating to the world, both yearning to transcend it and working to refine it.[5]

5. *Or HaTorah, Bereishit*, vol. 5, 1092a–1093a.

SIXTH READING

Genesis 49:27–50:20

Jacob concluded his blessings to his children by blessing them all with all the characteristics unique to each one individually.

Unity in Community

וַיְבָרֶךְ אוֹתָם אִישׁ אֲשֶׁר כְּבִרְכָתוֹ בֵּרַךְ אֹתָם: (בראשית מט, כח)

**[Jacob] gave them all the blessings that
he gave each one individually.**

Although we each have our unique roles in our Divine mission to make this world into G-d's home, we are all involved to some extent in the roles played by others, as well. There are three increasingly effective ways that we can do this:

- We all focus exclusively on our personal tasks, but since we are working toward the same goal, we all share in the results of our separate accomplishments.
- We invite and encourage one another to participate occasionally in the personal activity that we emphasize.
- When we periodically engage in tasks other than our forte, we immerse ourselves in them just as fully as we do when we engage in our personal task.

Participating in each other's endeavors fosters Jewish unity, making us worthy of G-d's blessings, including – and especially – the ultimate blessing, the Messianic Redemption.[6]

6. *Likutei Sichot*, vol. 25, pp. 287–291.

SEVENTH READING

Genesis 50:21–26

After concluding his blessings to his family, Jacob died. Joseph led his brothers to Canaan to bury their father in Hebron. After they returned to Egypt, Joseph continued to provide for his family. Before his own death, Joseph reminded the family of G-d's promise to return their descendants to the Land of Israel.

We Are Not Alone

וַיָּמָת יוֹסֵף...וַיִּישֶׂם בָּאָרוֹן בְּמִצְרָיִם: (בראשית נ, כו)

Joseph died and was placed in a coffin in Egypt.

Throughout their lives, our patriarchs and matriarchs clung to G-d and His plan for creation. They were therefore unaffected by our world's concealment of Divinity. Although our Divine consciousness is much lower, we have nonetheless inherited some of their ability to rise above the limitations of this world. This is what has enabled us to fulfill the Divine mission described in the next book of the Torah, Exodus. In the Book of Exodus, we will see the Jewish people receive the Torah and begin building a home for G-d out of this world.

To provide us with this inspiration, our ancestors, too, had to live in a state similar to exile. This happened when Jacob and his family descended to Egypt. Although they were never enslaved, they were still in "exile," banished from the Holy Land. By maintaining spiritual mastery over Egypt, Jacob and his sons gave us the strength to overcome the spiritual darkness of our own exile.

After the account of Jacob in Egypt, the Torah gives us the inspiration that will sustain us until the end of our exile: "Joseph was placed in a coffin in Egypt." We are not alone; Joseph is with us in exile, reminding us that we too can rise above exile and transform it into Redemption.[7]

---

7. *Likutei Sichot*, vol. 25, pp. 474 ff, vol. 30, pp. 249 ff.

EXODUS

Shemot

Slavery

Exodus 1:1–6:1

THE FIRST SECTION OF THE BOOK OF EXODUS OPENS BY LIST-
ing the names (*Shemot*, in Hebrew) of Jacob's sons, and then
chronicles the growth of their descendants into a nation and their
enslavement in Egypt. As the conditions of slavery progressively
worsen, the Jews cry out to G-d. G-d then charges Moses with
the mission of freeing the Jewish people from slavery in order to
receive the Torah. G-d informs them that the purpose of their
redemption is so they can assume their role as the moral leaders
of humanity, steering the world toward its Divine fulfillment as
G-d's true home.

FIRST READING

Exodus 1:1–17

G-d's promise that He would make Jacob's family into a great nation in Egypt was fulfilled quickly. In less than a century, the Jews' numbers increased so dramatically that Pharaoh was afraid that they might take over Egypt. He therefore began conscripting the Jews to labor in his building projects. Unfortunately, the Jews – except for the tribe of Levi – had begun to neglect their moral heritage, which left them susceptible to Pharaoh's artful appeal to their patriotic loyalty to Egypt. Thus, Pharaoh eventually succeeded in enslaving the Jews altogether, except for the Levites.

Jewish Identity

וְאֵלֶּה שְׁמוֹת בְּנֵי יִשְׂרָאֵל הַבָּאִים מִצְרָיְמָה וגו': (שמות א, א)

These are the names of the sons of Israel who came to Egypt.

The Jews' physical exile was their forced slavery; their spiritual exile was their psychological enslavement to their host's culture. Although many Jews assimilated because of their exile, others struggled to retain their Jewish identity, refusing to give up their Jewish names and language because of their faith in their destiny.

It was only after revealing their inner identity in response to the challenge of exile that the Jewish people could receive the Torah. The purpose of the Torah is to teach us how to bring Divine consciousness into the most mundane aspects of life, even those that initially oppose G-dliness. In exile, the Jewish people learned how to overcome even these forces.

The same applies to our present exile: holding on tenaciously to our traditions – even those that appear to be unimportant – will hasten our redemption. The challenges that we overcome purify and prepare us for the exalted Divine revelations that will accompany the imminent, final Redemption.[1]

1. *Torah Or* 49a ff; *Or HaTorah, Shemot*, p. 11. *Sefer HaMa'amarim* 5737, p. 118. *Likutei Sichot*, vol. 3, pp. 843–848, vol. 16, pp. 34–37, vol. 26, pp. 301–305.

SECOND READING
Exodus 1:18–2:10

Thirty years of conscripted labor did not succeed in breaking the Jews' spirit or curbing their fertility. So Pharaoh intensified their slavery by having them perform meaningless tasks. Five years after subjecting the Jews to this demoralizing labor, Moses was born to Amram, grandson of Jacob's son Levi, and Yocheved, Levi's daughter. Pharaoh's astrologers discerned that the Jews' future redeemer had been born, so Pharaoh attempted to prevent the redemption by decreeing that every newborn boy be killed.

Drowning in Egypt

וַיְצַו פַּרְעֹה לְכָל עַמּוֹ לֵאמֹר כָּל הַבֵּן הַיִּלּוֹד הַיְאֹרָה תַּשְׁלִיכֻהוּ וְכָל הַבַּת תְּחַיּוּן: (שמות א, כב)

Pharaoh gave orders to all his people: "You must cast every boy who is born into the Nile, but you must let every girl live."

By instructing his people to "let every girl live," Pharaoh meant that the Jewish girls should be raised as Egyptians. He thus decreed that the boys be killed physically and the girls be killed spiritually. The decree to throw the boys into the Nile also alludes to immersing the Jews in Egyptian culture, for the Egyptians worshipped the Nile as the source of their livelihood and culture.

Egypt is the prototype of all exiles. In all exiles, the ruling culture urges us to raise our children in its ways, promising that this is the path to attain material and social success. As in Egypt, resisting these promises and ensuring that our children grow up cherishing the Torah's values is what will guarantee their material, social, and spiritual happiness, as well as their freedom from the bonds of exile.[2]

2. *Likutei Sichot*, vol. 1, p. 111.

THIRD READING

Exodus 2:11–25

Moses' mother Yocheved placed him in a basket, which she hid among the reeds in the Nile River. He was discovered by Pharaoh's daughter, Bitya, who adopted him. Bitya employed Yocheved as Moses' wet nurse, and thus Moses grew up in his family's household. Yocheved kept Moses at home, so he joined Pharaoh's household only at age 12 or so. Pharaoh knew that Moses was a Jew, but he hoped that by raising him as an Egyptian, his exceptional intelligence and talents could be put to good use in Pharaoh's government. When Moses was about 18 years old, he saw an Egyptian taskmaster beating a Jew mercilessly, and killed the taskmaster. As Moses feared, Pharaoh heard of this and sentenced him to death.

In G-d We Trust

וַיִּשְׁמַע פַּרְעֹה אֶת הַדָּבָר הַזֶּה וְגוֹ': (שמות ב, טו)

Pharaoh heard about the incident.

Moses should have trusted in G-d's protection, but because he did not, he forfeited it. Pharaoh therefore heard about the incident and sought to kill him. Had Moses not been afraid – and not voiced this fear – nothing would have happened.

Similarly, when we face obstacles in fulfilling our Divine mission, we should realize that we can earn G-d's helpful intervention by trusting that He will help us. Feeling confident of G-d's help does not mean that we should not take whatever natural steps are necessary to avoid trouble or to solve our problems; it merely means that we should trust G-d to crown our efforts with success.

Our sages teach us that it was in the merit of their confidence in G-d that the Jews were delivered from Egypt. Similarly, our confidence that G-d will redeem us from the present exile will itself hasten the Redemption.[3]

---

3. *Likutei Sichot*, vol. 36, pp. 1–6, based on *Chovot HaLevavot, Sha'ar HaBitachon* 2, 3; *Ikarim* 4:46; *Kad HaKemach*, s.v. *Bitachon*, etc.

FOURTH READING
Exodus 3:1–15

Moses fled from Egypt, eventually arriving in Midian. At the age of 77, he married Tziporah, daughter of the local chieftain, Jethro, and went to work shepherding Jethro's flocks. Jethro had denounced idolatry, and was therefore ostracized by his people. In the meantime, the Jew's slavery in Egypt had intensified further, so G-d appeared to Moses on Mount Sinai, speaking to him from a bush that was burning but was miraculously not consumed.

Showing G-d that We Care

וַיֹּאמֶר מֹשֶׁה אָסֻרָה נָּא וְאֶרְאֶה אֶת הַמַּרְאֶה הַגָּדֹל הַזֶּה וגו': (שמות ג, ג)

[**When he saw the burning bush,**] **Moses said, "Let me turn away and go over there to behold this remarkable sight."**

When Moses said these words, he was voicing the aspiration that is the foundation of any relationship with G-d. This aspiration is what makes us human, i.e., beings that strive to rise above animal existence in search of intellectual depth and spiritual self-refinement.

This ambition enables us to focus our intellects in solitary meditation and climb the ladder of Divine consciousness. Whatever level of consciousness we achieve, we always aspire to ascend further. The force of this aspiration unlocks all our human potential, strengthening our intellect, emotions, and senses. We are constantly blessed with new insight and understanding, which in turn lead us toward a deeper relationship with G-d.

Thus, as stated in the next verse, it was only after "G-d saw that [Moses] had turned aside to look" that "He called to him from the midst of the bush."[4]

---

4. *Likutei Diburim* 138b–139a.

FIFTH READING
Exodus 3:16–4:17

G-d told Moses that He was now going to redeem the Jewish people in order to give them the Torah and to bring them to the Land of Israel. Moses asked how he should explain G-d's silence throughout the Jews' century of slavery. G-d replied that He indeed felt their pain throughout their exile. However, the exile had a purpose, and His mercy is operative at all times, even if it is hidden. G-d then told Moses that if he tells the people that the time of their redemption has arrived, they will believe him – despite their complaints about His treatment of them.

The Promise of the Redemption

פָּקֹד פָּקַדְתִּי אֶתְכֶם וְאֶת הֶעָשׂוּי לָכֶם בְּמִצְרָיִם: (שמות ג, טז)

[G-d told Moses to tell the people], "I have indeed remembered you and what is being done to you in Egypt."

Even though the Jews had sunk to a dangerously low spiritual state, even serving idols, G-d did not tell Moses to rebuke them or to warn them that if they do not mend their ways their exile will continue. Rather, G-d instructed him to remind them of the merit of their forbears and to announce that in this merit and in the merit of their suffering they were about to be redeemed. Only much later, when he had an alternative for them – a commandment for them to fulfill – did Moses tell the Jews to stop serving idols.

Similarly, the most effective way to draw the hearts of our fellow Jews closer to G-d is by first showing them the beauty of their heritage and uplifting them with the promise of the Redemption.[5]

5. *Sefer HaSichot 5751*, vol. 1, pp. 250, 252.

SIXTH READING
Exodus 4:18–31

Moses insisted that the Jews would not believe that G-d had sent him, so G-d gave him the power to perform some miracles that would prove that he was on a Divine mission. Finally, Moses argued that his speech impediment prevented him from being an effective leader. To this, G-d replied that Moses' older brother Aaron was a gifted speaker and would do the talking in his stead. G-d then informed Moses that Pharaoh would refuse to release the Jews, and that only after suffering miraculous plagues would he do so. G-d therefore instructed Moses to take his staff, with which he would perform these miracles.

The Staff of G-d

וַיִּקַּח מֹשֶׁה אֶת מַטֵּה הָאֱלֹקִים בְּיָדוֹ: (שמות ד, כ)

Moses took the staff of G-d in his hand.

Even though, as we will see, Moses gave Pharaoh the honor due a king and spoke to him respectfully, he made no compromises in his demands concerning the people's spiritual and physical needs. He spoke with "the staff of G-d in his hand," i.e., with authority and determination.

The lesson for us here is that whenever we are confronted with an "Egyptian king," i.e., someone who seeks to impose upon us elements of a lifestyle that goes against our values and principles – whether through kindness or force – we must recognize the inherent danger in succumbing to such pressure. In the end, this Pharaoh will tell us to drown ourselves (or our children) in material culture. We must therefore respectfully but resolutely insist on living according to the Torah's values.[6]

6. *Likutei Sichot*, vol. 16, pp. 11–12.

SHABBAT

SEVENTH READING
Exodus 5:1–6:1

Moses took leave of Jethro and set out for Egypt. As G-d had predicted, when Moses demanded that Pharaoh release the Jews, even for three days, Pharaoh refused. Instead, Pharaoh ordered that the Jews no longer be supplied with straw to make into bricks; they would have to produce the same daily quota of bricks but gather the necessary straw themselves. The Jews complained to Moses; feeling the Jews' suffering, Moses asked G-d why He had sent him on this mission if this was the result.

Questioning G-d's Ways

וַיָּשָׁב מֹשֶׁה אֶל ה' וַיֹּאמַר אֲדֹנָי לָמָה הֲרֵעֹתָה לָעָם הַזֶּה וְגו': (שמות ה, כב)

**Moses returned to G-d and said, "G-d, why
have You mistreated this people?"**

Deep down, Moses was not questioning G-d's justice, but was just seeking to understand it. Moses and the Jewish people had inherited their faith in G-d from the patriarchs and matriarchs. This faith was indeed very strong, but in order to be redeemed from Egypt and receive the Torah, it was not enough for their relationship with G-d to be an inheritance from their ancestors; they had to make it their own. Only when a person internalizes his faith and makes it his own can it permeate his whole being.

Ironically, the way we transform our inherited faith into our own possession is by *questioning* it – not out of doubt or for the mere sake of questioning, but in order to truly understand it.

Thus, in response to Moses' desire to understand G-d's ways, G-d told him that the purpose of the exile was to enable the people to reach an even higher level of Divine consciousness than they could by relying solely on their inheritance from the patriarchs.[7]

---

7. *Likutei Sichot*, vol. 16, p. 51.

Va'eira

The First Seven Plagues

Exodus 6:2–9:35

IN THE SECOND SECTION OF THE BOOK OF EXODUS, G-D begins the process that will lead to the redemption of the Jews from Egyptian slavery. He first informs Moses that it is crucial that he and the Jewish people demonstrate the same faith in G-d that the patriarchs did when He appeared (*Va'eira* in Hebrew) to them. After some additional preparations, G-d then begins to strike the Egyptians with plagues.

FIRST READING
Exodus 6:2–13

At the end of the previous section, Moses was troubled by the seeming contradiction between his faith in G-d's goodness and G-d's apparent mistreatment of the Jewish people. G-d therefore told Moses: "You must learn from the patriarchs and matriarchs. They believed in Me unquestioningly, even though I made promises to them that I did not fulfill during their lifetimes."

"Seeing" G-d

וַיְדַבֵּר אֱלֹקִים אֶל מֹשֶׁה וַיֹּאמֶר אֵלָיו אֲנִי ה': וָאֵרָא אֶל
אַבְרָהָם אֶל יִצְחָק וְאֶל יַעֲקֹב וגו': (שמות ו, ב-ג)

**G-d spoke to Moses, saying to him, "I am G-d. I
appeared to Abraham, Isaac, and Jacob."**

When it appears to us that something is wrong in the way G-d runs the world, G-d *wants* us to question Him. But at the same time, we must continue to believe absolutely in G-d's reality and goodness.

From where can we draw the power to believe in G-d so thoroughly that we virtually see Him even in the darkest moments of exile? G-d answers this question by saying, "I appeared to Abraham, Isaac, and Jacob." The patriarchs and matriarchs possessed this unshakable faith, and we inherit it from them. If we nurture it properly, we, too, will "see" G-d even when His goodness is not readily apparent.

This faith enables us to live out the final moments of our exile yearning for its end – and demanding it! – while maximizing our use of its remaining moments. In this merit, we will hasten the Messianic Redemption.[1]

---

1. *Hitva'aduyot 5743*, vol. 2, pp. 823–830.

SECOND READING
Exodus 6:14–28

The Torah then reviews the lineage of Moses and Aaron, for their lineage was an important factor contributing to the Jewish people's acceptance of them as leaders.

Moses and Aaron

הוּא אַהֲרֹן וּמֹשֶׁה וגו': (שמות ו, כו)

These are Aaron and Moses.

Moses was the transmitter of the Torah that he received from G-d. The "Moses" aspect of our lives is thus the study of G-d's Torah and the performance of His commandments. Aaron was the first high priest. The "Aaron" aspect of our lives is thus prayer, for prayer reaches up to G-d as did the sacrifices that were offered up by the priests.

The Torah sometimes mentions Moses before Aaron and sometimes mentions Aaron before Moses. This teaches us that sometimes we need to first study the Torah or fulfill some commandment in order to properly relate to G-d in prayer. At other times, we might need to connect to G-d through prayer before studying the Torah or fulfilling its commandments, in order to study or act in selfless devotion to G-d.[2]

2. *Likutei Torah* 3:88c.

THIRD READING

Exodus 6:29–7:7

G-d then gave specific instructions to Moses and Aaron regarding how to speak to Pharaoh.

How to Talk to Pharaoh

וַיֹּאמֶר ה' אֶל מֹשֶׁה רְאֵה נְתַתִּיךָ אֱלֹקִים לְפַרְעֹה וְגוֹ': (שמות ז, א)

**G-d said to Moses, "Observe! I have
made you master over Pharaoh."**

The purpose of Moses' respectful yet forceful speeches to Pharaoh was to break the forces of evil when their powers were strongest.

Similarly, there are times in our lives when our inner "Pharaohs," i.e., our animal drives, seem to have the upper hand. At such times, the best way to overcome these drives is to channel our inner "Moses" and rage against them, insult them, and humiliate them.

The same is true regarding our mission to oppose negativity in the world at large. Of course, we must always convey G-d's message in a pleasant and peaceful way, just as G-d commanded Moses to address Pharaoh respectfully. But at the same time, we must approach our "Pharaohs" fearlessly and forcefully. If we remain true to G-d's message, we can break the power of darkness and help bring G-d's redemptive light to the world.[3]

3. *Likutei Sichot,* vol. 16, pp. 74–76.

FOURTH READING
Exodus 7:8–8:6

As G-d instructed them, Moses and Aaron presented themselves before Pharaoh and his court, demanding that he release the Jews from slavery. Pharaoh requested proof that they were indeed sent by G-d. As G-d had instructed him to, Moses told Aaron to cast his staff to the ground, transforming it into a serpent. But Pharaoh was unimpressed by this marvel since his sorcerers were also able to do it. So G-d told Moses to transform the Nile River's water into blood, as the first of the ten plagues.

Warmth and Enthusiasm

הִנֵּה אָנֹכִי מַכֶּה בַּמַּטֶּה אֲשֶׁר בְּיָדִי עַל הַמַּיִם
אֲשֶׁר בַּיְאֹר וְנֶהֶפְכוּ לְדָם: (שמות ז, יז)

[G-d instructed Moses to tell Pharaoh,] "I am now going to strike the water in the river with the staff in my hand, and it will turn into blood."

The first of the ten plagues was the transformation of cold river water into warm blood, signifying the transformation of cold indifference toward Divinity into warm enthusiasm for it. This had to be the first of the plagues, because indifference would have prevented the Egyptians from being affected by any further demonstrations of G-d's power and involvement in life.

A similar lesson applies to anyone striving to leave the slavery of their inner "Egypt" – the tyranny of their material drives and not-yet-refined bodily desires. Our first step in this process is to replace any cold indifference to all things Jewish and holy with warm, passionate enthusiasm for G-d, His Torah, and His commandments.[4]

4. *Likutei Sichot*, vol. 1, p. 121.

FIFTH READING
Exodus 8:7–18

The plague of blood was followed by the plagues of frogs and lice.

The Purpose of Culture

וַיֹּאמֶר ה' אֶל מֹשֶׁה אֱמֹר אֶל אַהֲרֹן נְטֵה אֶת מַטְּךָ וְהַךְ
אֶת עֲפַר הָאָרֶץ וְהָיָה לְכִנָּם וגו': (שמות ח, יב)

**G-d instructed Moses to say to Aaron, "Raise your staff
and strike the dust of the earth, and it will turn into lice."**

The louse is a parasite; it lives off animals and people without
contributing anything to their lives. It is therefore a metaphor
for evil, since evil thrives by sucking the life force out of holiness
rather than by its own merits.

Just as a louse can attach itself to a person only if his hygiene is
lax, evil can only thrive when we allow our Divine consciousness
to lapse, falling either into misdeeds or the apathy toward holiness
that leaves us vulnerable to the enticements of materialism.

By infesting the Egyptians with lice, G-d was showing them
what their indifference to Divinity made them into: "parasites."
All their achievements in literature, art, architecture, science, and
so on, served only to inflate their egos and enhance their material lives. As such, they were draining vitality from the forces of
holiness in the world rather than aiding holiness.[5]

5. *Or HaTorah, Bereishit*, pp. 124b–125a, 444ab.

SIXTH READING
Exodus 8:19–9:16

The fourth plague was the sudden attack of a mixed horde of wild animals. G-d had Moses tell Pharaoh that this horde would not attack the province of Goshen, where the Jews lived.

Healthy Distinctions

וְשַׂמְתִּי פְדֻת בֵּין עַמִּי וּבֵין עַמֶּךָ וְגו': (שמות ח, יט)

[G-d instructed Moses to tell Pharaoh,] "I will make a redemptive distinction between My people and your people."

The most frightening facet of this plague was that the horde of wild animals attacked as a disorderly mixture rather than species by species. This anarchy and the terror it inspired are similar to what happens when the moral boundaries that keep society intact are breached.

There is value in questioning the established morals of secular society, but this can only be done when we are firmly grounded in our commitment to the Divine values of the Torah. Only when we are clear about what values are authentically holy can we properly evaluate each element of secular culture and choose what to co-opt and what to reject.

When we embrace this essential distinction between holy and unholy values, it is easier for us to enhance our connection with G-d.[6]

6. *Likutei Sichot*, vol. 11, pp. 32–33.

SEVENTH READING

Exodus 9:17–35

The fifth plague was an epidemic that struck the Egyptians' livestock. The sixth plague was a skin inflammation that erupted into blisters on the skin of the Egyptians and their cattle. The seventh plague was a rain of hail formed miraculously of ice together with fire.

Combining Mercy and Severity

וַיְהִי בָרָד וְאֵשׁ מִתְלַקַּחַת בְּתוֹךְ הַבָּרָד כָּבֵד מְאֹד וגו': (שמות ט, כד)

**The hail was very heavy, with flashing
lightning in the midst of the hail.**

Water and fire derive from and express the Divine attributes of mercy and severity, respectively. Thus, the uniqueness of the plague of hail was its blend of ice and fire, Divine mercy and severity. Similarly, although this was a particularly severe plague, as indicated by the harsh warning preceding it, this very warning included merciful instructions how to avert it.

Only G-d can override nature and combine fire and ice. In the same way, it is only by rising above our natural limitations and connecting ourselves to G-d that we can be both strict and merciful at the same time – both for our own benefit and for the benefit of others.[7]

---

7. *Likutei Sichot*, vol. 31, pp. 44–45, based on *Maskil LeDavid*.

Bo

The Last Three Plagues; The Exodus

Exodus 10:1–13:16

THE THIRD SECTION OF THE BOOK OF EXODUS OPENS AS G-D tells Moses to come (*Bo*, in Hebrew) to Pharaoh in order to announce the eighth plague. Two more plagues follow, after which the Jews are finally released from slavery and sent forth from Egypt. G-d tells the people to observe the anniversary of the Exodus as the holiday of Passover.

FIRST READING
Exodus 10:1–11

The eighth plague was a huge swarm of locusts that decimated Egypt's extensive grain fields.

Never Too Late

כִּי אִם מָאֵן אַתָּה לְשַׁלֵּחַ אֶת עַמִּי הִנְנִי מֵבִיא מָחָר אַרְבֶּה בִּגְבֻלֶךָ: (שמות י, ד)

[Moses said to Pharaoh,] "For if you refuse to send forth My people, I will bring locusts."

The fact that G-d warned Pharaoh that he would be punished for not obeying Moses' demand means that the door to repentance was still open. True, G-d had made Pharaoh stubborn, but that just meant that it was difficult for him to repent. Had Pharaoh summoned the inner strength to listen to his conscience, he still could have let the Jews go and spared himself and his country the impending ruin.

The lessons for us are as follows: First, no matter how estranged we may feel from G-d, even if it seems as though G-d has shut the door on us, nothing can resist our sincere efforts to return to Him. The apparent estrangement exists only in order to inspire us to summon a deeper, more powerful resolve.

Second, no matter how far another person may seem to have strayed from G-d, we must never despair of him. With true love and friendship, we can encourage him to mend his ways, and with G-d's help he will come back to his true, inner self.[1]

---

1. *Likutei Sichot*, vol. 6, pp. 64–68.

SECOND READING
Exodus 10:12–23

The ninth plague was absolute darkness that descended upon Egypt for six uninterrupted days. Like the other plagues, this darkness demonstrated to the Egyptians G-d's power over them. Additionally, the darkness enabled the Jews (who were not affected by it) to circulate among the Egyptians in order to see where they were hiding their wealth. Also, there were Jews who did not want to leave Egypt, and they died during the plague of darkness.

The Future Redemption

וַיֹּאמֶר ה' אֶל מֹשֶׁה נְטֵה יָדְךָ עַל הַשָּׁמַיִם וִיהִי
חֹשֶׁךְ עַל אֶרֶץ מִצְרָיִם וגו': (שמות י, כא)

G-d said to Moses, "Raise your arm toward the sky so that there will be darkness upon Egypt."

G-d did not force those Jews who did not want to leave Egypt to do so. By choosing to remain in Egypt, their lives lost all meaning and had spiritually ended. In contrast, in the future Redemption, even those Jews who do not consciously want to be redeemed will be taken out of exile. This is because when G-d gave us the Torah, He connected our essence with His essence, making it impossible for us to really oppose our connection with Him.

Of course, we can go through the motions of opposing our connection to G-d, but this is only superficial. Sooner or later, our deep, inner essence will surface, and this will make us all indeed worthy of being redeemed.[2]

2. *Likutei Sichot*, vol. 11, pp. 1–7.

THIRD READING
Exodus 10:24–11:3

After the plague of darkness, Pharaoh agreed to send forth the Jewish people – but on his own terms. When Moses refused these terms, Pharaoh reneged and angrily sent Moses away.

The Lust for Power

וַיֹּאמֶר לוֹ פַרְעֹה לֵךְ מֵעָלָי ...כִּי בְּיוֹם רְאֹתְךָ פָנַי תָּמוּת:
וַיֹּאמֶר מֹשֶׁה כֵּן דִּבַּרְתָּ וְגוֹ': (שמות י, כח-כט)

Pharaoh said [to Moses], "Leave my presence! The day you see my face you will die!" Moses replied, "You have spoken rightly."

Every evil thing is really a "fallen" version – i.e., a distortion – of some form of holiness. Pharaoh was the fallen expression of G-d's ability to override the limits of nature. In its fallen form, this power turned into Pharaoh's arrogant disregard of any authority other than his own. In this context, when Pharaoh told Moses that "the day you see my face you will die," he was (unknowingly) warning Moses that no one can behold G-d's infinity and live. Moses agreed: no finite, created being can experience G-d's infinity and continue existing as a finite being; he will be absorbed by the experience and "dissolve" into G-d's infinity.

However, G-d is not bound by His own rules; He can allow an individual to "survive" this experience. This is exactly what He did with Moses, in order to allow him to destroy Pharaoh's evil by revealing G-d's supernatural power through the plagues.

We all have our inner "Pharaoh," i.e., some stubborn opposition or hostility to holiness. When this "Pharaoh" is vanquished, the other obstacles toward living a positive, healthy life will follow suit.[3]

---

3. *Sefer HaSichot 5752*, vol. 1, p. 283; *Sefer HaSichot 5751*, volume 1, pp. 271–282. See *Sefer HaMa'amarim 5704*, pp. 119, 127.

FOURTH READING

Exodus 11:4–12:20

In the tenth and final plague, all the Egyptian firstborn died instantaneously at midnight of 15 Nisan. Before this, G-d instructed the Jewish people to prepare a lamb or kid goat to slaughter and eat that night.

Fleeing Exile

וַאֲכַלְתֶּם אֹתוֹ בְּחִפָּזוֹן וגו׳: (שמות יב, יא)

[G-d instructed Moses to tell the people,] "You must eat [the lamb or kid goat] in haste."

Although the Jews had renounced their involvement in Egyptian culture, the glamour of Egyptian materialism still maintained an inner grip on them. G-d therefore had to hurry them out of Egypt while they were still sufficiently impressed by the ten plagues that they were willing to leave the only home they knew and venture into the double unknown of the inhospitable desert and a lifestyle of holiness.

The same is true whenever we go out of a personal "Egypt," i.e., whenever we leave behind the familiarity of a previous way of living and rise to a new level of Divine consciousness and its accompanying way of life. In order to stay on our new path, it is crucial to sustain our momentum and take all necessary measures in order not to slide back into previous habits.

In the Messianic Redemption, however, this caution will be unnecessary. Since this redemption will be absolute and encompass all reality, there will be no possibility of backsliding into the mentality of materialism.[4]

4. *Tanya,* chapter 31; *Or HaTorah, Bo,* pp. 291–2; *Torat Shmuel, VeKachah (5637),* chapters 1–4; *Sefer HaMa'amarim 5737,* pp. 191–199.

FIFTH READING
Exodus 12:21–28

G-d told the Jews that the animal they were to eat this night would be called the "Passover" animal. He gave them further instructions regarding how they were to prepare it and eat it.

Preparing for Personal Redemption

וּלְקַחְתֶּם אֲגֻדַּת אֵזוֹב... וְהִגַּעְתֶּם אֶל הַמַּשְׁקוֹף וְאֶל שְׁתֵּי
הַמְּזוּזֹת מִן הַדָּם אֲשֶׁר בַּסָּף וְגוֹ': (שמות יב, כב)

[G-d instructed Moses to tell the people,] "You must take a bundle of hyssop and [with it] apply some of the blood [of the Passover animal] to the lintel and the two doorposts."

The right doorpost signified good deeds; the left doorpost signified prayer, and the lintel above them signified the study of the Torah. Together, these three constitute a complete, balanced life that enables us to fulfill our Divine mission of making the world into G-d's home.

The door itself signified our readiness to obey G-d's will, since this commitment is the entrance into our active partnership with G-d to rectify the world. The lowly hyssop used to apply the blood to the door frame signified the self-abnegation we must cultivate in order to be receptive to G-d's presence in our lives. The blood itself signified the vitality of our animating soul, with which we must perform good deeds, pray, and study the Torah.

Every personal exodus from an "Egypt" requires that we humbly apply our vitality to action, prayer, and study of the Torah, all performed with renewed commitment to our Divine mission in life.[5]

---

5. *Sefer HaMa'amarim 5632*, vol. 1, pp. 129, 284–285; *Sefer HaMa'amarim 5678*, pp. 239, 244–245; *Sefer HaMa'amarim 5706*, pp. 69–70, 76.

SIXTH READING
Exodus 12:29–51

As Moses had said, all the firstborn Egyptian males died precisely at midnight. The Egyptians urged the Jews to leave, showering them with silver, gold, and clothing. The Jewish women, confident that G-d would perform miracles for them, also brought timbrels to celebrate with.

Faith in the Redemption

וּבְנֵי יִשְׂרָאֵל...וַיִּשְׁאֲלוּ מִמִּצְרַיִם כְּלֵי כֶסֶף וּכְלֵי זָהָב וּשְׂמָלֹת: (שמות יב, לה)

**The Israelites ... requested silver and gold
utensils and clothing from the Egyptians.**

By also bringing along timbrels, the women demonstrated more faith and trust in G-d than did the men. The women of our generation, too, can lead the way by demonstrating their faith that the final Redemption is imminent. To be sure, until the moment of redemption arrives, we should all feel the bitterness of the exile and pray fervently that G-d bring it to an end. But at the same time, our unshakable confidence that G-d will fulfill His promise of redemption should fill us with overflowing joy. Women, on the strength of their innately more deep-seated faith, can already begin celebrating the Redemption – even with music and dance – and this will inspire the men to follow suit.[6]

6. *Sefer HaSichot 5752*, vol. 1, pp. 303–307.

SEVENTH READING
Exodus 13:1–16

G-d then told the Jews that they must celebrate the anniversary of the Exodus every year as the holiday of Passover. A central feature of this celebration would be the retelling of the story of the Exodus to the children.

For the Children

וְהִגַּדְתָּ לְבִנְךָ בַּיּוֹם הַהוּא לֵאמֹר וגו': (שמות יג, ח)

You must tell your child on that day.

Interestingly, the commandment to retell the story of the Exodus – which is the source for the annual Passover *Seder* – is given in the context of describing "the child who does not know how to ask," the most immature of all the four types of children to whom we must tailor our description of the Exodus. This teaches us that our duty to retell the Exodus applies *mainly* to this uninitiated child. We must find the words to inspire even this type of child with gratitude to G-d for liberating us from Egypt and from all past, present, future, personal, and collective Egypts.

This is so because the Exodus from Egypt was absolute: not one Jew remained in Egypt. Since the Exodus was so all-encompassing, the transmission of its message must also encompass each and every individual that can possibly understand it, even if this takes extraordinary effort.

By ensuring that even "the child who does not know how to ask" understands the meaning of the Exodus, we ensure that the other children will understand it, too, much as lifting up the bottom of any structure automatically raises the rest of the structure, as well.[7]

---

7. *Sefer HaMa'amarim 5734–5735*, pp. 347–353.

Beshalach

The Splitting of the Sea
Exodus 13:17–17:16

THE FOURTH SECTION OF THE BOOK OF EXODUS BEGINS AS Pharaoh "sent forth" (*Beshalach*, in Hebrew) the Jews from Egypt. The Jews proceed toward Mount Sinai to receive the Torah, but are pursued by Pharaoh and the Egyptian army. G-d splits the Sea of Reeds, allowing the Jews to pass to safety and then drowning the Egyptians in it. The Jews then continue on toward Mount Sinai, with G-d miraculously providing them with food (manna) and water from a rock. Just as they approach their destination, the Jews are attacked by the nation of Amalek.

FIRST READING
Exodus 13:17–14:8

Joseph had left instructions for the Jews to take his remains out of Egypt when they would leave. Moses therefore took Joseph's remains along when the Jews left Egypt. Joseph's remains were eventually interred in Shechem.

Joseph's Bones

וַיִּקַּח מֹשֶׁה אֶת עַצְמוֹת יוֹסֵף עִמּוֹ וְגו': (שמות יג, יט)

Moses took the bones of Joseph with him.

The Hebrew word for "bone" (*etzem*) also means "essence." The Jewish people were about to embark on a journey through a desert whose barrenness and perils were a reflection of its spiritual desolation. In order to be able to survive this journey, Moses ensured that the Jewish people were accompanied by the essence and spirit of Joseph.

Joseph's essence is expressed in his name, which means "May He add," for when he was born, his mother Rachel prayed, "May G-d add for me another son."[1] This wish includes the desire to welcome the estranged Jew back into the fold. In a more general sense, it includes the desire to transform all mundane reality into the vehicle for holiness it was originally intended to be.

The odyssey of exile is likened to a journey through a barren, perilous desert.[2] In order for us to persevere through periods of spiritual desolation, we must take our cue from Joseph's essence. We must strive to bring even the most distant and rebellious individuals back to the fold, showing them that they are truly G-d's beloved children. When we remain true to this objective, we are assured that in the end, no Jew will be left behind.[3]

---

1. Genesis 30:24.
2. See Ezekiel 20:35; Rabbeinu Bachaye and *Or HaChaim* on Numbers 33:1 ff.
3. *Likutei Sichot*, vol. 26, pp. 85–89.

SECOND READING

Exodus 14:9–14

G-d knew that the Jewish people would not feel totally free of Pharaoh's clutches as long as he remained alive, and that the potential threat of his pursuit would prevent them from receiving the Torah fully. So G-d again made Pharaoh stubborn, inspiring him to pursue the Jews to the shore of the Sea of Reeds (the Gulf of Suez). Seeing him approaching, the Jews panicked.

Embracing Spiritual Challenges

וּפַרְעֹה הִקְרִיב וגו': (שמות יד, י)

Pharaoh drew near.

The Midrash offers another interpretation: By chasing them, Pharaoh drew *the Jews* nearer *to G-d*, as evidenced by their crying out to Him when they saw the Egyptian army approaching. Indeed, it is often opposition that awakens our deepest reserves of energy.

When we are confronted with a challenge, we should view it as an opportunity for spiritual growth rather than try to avoid it. Comfort and contentment can cause us to lose sight of priorities, weakening our sense of urgency in our Divine mission. Physical or spiritual adversity can shock us out of this indifference, undermining our self-assurance and affording us the opportunity to advance in our relationship with G-d by breaking through the obstacle.[4]

---

4. *Torah Or* 61c; *Sefer HaMa'amarim 5721*, pp. 257–258; *Sichot Kodesh 5721*, pp. 62–63; *Sichot Kodesh 5726*, pp. 209–210.

THIRD READING

Exodus 14:15–25

Moses tried to calm the Jews and started to pray to G-d for deliverance. But G-d told Moses that there was no need to pray; all that was necessary was that he lift his staff over the sea and it would split, enabling the Jews to pass through it to safety.

Eliciting G-d's Blessings

וְאַתָּה הָרֵם אֶת מַטְּךָ וּנְטֵה אֶת יָדְךָ עַל הַיָּם וְגו': (שמות יד, טז)

**[G-d told Moses,] "Take up your staff
and raise your arm over the sea."**

The splitting of the Sea of Reeds was a miraculous and supernatural event. Yet there had to be a natural action to "ignite" the miracle: G-d instructed the people to journey forward and Moses to lift his staff over the water. G-d always demands some human act first and only then does He perform miracles.

This is because events that occur without our involvement do not truly affect us. Only when we expend some effort do we appreciate G-d's miracle. The same applies in all areas of life. Asking for G-d's blessings is not sufficient; we must make some effort that can serve as a conduit for the blessing.[5]

5. *Hitva'aduyot 5742*, vol. 2, pp. 561–562.

FOURTH READING
Exodus 14:26–15:26

The sea split and the Jews passed through it to safety. The Egyptians followed them into the dry sea, but G-d let the water return to its natural state, drowning them all. When the waves of the sea threw the dead Egyptians upon the shore, Moses led the men, and his sister Miriam led the women, in praising G-d for rescuing them. After this, the Jews collected the gold, silver, and precious jewels with which the Egyptians had adorned their horses. There was so much wealth that the next day, 22 Nisan, they were still busy collecting it, so Moses had to force them to move on.

Changing Direction

וַיַּסַּע מֹשֶׁה אֶת יִשְׂרָאֵל מִיַּם סוּף וְגו׳: (שמות טו, כב)

**Moses had to forcibly make the Israelites
set out from the Sea of Reeds.**

The Jewish people did not tarry out of greed. They were fulfilling G-d's commandment to empty Egypt of its wealth. The spiritual dimension of this directive was to salvage all the potentials of holiness present in this wealth.

From this we learn two lessons: First, once we know what our Divine mission in life is, we must be so devoted to it that doing anything else seems unthinkable. On the other hand, as soon as it is clear that it is time to change direction, we must not hesitate. We should apply ourselves to our new mission with the same enthusiasm we gave to our previous mission.

Second, just as the Jews did not want to leave a single piece of Egyptian wealth unelevated, we should desire to bring every last individual closer to G-d. Until we receive a clear directive to focus on something else, we must view every individual estranged from G-d as a priceless pearl waiting to be redeemed from Egypt.[6]

6. *Likutei Sichot*, vol. 21, pp. 77–82.

FIFTH READING

Exodus 15:27–16:10

Led by G-d's pillar of cloud, the people proceeded on their journey toward Mount Sinai. On 15 Iyar, the Jews ran out of matzo.
G-d then began to feed them with manna, a type of bread that
descended from heaven each morning.

The Lesson of the Manna

וַיֹּאמֶר ה' אֶל מֹשֶׁה... וְיָצָא הָעָם וְלָקְטוּ דְּבַר יוֹם בְּיוֹמוֹ וְגוֹ': (שמות טז, ד)

**G-d told Moses [to tell the people...] "The people will
go out and gather each day's portion on that day."**

Even if we believe that everything is in G-d's hand, we still tend to
think that our own efforts also play a role in acquiring our physical
sustenance. In contrast, manna was not acquired through human
effort, and so left no room for such misconceptions.

Even so, G-d did not allow the people to collect more than
one day's worth of manna at a time, for whenever the pantry
would have been full, the people would not have felt dependent
upon G-d.

On the other hand, G-d did require the people to go out and
gather the manna, rather than deliver it to their doorsteps. In this
way, He prepared them for their eventual entry into the real world.
If acquiring the manna had not required any human effort, the
people would have dismissed it as an isolated miracle, irrelevant
to real life. By being required to collect the manna, they learned
that human effort and G-d's blessings work together.

The manna taught us that our sustenance comes from heaven.
Even when it appears to be the fruit of our own labor, it is in fact
a gift from G-d.[7]

7. *Likutei Sichot*, vol. 16, pp. 177–178.

SIXTH READING
Exodus 16:11–36

The manna did not descend on the Sabbath. Instead, a double portion descended on Friday. This was the only exception to G-d's directive not to save manna from one day for the next.

The Sabbath

שַׁבָּתוֹן שַׁבַּת קֹדֶשׁ לַה' מָחָר וגו': (שמות טז, כג)

[On Friday, Moses told the people,] "Tomorrow will be a day of rest, a holy Sabbath unto G-d."

This is the first explicit mention in the Torah of the obligation to observe the Sabbath. It is appropriate that the Sabbath is introduced in connection with the manna, for the Sabbath and the manna share a common purpose – to underscore our complete dependency upon G-d as the true source of all sustenance. Belief that human effort is the sole determining factor for success makes it hard to justify giving up a full day's income. Not working on the Sabbath is a clear affirmation of our faith that sustenance lies in G-d's hands and that our work is no more than a vessel through which G-d's blessings can flow.[8]

8. See *Likutei Sichot*, vol. 16, pp. 173–182.

SHABBAT

SEVENTH READING
Exodus 17:1–16

At the next stop, there was no water to drink, but instead of trusting that G-d would provide for them, the people complained. G-d had Moses strike a rock with his staff, and this rock miraculously gave forth enough water for all the people's needs. This "well" accompanied the Jews throughout their trek through the desert. The Jews were then attacked by the nation of Amalek.

Silencing Inner Doubts

וַיָּבֹא עֲמָלֵק וַיִּלָּחֶם עִם יִשְׂרָאֵל בִּרְפִידִם: (שמות יז, ח)

Amalek came and fought against Israel at Refidim.

The physical attack of the nation of Amalek was the outer manifestation of the spiritual attack of the people's inner Amalek – their doubt regarding G-d's care and involvement in their lives.

This inner Amalek continues to plague us today, attempting to sow doubt and cool our religious fervor. It acknowledges that G-d exists, but tries to convince us that G-d is too great to care about the details of our Jewish observance. Doubt leads to doubt, and eventually our inner Amalek convinces us that G-d is not involved in human life altogether. That, in turn, causes us to abandon our search for G-dliness and spirituality.

Thus, just as the Exodus from Egypt reoccurs in every generation and every day, so does the war with Amalek. Every day, we must silence the voice of doubt that seeks to halt our spiritual progress. Once we successfully leave our inner Egypt and overcome our inner Amalek, we are ready to receive the Torah anew and enter our Promised Land.

Successfully implementing this process of spiritual growth on an individual basis will hasten its collective fulfillment, bringing the world to its Messianic Redemption.[9]

9. *Sichot Kodesh 5739*, vol. 2, pp. 144–145; *Torah Or* 84b–85b; *Sefer HaMa'amarim 5747–5751*, pp. 101–105.

Yitro

The Giving of the Torah
Exodus 18:1–20:23

THE FIFTH SECTION OF THE BOOK OF EXODUS BEGINS WITH the account of how Moses' father-in-law, Jethro (*Yitro* in Hebrew) joins the Jewish people at Mount Sinai. It continues with the culmination of all human history from the creation of the world until that point: the Giving of the Torah. Sandwiched in between these two accounts is the narrative of how Jethro advised Moses – after Moses' descent from Mount Sinai – to set up a judicial system.

FIRST READING
Exodus 18:1–12

After hearing about the Exodus from Egypt, the Splitting of the Sea, and the war with Amalek, Jethro went to meet Moses and the Jewish people, who were camped at Refidim, a short distance from Mount Sinai. Although he had already renounced idolatry, he now felt it was time to take the next step and become a Jew.

Receiving the Torah Each Day

וַיִּשְׁמַע יִתְרוֹ...אֵת כָּל אֲשֶׁר עָשָׂה אֱלֹקִים
לְמֹשֶׁה וּלְיִשְׂרָאֵל עַמּוֹ וְגוֹ': (שמות יח, א)

**Jethro heard about all that G-d had done
for Moses and for His people Israel.**

The Splitting of the Sea, the war with Amalek, and Jethro's conversion to Judaism were all prerequisites to the Giving of the Torah.

We must relive these events in our daily lives, for G-d gives us the Torah anew each day, granting us new and higher insights into life every day from the infinite well of the Torah. But before this can happen, we must first subdue our inner Amalek, i.e., silence our doubts about Divine providence. Then, we must convert our inner Jethro, i.e., win over the part of us that still prefers to serve the idols of excessive material desires.

But in order to take these steps, we must first "split the sea and enter it," i.e., temporarily immerse ourselves totally in holiness, through our morning prayers and regular Torah study. The Divine consciousness we experience this way enables us to bring a higher awareness into all aspects of our daily lives: eating, earning a living, interacting with others, and so on. Then, when we make time during our day to study the Torah, we will be able to uncover new insights that make it eternally relevant, thus hearing G-d's voice from Sinai on a day-to-day basis.[1]

---

1. Based on *Likutei Sichot*, vol. 11, pp. 74 ff and vol. 4, pp. 1271–1272.

SECOND READING

Exodus 18:13–23

In order to complete the story of Jethro, the Torah now jumps four months ahead to 11 Tishrei 2449, the day after Moses descended Mount Sinai for the last time.

Infinite Ascents

וַיְהִי מִמָּחֳרָת וַיֵּשֶׁב מֹשֶׁה לִשְׁפֹּט אֶת הָעָם וגו': (שמות יח, יג)

On the day following [Moses' descent from Mount Sinai], Moses sat to judge the people.

When our spiritual lives seem to flow smoothly, we may think that we have overcome the challenges of life and can sit back and relax. For the proper response to this sentiment, we need only look at Moses' example. While on Mount Sinai, Moses reached the peak of spirituality, yet, as soon as he rejoined the people, he plunged directly into his new task of judging the cases that the people brought before him.

Similarly, even when it feels as though we have reached the pinnacle of holiness, there is still tomorrow – when, like Moses, we should set our sights even higher.[2]

2. *Hitva'aduyot 5742*, vol. 2, pp. 871–872.

THIRD READING

Exodus 18:24–27

At first, Moses tried to answer all the people's questions and settle all their disputes himself. Jethro pointed out various shortcomings in this approach, and suggested that Moses set up a hierarchy of judges, reserving for himself only those cases that were too difficult for the judges of the lower courts. G-d told Moses that Jethro's plan was superior to Moses' approach.

The Torah's Universal Relevance

וַיִּבְחַר מֹשֶׁה . . . שָׂרֵי אֲלָפִים שָׂרֵי מֵאוֹת שָׂרֵי
חֲמִשִּׁים וְשָׂרֵי עֲשָׂרֹת: (שמות יח, כה)

**Moses appointed leaders of thousands, of
hundreds, of fifties, and of tens.**

In Jethro's plan, the people would be under the authority of judges who were beneath Moses' stature. Nonetheless, G-d approved of this system, because this way even the simplest among the people would be able to solve their problems according to the Torah's legal system, thereby submitting their lives to its authority. If Moses had remained the people's sole judge, some of the people would have been too intimidated by his awe-inspiring presence and spiritual stature to approach him with their problems. This might have led these people to feel alienated, or beyond the Torah's concern.

This would have been most unfortunate, for the Torah was given to everyone, including unsophisticated, average people. It is to the Torah's credit, and a demonstration of its truth, that its laws govern not only our most sublime moments but also the seemingly trivial concerns that crop up in our daily affairs.[3]

3. *Likutei Sichot*, vol. 16, pp. 209–210.

FOURTH READING
Exodus 19:1–6

The Torah then returns to the events following the Splitting of the Sea, the war with Amalek, and Jethro's arrival at Mount Sinai. The Jews arrived at the foot of Mount Sinai on 1 Sivan, 2448.

Brotherly Love

וַיִּחַן שָׁם יִשְׂרָאֵל נֶגֶד הָהָר: (שמות יט, ב)

Israel encamped there [as one united people] facing the mountain.

G‑d's presence refuses to dwell amid discord and disharmony. Only when the Jews were unified in harmony with each other could they achieve the harmony with G‑d necessary in order to receive His Torah.

The same applies today. Anyone can study the Torah, of course, but the Divine inspiration that grants us additional insight and allows us to sense G‑d's presence in the Torah is ours only when we are actively concerned for our fellow human beings.

There is an additional lesson here. The Jews were able to unite at Mount Sinai *because* they were "facing the mountain" – i.e., focused on the Torah. Since we all possess different intellectual faculties, emotions, character traits, and viewpoints, there is no natural way that we can maintain our individuality and still function as one unified body. Only if we are focused on G‑d do our differences suddenly cease to be obstacles to unity. Our differences still exist, for they are all necessary in order to fulfill our collective Divine mission. But our shared devotion to G‑d's will transforms these differences into stepping-stones toward our goal rather than barriers to it.[4]

4. *Likutei Sichot*, vol. 11, p. 250.

THURSDAY

FIFTH READING

Exodus 19:7–19

During the next six days, G-d had the Jewish people prepare for the Revelation of the Giving of the Torah. On the morning of 6 Sivan, G-d began to reveal Himself on Mount Sinai.

The Power of Enthusiasm

וְהַר סִינַי עָשַׁן כֻּלּוֹ מִפְּנֵי אֲשֶׁר יָרַד עָלָיו ה' בָּאֵשׁ וגו': (שמות יט, יח)

**The whole of Mount Sinai was asmoke because
G-d had descended upon it in fire.**

The fact that the mountain was asmoke indicated that the Giving of the Torah enabled the physical world to be affected by spirituality. This teaches us that the key to transforming all aspects of life – space, time, and consciousness – is making sure that all aspects of our religious life are imbued with "fire," i.e., warmth and enthusiasm for G-d and His Torah.[5]

---

5. *Sefer HaMa'amarim 5701*, p. 129; *Likutei Sichot*, vol. 13, p. 151.

SIXTH READING
Exodus 19:20–20:14

G-d then gave the Jewish people the 613 commandments contained in the Torah. Of these, He gave ten explicitly: to believe in G-d, not to serve idols, to respect G-d's name, to observe the Sabbath, to honor parents, not to murder, not to commit adultery, not to kidnap, not to lie when testifying, and not to desire other people's homes, spouses, or possessions. The remaining 603 commandments were implicit within these.

The Cure for Envy

לֹא תַחְמֹד בֵּית רֵעֶךָ וְגוֹ': (שמות כ, יד)

You must not desire your fellow's house.

G-d provides each of us with all the resources – possessions, talents, and strengths – that we require to fulfill our unique mission in life. We each achieve our ultimate fulfillment by dedicating these resources to our Divine mission and utilizing them to heighten the awareness of G-d in the world. Any resources that G-d has *not* provided us with at any given moment are thus not necessary for fulfilling our mission, and would in fact sidetrack us from the development of our fullest potential. Reflecting on this truth will cure us of any envy.[6]

6. *Hitva'aduyot 5742*, vol. 3, pp. 1661–1662.

SEVENTH READING
Exodus 20:15–23

After the Giving of the Ten Commandments, G-d told Moses to ascend Mount Sinai and remain there for 40 days in order to learn the rest of the Torah. Some of the laws that G-d taught Moses concerned how to build an altar for sacrifices. One of these laws was that the altar must be ascended by means of a ramp, rather than by stairs.

The Importance of Simple Things

וְלֹא תַעֲלֶה בְמַעֲלֹת עַל מִזְבְּחִי אֲשֶׁר לֹא תִגָּלֶה עֶרְוָתְךָ עָלָיו: (שמות כ, כג)

**You must not ascend My altar on steps, so that
your nakedness not be exposed over it.**

The priests wore trousers under their tunics, so their bodies would not have been exposed to the altar even on a staircase. Nonetheless, since walking up a staircase gives the *impression* of exposing one's uncovered body, it is more modest to use a ramp. If G-d requires us not to offend unfeeling stones, all the more so does He require us to respect the feelings of our fellow human beings.

The requirement to show respect to the stones of the altar teaches us to safeguard the honor of other people even when they are not aware that they are being disrespected, even when we do not mean to offend them.

Thus, this last verse of this section of the Torah sums up the message of G-d's revelation at Mount Sinai: G-d is found in even the most mundane things. Our relationships with other people are part and parcel of our relationship with G-d. And in a positive sense, loving other people is in truth loving our Creator.[7]

7. *Likutei Sichot*, vol. 21, p. 124.

Mishpatim

Laws

Exodus 21:1–24:18

AFTER GIVING THE TORAH TO THE JEWISH PEOPLE, G-D TOLD Moses to ascend Mount Sinai again – this time for 40 days – in order to teach him the details of the Torah's laws. The sixth section of the Book of Exodus is primarily a selection of the laws (*Mishpatim*, in Hebrew) that G-d taught Moses while he was on Mount Sinai.

FIRST READING
Exodus 21:1–19

G-d prefaced His explanation of the laws by saying that the Jewish people are required to set up a system of courts in order to try all cases of criminal, civil, and ritual law. G-d then explained the laws pertaining to servants, marital obligations, murder, honoring parents, kidnapping, and compensation for injuries.

Physical and Spiritual Physicians

רַק שִׁבְתּוֹ יִתֵּן וְרַפֹּא יְרַפֵּא: (שמות כא, יט)

**[If someone injures someone else, the injurer] must
pay for [the injured party's] complete cure.**

Whenever we are ill, G-d requires us to seek the help of qualified physicians and follow all of their instructions. Likewise, G-d has empowered physicians to heal the sick. But whereas doctors are merely *encouraged* to heal whoever is sick, they are *obligated* to try to save someone's life when it is threatened.

Just as there are both life-threatening and non-life-threatening bodily illnesses, so it is with spiritual "illnesses." Spiritually, a person is in "mortal danger" when his condition has begun to affect his ability or desire to fulfill the Torah's commandments, since it is through our performance of the commandments that our spiritual vitality flows into us.

The rules pertaining to a physical doctor also apply to a spiritual "doctor" – i.e., anyone who is capable of helping someone who is spiritually "ill." When someone is suffering from a minor spiritual "ailment," we are encouraged to offer spiritual assistance. But when someone is in spiritually "mortal danger" – i.e., his fulfillment of G-d's commandments is threatened – we are *obligated* to offer assistance, not allowing any other considerations to get in the way.[1]

---

1. *Likutei Sichot*, vol. 2, pp. 529–530.

SECOND READING

Exodus 21:20–22:3

G-d also taught Moses the laws pertaining to damages caused by a person's animals or property, including a pit that someone digs in the public domain.

Care in Receiving; Care in Giving

וְכִי יִפְתַּח אִישׁ בּוֹר אוֹ כִּי יִכְרֶה אִישׁ בֹּר . . . וְנָפַל שָׁמָּה שׁוֹר
אוֹ חֲמוֹר: בַּעַל הַבּוֹר יְשַׁלֵּם וְגו': (שמות כא, לג-לד)

**If a person uncovers or digs a pit . . . and an ox
or donkey falls into it, the one responsible
for the pit must pay [for the damage].**

The same law that applies to a pit (i.e., a sunken hazard) applies to a raised barrier or other obstacle (i.e., a protruding hazard).

Spiritually, a pit represents our ability to receive and a protrusion represents our ability to give. Properly used, these abilities can be beneficial; without proper supervision, however, they may cause damage. If we give and receive haphazardly – not paying heed to what or how much we are giving or receiving, or to whom we are giving or from whom we are receiving – we will become a danger to society. But if we choose to accept only positive influences and spread only positivity throughout our surroundings, we will become a source of blessing to all around us.[2]

2. *Hitva'aduyot 5747*, vol. 1, pp. 488–489.

THIRD READING

Exodus 22:4–26

G-d continued with the laws governing cases of theft; responsibilities of borrowers, guardians, and renters; seduction; sorcery; bestiality; idolatry; exploitation; and loans.

Fixing Previous Incarnations

אִם כֶּסֶף תַּלְוֶה אֶת עַמִּי וגו': (שמות כב, כד)

When you lend money...

The commandment to lend money applies even if the borrower owns possessions that he can theoretically sell. Thus, the commandment to lend money, unlike the commandment to give charity, is intended to benefit not only the poor but also the rich.

If, at times, we are reluctant to lend money to someone who is not poor, we should consider the possibility that in a previous lifetime, the present roles may have been reversed: we may have been the beneficiary of a loan or some other form of help from the person presently requesting a loan from us. This is our opportunity to repay his good deed.[3]

---

3. *Sichot Kodesh 5713*, p. 191.

FOURTH READING

Exodus 22:27–23:5

G-d continued with the laws governing respect for authority, donations to be given to the tribe of Levi, truth in the administration of justice, and behavior toward enemies.

Helping the Body Help the Soul

כִּי תִרְאֶה חֲמוֹר שֹׂנַאֲךָ רֹבֵץ תַּחַת מַשָּׂאוֹ . . . עָזֹב תַּעֲזֹב עִמּוֹ: (שמות כג, ה)

When you see your enemy's donkey crouching under its load . . . you must help [him].

G-d gave us the Torah and its commandments for the benefit of our bodies as well as our souls. Nonetheless, since the body (our beast of burden, or "donkey") naturally seeks its own comfort, it is likely to consider the study of G-d's Torah and the fulfillment of His commandments a burden. It may rebel ("crouch"), positioning itself as the soul's "enemy." Therefore, since for most of us, our body's voice is louder than our soul's, we are likely to initially view the Torah as an oppressive burden.

This only means, however, that we have not yet integrated the Torah into our lives. Rabbi Yisrael Ba'al Shem Tov, the founder of Chasidism, taught that we should not despise the body because of its natural attitude. Rather, we should work with it, strengthening its health while "educating" it to realize that accepting the Torah's dictates is in its own best interest. Once we realize that G-d's Torah and His commandments are the truest source of life, our bodies will view them as a gift, joining our souls enthusiastically in their fulfillment.[4]

4. *Hitva'aduyot 5710*, pp. 111–112.

FIFTH READING
Exodus 23:6–19

G-d continued with the laws governing the sabbatical year, the yearly cycle of holidays, and mixing milk and meat.

The Sin of Cruelty

לֹא תְבַשֵּׁל גְּדִי בַּחֲלֵב אִמּוֹ: (שמות כג, יט)

You must not eat a young animal cooked in its mother's milk.

Cooking a young animal in its mother's milk is an act of consummate cruelty. The Torah therefore forbids us not only to cook a young animal in its mother's milk, but to cook any animal in any other animal's milk, to eat such a mixture, or even to derive any other benefit from it.

　We see here what extremes the Torah goes to in forbidding cruelty towards animals. The precautions the Torah takes to distance us from causing suffering to an *animal* demonstrate how much care we must take to avoid causing suffering to a fellow human being.[5]

5. *Likutei Sichot*, vol. 6, p. 151.

SIXTH READING
Exodus 23:20–25

G-d continued with the laws governing the conquest of the Land of Israel and the eradication of idolatry.

Supernatural Living

וַעֲבַדְתֶּם אֵת ה' אֱלֹקֵיכֶם וגו': (שמות כג, כה)

[Rather than serve idols,] you must serve G-d, your G-d.

G-d established the laws of nature when He created the world; sometimes He acts within these laws and sometimes He overrides them. The two names of G-d used in this verse refer to these two ways in which G-d relates to the laws of nature. The first name ('ה) refers to Him when He *ignores* the limitations of nature; the second (אלקים) refers to Him when He works *within* the laws of nature.

Thus, in this verse, G-d is telling us to spiritually refine ourselves ("to serve") until the supernatural becomes natural for us, becoming our "second nature." When we rise to this level of consciousness, we view everything in life from G-d's perspective, and see everything that happens as part of His all-encompassing providence.[6]

6. *Torah Or* 78d-79a.

SEVENTH READING
Exodus 23:26–24:18

After concluding its account of how G-d taught Moses the Torah's laws on Mount Sinai, the narrative returns to its account of the Giving of the Torah. This time, it focuses on the covenant that G-d forged between Himself and the Jewish people by giving them the Torah. The day before the Giving of the Torah, Moses informed the people that receiving the Torah would involve both studying it and performing G-d's commandments.

Unconditional Commitment

וַיֹּאמְרוּ כֹּל אֲשֶׁר דִּבֶּר ה' נַעֲשֶׂה וְנִשְׁמָע: (שמות כד, ז)

[The people] responded, "We will do and we will learn everything that G-d has spoken."

By saying "we will do" before "we will learn," the Jewish people declared that they were prepared to fulfill G-d's will unconditionally – accepting His commandments even before they knew what they were. It is still on the condition of this commitment that G-d continues to "give us the Torah" today – i.e., revealing Himself and His will to us as we study the Torah and perform its commandments.

Conventional thinking may deem it irrational to commit oneself to a contract before the terms of the contract are spelled out. And we can indeed connect to G-d as He reveals Himself within creation without first committing ourselves to do whatever He wants. But the only way we can connect to G-d *Himself* – i.e., as He is beyond creation and rationality – is by likewise rising above the limits of rationality. Therefore, nowadays, just as when the Torah was first given, the way we connect with G-d Himself is by devoting ourselves to His Torah unconditionally.[7]

---

7. *Likutei Sichot*, vol. 23, p. 92 ff; *Sichot Kodesh 5739*, vol. 3, pp. 295–297; *Igrot Kodesh*, vol. 7, p. 28; *Hitva'aduyot 5748*, vol. 3 pp. 234–235; *Sichot Kodesh 5741*, vol. 4, pp. 31–32.

Terumah

The Tabernacle

Exodus 25:1–27:19

AS THE TORAH WILL RECOUNT LATER, WHEN THE JEWS became convinced that Moses was not going to come down from Mount Sinai, they committed the sin of making a golden calf. Some of the people worshipped this calf as an idol; as a result, G-d withdrew His presence from the people as a whole. In order to reinstate His presence among the Jewish people, G-d commanded them to construct a portable "housing" for His presence, consisting of a tent-sanctuary (the "Tabernacle"), a surrounding Courtyard, and various furnishings placed in specific positions within this sanctuary and its enclosure. The seventh portion of the Book of Exodus opens with G-d's command for the Jewish people to contribute (*Terumah* in Hebrew) toward the construction of this Tabernacle.

FIRST READING

Exodus 25:1–16

G-d began His instructions regarding the Tabernacle by listing the materials needed for its construction, as well as defining its purpose.

How G-d Dwells with Us

וְעָשׂוּ לִי מִקְדָּשׁ וְשָׁכַנְתִּי בְּתוֹכָם: (שמות כה, ח)

They must make Me a sanctuary, so that I may dwell in their midst.

Not "in *its* midst" but "in *their* midst": G-d told us to make a sanctuary so He may dwell within us. There are three types of sanctuaries included in this commandment: the physical Tabernacle that the Jews built in the desert; the personal, inner sanctuary that each of us must construct out of our lives and our sphere of influence in the world; and finally, the world at large, which we must transform into G-d's home.

In all three cases, the task is possible only because we are simply revealing the hidden, true nature of reality. The world at large and everything in it exist only because of the Divine energy pulsing within them, so making the world into a place where Divinity is revealed is simply a matter of removing the obstructions that hide this reality. Similarly, the essence of every one of us is our Divine soul, so making our lives into a Tabernacle for G-d is nothing more than allowing our inner essence to shine through the excess material baggage we have accumulated during our journey through life.[1]

1. *HaYom Yom*, 21 Tamuz.

SECOND READING
Exodus 25:17–30

The first furnishing of the Tabernacle that G-d instructed the Jews to make was the Ark of the Covenant, an open, gold-covered wooden box that housed the two Tablets of the Covenant upon which G-d had engraved the Ten Commandments. This Ark was sealed by a golden Cover, upon which were two figurines of winged angels with infant faces, known as the cherubim.

The Inner Child

וְעָשִׂיתָ שְׁנַיִם כְּרֻבִים זָהָב וגו': (שמות כה, יח)

You must make two golden cherubim.

The infant-like faces of the cherubim signified that our intrinsic bond with G-d is akin to the essential bond between parent and child. Despite any fluctuations that might arise in their relationship, the bond between parent and child can never be broken. The fact that the cherubim were situated above the Tablets of the Torah and faced each other signified that by studying the Torah, we can reach the root of our Divine soul, allowing our consciousness to merge totally with G-d. The infant faces of the cherubim also alluded to the fact that the Torah as we know it is a diluted, simplified version of the heavenly Torah, G-d's infinite wisdom. G-d contracted His infinite wisdom into a form we can understand and digest, much as an expert teacher contracts his grasp of a subject in order to convey it to his pupils.

The fact that the cherubim's wings were spread protectively over the Ark alludes to the fact that the Torah-education of young children ensures the preservation and continuity of the transmission of the Torah.[2]

2. *Torah Or* 79d; *Reshimot* 108; *Sichot Kodesh 5741*, vol. 2, pp. 395–397; *Likutei Sichot*, vol. 26, pp. 180–182.

THIRD READING
Exodus 25:31–26:14

Next, G-d commanded the people to make a golden Table specifically designed to hold twelve loaves of bread that would be placed on it every Sabbath. After this, G-d commanded the people to make an ornate, seven-branched golden Candelabrum.

How to Light up the World

וְעָשִׂיתָ מְנֹרַת וְגוֹ': (שמות כה, לא)

You must make a Candelabrum.

We are taught that Moses did not understand all of G-d's instructions how to make the Candelabrum, so G-d showed him an image of a fiery Candelabrum. But even so, the Candelabrum was still too complicated for Moses to envision, so G-d told him to simply throw the gold into a fire and the Candelabrum would miraculously take form.

Besides the Candelabrum's physical construction, what Moses found most difficult to grasp was how such a physical object could spread the light of Divine consciousness to the outside world. By showing Moses the fiery Candelabrum, G-d affirmed his hesitations. He informed him that indeed, using physical objects to spread Divine awareness in the world is impossible for us to do on our own. He therefore told Moses to cast the gold into the fire and that the Candelabrum would take form by itself.

Similarly, G-d requires us to transform all our material pursuits and possessions into sources of Divine light, but He also knows that we cannot do this on our own. All He asks is that we cast it all into the fire of our hearts – i.e., to let our love for Him permeate all we do – and He will miraculously do the rest.[3]

3. *Likutei Sichot*, vol. 1, p. 174.

FOURTH READING
Exodus 26:15–30

G-d next instructed the Jews how they were to construct the Tabernacle itself. The roof of the Tabernacle was to be formed out of three layers of material: a woven tapestry, a cover made of goat's hair, and a cover made of the skins of rams and another, now-extinct animal. The walls were to be made out of vertical planks of acacia wood.

Holy Foolishness

וְעָשִׂיתָ אֶת הַקְּרָשִׁים לַמִּשְׁכָּן עֲצֵי שִׁטִּים עֹמְדִים: (שמות כו, טו)

**You must make the planks for the Tabernacle
out of acacia wood, [placed] vertically.**

The Hebrew word for "acacia" (*shitah*) means "bending." The acacia tree is called the "bending" tree because it bends to the side as it grows, rather than growing straight up. The Hebrew word for "foolishness" (*shetut*) is another form of this word, since foolishness is an act of "bending" from the path dictated by logic.

Foolishness can be either holy or unholy. Unholy foolishness is the illogical thinking that leads us to go against G-d's will. Holy "foolishness" is our willingness to go beyond the strict requirements of the Torah in fulfilling our Divine mission or in refining ourselves.

Allegorically, then, placing the "bending" acacia planks *vertically* means using our power to be "foolish" for holy purposes. We can thereby turn this often negative character trait into a positive force in our lives, enabling us to reach levels of dedication to G-d and union with Him that we would not be able to reach otherwise.[4]

4. *Sefer HaMa'amarim 5710*, p. 114.

FIFTH READING
Exodus 26:31–37

The inside of the Tabernacle was divided by a curtain into an outer chamber (which is described as being "Holy") and an inner chamber (or "Holy of Holies").

Transcending the Intellect

וְהִבְדִּילָה הַפָּרֹכֶת לָכֶם בֵּין הַקֹּדֶשׁ וּבֵין קֹדֶשׁ הַקֳּדָשִׁים: (שמות כו, לג)

**The Curtain will separate for you between
the Holy and the Holy of Holies.**

The outer chamber of the Tabernacle contained three furnishings: the Candelabrum, the Table of twelve loaves (both of which are discussed in this section of the Torah), and the incense Altar (which is discussed in the next section). The Holy of Holies, in contrast, contained only one furnishing: the Ark of the Covenant.

The two chambers of the Tabernacle signify the two stages of achieving Divine consciousness. In the Tabernacle's outer chamber, we begin to orient our consciousness toward Divinity by focusing our intellect on G-d. This is why there were three furnishings in the outer chamber; they signify the three components of the intellect: the ability to gain insight (*chochmah*, in Hebrew), the ability to comprehend (*binah*) the meaning of that insight, and the ability to make what we comprehend relevant to our own lives (*da'at*).

Once we arrive at an intellectual consciousness of G-d, we can proceed to the next level, supra-rational consciousness of Him. This is the consciousness of the inner chamber and the Ark contained within it. At this level, not only our intellect but our entire being is engulfed in Divine consciousness.[5]

5. *Reshimot* 108.

SIXTH READING
Exodus 27:1–8

G-d then gave the instructions for constructing the Altar used for sacrifices. This Altar was situated in the Courtyard, outside the Tabernacle itself.

Consecrating our Inner Animal

וְעָשִׂיתָ אֶת הַמִּזְבֵּחַ וְגו': (שמות כז, א)

You must make the [Outer] Altar.

The Outer Altar was used for offering three types of animals: cattle, sheep, and goats. The animal sacrifices we offer up in our personal, inner sanctuaries are the various facets of the "animal" side of our personalities. Our inner "cattle" are our impulses to be confrontational, to oppose the directives of the Divine side of our personalities. Our inner "sheep" are our impulses to conform, to follow the crowd in pursuit of creature comforts because we are too weak to assert our Divine nature. Our inner "goats" are our impulses to be stubborn, brazenly refusing to budge from our preconceived notions.

We "slaughter" our inner animal by renouncing our animalistic orientation toward life. We "sprinkle its blood" and "place its fat" on the Altar by re-orienting our enthusiasm (warm blood) and sense of delight (fat) toward G-dliness. We "burn up" our inner animal on the Altar by allowing the Divine side of our personality to consume our animal drives.

The fact that the sacrificial Altar was situated outside the Tabernacle, in the Courtyard, teaches us that refining the animal side of our personalities is prerequisite to entering the realm of holiness and Divine consciousness, represented by the Tabernacle itself.[6]

6. *Reshimot* 108.

SEVENTH READING
Exodus 27:9–19

G-d then gave the instructions for demarcating the Courtyard with netted hangings suspended from copper-plated wooden pillars. The hangings were anchored to the ground by copper stakes.

Infusing Divinity

וְכָל יִתְדֹת הֶחָצֵר נְחֹשֶׁת: (שמות כז, יט)

All the stakes of the Courtyard must be made of copper.

The stakes were hammered into the earth, indicating that the holiness of the Tabernacle actually penetrated the ground. By building the Tabernacle in the desert, and by "building" our personal, inner Tabernacles, we infuse Divinity even into those places that appear to be, like the ground, inanimate and lifeless.[7]

7. *Likutei Sichot*, vol. 6, pp. 166–168.

Tetzaveh

The Priests

Exodus 27:20–30:10

THE EIGHTH SECTION OF THE BOOK OF EXODUS BEGINS AS
G-d tells Moses to command (*Tetzaveh*, in Hebrew) the Jewish
people to provide the olive oil to be used to fuel the lamps of the
Tabernacle's Candelabrum. He then described the special garments that the priests – Moses' brother Aaron and Aaron's present
and future descendants – would wear whenever they officiated in
the Tabernacle. Aaron's sons became the first "ordinary" priests,
who officiated in a uniform comprising four garments; Aaron
became the first "high priest," who wore an eight-garment uniform and was entrusted with duties and privileges beyond those
of ordinary priests. After describing the priests' garments, G-d
instructed Moses to follow a week-long ritual in order to install his
brother and nephews into their priestly office. This is followed by
the description of the Altar for incense, which was positioned in
the outer chamber of the Sanctuary, near the Candelabrum and
the Table of twelve breads.

FIRST READING
Exodus 27:20–28:12

G-d taught Moses the procedure for kindling the lamps of the Candelabrum. He then began to describe how to fashion the special garments of the priests.

The Priest Within

וְאַתָּה הַקְרֵב אֵלֶיךָ אֶת אַהֲרֹן אָחִיךָ וְאֶת בָּנָיו
אִתּוֹ . . . לְכַהֲנוֹ לִי וְגו': (שמות כח, א)

[G-d told Moses,] "You must draw your brother Aaron to you, together with his sons, to minister to Me [as priests]."

It would seem that we should all want to be priests, consecrated to G-d and totally steeped in Divine consciousness. This is indeed a worthy ideal, but if it were put into practice, it would undermine the purpose of Creation. G-d created us not to be angels but human beings who live in the mundane world. Only this way can we can elevate the world, refine it, and fill it with Divine consciousness.

On the other hand, in order to elevate the world, we need to preserve an image of the totally Divine way of living that we are striving to elevate it to. Hence, a select minority of the people had to live out this ideal in practice; they were the priests. Similarly, we must all consecrate a portion of our personality to the sole purpose of serving G-d. By creating ("installing") this "inner priest," we can then relate to the world at large as we are meant to, guiding and leading it to its Divine fulfillment. This is how we fulfill G-d's promise to us when He gave us the Torah: "You will be unto Me a kingdom of priests and a holy nation."[1]

---

1. Exodus 19:6. Based on *Sefer HaSichot 5752*, vol. 2, pp. 410 ff.

SECOND READING

Exodus 28:13–30

The first two garments that G-d described were the high priest's Ephod and Breastplate. The Ephod was an apron-like garment tied around the waist, possessing two straps that rose in the back from the waist up to and over the shoulders. A precious stone was attached to the upper end of each of these straps; the names of six of the twelve tribes were engraved on one stone and the other six on the other stone. The Breastplate was a square piece of material onto which were fastened twelve different precious stones; each one was inscribed with the name of one of the twelve tribes. The Breastplate was tied to the Ephod at the top and bottom with wool cords.

The Sublime and the Mundane

וְלֹא יִזַּח הַחֹשֶׁן מֵעַל הָאֵפוֹד: (שמות כח, כח)

[G-d told Moses,] "The Breastplate must not come loose from the Ephod."

The Ephod hung from the high priest's back down to his heels, while the Breastplate rested in front, opposite his heart. The "back" represents that which is external and mundane – the aspects of life that may be necessary but are not the focus of our main interest. In contrast, the "front" signifies the internal and sublime – the real focus of our interest – just as our face, which expresses our inner thoughts and feelings, is on the front of our body.

The fact that the Breastplate must not become disconnected from the Ephod therefore means that the high priest was not allowed to have any gap between the sublime and the mundane, the essential and the external aspects of his life. What is true in our idealistic and inspired hearts must express itself even in our "heels," i.e., the mundane and routine aspects of our lives.[2]

2. *Sefer HaSichot 5748*, vol. 1, p. 314.

THIRD READING
Exodus 28:31–43

The high priest's ankle-length Robe was worn under the Ephod and Breastplate. The bottom seam of this Robe was adorned all around with small golden bells and woolen pomegranates.

The Necessity for Jewish Unity

וְהָיָה עַל אַהֲרֹן לְשָׁרֵת וגו': (שמות כח, לה)

**[G-d told Moses,] "[The Robe] must be worn by
Aaron in order [for him] to serve [as high priest]."**

The unity of the Jewish people was reflected in the three primary garments of the high priest: The names of the tribes that were engraved on the Breastplate, resting on the high priest's heart, signified the righteous among us. The names of the tribes that were engraved on the stones of the Ephod, which mainly covered the high priest's back, signified those Jews still struggling with their evil inclinations. The bells and pomegranates of the Robe signified those Jews who are still under the sway of their evil inclinations; despite their low spiritual state, these Jews are "as full of good deeds as a pomegranate is full of seeds."[3] All of these Jews must be represented when the high priest enters the Sanctuary, for he must invoke the merit that is common to *all* his people.

Similarly, when we see people in need of a spiritual boost, we must first make them aware of their inherent worth: that they possess a soul that is truly a part of G-d. By welcoming them back into Jewish observance, we help them reconnect with their true selves. After this, we can help them shed whatever negativity remains in their lives and increase their performance of deeds of light and goodness.[4]

3. *Berachot* 57a.
4. *Likutei Sichot*, vol. 21, pp. 184–189.

FOURTH READING
Exodus 29:1–18

The high priest also wore a golden Forehead-Plate; a Tunic, which he wore under his Robe; a Sash, which he tied around his Robe; and a Turban. The ordinary priests wore tunics, sashes, and hats. Both the high priest and the ordinary priests wore knee-length trousers under the rest of their uniform. As part of the rituals that would install the priests in their office, Moses had to anoint Aaron and his sons, as well as some of the sacrifices, with olive oil compounded with spices according to a specific formula.

Holy vs. Secular Intellect

וְלָקַחְתָּ אֶת שֶׁמֶן הַמִּשְׁחָה וְיָצַקְתָּ עַל רֹאשׁוֹ וגו': (שמות כט, ז)

[G-d told Moses,] "You must take some of the anointing oil and pour it on [Aaron's] head.

The oil was smeared in the form of the Greek letter lambda (Λ), which is the angled form of the Hebrew letter *kaf* (כ), the initial of the word for "priest," *kohen*.

Whereas the Greeks believed human intellect to be the highest arbiter of truth, Judaism asserts that G-d's supra-human intellect is the source of truth. These two worldviews are sometimes at odds, for the Torah's demands sometimes transcend human intellect. This is why the followers of Greek philosophy fought the Jews and the Torah in the struggle that resulted in the miracle of Chanukah. It therefore seems hardly appropriate to introduce a Greek symbol into the installation rites of the Tabernacle, the spiritual center of Judaism!

The reason why this was done is because G-d's intellect, as it is expressed in the Torah, is meant to sanctify human intellect. This is why specifically the Greek form of the letter *kaf* was used in the rites initiating the Tabernacle.[5]

5. *Likutei Sichot*, vol. 26, pp. 246–247.

FIFTH READING
Exodus 29:19–37

In addition to installing the priests, G-d told Moses to install the Altar by anointing it and offering up specific sacrifices upon it. An expression of the Altar's holiness is the fact that once something has been placed upon it, it must remain there to be burnt up, even if it had become disqualified for use as a sacrifice.

The Power of Holiness

כָּל הַנֹּגֵעַ בַּמִּזְבֵּחַ יִקְדָּשׁ: (שמות כט, לז)

[G-d told Moses,] "Whatever touches
the Altar will become sanctified."

Spiritually, this principle applies to each of us in our relationship with holiness. Even if all we do is "touch" holiness – without taking the relationship any deeper than an external touch – we become holy. Once we have had a spiritual experience, we are forever changed. We may try to forget, ignore, or run away from it, but our contact with the Divine realm will never again allow us to completely immerse ourselves in mundane life, whether to indulge in empty diversions or to try to improve the world through purely secular means.

True, the rule that whatever touches the Altar becomes sanctified applies only to things that are worthy of being brought upon the Altar in the first place. But spiritually, each of us falls into that category, for every Jew possesses intrinsic holiness; the true desire of every Jew is to do what G-d commands.[6]

---

6. *Hitva'aduyot 5747*, vol. 2, pp. 557–559.

SIXTH READING
Exodus 29:38–46

G-d concluded His description of the installation rites by naming the Tabernacle the "Tent of Meeting." This term implies that the Tabernacle would be the place where G-d would "meet" with Moses in order to communicate with him, and the place where G-d would "meet" the Jewish people whenever they would gather there to pray or listen to what G-d told Moses.

Rewards

וְיָדְעוּ כִּי אֲנִי ה' אֱלֹקֵיהֶם אֲשֶׁר הוֹצֵאתִי אֹתָם מֵאֶרֶץ
מִצְרַיִם לְשָׁכְנִי בְתוֹכָם וְגו': (שמות כט, מו)

**[G-d told Moses, "The Jewish people] will know
that I am G-d, their G-d, who brought them out
of Egypt in order to abide among them."**

There are those who complain, "The way of Torah puts us at a disadvantage. We have to observe the Sabbath and the holidays, but we have to compete in business with people who don't. Before going to work in the morning, we have to pray and study the Torah. Right in the middle of our workday, we have to stop and pray again. When we finally get home in the evening, there's still one more prayer to be recited. At work, we have to be careful to stay away from dishonesty or illegal business practices. We are not even allowed to compete with someone else's business under many circumstances. How can we survive under these circumstances?"

G-d replies, "I took you out of Egypt. Until then, not a single slave had ever managed to escape from Egypt. Yet, I took several million of you out, and showered you with great wealth. So you see, I am not bound by the restrictions of nature. If you fulfill My directives, I will reward you supernaturally and ensure that you have an abundance of everything that you need."[7]

---

7. *Likutei Sichot*, vol. 2, p. 325.

SEVENTH READING
Exodus 30:1–10

Having concluded His instructions for installing the priests through their special uniforms and installation rites, G-d taught Moses how to construct the incense Altar. This Altar was placed in the outer chamber of the Tabernacle.

The Inner Life

וְעָשִׂיתָ מִזְבֵּחַ מִקְטַר קְטֹרֶת וגו': (שמות ל, א)

You must make an Altar for burning incense.

One reason why the passage about the Inner Altar is placed at the very end of all of the discussions pertaining to the Tabernacle and all that was in it, is in order to indicate that the Inner Altar has a unique status, above and beyond all of the other furnishings of the Tabernacle.

What was different about the Inner Altar was that every other ritual that was performed in the Tabernacle had spectators. When the incense was burned on the Inner Altar, however, there was no one present – only the priest burning it and G-d Himself. Furthermore, we are taught that it was specifically this private service that caused the Divine Presence to be most felt in the Tabernacle.

This lesson of the incense is very relevant in our modern – and loud – world. The ultimate in holy living, and especially in areas of kindness and charity, is when no one is present – when we exhibit generosity without publicity, purely because it is the right thing to do.[8]

8. *Likutei Sichot*, vol. 1, pp. 171–172.

Tisa

The Golden Calf
Exodus 30:11–34:35

THE NINTH SECTION OF THE BOOK OF EXODUS BEGINS WITH
G-d's final instructions regarding the Tabernacle. G-d tells Moses
to take (*Tisa*, in Hebrew) a census of the adult male Jews by collecting a silver half-shekel coin from each one. The silver thus collected was used to purchase those sacrifices offered up on behalf
of the people as a whole. G-d then proceeds to instruct Moses
how to construct the Urn used by the priests to wash their hands
and feet before officiating in the Tabernacle, how to make and use
the anointing oil and incense, and whom he should appoint to
oversee the construction of the Tabernacle and the fashioning of
its furnishings and utensils. All of this is followed by the account
of the incident of the Golden Calf and its aftermath.

FIRST READING

Exodus 30:11–31:17

G-d told Moses to take two censuses of the Jewish people: one when he came down from Mount Sinai, and another when the Tabernacle was erected. In both cases, the male Jews age 20 and over were to be counted by having each one contribute a half-shekel coin. The silver from the first census was used to make the bases of the planks that made up the Tabernacle's walls. The silver collected from the second census was used to purchase the "communal" sacrifices, i.e., sacrifices offered up on behalf of the Jewish people as a whole. (In contrast, private sacrifices were purchased individually by the person offering them up).

No One is More than Half

זֶה יִתְּנוּ... מַחֲצִית הַשֶּׁקֶל בְּשֶׁקֶל הַקֹּדֶשׁ עֶשְׂרִים גֵּרָה הַשֶּׁקֶל וְגוֹ': (שמות ל, יג)

[G-d told Moses,] "This is what everyone must give:
a half-shekel; [specifically, half] of the shekel used
for holy [purposes], which weighs 20 *geirah*."

The half-shekel was an expression of Jewish unity – rich and poor alike gave the same amount. Everyone gave only *half* a shekel in order to teach us that we can only achieve unity when we all recognize that we are just halves. To be a complete shekel, we must unite with our fellow.

Similarly, we are also only "half" in our relationship with G-d. The ten powers of the soul – our intellect and emotions – parallel the ten powers that G-d used in creating the world and continues to use in order to constantly re-create it. When we channel all ten powers of our soul – every nuance of our being – toward uniting with G-d and fulfilling our Divine mission, we align our soul-powers with G-d's attributes. Our ten becomes twenty – a holy shekel.[1]

---

1. *Sefer HaSichot 5752*, vol. 2, pp. 440–441.

SECOND READING
Exodus 31:18–33:11

Moses had told the Jews that he would be spending 40 full days on Mount Sinai, but the Jews mistakenly counted the first half-day as one of the 40. When Moses failed to appear on what they had calculated to be the 40th day, some of the Jews became convinced that Moses had died and that it was necessary to find a substitute for him. They knew that G-d would later communicate with them through gold figurines in the Tabernacle (the cherubim). They imagined that if Aaron were to make a gold figurine, G-d would consent to communicate with them through it. Although Aaron was opposed to this idea, he thought that by working slowly, he could calm the people down until Moses would arrive. When the Golden Calf was finished, some people worshipped it as an idol.

The Heights of Repentance

וַיַּעֲלוּ עֹלֹת וַיַּגִּשׁוּ שְׁלָמִים וגו': (שמות לב, ו)
They sacrificed [to the calf].

How could the people who witnessed G-d's miracles and experienced His revelation at Mount Sinai commit such a blatant transgression so soon afterward? True, only a small percentage of the people worshipped the Calf, but even this is hard to imagine.

The sages of the Talmud therefore teach us that indeed, the Jews at that point were incapable of sinning. In order to enable the people to rise to the heights of spiritual achievement only attainable through repentance, G-d "forced" the entire incident upon them.

In this light, we can all focus on our past misdeeds as opportunities through which we can scale spiritual heights that we could not rise to otherwise.[2]

2. *Likutei Sichot*, vol. 16, pp. 412–413.

THIRD READING

Exodus 33:12–16

While Moses was still on Mount Sinai, G-d told him that some of the people were worshipping the Golden Calf, and that He was planning on holding the entire community responsible for not protesting the misdeeds of this minority. Moses pleaded with G-d to forgive the people; G-d agreed only to punish the guilty minority, but insisted that His presence could no longer accompany the people. When Moses saw the people worshipping the Golden Calf, he understood that the Jewish people were not yet ready to receive the Torah. He threw down the tablets on which G-d had inscribed the Ten Commandments, breaking them. He then ascended Mount Sinai again for another 40 days, during which He secured G-d's forgiveness for the people. After descending from his second stay on Mount Sinai, Moses asked G-d to again let His presence dwell among the people, and G-d agreed.

Following Moses' Example

וַיֹּאמַר פָּנַי יֵלֵכוּ וְגוֹ': (שמות לג, יד)

G-d told [Moses,] "My Presence will [again] go with you."

Moses asked G-d to omit his name from the Torah if He would refuse to forgive the Jews. Moses was willing to sacrifice his connection with the Torah for the sake of his people – all of his people, even those who worshipped the Golden Calf.

We can all emulate Moses' self-sacrifice for the Jewish people. It is not sufficient to simply fulfill the commandment to "love your fellow as yourself"; we must be ready to sacrifice even that which we hold most dear for the benefit of the Jewish people in general and for every single Jew in particular – no matter how far away he may seem at that moment from G-d and His Torah.[3]

---

3. *Likutei Sichot*, vol. 21, pp. 175–177.

FOURTH READING

Exodus 33:17–23

Moses asked G-d further to show Him how everything He does is out of kindness. G-d replied that it is only possible for the human mind to grasp this "from the back," i.e., after the fact.

The Face of G-d

וְרָאִיתָ אֶת אֲחֹרָי וּפָנַי לֹא יֵרָאוּ: (שמות לג, כג)

[G-d told Moses,] "You may see My 'back,' but My 'face' may not be seen."

It is only necessary to negate something that is possible, not something that is impossible. Thus, when G-d said "My face may not be seen," He meant that the workings of Divine providence *can* be perceived, but not directly.

To explain: There are two ways of grasping a concept: by understanding what it is and by understanding what it is not. If a concept is within our sphere of experience, we can understand what it is. If a concept is outside our sphere of experience, we cannot understand what it is, but we can understand what it is *not*. We mentally remove it from possibility after possibility until, by process of elimination, we gain a glimpse of it.

Thus, G-d's statement, "My face may not be seen," means that we cannot understand Divine providence directly, but we can understand it by negating what we know it not to be.[4]

---

4. *Sefer HaSichot 5748*, vol. 1, pp. 299–300.

FIFTH READING
Exodus 34:1–9

G-d then summoned Moses to Mount Sinai for a third 40-day stay. During this stay, G-d revealed His thirteen attributes of mercy to Moses. By invoking these attributes, it would always be possible to secure G-d's forgiveness.

Elevating the Power within Sin

נֹשֵׂא עָוֹן וָפֶשַׁע וְחַטָּאָה וגו׳: (שמות לד, ז)

[The 10th, 11th, and 12th attributes of Divine mercy are that G-d can] forgive premeditated misdeeds, rebellious misdeeds, and unintentional misdeeds.

The Hebrew word for "forgive" used in this verse literally means "carry" or "lift." Based on this, Rabbi Yisrael Ba'al Shem Tov, the founder of Chasidism, taught that G-d elevates the spark of holiness in the misdeed. Nothing, not even a sin, can exist unless it contains a spark of holiness. When a person repents, G-d elevates the Divine spark in his misdeed and returns it to its Divine source.

Rabbi Shneur Zalman of Liadi, the founder of the Chabad branch of Chasidism, explained this idea as follows: It is indeed impossible to elevate a sinful *act*; such an act is evil, and the only proper treatment for it is to renounce it. In contrast, the *power of desire* vested in the act is not evil, for it is possible to utilize this power to desire good as well as evil. When we repent properly, we divest our power of desire of its veneer of evil and restore it to its holy source.[5]

5. *Likutei Torah* 4:61d.

SIXTH READING

Exodus 34:10–26

G-d then renewed the covenant He forged with the Jewish people at Mount Sinai, which had been rendered null and void by the sin of the Golden Calf. Part of this covenant was G-d's promise to give the Jews the Land of Israel, which was then occupied by the seven Canaanite nations.

Purifying Thought, Speech, and Action

הִנְנִי גֹרֵשׁ מִפָּנֶיךָ אֶת הָאֱמֹרִי וְהַכְּנַעֲנִי וְהַחִתִּי

וְהַפְּרִזִּי וְהַחִוִּי וְהַיְבוּסִי: (שמות לד, יא)

[G-d instructed Moses to tell the Jewish people,] "I am going to drive out before you the Amorites, the Canaanites, the Hittites, the Perizites, the Hivites, and the Jebusites."

Only six of the seven Canaanite nations are mentioned here; the Girgashites are missing from the list. This is because the first six Canaanite nations personified the six unrectified emotions of the animal soul, while the Girgashites personified the animal soul's drive to express these unrectified emotions in thought, speech, and action. When we rectify the six emotions of our animal soul, we will not have to worry about combating any drive to express them.

But until this process is complete, we must control our faculties of thought, speech, and action in order to ensure that they serve only holy purposes and not those of the six unrectified emotions of our animal soul. The next verse therefore enjoins us to "beware, lest you make a treaty with the inhabitants of the land that you are entering, lest they become a snare in your midst."[6]

---

6. *Likutei Sichot*, vol. 21, pp. 229 ff.

SEVENTH READING
Exodus 34:27–35

After his third 40-day stay on Mount Sinai, Moses descended on
10 Tishrei 2449, carrying the second set of tablets, which replaced
the first set that Moses broke when he saw the Jews worshipping
the Golden Calf. Moses' extended stay in G-d's presence had left
a lasting impression on his body: his face radiated light.

A Shining Face

וּמֹשֶׁה לֹא יָדַע כִּי קָרַן עוֹר פָּנָיו וגו': (שמות לד, כט)

**Moses was not aware that the skin of
his face had become radiant.**

G-d Himself chiseled the first set of tablets out of the rocks on
Mount Sinai, whereas the second tablets were chiseled by Moses.
Nevertheless, it was specifically after receiving the second set of
tablets, rather than the first set, that Moses' face shone.

This is because when something is given to us from G-d without our having worked to earn it, it does not penetrate our very
being. It is thus no accident that the first tablets were broken,
whereas the second set never were. When we work for something,
it can remain with us permanently; something that is received
unearned can be more easily lost.

Because Moses chiseled the second tablets himself, their
holiness could penetrate his physical body, and therefore his face
shone. Similarly, the effort we expend in studying the Torah and
fulfilling G-d's commandments refines even our physical bodies.
If we exert ourselves to the point that the Torah penetrates us,
our faces glow.[7]

Vayakheil

Constructing the Tabernacle
Exodus 35:1–38:20

THE TENTH SECTION OF THE BOOK OF EXODUS OPENS AS
Moses comes down from Mount Sinai for the third and final time
and immediately assembles (*Vayakheil,* in Hebrew) the Jewish
people. Moses informed them that G-d had forgiven them for
the sin of the Golden Calf and had instructed them to build the
Tabernacle as a sign of this forgiveness.

FIRST READING
Exodus 35:1–20

Moses prefaced his instructions for the Tabernacle by reminding the Jewish people that they must keep the Sabbath. They must not let their enthusiasm for building the Tabernacle lead them transgress the prohibition to work on the seventh day.

What it Means to Rest on the Sabbath

שֵׁשֶׁת יָמִים תֵּעָשֶׂה מְלָאכָה וּבַיּוֹם הַשְּׁבִיעִי יִהְיֶה
לָכֶם קֹדֶשׁ שַׁבַּת שַׁבָּתוֹן וגו': (שמות לה, ב)

**[Moses told the Jewish people], "Work may be
done for six days, but the seventh day must be
holy for you, a complete rest from work."**

Spiritually, every week is a repetition of the week of Creation: G-d re-creates the world during the six workdays and "rests" every Sabbath. G-d "rests" by re-experiencing the original idea that gave rise to the creation of the world. During the six original days of Creation, G-d attended to the details of executing His designs; after the master architect completed His masterpiece, He surveyed it and reviewed it as the fulfillment of His plan.

Thus, during the six workdays, the world is re-created by G-d's "creative" energy, whereas on the Sabbath, the world is created by G-d's "resting" energy.

Therefore, our task on the Sabbath is not to labor in rectifying creation, but to experience creation as the Divine dwelling we have worked to make it into during the week. We enter into this state of consciousness by refraining from the 39 categories of creative work we do in our weekday lives.[1]

---

1. *Or HaTorah, Shemot*, vol. 6, p. 2113.

SECOND READING

Exodus 35:20–29

After Moses told the people what was needed in order to construct the Tabernacle, the people started bringing their contributions.

How to Educate Successfully

חָח וָנֶזֶם וְטַבַּעַת וְכוּמָז וגו': (שמות לה, כב)

[The people brought their gold] bracelets, nose-rings, finger-rings, and chastity belts.

The medieval Biblical scholar Rabbi Avraham Ibn Ezra translates this list of items slightly differently, as "earrings, nose-rings, finger-rings, and bracelets."

The four items that the women donated allude to the four aspects of proper child-rearing and Jewish education:

Earrings: Listening carefully to children's conversations with their peers, for children learn how to talk from their elders' example; if something is amiss in how they speak, it means something is amiss in how their role models speak.

Nose-rings: Developing a keen sense of *"smell"* to determine if children's friendships with other children are beneficial.

Finger-rings: Pointing children to the proper path, by gently guiding them to adhere to the Torah's teachings and not to follow harmful paths.

Bracelets: Being strong-*armed* – for even if children are well-behaved, it is necessary to be firm with them in order to foster their enthusiasm for their studies.[2]

2. *Likutei Diburim*, vol. 3, pp. 573–574.

THIRD READING

Exodus 35:30–36:7

As G-d instructed him to, Moses then appointed the artisans Betzalel and Aholi'av to oversee the work.

Everyone's Unique Contribution

לַעֲשֹׂת בַּזָּהָב וּבַכֶּסֶף וּבַנְּחֹשֶׁת: (שמות לה, לב)

[**Moses said, "G-d has endowed them with the capacity**] **to work in gold, silver, and copper."**

Silver, gold, and copper represent three types of Jews: Silver represents those among us who are not fazed by the spiritual darkness of the mundane world but who, on the contrary, channel Divine consciousness into it. Gold represents those of us who used to be entrenched in the mundane world, but have overcome the stranglehold of its materialism. Copper represents those of us who are still struggling to overcome the materialism of the mundane world.

The Torah requires that all three metals be used for the construction of the Tabernacle. This is a lesson both for those who perceive themselves as gold and silver as well as to those who think of themselves as copper. The "silver" among us must not shy away from involvement in the physical world, preferring instead to occupy themselves with only spiritual matters. Similarly, the "gold" among us, who overcame materialism and therefore might feel immune to its dangers, are still not exempt from elevating the physical world. Finally, the "copper" among us might think that they first have to refine themselves before they can elevate the world, but the Torah tells them otherwise: they, too, must do their part in building G-d's home in this world.[3]

3. *Likutei Sichot*, vol. 6, pp. 157–160.

FOURTH READING
Exodus 36:8–19

The first articles the artisans made were the tapestries that formed the covering of the Tabernacle.

The Dynamics of Relationship

שֵׁשׁ מָשְׁזָר וּתְכֵלֶת וְאַרְגָּמָן וְתוֹלַעַת שָׁנִי וגו': (שמות לו, ח)

[**The artisans made the tapestries out of**] **linen, turquoise wool, purple wool, and scarlet wool.**

These four materials allude to the four bases of our emotional relationship with G-d.

Scarlet wool is red, alluding to fire. The fire within our soul is the fiery love of G-d that results from contemplating His infinity. When we realize the extent to which G-d is beyond creation and that He is the true reality, we are overcome with a passionate desire to escape the limitations of the world in order to know Him and to merge with Him.

Turquoise wool is the color of the sky, alluding to our experience of G-d's majesty. In this experience, we also contemplate G-d's infinity, but focus on our own insignificance in comparison. This fills us with feelings of awe.

Purple wool is a blend of blue and red, of love and awe, alluding to pity, which is compounded of love and anger: love for the ideal, anger over how the ideal goes unfulfilled. Specifically, we pity our Divine soul when we consider its plight, having to live so spiritually distant from its natural home, i.e., in G-d's presence.

Linen is white, alluding to our basic, inherent love of G-d, a feeling that is above and beyond rationality. This love is what makes us capable of self-sacrifice for G-d's honor, as it expresses our invincible bond with G-d.[4]

4. *Sefer HaMa'amarim 5708*, pp. 138 ff.

FIFTH READING
Exodus 36:20–37:16

After fashioning the coverings and walls of the Tabernacle, the artisans proceeded to fashion its furnishings, first of which was the Ark of the Covenant.

Breaking in Order to Build

אַמָּתַיִם וָחֵצִי אָרְכּוֹ וְאַמָּה וָחֵצִי רָחְבּוֹ וְאַמָּה וָחֵצִי קֹמָתוֹ: (שמות לז, א)

[**The artisans made the Ark, as instructed,**] **two
and a half cubits long, one and a half cubits
wide, and one and a half cubits high.**

Unlike the other furnishings of the Tabernacle, the dimensions of the Ark were all incomplete measurements. Inasmuch as the Ark housed the Torah, this alludes to the idea that the Torah must "break" us: It must be learned in such a way that it breaks our ingrained habits and negative personality traits.[5]

5. *Sefer HaMa'amarim Kuntresim*, vol. 1, p. 318.

SIXTH READING

Exodus 37:17–29

Next the artisans fashioned the Table of 12 loaves. After this, Moses threw gold for the Candelabrum into the furnace, and G-d fashioned the Candelabrum.

Seven Ways to Light up the World

וַיַּעַשׂ אֶת הַמְּנֹרָה זָהָב טָהוֹר וְגוֹ': (שמות לז, יז)

[G-d] made the Candelabrum out of pure gold.

The Candelabrum, the source of light in the Tabernacle, signified insight and enlightenment. The sudden and elusive flash of insight and illumination in the mind is similar to a bolt of lightning flashing across a dark sky.

Every Divine soul is a source of Divine illumination. It is in this sense that the soul is metaphorically termed "the lamp of G-d." The seven lamps of the Candelabrum signify the seven basic types of Jewish souls. Each type has its particular path in revealing Divinity, based on the seven basic emotions: (1) the love of G-d, (2) the awe of G-d, (3) connecting to G-d through studying the Torah, (4) overcoming obstacles opposing G-dliness in the world, (5) appreciating G-d's goodness, (6) the pride in being G-d's emissary in the world, and (7) humility.[6]

6. *Likutei Torah* 3:29b.

SEVENTH READING
Exodus 38:1–20

The artisans then fashioned the Inner Altar and the Outer Altar. These were followed by the Laver and the pillars of the Courtyard.

Blending Assertiveness with Humility

נָבוּב לֻחֹת עָשָׂה אֹתוֹ: (שמות לח, ז)

[As instructed, the artisans made the Outer, copper Altar] as a hollow structure.

The Outer Altar is where the process of refining our animal natures took place. The material and form of the Outer Altar allude to the two opposite attitudes we need to cultivate in order to accomplish this:

On the one hand, we must be resolute in our dedication to spiritual advancement. The Jews are called "a stiff-necked people"; this can be a positive quality when it is expressed as determination and obstinacy in realizing spiritual goals. This quality is alluded to by the fact that the Altar was made of copper, since the Hebrew word for "copper" (*nechoshet*) is related to the Hebrew word for "brazen (*nechush*) stubbornness."

On the other hand, the hollow Altar was filled with earth. Similarly, while we must be externally stubborn, internally we must be humble as earth. As we say in our prayers, "and may my soul be as dust to all."[7]

---

7. *Reshimot* 108.

Pekudei

Erecting the Tabernacle
Exodus 38:21–40:38

THE ELEVENTH AND FINAL SECTION OF THE BOOK OF EXODUS
opens by informing us whom Moses appointed (*Pekudei*, in
Hebrew) over the functioning and transport of the Tabernacle.
Having concluded the account of how the artisans fashioned the
various components of the Tabernacle, the Torah proceeds to
describe how these same artisans fashioned the priestly garments
and how the Tabernacle was finally erected.

FIRST READING
Exodus 38:21–39:1

In discussing how Moses appointed various people over the functioning and transport of the Tabernacle, the Torah refers to the Tabernacle for the first time as a "testimony."

Second Innocence

אֵלֶּה פְקוּדֵי הַמִּשְׁכָּן מִשְׁכַּן הָעֵדֻת וגו': (שמות לח, כא)

**These are the appointments over the Tabernacle.
The Tabernacle was a testimony.**

The Torah refers to the Tabernacle as a "testimony" because it testified that G-d forgave the Jewish people for the sin of the Golden Calf.

Moreover, the Hebrew word for "testimony" (*eidut*) is related to the word that the Torah uses for the "jewelry" (*edi*) – i.e., the spiritual crowns – that the people received at the Giving of the Torah and had to remove after the incident of the Golden Calf. Thus, the Tabernacle is also called "the Tabernacle of the jewelry." This indicates that the Tabernacle was also the means by which G-d enabled the Jewish people to regain the spiritual heights and Divine consciousness that they attained when G-d first gave them the Torah – before the sin of the Golden Calf.

Similarly, by constructing our inner, personal spiritual Tabernacle, we, too, can overcome any spiritual handicaps we may have accrued during our lives, thereby attaining something of the pristine Divine consciousness G-d bestowed upon us when the Torah was first given.[1]

---

1. *Or HaTorah, Shemot*, vol. 6, p. 2233.

SECOND READING

Exodus 39:2–21

The Torah then describes how the artisans fashioned the priestly garments, including the high priest's Ephod. Two onyx stones were attached to the upper ends of the two shoulder straps of the Ephod.

The Common Denominator

וַיַּעֲשׂוּ אֶת אַבְנֵי הַשֹּׁהַם . . . מְפֻתָּחֹת פִּתּוּחֵי חוֹתָם
עַל שְׁמוֹת בְּנֵי יִשְׂרָאֵל: (שמות לט, ו)

[The artisans] made the onyx stones . . . engraved
with the names of Israel's [i.e., Jacob's] sons.

Some of Jacob's sons were singled out for leadership roles: Judah was the father of the royal line of David, Levi was the father of the priests, and Joseph was selected to lead the family after Jacob's death. Nonetheless, the names of Jacob's sons were inscribed on the Ephod's two shoulder stones in the order of their birth, rather than in the order of their importance or prestige. This underscores their common, unifying factor – the fact that they are all Jacob's sons.

Jacob was the only patriarch whose children all remained faithful to the Divine mission and ideology that Abraham began. All of Jacob's sons learned how to channel their individual differences and strengths toward perpetuating Judaism. This unity made their inscribed names a source of merit for us as the high priest entered the Tabernacle to represent us before G-d. Just as parents are happy to grant their children's wishes when they all cooperate lovingly, G-d is more ready to shower us with His beneficence when we follow in the footsteps of Jacob's sons and unite in our devotion to the ideals of Judaism.[2]

2. *Likutei Sichot*, vol. 36, pp. 146–152.

THIRD READING
Exodus 39:22–32

One of the high priest's garments was the golden Forehead-plate.

Positive Stubbornness

וַיַּעֲשׂוּ אֶת צִיץ... וַיִּכְתְּבוּ עָלָיו מִכְתַּב פִּתּוּחֵי חוֹתָם קֹדֶשׁ לַה': (שמות לט, ל)

[The artisans] made the Forehead-plate, and inscribed upon it "Holy unto G-d."

The high priest was required to wear the Forehead-plate because the forehead represents stubborn determination. We all naturally wrinkle our forehead muscles whenever we resolve to see something through despite all odds.

Stubbornness can be positive or negative. Brazen nerve or arrogance in showing contempt for G-d's law is negative. It is no coincidence that the stone thrown from David's slingshot hit and killed Goliath in the forehead, for Goliath brazenly and openly defied G-d. We are therefore taught that the high priest's Forehead-plate atoned for the sin of arrogance.

An example of positive stubbornness is the resolve that enables us to stay true throughout the day to the spiritual awakening that we feel during our morning prayers. As we go about our daily business, it may be difficult to maintain the heightened Divine consciousness that we aspire to in prayer. But we can certainly maintain the attitude toward life implicit in this heightened awareness: that our Divine mission is our primary concern and the purpose of our involvement in the material world is to elevate it by using it for G-dly purposes. Our goal of making everything "Holy unto G-d" was therefore inscribed on the Forehead-plate.[3]

3. *Or HaTorah, Shemot*, vol. 5, pp. 1713–1715.

FOURTH READING

Exodus 39:33–43

After all the components of the Tabernacle were fashioned, the people brought them to Moses. Moses inspected their work and found that everything had been prepared exactly according to the instructions that he received from G-d. He then blessed the Jewish people, praying that G-d rest His presence on their handiwork, as He had promised.

The Need for a Moses

וַיָּבִיאוּ אֶת הַמִּשְׁכָּן אֶל מֹשֶׁה וגו': (שמות לט, לג)

[The Jewish people] brought the Tabernacle to Moses.

The people knew that Moses had to erect the Tabernacle, even though they had done all the work of constructing and preparing its components themselves.

The same applies to the inner, spiritual Tabernacle that we are to construct within ourselves. We must do all we can on our own to form and prepare all its parts, but after that we must enlist the aid of our "Moses" – the mentor who teaches us the Torah and shows us how to live according to it – whose task it is to connect us with G-d. Then we can be assured that all the pieces of our inner Tabernacle will unite seamlessly to perform their function in the fullest way.[4]

4. *Likutei Sichot*, vol. 11, p. 172.

FIFTH READING
Exodus 40:1–16

G-d then gave Moses specific instructions how to erect the Tabernacle. Included in these instructions was where to place the Laver – the urn from which the priests washed their hands and feet in preparation for officiating in their roles.

The Elevation of Sensuality

וְנָתַתָּ אֶת הַכִּיֹּר בֵּין אֹהֶל מוֹעֵד וּבֵין הַמִּזְבֵּחַ וְגוֹ': (שמות מ, ז)

[G-d told Moses,] "You must place the Laver between the Tent of Meeting and the Altar."

The Laver was made out of the mirrors that the Jewish women donated for the construction of the Tabernacle. The women had used these vanity mirrors to make sure that the Jewish people would continue to exist: When the men returned home, beaten and exhausted after toiling all day in slave labor in Egypt, their wives had them look at the two of them together in their mirrors, arousing their husbands' marital passion.

Spiritually, the Laver signifies the necessity to cleanse ourselves from even the slightest tinge of materialism before entering our inner Tabernacle. It therefore seems illogical that the Laver was made out of mirrors that were used to *arouse* sensuality. Indeed, for this very reason, Moses originally wanted to reject this donation.

The sensual drive is undoubtedly the most powerful form of lust. Yet the fact that the Laver was made from the Jewish women's mirrors teaches us that physical intimacy can not only be a holy act, but – when used to reach greater spiritual heights – it can even assist us in purifying ourselves of our worldly, materialistic, and physical orientation.[5]

5. *Reshimot* 108.

SIXTH READING
Exodus 40:17–27

On 1 Nisan 2449, Moses erected the Tabernacle according to G-d's instructions. As mentioned previously, one of the Tabernacle's furnishings was the Inner Altar, on which was burned a daily offering of incense.

FRIDAY

Inclusiveness

וַיַּקְטֵר עָלָיו קְטֹרֶת סַמִּים כַּאֲשֶׁר צִוָּה ה' אֶת מֹשֶׁה: (שמות מ, כז)

**[Moses] burned an incense offering on [the
Inner Altar], as G-d had commanded him.**

One of the ingredients of the incense was galbanum. Because of its foul smell, this herb alludes to the wrongdoers of our people. The fact that galbanum was an essential component of the incense teaches us that all Jews are an essential part of the Jewish nation, even if their behavior is sometimes inappropriate.

We must therefore never exclude one of our fellow Jews from the community, even if there are aspects of their behavior that would seem to justify this. In fact, our sages teach us that any public prayer or fast from which sinners are intentionally excluded will not be effective! This is because, by virtue of their Divine souls, every Jew possesses inestimable worth and is in fact full of good deeds. Each of our unique personalities plays a crucial role in the destiny of the Jewish people and the world in general.[6]

6. *Likutei Sichot*, vol. 21, pp. 179.

SEVENTH READING
Exodus 40:28–38

When the Tabernacle was set up and all its furnishings put in place, Moses performed the rites that inaugurated the Tabernacle and the priests. As a sign that all was done properly and the Tabernacle was indeed ready to serve as a place where G-d's presence could be felt, a cloud materialized and hovered above the Tabernacle.

The Mystical Dimension

וְלֹא יָכֹל מֹשֶׁה לָבוֹא אֶל אֹהֶל מוֹעֵד כִּי שָׁכַן עָלָיו הֶעָנָן
וּכְבוֹד ה' מָלֵא אֶת הַמִּשְׁכָּן: (שמות מ, לה)

Moses could not enter the Tent of Meeting, for the cloud had rested upon it, and G-d's glory filled the Tabernacle.

Clouds conceal what is within and behind them, and are therefore a metaphor for the incomprehensible infinity of G-d, which is beyond the ability of the human mind to grasp. This is why once G-d's presence rested upon the Tabernacle, even Moses could not enter it.

Yet, in the beginning of the very next book of the Torah, Leviticus, G-d calls to Moses from within the Tabernacle, thereby enabling him to enter it despite the Divine cloud resting on it and G-d's glory filling it.

We are taught that in the absence of the Tabernacle (and its successor, the holy Temple in Jerusalem), G-d reveals Himself to us through the Torah. We all possess an inner "Moses," i.e., the ability to selflessly devote ourselves to G-d and His will. G-d calls out to us through this inner Moses, enabling us to enter the mysteries of the Torah and commune with His presence. By fulfilling G-d's commandments and praying, we refine ourselves so that we can perceive G-d's presence ever clearer in our study of His Torah.[7]

7. *Likutei Torah* 2:1a–2b.

LEVITICUS

Vayikra

Sacrifices

Leviticus 1:1–5:26

LEVITICUS, THE THIRD BOOK OF THE TORAH, CONTAINS VERY little "action"; it is primarily devoted to the rules governing the relationship of G-d with the Jewish nation and with each person as an individual. The first two-and-a-half sections describe the procedures for offering sacrifices. The first section of the Book of Leviticus opens as G-d calls out (*Vayikra* in Hebrew) to Moses, bidding him to enter the Tabernacle so He can teach him these procedures.

FIRST READING

Leviticus 1:1–13

After the Tabernacle was erected on 1 Nisan, 2449, G-d called Moses into the Tabernacle and began instructing him regarding the procedures for the sacrifices. There are four broad categories of sacrifices: ascent-offerings, peace-offerings, sin-offerings, and guilt-offerings. G-d first taught Moses the procedures for ascent-offerings.

Getting Close

אָדָם כִּי יַקְרִיב מִכֶּם קָרְבָּן וגו': (ויקרא א, ב)

[**G-d said to Moses,**] "**When someone brings a sacrifice…**"

The notion of sacrifices seems to run counter to the Jewish conception of G-d: G-d has no need to "consume" or be "bribed" by our sacrifices. Yet we see in this section of the Torah that G-d not only accepts sacrifices but explicitly sets down the procedures for them, giving every indication that He actually *wants* them!

In fact, the Hebrew word translated as "sacrifice" or "offering" – *korban* – means "getting close." Although we generally associate sacrifices with atonement for sin, the first sacrifices mentioned in this section are voluntary offerings, which an individual brings to G-d not to atone for sin but out of the desire to draw closer to Him. Of course, some of the sacrifices are indeed sin-offerings. This simply indicates that G-d calls out to all of us to draw close to Him – not only to the guiltless among us – at all times.

Nowadays, in the absence of the Tabernacle (or its permanent successor, the holy Temple in Jerusalem), there are three ways that we draw close to G-d: through studying the Torah – particularly its teachings about sacrifices; through prayer, the liturgy of which is modeled after the sacrifices; and through acts of charity and kindness.[1]

---

1. Based on *Likutei Sichot*, vol. 7, pp. 24–26; ibid., vol. 32, pp. 1–5.

SECOND READING
Leviticus 1:14–2:6

The five types of animals that could be brought as sacrifices were cattle, goats, sheep, pigeons, and doves. Fish are not brought as sacrifices.

Spiritual Walking, Flying, and Swimming

וְאִם מִן הָעוֹף עֹלָה קָרְבָּנוֹ לַה' וגו': (ויקרא א, יד)

**[G-d told Moses,] "If someone's sacrifice
to G-d is an ascent-offering of fowl."**

Mammals allude to those among us whose animal nature is relatively pronounced. Fowl, because they can fly, allude to those of us who are less "earth-bound," i.e., who live a more intellectual life and can therefore "fly" above a purely animal existence. Nonetheless, just as fowl need to periodically rest from flight, human intellect is limited by nature. Therefore, fowl, like mammals, are used as sacrifices, since both our animal natures and our intellects need to be spiritually refined and uplifted.

In contrast, fish, which must remain constantly in water, allude to those of us who have so refined themselves that they remain always connected to G-d, "swimming" constantly in Divine consciousness. Since the Divine side of our personality does not need the elevation that our animal side does, fish are not used for sacrifices.[2]

2. *Igrot Kodesh*, vol. 1, pp. 46–47, 130–131.

THIRD READING

Leviticus 2:7–16

All sacrifices were salted just before they were burned on the Altar.

Elevating the Four Kingdoms

עַל כָּל קָרְבָּנְךָ תַּקְרִיב מֶלַח: (ויקרא ב, יג)

[G-d told Moses,] "You must offer up salt on all your sacrifices."

All four kingdoms of creation are incorporated in the sacrifices: Salt is the mineral element; the oil, wine, and flour that accompany sacrifices are the vegetative element; the animal itself is the animal element; the person offering the sacrifice and the priest officiating at the sacrifice are the human element. Through these representatives, the sacrifice elevates all four kingdoms of creation into holiness.

Similarly, the animal and vegetable food that we eat is our own personal "sacrifice," since by eating it, we transform it into the fuel that enables us to fulfill G-d's commandments, thereby elevating it into holiness. In this context, our tables are our own personal "altars." Traditionally, the bread that we eat is first dipped in salt. In this way, we elevate all four kingdoms of creation at our table, just as they were in the sacrifices.[3]

3. *Sefer HaMa'amarim 5745*, pp. 3, 129

FOURTH READING

Leviticus 3:1–17

In teaching Moses the procedures for the sacrifices, G-d referred to them several times as "bread for the fire [of the Altar]."

"Feeding" G-d

וְהִקְטִירוֹ הַכֹּהֵן הַמִּזְבֵּחָה לֶחֶם אִשֶּׁה לַיהֹוָה: (ויקרא ג, יא)

[G-d told Moses,] "The priest must burn [the sacrifice] on the Altar, as food for the fire, to G-d."

Throughout the Torah, G-d refers to the sacrifices repeatedly and figuratively as His "bread." Just as consuming bread – and food in general – keeps our souls connected to our bodies, the "bread" of G-d – the sacrificial service – keeps G-d, the soul and life-force of the world, bound together with the world. In this way, through the sacrificial rituals, Divine energy is drawn into the world.

The same is true of our personal "sacrificial services": Our study of the Torah, our prayers, our charitable deeds, and our ongoing refinement and elevation of the physical world in general, are G-d's "bread," connecting the world with G-d.[4]

4. *Sefer HaMa'amarim 5643*, p. 104.

FIFTH READING

Leviticus 4:1–26

After G-d taught Moses the procedures for ascent-offerings and peace-promoting-offerings, He taught him the procedures for sin-offerings. These sacrifices atoned principally for unintentional misdeeds.

Unintentional Misdeeds

נֶפֶשׁ כִּי תֶחֱטָא בִשְׁגָגָה וְגו': (ויקרא ד, ב)

[G-d told Moses,] "If a person unintentionally transgresses."

The reason why sacrifices were offered for unintentional misdeeds is because our deepest interests and aspirations, as well as our most intimate cares and concerns, are revealed specifically by our impulsive actions. It is through these actions that our "subconscious" self involuntarily surfaces. We do not need to atone for the misdeed itself, since it was done unintentionally. What we need to atone for is all the previous conduct and laxity that molded our inner selves into someone whose interests run contrary to G-d's will and who spontaneously rejected it.

In this light, our unintentional misdeeds warrant greater atonement than our intentional ones, for unintentional deeds indicate that we have a deep, subconscious attachment to a type of behavior that is contrary to G-d's will. Intentional misdeeds do not necessarily indicate that we suffer from this hidden flaw.[5]

5. *Likutei Sichot*, vol. 3, pp. 944–945.

SIXTH READING
Leviticus 4:27–5:10

In contrast to sin-offerings, which atone for unintentional sins, the guilt-offering can atone for certain intentional sins. Female goats or sheep can be used as personal sin-offerings, whereas only male sheep are used for guilt-offerings.

Male and Female Repentance

שְׂעִירַת עִזִּים תְּמִימָה נְקֵבָה וגו': (ויקרא ד, כח)

[G-d told Moses that an individual's sin-offering can be brought from] an unblemished female goat [or sheep].

There are two basic explanations of how sacrifices atone:

- We should imagine that everything being done to the animal is being done to us. The sacrifice thus jolts us out of our negative ways.
- The animal personifies our animal instincts, which led to the misdeed, in contrast to our Divine soul, which did not participate in the misdeed. The sacrifice stirs our Divine soul, inspiring us to serve G-d better than we did previously.

The first explanation is harsher than the second, and is therefore appropriate for more severe misdeeds. Therefore, the guilt-offering, which can atone for deliberate misdeeds, is brought from male animals, suggesting the "male" meditation necessary to shake a person free from deliberate misbehavior. The second, gentler, more "female" meditation is more appropriate for unintentional misdeeds; therefore, the sin-offering, which atones for such misdeeds, is brought from female animals.

When we feel estranged from G-d and seek to draw closer to Him, we need to evaluate the cause of our estrangement. We can then meditate on our relationship with G-d in the way appropriate to our situation and take the appropriate corrective action.[6]

6. *Likutei Sichot,* vol. 32, pp. 16–17.

SEVENTH READING
Leviticus 5:11–26

One of the sins atoned for by the guilt-offering is robbery. In order for the sacrifice to atone for this sin, however, the robber had to first return the article that he robbed.

Returning Spiritually Robbed Goods

וְהֵשִׁיב אֶת הַגְּזֵלָה אֲשֶׁר גָּזָל וגו': (ויקרא ה, כג)

**[G-d told Moses that if a robber wishes to atone
for his sin by offering up a guilt-offering,] he must
[first] return the article that he had robbed.**

Spiritually, "robbed articles" are anything that we, by sinning, have "robbed" from G-d and given over to the forces of evil, whether a physical object, a moment in time, or human potential.

Our task in life is to return the world's robbed entities to their rightful owner, i.e., to reorient everything that has been given over to the cause of evil toward Divinity, beginning with whatever we ourselves have "robbed" from G-d through our misdeeds. This is the essence of repentance: restoring the world to its natural, Divine state. Through repentance, it is further possible for us to reach even greater heights than we had attained before sinning.[7]

---

7. *Likutei Sichot*, vol. 25, pp. 398, 455–457.

Tzav

Details of the Sacrifices; The Installation Rites
Leviticus 6:1–8:36

THE SECOND SECTION OF THE BOOK OF LEVITICUS IS THE continuation and completion of the preceding section, and opens as G-d tells Moses to command (*Tzav*, in Hebrew) Aaron and his sons to follow the procedures for offering up sacrifices. The second half of the section describes the weeklong installation rites by which the priests and the Tabernacle were inaugurated.

FIRST READING

Leviticus 6:1–11

G-d told Moses that once a sacrificial animal has been slaughtered, the parts of it that are to be burned should preferably be placed on top of the Altar during the day. However, if this is not possible, they may still be placed on the Altar-fire any time throughout the following night.

The Eternal, Inner Flame

וְאֵשׁ הַמִּזְבֵּחַ תּוּקַד בּוֹ: (ויקרא ו, ב)

[G-d told Moses that a sacrifice is still valid if it is placed on the Altar at night,] for the fire of the Altar must burn on it [throughout the night].

The Altar fire that was kept burning throughout the night was kindled during the day.

The Altar alludes to the Jewish heart. Even when we find ourselves in situations of spiritual darkness, we must keep the Divine fire of enthusiasm for G-d, His Torah, and His commandments, always burning in our hearts.[1]

---

1. See *Or HaTorah, Vayikra*, vol. 1, p. 13.

SECOND READING
Leviticus 6:12–7:10

The high priest was required to offer up a special grain-offering every morning and every evening.

Channeling the Inner High Priest

וְהַכֹּהֵן הַמָּשִׁיחַ תַּחְתָּיו מִבָּנָיו יַעֲשֶׂה אֹתָהּ וְגו': (ויקרא ו, טו)

The priest from among [Aaron's] sons who is anointed [as high priest] must offer up [this grain-offering].

Our inner "high priest" is the innermost aspect and core of our soul, which is permanently bound to G-d. This aspect of our soul is that part of us that refuses to participate in any act that is a denial of our connection with G-d.

The classic example of something that disconnects us from G-d is idolatry. But really, any violation of G-d's will can be considered a form of idolatry, for when we violate G-d's will we are serving something other than G-d (whether it be money, fame, pleasure, or despair). If we would only realize this fact, nothing could entice us away from fulfilling G-d's will – whether by dwelling on unholy or depressing thoughts, by speaking unholy or insensitive words, or by performing unholy or destructive actions.

In this context, our personal "high-priestly" grain-offering is the meditative contemplation through which we channel the innermost core of our souls. Like the high priest's offering, drawing upon the power of this core is necessary both in the figurative "morning," i.e., when we feel enlightened and inspired, in order to ensure that we channel our energy in accordance with G-d's will, and in the figurative "evening," i.e., when we feel confused or uninspired, in order to ensure that we resist the temptation to go against what we know we should be doing.[2]

2. *Hitva'aduyot 5746*, vol. 2, pp. 701–702.

THIRD READING

Leviticus 7:11–38

A person was required to offer up a thanksgiving-offering whenever he or she experienced some open example of G-d's protection or help.

Always Being Thankful

אִם עַל תּוֹדָה יַקְרִיבֶנּוּ וְגו': (ויקרא ז, יב)

**If [a person] is bringing [a sacrifice]
in order to give thanks...**

In the Messianic era, communal sacrifices will continue to be
offered up, but there will no longer be personal sacrifices. The
sole exception will be the thanksgiving-offering. Similarly, we
are taught that in the Messianic era, all forms of prayer will cease
except for prayers of thanksgiving.

The purpose of personal sacrifices (other than the thanksgiving-offering) is to orient our animal soul toward Divinity. Once
the process of atonement will have been completed – and we will
no longer have the desire to sin – these types of sacrifices will
become obsolete. Only the thanksgiving-offering will remain,
for its function is to express our acknowledgement of our dependence upon G-d, and this will continue to be the case.

Similarly, we will no longer need to pray for our needs: we
will not lack anything, illness and poverty will be matters of
the past, and harmony and spiritual sensitivity will become the
hallmarks of society. Prayer will consist only of giving thanks, as
we continuously acknowledge G-d's benevolence and wonders.

We can hasten the Messianic era by emphasizing in our present lives what will be true in Messianic times. Thus, by placing
the emphasis in our prayers on appreciating G-d's goodness, we
hasten the time when this will indeed be our prayers' sole focus.[3]

3. *Or HaTorah, Vayikra*, p. 23; ibid., *Tehilim*, p. 369; ibid., *Nach*, vol. 2, pp.
963–964.

FOURTH READING

Leviticus 8:1–13

Having completed the instructions regarding the procedures for the sacrifices, the Torah describes how Aaron and his four sons were installed into the priesthood. Moses assembled the entire Jewish people at the entrance to the Tabernacle so they could witness these rituals.

The Purpose of the Priest

וַיֹּאמֶר מֹשֶׁה אֶל הָעֵדָה זֶה הַדָּבָר אֲשֶׁר צִוָּה ה' לַעֲשׂוֹת: (ויקרא ח, ה)

Moses said to the community: "This procedure is what G-d commanded [me] to do."

Aaron and his son were installed into the priesthood through two types of offerings: specific sacrifices that Moses offered up on their behalf every day for a full week when the Tabernacle was first erected, and a grain-offering that every priest was required to offer up on the first day of his service (and which the high priest was required to offer up twice every day). The purpose of these sacrifices was to awaken within Aaron and his sons the qualities that would enable them to act as the Jewish people's representatives before G-d, whether by securing atonement for their misdeeds or by raising them to higher levels of Divine consciousness.

Every one of us has the inner power to not only overcome spiritual darkness but to transform it into light. But this inner power is not always readily available to us, for various reasons. We must therefore seek out individuals who are steeped in the Torah and further along the path of spiritual refinement than we are, so we can benefit from their inspiration and guidance. At the same time, we must also develop our inner "priest," both in order to transform our own inner darkness into light, as well as to help others do the same for themselves.[4]

4. *Likutei Sichot*, vol. 7, pp. 39, 46–47.

FIFTH READING
Leviticus 8:14–21

The sacrifices that Moses offered up in order to install Aaron and his sons included ascent-offerings, sin-offerings, and peace-offerings.

Study vs. Action

וַיַּקְרֵב אֵת אֵיל הָעֹלָה וגו': (ויקרא ח, יח)

[Moses] brought forth the ascent-ram.

The sages teach us that, in the absence of the holy Temple, someone who studies the laws of a given sacrifice is considered as if he had offered it up. But if the study of the laws of a sacrifice accomplishes the same thing as offering it up, why should we bother with the sacrifice itself, even when the Temple will be rebuilt?

The difference between the "virtual" sacrifice and the actual one is their effect on the world. While a sacrifice "offered up" by studying its laws elevates the person, it does not elevate the world around him. Only the physical sacrifice, which includes all aspects of creation – human (the priest offering up the sacrifice), animal (the sacrifice itself), vegetable (the wood of the fire), and mineral (the salt added to all sacrifices) – elevates the world at large.

Thus, we should always seek a practical, tangible way to apply the spiritual inspiration or insight we garner, in order for it to affect and elevate not merely ourselves, but the entire world.[5]

---

5. *Hitva'aduyot 5742*, vol. 2, pp. 1137, 1145–1146.

SIXTH READING
Leviticus 8:22–29

As was the case with most sacrifices, parts of the sacrifices of the installation rituals were burned on the Outer Altar.

The Inner Sacrificial Altar

וַיִּקַּח מֹשֶׁה אֹתָם מֵעַל כַּפֵּיהֶם וַיַּקְטֵר הַמִּזְבֵּחָה וְגוֹ': (ויקרא ח, כח)

**Moses took [specific parts of the slaughtered
sacrifices] from the hands [of Aaron and his
sons] and burned them up on the Altar.**

The procedures for the sacrifices all allude to inner, psychological processes that we must undergo in order to draw close to G-d. (As mentioned above, the Hebrew word for "sacrifice" [*korban*] means "drawing close.")

Slaughtering the animal alludes to how we slaughter – i.e., renounce – our animalistic orientation toward life. *Sprinkling the blood on the Altar* alludes to how we then re-orient our enthusiasm (signified by our warm blood) toward G-dliness. *Placing the fat of the slaughtered animal on the Altar* alludes to how we re-orient our sense of delight (signified by fat, which results from indulging in eating foods that trigger feelings of delight in our brain) toward G-dliness. *Burning the animal by fire on the Altar* alludes to the consumption of our animal nature by Divinity, meaning that our formerly animalistic drives become drives for goodness, as we transform the world into G-d's home.[6]

6. *Reshimot* 108.

SEVENTH READING
Leviticus 8:30–36

The installation rituals were repeated every day for a full week.

Bringing Creation to its Fulfillment

כִּי שִׁבְעַת יָמִים יְמַלֵּא אֶת יֶדְכֶם: (ויקרא ח, לג)

[**Moses told Aaron and his sons,**] "[**G-d**] **will
install you** [**by these rituals**] **for seven days.**"

When the world was first created, G-d's Presence rested on earth.
But the misdeeds of successive generations banished it to further
and further spiritual realms. This process began to be reversed
by Abraham, and was consummated by the construction of the
Tabernacle.

Thus, the seven days of installation rites returned the world
to its original state of completeness and holiness, the way it was
during the original seven days of Creation.

If we look deeper, however, we can see that the seven days of
the installation rites brought the world to an even greater level of
completion than it possessed during the seven days of Creation.
The Divine revelation that accompanied the construction of
the Tabernacle was able to overcome the spiritual darkness that
had spread throughout the world as a result of the progressive
departure of the Divine Presence, not to mention the spiritual
darkness into which the world was plunged by the incident of
the Golden Calf.

Similarly, by focusing our attention on our Divine mission of
making our lives into a "Tabernacle," an environment where G-d
can feel at home, we bring ourselves to a higher level of Divine
consciousness than we possessed originally. Our return to G-d
affects all our seven basic emotions, just as the installation rites
of the priests had to take place over seven full days.[7]

7. *Sefer HaSichot 5748*, vol. 1, p. 363.

Shemini

The Conclusion of the Installation Rites; Kashrut

Leviticus 9:1–11:47

THE THIRD SECTION OF THE BOOK OF LEVITICUS OPENS WITH
the description of the eighth (*Shemini*, in Hebrew) and final day
of the installation rituals. After this, it records which animals are
permitted for Jewish consumption.

FIRST READING
Leviticus 9:1–16

During the week of 23–29 Adar 2449, Moses installed Aaron and his sons as priests. On the eighth day, 1 Nisan, Aaron officiated for the first time as high priest and his sons as regular priests. During the seven installation days, no fire descended from heaven to consume the sacrifices. Only when Aaron officiated, on the eighth day, did this miraculous sign of G-d's acceptance of the sacrifices occur.

When Aaron is Superior to Moses

וַיְהִי בַּיּוֹם הַשְּׁמִינִי קָרָא מֹשֶׁה לְאַהֲרֹן וּלְבָנָיו וגו' : (ויקרא ט, א)

On the eighth day, Moses summoned Aaron and his sons.

Due to the limitations of our finite human minds, we cannot attain ultimate Divine consciousness on our own. G-d therefore revealed Divinity in such a way that we can grasp it, by giving us the Torah. Once this had been accomplished, the next step was to prepare the world to absorb the G-dliness that is inherent in the Torah, for without preparation on our part, Divine revelation cannot be absorbed into our being, and therefore cannot elevate us in any meaningful or lasting way.

G-d gave us the Torah through Moses, but Aaron was the one who made society receptive to G-dliness by inspiring the people to aspire to the spiritual life. It was therefore Aaron who completed the process of Divine revelation begun by Moses. The rites that Moses performed in the Tabernacle's installation rites did not reveal G-d's presence; only those that Aaron performed accomplished this.

We all desire to feel G-d's presence in our lives. In order for this to occur, we must imitate Aaron: "love peace and pursue peace; love your fellow creatures and bring them close to the Torah."[1]

---

1. *Likutei Sichot*, vol. 7, pp. 298–299.

SECOND READING
Leviticus 9:17–23

After Aaron finished performing his sacrificial rites, he blessed the Jewish people.

Consummate Humility

וַיִּשָּׂא אַהֲרֹן אֶת יָדָו אֶל הָעָם וַיְבָרֲכֵם וגו': (ויקרא ט, כב)

**Aaron lifted up his hands toward the
people and blessed them.**

Although Aaron was aware that it was his performance of this special day's rituals that would bring G-d's presence into the Tabernacle, and he did everything exactly as Moses instructed, he still felt unworthy of his role. The memory of his participation in the incident of the Golden Calf still weighed heavily on him.

Aaron expressed these sentiments when he blessed the people, applying the text of the priestly blessing to the day's unique circumstances: He said, "We know that G-d's presence can only dwell in this Tabernacle if He has forgiven us for the incident of the Golden Calf. Since I played a central role in this incident, His forgiveness for all of us depends upon His forgiving me. Therefore, until we know that G-d has forgiven me, I cannot bless your efforts by myself. Therefore, I must appeal to G-d Himself *to bless you and watch over you. May G-d shine His face to you and grace you* with His presence, as a result of His *being partial toward you,* forgiving you the sin of the Golden Calf, and thereby *granting you peace.*"

Like all great Jewish leaders, it was Aaron's feelings of inadequacy that truly made him fit for his role.[2]

2. *Likutei Sichot,* vol. 22, pp. 39–44.

THIRD READING
Leviticus 9:24–10:11

After Aaron's blessing and Moses' prayer, fire did descend from heaven and consume the parts of the sacrifices that had been placed on the Altar. When the Jewish people saw this, they were ecstatic that G-d's presence appeared to them again openly. Their efforts in donating material for the Tabernacle and working diligently in constructing it, as well as their inner "work" of repenting for the incident of the Golden Calf, had borne fruit. But then, two of Aaron's four sons, Nadav and Avihu, offered up some incense on their own initiative. To everyone's horror, Divine fire again descended, but this time in the form of two pairs of flames that entered Nadav's and Avihu's nostrils, killing them instantly.

Managing Ecstasy

וַתֵּצֵא אֵשׁ מִלְפְנֵי ה' וַתֹּאכַל אוֹתָם וגו': (ויקרא י, ב)

A fire went forth from before G-d and consumed them.

Nadav and Avihu were swept up in the ecstasy of the moment. In their intense desire to cleave to G-d, which they expressed through their unauthorized incense offering, they rose through spiritual heights even as they felt their souls leaving them. From this perspective, their death was not a punishment but a fulfillment of their wish to dissolve into G-d's essence.

Nevertheless, we are not intended to imitate their example; on the contrary, we are expressly forbidden to pursue such suicidal spiritual rapture. Although it is necessary to seek inspiration and renew it constantly, the purpose of reaching increasingly higher planes of Divine consciousness is to bring the consciousness that we acquire down into the world, thereby making the world increasingly more conscious of G-d, transforming it into His home.[3]

3. *Likutei Sichot*, vol. 3, pp. 987–991.

FOURTH READING
Leviticus 10:12–15

Moses comforted Aaron and his sons over the death of Nadav and Avihu. Even though it is normally forbidden for a priest who is in mourning to officiate, Moses instructed Aaron and his two surviving sons to continue with the sacrificial service – including eating their designated portions of the sacrifices – as an exceptional case.

Eliciting the Supernatural

וַאֲכַלְתֶּם אֹתָהּ . . . כִּי כֵן צֻוֵּיתִי: (ויקרא י, יג)

[Moses said to Aaron and his sons,] "You must eat [your portions of the sacrifices...] for so have I been commanded [by G-d]."

The normal rules governing the behavior of the priests were suspended on the eighth day of the installation rites because the day's essential message was that G-d can override His own rules. Whereas the number seven signifies the natural order, the number eight signifies the miraculous transcendence of natural order.

Nevertheless, there could not have been a miraculous eighth day of the Tabernacle's inauguration without the preceding seven non-miraculous days. This is because G-d makes His miraculous intervention in life dependent upon us.

The ultimate transcendence of the natural order will occur in the Messianic era. The miraculous revelations of the future will be the result of the preparations we make now. As we continue to refine the world through natural means, we should bear in mind that the results of our efforts will be beyond whatever we can imagine.[4]

4. *Likutei Sichot*, vol. 17, pp. 92–99.

FIFTH READING
Leviticus 10:16–20

Moses assumed that G-d's instruction that the priests eat their designated portions of the day's sacrifices applied to *all* the sacrifices of the day, while Aaron assumed that it applied only to the special sacrifices that were offered up on this day. When Moses saw that Aaron and his sons had not eaten their portions of one of the regular sacrifices, he demanded an explanation. When Aaron explained his perspective, Moses agreed that he was right.

The Absolute vs. the Relative

וַיְדַבֵּר אַהֲרֹן אֶל מֹשֶׁה... וְאָכַלְתִּי חַטָּאת הַיּוֹם הַיִּיטַב בְּעֵינֵי ה': (ויקרא י, יט)

Aaron said to Moses, "If I had eaten a [regular] sin-offering today, would it have pleased G-d?"

Moses' and Aaron's perspectives on the difference between the special sacrifices of the day and those that would be offered up on a regular basis reflect their emphases in our relationship with G-d. Moses was devoted to transmitting G-d's Torah to the people, whereas Aaron was devoted to elevating the people to the Torah.

The Torah is unchanging truth, whereas human beings are constantly changing. Moses saw the Torah's truth as being uniformly applicable in all situations, whereas Aaron realized that each situation must be assessed in order to know how to apply the Torah's unchanging truth effectively. Aaron saw that a one-time sacrifice is different than one that would be offered up regularly, that G-d's truth can be reflected differently in different contexts.

In our own lives, we must meld Moses' and Aaron's perspectives. For ourselves, we must be like Moses, devoted to the Torah's absolute and unchanging truth. When interacting with others, we, like Aaron, must take into account their moods and inclinations, drawing them closer to the Torah through forgiving love.[5]

5. *Likutei Sichot*, vol. 17, pp. 113–116.

SIXTH READING

Leviticus 11:1–32

G-d has endowed the Jewish people with Divine souls tailored to their Divine mission. In order to maintain the health of these unique souls, the Jewish people are required to follow a special diet: the laws of Kashrut.

Cloven Feet

כֹּל מַפְרֶסֶת פַּרְסָה וְשֹׁסַעַת שֶׁסַע פְּרָסֹת וְגוֹ': (ויקרא יא, ג)

[G-d instructed Moses to tell the Jewish people, "You may only eat animals] whose feet are [not only partially] cloven but completely split into [at least two sub-]feet."

The first sign of a kosher animal is its split foot. The foot both touches the ground and separates us from the ground. It therefore alludes to the notion that in our involvement with the physical world, we must remain separate from it, aloof in our dealings with materiality. The fact that the foot must be split alludes to the notion that there must be an opening in this barrier: We must make sure that the light of holiness permeates even the most mundane aspects of creation, and make sure to retain Divine consciousness even when we are involved in the mundane aspects of our lives.

The other sign of kosher land animals is rumination. This alludes to the necessity of deliberating before engaging the mundane aspects of life. First, we must weigh our intentions, ensuring that they are solely toward elevating the world, purging them of any desire to simply indulge in sensuality for its own sake. Second, we must weigh the methods we employ in elevating the world, ensuring that they conform to the guidelines set forth in the Torah.[6]

6. *Likutei Sichot*, vol. 1, pp. 224–226.

SEVENTH READING
Leviticus 11:33–47

After detailing which land-animals, fish, and fowl are permitted for Jewish consumption, G-d instructed Moses to teach the Jewish people the laws of ritual defilement. The purpose of these laws is to emphasize that, as Jews, we must value and emphasize life in this world, distancing ourselves from contact with the negativity and depression associated with death. Ritual defilement is contracted either through contact with certain dead animals or a dead person, or through some bodily condition that takes the individual close to the boundary between life and death. Contracting ritual defilement prevents an individual from entering the Tabernacle and/or consuming sacrifices and other types of ritually sacred food.

Avoiding Being Duped

לְהַבְדִּיל בֵּין הַטָּמֵא וּבֵין הַטָּהֹר וגו': (ויקרא יא, מז)

**[G-d instructed Moses to teach the Jewish people how]
to distinguish between the defiled and the undefiled.**

Spiritually, this decree refers to making the moral distinction between what is acceptable, healthy behavior and what is not. This distinction is easy enough when matters are clear and obvious. But all too often, the distinction is blurred, and what is in fact defiled can easily be taken as being undefiled.

By studying the Torah, we remain connected to G-d, who is not subject to the limited reach of human intellect. Thus attuned to Divine consciousness, we instinctively know what is spiritually healthy and what is not.[7]

---

7. *Likutei Sichot*, vol. 7, pp. 72–73.

Tazri'a

Tzara'at

Leviticus 12:1–13:59

THE PRECEDING SECTION OF THE BOOK OF LEVITICUS DIS-
cussed the laws of ritual defilement imparted by dead animals. In
this section, the Torah proceeds to the laws of defilement associated with human beings. It first discusses the defilement that
automatically rests upon any Jewish woman who gives birth (after
having conceived – *Tazri'a*, in Hebrew). The justified pride that a
woman is likely to feel after the miracle of giving birth prevents her
from feeling the absolute humility before G-d required in order
to enter His Tabernacle. She is therefore obligated to undergo
a fixed period of recuperation and a purification process, after
which she can again visit the Tabernacle and participate in its
rituals. The second type of defilement discussed in this section
is an extinct disease known as *tzara'at,* that appeared on a Jewish
man or woman's skin, garments, or home.

FIRST READING
Leviticus 12:1–13:5

The reason why *tzara'at* no longer exists is that it afflicted only people who had refined their behavior and had risen to extremely high levels of Divine consciousness; these levels of consciousness are available to us only when the Tabernacle – or its successor, the holy Temple – is standing.

Healing Subconscious Flaws

אָדָם כִּי יִהְיֶה בְעוֹר בְּשָׂרוֹ . . . וְהוּבָא אֶל אַהֲרֹן הַכֹּהֵן וְגו': (ויקרא יג, ב)

[G-d told Moses,] "If a person develops [certain kinds of lesions on the skin,] he must be brought to Aaron the priest [in order to determine if he is afflicted with *tzara'at*]."

The first types of *tzara'at* that the Torah discusses are those that appear on a person's skin. The skin is the external layer of our body; this type of *tzara'at* therefore alludes to an imperfection in our external behavior. Specifically, it afflicts people who are guilty of unintentional, spontaneous injurious gossip or slander.

We can indeed purify our deliberate behavior, speech, and thought of negativity. Nevertheless, some subconscious negativity might remain, lurking so deep within that we might never become aware of it on our own. When the only trace of negativity remaining within us is this delicate, the only way it can surface is in spontaneous behavior, such as unpremeditated gossip – the casual remark that slips through otherwise innocent conversation. Spontaneous speech discloses the inner recesses of the heart.

When the Tabernacle or Temple stood, G-d let people know when they still possessed this slight imperfection of character by afflicting them with *tzara'at*. Although we lack this open sign today, we can still notice the slips of our tongue and take them as cues to refine ourselves accordingly.[1]

---

1. *Likutei Torah* 2:22b; *Likutei Sichot*, vol. 22, pp. 65–69, 74–75.

SECOND READING
Leviticus 13:6–17

Paradoxically, *tzara'at* on a person's skin renders him ritually defiled only if it covers part of his body. If it spreads over his whole body, he is not ritually defiled.

A Light Unto the Nations

וְהִנֵּה כִּסְּתָה הַצָּרַעַת אֶת כָּל בְּשָׂרוֹ וְטָהַר וְגו': (ויקרא יג, יג)

If the *tzara'at* has covered all his flesh, he is not defiled.

One of the signs given by the sages that the Messiah's arrival is imminent is that "the government has become heretical." This notion is alluded to in the law that if *tzara'at* covers the entire body, the person is not defiled.

There are two ways that the world's governments can be considered to have become "heretical." The negative way is for heresy to indeed infect all the world's governments. The positive way is for the truth of the Torah to become so self-evident that it will be universally acknowledged that any government that does *not* submit to the Torah's rules is "heretical."

It is our hope and prayer that redemption occur the second way. It is therefore imperative that the Jewish people encourage the nations of the world to fulfill the commandments that the Torah obligates them to observe (the "Noahide" laws). By acknowledging the Torah as the sole possible basis for true ethical behavior and moral justice, the non-Jewish world will come to recognize and appreciate the Jewish people as the vanguards of universal justice, morality, and peace. This will pave the way for the ultimate, Messianic Redemption.[2]

2. *Likutei Sichot*, vol. 32, pp. 77–83.

THIRD READING
Leviticus 13:18–23

Tzara'at of the skin can develop out of a lesion, an inflammation, or a burn. In all these cases, the first symptom of this affliction is a white spot on the flesh.

Symptoms of Spiritual Blockage

שְׂאֵת לְבָנָה אוֹ בַהֶרֶת לְבָנָה...וְנִרְאָה אֶל הַכֹּהֵן: (ויקרא יג, יט)

If a white spot [develops, the person] must be shown to the priest [in order to determine if he is afflicted with *tzara'at*].

When G-d causes *tzara'at* to appear on a person's skin, He does so by limiting the circulation of blood in a specific area of the skin, which then turns white. This blockage in the circulation is the physical symptom of a similar, spiritual blockage.

The spiritual blockage that results in physical *tzara'at* occurs when our feelings of spiritual inspiration fail to humble us as they should. Instead of making us into better people, our enhanced awareness of G-d inflates our ego. This amplified sense of self-worth intoxicates us with overconfidence. If left unchecked, this self-righteousness can corrupt us in many ways.

It is therefore important to make sure that no such spiritual blockage occurs, that spiritual inspiration always humbles us and is expressed in our concern for others.[3]

3. *Likutei Torah* 2:23b, 24a, 24c ff; *BeSha'ah sheHikdimu 5672*, vol. 1, p. 370; *Sefer HaMa'amarim 5714–5716*, p. 511.

FOURTH READING
Leviticus 13:24–28

As explained above, the first symptom of *tzara'at* of the skin is a white spot on the flesh.

Getting Carried Away

וְהָיְתָה מִחְיַת הַמִּכְוָה בַּהֶרֶת לְבָנָה וגו': (ויקרא יג, כד)

If the healed area of the burn turns into a white spot . . .

White is a symbol of purity and innocence. Therefore, the appearance of an abnormally white spot on the flesh can also indicate an overabundance of holy spiritual energy. This can happen when our experience of holy rapture is not balanced by an equal sense of humble commitment to our Divine mission.

In this context, the sin of gossip – which *tzara'at* is meant to indicate – can be seen as too much of what could have (and should have) been a good or even holy thing, but instead degenerated into the opposite. We are all aware of how powerful speech can be in forging social ties and promoting peace. Whether we are conscious of it or not, this is why we enjoy social conversation, clarifying issues with each other until we reach a mutual understanding. When, however, a hidden excess of ego insists that our reputation or esteem take precedence over the advancement of social harmony, some gossip or slander is inadvertently released in the excitement of conversation. It is therefore crucial that we remain constantly on guard, so only good come out of our social conversation.[4]

---

4. *Likutei Torah* 2:22b, 25b; *Likutei Sichot*, vol. 37, pp. 33–36; *Sefer HaSichot 5751*, vol. 2, pp. 492–494.

FIFTH READING

Leviticus 13:29–39

Special laws apply to *tzara'at* that appears on the head.

Pride and Arrogance

וְאִישׁ אוֹ אִשָּׁה כִּי יִהְיֶה בוֹ נָגַע בְּרֹאשׁ וגו': (ויקרא י"ג, כט)

If a man or a woman has a lesion on the head . . .

The eruption of *tzara'at* on the head is caused by self-pride and arrogance, as opposed to *tzara'at* elsewhere on the body, which is the result of gossip or slander. The reason for this difference is that gossip and slander are superficial misdeeds, as explained above, which therefore affect the skin elsewhere on the body. Pride and arrogance, in contrast, are warped *mental attitudes*, and therefore they affect the head.

We should continuously strive to eliminate these character imperfections.[5]

5. *Likutei Sichot*, vol. 27, p. 99.

SIXTH READING
Leviticus 13:40–54

When a person has been declared by the examining priest to have contracted *tzara'at* on his skin, he must dwell outside the city until the *tzara'at* disappears. This is appropriate corrective action for the antisocial gossip of which he was guilty. *Tzara'at* appears on the walls of a person's home and on his garments before it appears on his skin.

Purging Negativity

וְהַבֶּגֶד כִּי יִהְיֶה בוֹ נֶגַע צָרָעַת וְגו': (ויקרא יג, מז)

A garment that has the lesion of *tzara'at* on it...

Our skin, clothing, and homes are three increasingly external layers that envelop us. *Tzara'at* first affected the outermost "garment," the house, because at first, gossip is a totally superficial symptom. If the individual did not take this cue, neglecting to purge himself of his hidden negativity, *tzara'at* broke out on his clothing. This indicated that his hidden flaws had started to seep into him from the outside. If he ignored this cue as well, *tzara'at* broke out on his skin, indicating that his inner evil, although still superficial, was now part of him. At this stage, he had to be ostracized from society, with the hope that this demonstration of the consequences of his misbehavior would inspire him to mend his ways.[6]

6. *Likutei Torah* 2:22b; *Likutei Sichot*, vol. 22, pp. 65–69, 74–75; *Igrot Kodesh*, vol 11, p. 248.

SEVENTH READING
Leviticus 13:55–59

Only a priest was empowered to declare a person, article of clothing, or house afflicted with *tzara'at* or free of it.

Looking at Others Positively

וְרָאָה הַכֹּהֵן וְגוֹ': (ויקרא יג, נה)

The priest must examine [the article to determine if it is afflicted with *tzara'at*].

The Torah specifically requires the priests to judge cases of *tzara'at* because they are the spiritual heirs of the very first priest, Aaron, who was famous for promoting brotherly love among the Jewish people. Because of their love for their fellow Jews, the priests – while taking care not to bend the law of the Torah in any way – will make absolutely sure that the law indeed requires them to pronounce the sufferer defiled before doing so. And if the priests do have to declare a person defiled, they will do whatever it takes to declare him undefiled at the earliest possible opportunity.

Similarly, when we encounter someone who appears to be afflicted with some negative character trait, we should not rush to reject him. Rather, we should first examine ourselves, in order to determine how well we exemplify the ideals of brotherly love. If we are in any way lacking in this regard, we have no right to pass judgment on others, for it could well be that our perception is skewed by our unrefined feelings.

By learning from Aaron how to love our fellows regardless of their objective behavior, we counteract the cause of our present exile, unwarranted hatred. This will hasten the final, Messianic Redemption.[7]

7. *Likutei Sichot*, vol. 27, pp. 88–91.

Metzora

Purification from *Tzara'at*

Leviticus 14:1–15:33

CONTINUING THE CONTENT OF THE PRECEDING SECTION,
the fifth section of the Book of Leviticus opens with the rituals that someone who was afflicted with *tzara'at* (*Metzora*, in
Hebrew) must undergo in order to be allowed into the Tabernacle
again. It then describes how *tzara'at* can appear on buildings and
how affected buildings are purified from it. Finally, it discusses
the various forms of ritual defilement that result from certain
bodily discharges.

FIRST READING
Leviticus 14:1–12

Once *tzara'at* has disappeared from the body, the formerly afflicted person has to offer up specific sacrifices and follow specific rituals, including immersing himself and his clothes in a *mikveh* (ritual pool) and shaving off all his hair.

Combating Excess with Excess

זֹאת תִּהְיֶה תּוֹרַת הַמְּצֹרָע וגו': (ויקרא יד, ב)

[G-d told Moses,] "The following is the law regarding the person afflicted with *tzara'at*."

The Hebrew word for a person afflicted with *tzara'at* (*metzora*) can be seen as a contraction for the Hebrew phrase for "slanderer" (***motzi shem ra***), which literally means "someone who gives [someone else] a bad name." This reflects the fact that *tzara'at* afflicted people whose hidden evil surfaced in spontaneous harmful gossip and slander.

Good deeds generate positive energy and misdeeds generate negative energy. Therefore, when we set out to repair the damage caused by a misdeed, we also need to neutralize the negative energy it generated. Gossip and slander result from using the power of speech excessively. Therefore, the way to rectify the damage they caused is by excessive speech in a positive way – by studying the Torah (which should be done out loud). This draws positive, holy energy into the world.

We are taught that the Torah's letters are all "names" of G-d – i.e., channels through which Divine energy enters the world. Thus, the positive energy that is brought into the world through the study of the Torah counteracts the negative energy that produces *tzara'at*, replacing the destructive, evil "bad names" with constructive, Divine "names."[1]

---

1. *Likutei Torah* 2:24c– 25a; *Likutei Sichot*, vol. 12, pp. 81–82.

SECOND READING
Leviticus 14:13–20

In the course of the sacrificial rites performed on the formerly afflicted person, the officiating priest must apply some of the blood of one of the sacrifices to various points on the person's body.

A Pure and Humble Heart

וְלָקַח הַכֹּהֵן מִדַּם וגו': (ויקרא יד, יד)

The priest must take some of the blood.

As just mentioned, the excess negative energy generated by the sins of gossip and slander is counteracted and overcome by studying the Torah "excessively"; this generates an excess of positive energy. However, in order for our study of the Torah to indeed elicit Divine energy and infuse it into creation, we must study it with pure motives, namely, in order to fulfill G-d's will and disseminate Divine consciousness, rather than for personal interest or as an intellectual pursuit. Therefore, just as a priest had to officiate at the purification process of a person formerly afflicted with *tzara'at*, our study of the Torah must be overseen by our inner "priest." The priest in the Tabernacle (and later, in the holy Temple) personified total self-nullification to G-d; similarly, we should strive to study the Torah with a pure and humble heart.[2]

2. *Likutei Torah* 2:24c- 25a; *Likutei Sichot*, vol. 12, pp. 81–82.

THIRD READING

Leviticus 14:20–32

If the person formerly afflicted with *tzara'at* could not afford the lambs required for his sacrifices, he could substitute fowl.

Achieving Spiritual Balance

זֹאת תּוֹרַת אֲשֶׁר בּוֹ נֶגַע צָרָעַת...בְּטָהֳרָתוֹ: (ויקרא יד, לב)

This is the law regarding someone suffering from a lesion of *tzara'at*...when he is to be purified.

The fact that the symptom of *tzara'at* was a white spot on the flesh indicates that *tzara'at* resulted when holy rapture is not balanced by an equal sense of humble commitment to our Divine mission. Divine rapture is an expression of our love of G-d, whereas humble devotion to His will is an expression of our fear of G-d and submission to His will. Love of G-d and fear of G-d are identified in Jewish mystical texts as the "right hand" and "left hand" of our soul, respectively. Thus, favoring one over the other upsets our spiritual balance.

Opposite forces can only be harmonized by using a third force that surpasses and encompasses them both – the study of the Torah. Studying the Torah with a sense of self-nullification to G-d enables us to rise above the limitations of logic and nature. We can harmonize the opposites of love and fear, and restore the healthy balance between them. This is another way in which the study of the Torah is the antidote for gossip and slander, bringing healing and harmony into the world.[3]

3. *Sefer HaSichot 5751*, vol. 2, pp. 493–494.

FOURTH READING
Leviticus 14:33–53

There was an additional reason for *tzara'at* breaking out on someone's house, aside from the reasons given above. When the pagan Canaanites heard that the Jewish people were planning on driving them out of the Land of Israel, they hid their precious wealth in the walls of their homes, hoping that they would eventually return to them. By causing *tzara'at* to break out on such a house, G-d forced its new Jewish owner to demolish its wall, revealing this hidden treasure.

Even Righteous People Can Repent

וְנָתַתִּי נֶגַע צָרַעַת בְּבֵית וְגוֹ': (ויקרא יד, לד)

I will place a *tzara'at*-lesion on a house.

Sincere repentance elevates us to degrees of Divine consciousness that we could not have attained otherwise. Since *tzara'at* struck specifically people who seemingly had nothing to repent for, it enabled even these people to achieve the closeness to G-d normally reserved for people who have repented for some misdeed.

Although this held true of *tzara'at* in general, it was most clearly seen in the *tzara'at* of homes, where the sufferer was rewarded openly by suddenly acquiring the worldly wealth hidden in his walls. This physical windfall reflected the spiritual windfall that the person acquired: his newfound closeness to G-d.

This is how we should view any apparent misfortune or seeming setback in life. It is G-d's way of elevating us to a level of relationship with Him that we could not have reached on our own.[4]

---

4. *Likutei Sichot*, vol. 27, pp. 107–114.

FIFTH READING
Leviticus 14:54–15:15

The Torah now turns to the laws regarding ritual defilement caused by bodily discharges. The first of these it discusses is urethral discharges in men.

To Overcome and Be Purified

אִישׁ אִישׁ כִּי יִהְיֶה זָב מִבְּשָׂרוֹ וְגוֹ': (ויקרא טו, ב)

If a man has a discharge from his reproductive organ...

Even if a non-seminal discharge issues from a man's body against his will, it can, in certain cases, render him ritually defiled. This is so because even inadvertent discharges are caused by improper attitudes that the man willfully adopted.

Similarly, if a person immerses his thoughts repeatedly and deeply in negative notions, negativity can begin to influence him against his will.

Nonetheless, the Torah offers a person suffering from non-seminal discharges the opportunity to regain ritual purity, by offering up the appropriate sacrifice. The same applies to someone who has unfortunately overly immersed himself in negative ways of thinking: he must never despair of himself. Even if he feels that negativity is gaining the upper hand, he can always overcome it and reinstate his former innocence.[5]

5. *Likutei Sichot*, vol. 37, pp. 42–46.

SIXTH READING
Leviticus 15:16–28

The Torah then discusses the laws regarding ritual defilement caused by discharges from women's reproductive organs. It first discusses the laws of normal menstrual bleeding.

The Lessons of the Feminine Cycle

וְאִשָּׁה כִּי תִהְיֶה זָבָה וגו': (ויקרא טו, יט)

If a woman has a discharge...

Before they ate from the Tree of Knowledge of Good and Evil, Adam and Eve were paragons of spiritual perfection and purity. By eating the Tree's fruit, they opened the door for the mixture of good and evil, causing the world to fall from its previous degree of spiritual purity. Female menstruation and its resultant ritual defilement also began only after Adam and Eve ate from the fruit of the Tree of Knowledge, as a result of the intermixture of good and evil that became an integral part of nature.

The Jewish people are G-d's "bride." When the Holy Temple was standing, we were closer to G-d, whose presence we could feel openly. During exile, however, we are like a menstruating wife, who is not allowed to have marital relations with her husband.

It is important to realize that the intermixture of good and evil will not continue forever. In the future, G-d will "cause the spirit of defilement to pass from the world." The Talmudic sages teach us that this means that women will no longer menstruate. Similarly, with the coming of the Redemption, G-d's "bride," the Jewish people, will once again unite with Him, this time forever.

The inner purpose of studying the Torah and fulfilling G-d's commandments at present is to hasten the long-awaited reinstatement of our close, loving bond with G-d in its fullest revelation.[6]

6. *Reshimot 12; Likutei Sichot, vol. 3, pp. 983–987; ibid., vol. 14, pp. 26–28.*

SEVENTH READING
Leviticus 15:29–33

The Torah then discusses the laws regarding ritual defilement brought about by abnormal, non-menstrual bleeding.

There is Always Hope

וּבַיּוֹם הַשְּׁמִינִי וגו': (ויקרא טו, כט)

On the eighth day...

Abnormal uterine bleeding, i.e., that occurs outside the menstrual cycle, alludes to an abnormal exaggeration of self-centeredness. Just as abnormal uterine bleeding imparts a more serious degree of ritual defilement, requiring more elaborate rituals designed to enable the woman to restore herself to full ritual purity, so does exaggerated self-centeredness require more intense spiritual treatment than normal.

Nonetheless, the fact that the Torah prescribes purification rituals for abnormal uterine bleeding teach us that the power of repentance is such that even someone who is suffering from excessive spiritual "maladies" can still be cured.[7]

7. *Likutei Sichot*, vol. 14, pp. 26–28.

Acharei

Yom Kippur
Leviticus 16:1–18:30

THE SIXTH SECTION OF THE BOOK OF LEVITICUS OPENS AS G-d addresses Moses after (*Acharei*, in Hebrew) the death of his brother Aaron's two oldest sons (which was recounted in the third section, *Shemini*). G-d gives Moses the laws regarding the Day of Atonement (*Yom Kippur*). This is followed by a list of various types of behavior that G-d has forbidden to the Jewish people as a result of having made them into "a kingdom of priests and a holy nation" at the Giving of the Torah.

FIRST READING
Leviticus 16:1–17

Repentance makes it possible to restore our original innocence before G-d, and even forge a better relationship with Him than had existed previously. When the Tabernacle or the holy Temple stood, the most severe misdeeds were atoned for through the rituals and sacrifices of the annual Day of Atonement (*Yom Kippur*). These rituals can only be performed by the high priest. Some of these rituals take place in the innermost chamber of the Tabernacle, the Holy of Holies.

The High Priest's Wife

וְהִקְרִיב אַהֲרֹן אֶת פַּר הַחַטָּאת אֲשֶׁר לוֹ וְכִפֶּר בַּעֲדוֹ וּבְעַד בֵּיתוֹ: (ויקרא טז, ו)

Aaron must bring forward his sin-offering bull and atone for himself and for his household [i.e., his wife].

In order for the *Yom Kippur* rites to be valid, the high priest must be married, and return directly home to his wife after completing the *Yom Kippur* rites. The purpose of his attaining high levels of Divine consciousness in the Holy of Holies is that he apply this inspiration to everyday life. Since women personify our drive to make the world into G-d's home, the high priest's return home to his wife – sharing his Divine inspiration with her, thereby enabling her to develop and expand her own Divine consciousness – is the culmination of the intense spiritual work of the day.

The *Yom Kippur* rites instruct us how to renew our relationship with G-d. Thus, fostering our own marital harmony is an integral part of fostering our relationship with G-d. Husbands must encourage their wives' spiritual development. And we must all strive to harmonize our "male" sides, i.e., our aspiration to spirituality, with our "female" sides, i.e., our aspiration to bring spirituality into our daily lives.[1]

1. *Likutei Sichot*, vol. 32, pp. 110–111.

SECOND READING

Leviticus 16:18–24

The high priest was required to change into special garments of simple linen in order to enter the Holy of Holies.

Becoming a New Person

וּפָשַׁט אֶת בִּגְדֵי הַבָּד אֲשֶׁר לָבַשׁ בְּבֹאוֹ אֶל הַקֹּדֶשׁ וְהִנִּיחָם שָׁם: (ויקרא טז, כג)

**[Aaron] must remove the linen garments that
he wore when he entered the Holy [of Holies],
and leave them [in the Tabernacle].**

The linen garments worn by the high priest on *Yom Kippur* must never be worn again. The reason for this rule is that when a person repents sincerely, he or she is transformed into a new person. Inasmuch as the essence of *Yom Kippur* is repentance, the garments used by the high priest to perform the *Yom Kippur* rituals had to be new each year.[2]

---

2. *Likutei Sichot*, vol. 28, pp. 224–225.

THIRD READING
Leviticus 16:25–34

The rituals that were performed by the high priest in the Tabernacle on *Yom Kippur* atoned principally for the collective misdeeds of the community. In contrast, each individual atones for his or her own personal misdeeds on *Yom Kippur* through repentance, fasting, and refraining from working on this day.

The Power of Yom Kippur

כִּי בַיּוֹם הַזֶּה יְכַפֵּר עֲלֵיכֶם לְטַהֵר אֶתְכֶם וְגוֹ': (ויקרא טז, ל)

**For on this day, [G-d] will effect atonement
for you in order to purify you.**

Rather than "surgically" removing our misdeeds from us, *Yom Kippur* removes us from our misdeeds, by elevating us far above them. Therefore, the focus on *Yom Kippur* is on our relationship with G-d rather than on our misdeeds per se. What is required of us on this day is to yearn to be reconciled with G-d in a general sense, and to express this yearning by observing *Yom Kippur* properly.

Yom Kippur elevates us this way because the day itself reveals the intrinsic connection that every Jew shares with G-d by virtue of his or her Divine soul. The connection between our essence and G-d's essence has existed since before Creation and is therefore not limited by time or space. For this reason, it cannot be damaged by any misdeeds we might have committed. Thus, the very day of *Yom Kippur* – by revealing this intrinsic connection between ourselves and G-d – wipes our slate completely clean.[3]

3. *Likutei Sichot,* vol. 27, pp. 124–131.

FOURTH READING
Leviticus 17:1–7

G-d gave Moses further instructions regarding sacrifices, stipulating that they may be offered up only in the Tabernacle (or in its successor, the holy Temple).

The Power of Sacrifice

לְמַעַן אֲשֶׁר יָבִיאוּ בְּנֵי יִשְׂרָאֵל אֶת זִבְחֵיהֶם . . . לה' וְגו': (ויקרא יז, ה)

The Israelites should bring their feast-offerings to G-d.

Offering up animal sacrifices to G-d seems to go against the Torah's respect for animal life. Even with regard to non-animal sacrifices, why would G-d ask us to take valuable property and burn it up for no apparent benefit? Furthermore, of all G-d's commandments, why does the Torah refer only to sacrifices as being "pleasing" to G-d? Surely it pleases G-d when we perform any of His commandments!

The answer is that sacrifices please G-d in the purest way *precisely because* the only possible reason for offering them up is in order to fulfill His will. Unlike other commandments, there is no possible "ulterior motive" for sacrifices. Since they fly blatantly in the face of logic, no self-interest can be involved. Clearly, this is a much greater state of self-nullification than that required to fulfill any of the Torah's other commandments.

Today, our daily prayers are a reflection of the sacrifices offered up in the Tabernacle. Just as with the sacrifices, it may seem illogical to "waste" our valuable time on praying when we could be actually "doing" something – even holy deeds, such as studying the Torah or performing some "practical" commandment. Yet it is precisely by dedicating our valuable time and concentration to nothing other than getting closer to G-d that we connect to Him in the most profound, intimate way.[4]

4. *Likutei Sichot*, vol. 32, pp. 1–5.

FIFTH READING
Leviticus 17:8–18:5

G-d then instructed Moses regarding the laws governing forbidden relations. G-d prefaced these laws by stating that their purpose is to enhance the Jewish people's lives and to refine them so they can be admitted into the afterlife.

Bringing Life to the Commandments

וּשְׁמַרְתֶּם אֶת חֻקֹּתַי וְאֶת מִשְׁפָּטַי אֲשֶׁר יַעֲשֶׂה
אֹתָם הָאָדָם וָחַי בָּהֶם וְגוֹ': (ויקרא יח, ה)

**You must safeguard My rules and My ordinances,
which a person must do to live by them.**

The Hebrew phrase "to live by them" can also be read, "in order to imbue them with life-force." This teaches us that not only do G-d's commandments enhance our lives; by observing them, *we* bring *them* to life. For example, even the most carefully crafted *tefilin* cannot accomplish their purpose – thereby effecting a positive change in reality – until a Jewish man wears them.

Thus, we bring G-d's plan for creation to fruition through fulfilling His commandments. Of course, in order to "enliven" G-d's commandments, we ourselves must be "alive," i.e., healthy, strong, happy, enthusiastic, and optimistic.[5]

---

5. *Igrot Kodesh Mehorayatz*, vol. 4, p. 308; *HaYom Yom*, 10 Shevat; *Likutei Sichot*, vol. 1, p. 152; *Hitva'aduyot 5746*, vol. 2, pp. 394–395; ibid., vol. 4, p. 294, note 90; ibid., pp. 326–327.

SIXTH READING
Leviticus 18:6–21

Most of the forbidden relations are prohibited on account of being incestuous.

The Child's Environment

אִישׁ אִישׁ אֶל כָּל שְׁאֵר בְּשָׂרוֹ לֹא תִקְרְבוּ לְגַלּוֹת עֶרְוָה אֲנִי ה': (ויקרא יח, ו)

**No man may come near to any of his close
relatives to "uncover [their] nakedness."**

The patriarchs – Abraham, Isaac, and Jacob – observed the Torah's laws before they were formally given on Mount Sinai. Nonetheless, we have seen that Jacob's sons married their sisters. The reason for this was because society was so morally depraved in the patriarchs' times that there were simply no suitable choices for marriage partners outside the family circle. In those early days, it was crucial to preserve the spiritual and moral integrity of the family that was being groomed to become the Jewish people. Therefore, in order to ensure that their children not inherit negative traits from unworthy mothers or absorb negative attitudes while being raised by these women, Abraham's male descendants were forced not to honor these prohibitions, which in any case would only become legally binding with the Giving of the Torah on Mount Sinai.

We learn from this how much care we should take to ensure that our children's upbringing and environment support and encourage their absorption of the Torah's teachings and values.[6]

6. *Igrot Kodesh*, vol. 20, pp. 262–263.

SEVENTH READING

Leviticus 18:22–30

At the end of the list of forbidden relations, G-d authorized the Jewish courts to impose on the Jewish people any additional restrictions they deem necessary in order to safeguard the observance of these laws.

The Need for Precaution

וּשְׁמַרְתֶּם אֶת מִשְׁמַרְתִּי וגו': (ויקרא יח, ל)

[G-d told Moses,] "You must safeguard My charge."

This injunction also includes the directive that each of us take our own, added precautions when we see that these are necessary in order to avoid transgressing any of the Torah's prohibitions.

The fact that the Torah encourages such "safeguards" teaches us that we should never underestimate their importance. Since we are all naturally prone to overestimating our ability to resist evil, it is necessary for us to periodically evaluate our spiritual health – preferably by consulting regularly with a qualified spiritual counselor – in order to determine when additional stringencies are necessary.[7]

7. *Likutei Sichot*, vol. 1, pp. 253–254.

Kedoshim

Holiness

Leviticus 19:1–20:27

THE SEVENTH SECTION OF THE BOOK OF LEVITICUS CONTIN-
ues the theme of the preceding section. The Jewish people, having
been made into "a kingdom of priests and a holy nation" at the
Giving of the Torah, must adhere to a specific code of conduct
in order to fulfill this role properly. Thus, this section opens as
G-d instructs Moses to tell the Jewish people that they must be
"holy" (*Kedoshim*, in Hebrew), i.e., that they must hold themselves
to this standard of conduct.

FIRST READING
Leviticus 19:1–14

G-d began to instruct Moses regarding the code of conduct the Jewish people are called upon to follow in order to be holy. While some of these rules do go beyond what most people would consider normally required behavior, many (such as honoring parents, not stealing or robbing, etc.) do not fall into this category.

What it Means to be Holy

קְדֹשִׁים תִּהְיוּ כִּי קָדוֹשׁ אֲנִי ה' אֱלֹקֵיכֶם: (ויקרא יט, ב)

[G-d instructed Moses to tell the Jewish people,] "You must be holy, for I – G-d, your G-d – am holy."

The Hebrew word for "holy" (*kadosh*) means "separate," "removed," and "beyond." G-d is absolutely and infinitely holy, for inasmuch as He created the world, He is beyond it, unlimited by time, space, or any other of its attributes. Thus, by being told that we are to be holy because G-d is holy, we are being told that we are able to partake of G-d's otherness, that the heights of holiness we can reach are infinite, just as G-d is infinite.

This means that as Jews, we are intended to live with the awareness that the laws of nature pose no contradiction to Divinity. There is no aspect of life that is beyond our capacity to elevate, so long as we are connected to G-d and act in accordance with His will. Therefore, we can "sanctify" all aspects of our lives, even the most self-understood and commonplace. We should consider everything that we do to be part of our Divine mission, a way of bringing G-d into the world and making it into His home.[1]

---

1. *Likutei Sichot*, vol. 27, pp. 116–123.

SECOND READING
Leviticus 19:15–22

One of the prohibited forms of behavior is gossip.

The Power of Thought and Speech

לֹא תֵלֵךְ רָכִיל בְּעַמֶּיךָ וגו': (ויקרא יט, טז)

[G-d instructed Moses to tell the Jewish people,]
"You must not go around as a gossipmonger."

According to the Talmud, gossip "kills" three people: the speaker, the listener, and the object of the gossip. That the speaker and listener deserve to be punished is understandable, but why should the person about whom they are gossiping suffer? The answer is that speaking about another person's shortcomings does more than just belittle him. Words have the power to bring latent energy into actuality. When we speak about a person's negative traits, it causes him to continue to manifest them, which in turn reinforces them. As a result, his behavior takes a turn for the worse and he thus incurs punishment.

Conversely, when we speak about the good traits of another person, we reveal and reinforce those traits. We can thus be a positive or negative influence on people; the choice is ours.

It is not only prohibited to speak derogatorily about someone; it is also prohibited to *think* about them derogatorily. In some ways, thinking negatively about someone is more serious than speaking negatively about them.[2]

2. *Likutei Sichot*, vol. 27, p. 163; *Igeret HaKodesh* 22.

THIRD READING
Leviticus 19:23–32

G-d told the Jewish people that when they would enter the Land of Israel and plant fruit trees, they must not eat the fruit that any newly-planted tree produces during the first three years of its growth. The fruit that the tree produces during its fourth year is to be considered holy, which in this context means that it must be taken to the Tabernacle (or its successor, the holy Temple) in order to be eaten in the surrounding area (or Temple-city). Only the fruit of the fifth year and on can be eaten freely.

Infusing Holiness into Life

לְהוֹסִיף לָכֶם תְּבוּאָתוֹ וגו': (ויקרא יט, כה)

[G-d instructed the Jewish people to refrain from eating the fruit of their trees for the first three years, and to treat its fourth-year fruit as holy] "in order that it increase its produce for you."

Surprisingly, G-d tells us that the purpose of observing these restrictions on eating the fruit from a tree during its first four years is for the sake of the fifth year and beyond. Shouldn't the focus of this process be the holiness of the fourth year, rather than the mundaneness of the fifth year and beyond?

The answer is that holiness per se is not the goal of life; the goal is to fill the mundane with holiness, for only thus can we make all facets of life into G-d's home, thereby fulfilling the purpose of creation. When we take the fruit of the fifth and following years, which is not intrinsically holy, and make use of it for holy purposes, we are accomplishing precisely that. This is especially true when we recognize that the bountiful blessings of the fifth year come to us as a direct result of our having heeded G-d's instructions regarding the fruit of the preceding four years.[3]

---

3. *Likutei Sichot*, vol. 7, pp. 134–138.

FOURTH READING
Leviticus 19:33–37

Another form of prohibited behavior is possessing inaccurate weights and measures.

Honesty in Business

מֹאזְנֵי צֶדֶק אַבְנֵי צֶדֶק אֵיפַת צֶדֶק וְהִין צֶדֶק יִהְיֶה לָכֶם וְגוֹ': (ויקרא יט, לו)

[G-d instructed Moses to tell the people,] "You must possess [only] accurate scales, weights, and measures."

The Torah prohibits us from possessing false measures even if we never use them. This is because false measures involve not only theft but deception: the merchant pretends to charge his customer correctly, but is really cheating him. This trickery ultimately leads to overt theft and worse.

The same applies with regard to our relationship with G-d. Our evil inclination, aware that any attempt to convince us to openly rebel against our Creator will undoubtedly fail, attempts to ensnare us through deception. "I agree," he begins, "that our every action must be 'measured,' carried out in full compliance with Jewish law. But what would be so terrible if the 'measures' were slightly off? Even if you do insist on keeping an honest measure," he continues, "keep another one as well: Apply G-d's laws to your life fully when dealing with spiritual matters. But when interacting with the material world or conducting business, surely there is room for compromise."

Scrupulousness in maintaining accurate measures, as well as in all business dealings, is the prerequisite to fulfilling the entire Torah. In the words of the great Talmudic sage Hillel, "What is hateful to you, do not do to your fellow – this is the entire Torah, and the rest is commentary. Go and study it!"[4]

4. *Likutei Sichot*, vol. 27, pp. 149–157.

FIFTH READING

Leviticus 20:1–7

In the course of teaching Moses the laws of holiness, G-d promised that it is indeed possible for people to hold themselves to these standards of behavior.

Help in Becoming Holy

וְהִתְקַדִּשְׁתֶּם וִהְיִיתֶם קְדֹשִׁים וגו': (ויקרא כ, ז)

[G-d instructed Moses to tell the people,] "You must sanctify yourselves and be holy."

The Talmudic sages assure us that when we sanctify ourselves even in some small way, G-d helps us become holy in a great way. When we resist the urge to indulge in some material pleasure, we generate an increase of holiness and of positive spiritual energy, which then descends and rests upon us.

This verse, then, can be interpreted as follows: "Sanctify yourself," i.e., act in some holy way, even if such behavior seems to be beyond your present spiritual level, and you will "be holy" – ultimately you will attain that level of holiness, on account of the great holy energy that you have generated, which will then descend upon you.[5]

5. *Tanya*, end of chapter 27.

SIXTH READING

Leviticus 20:8–22

One of the forbidden forms of behavior is cursing one's parents, whether during their lifetime or after they have died.

Honoring Parents

כִּי אִישׁ אִישׁ אֲשֶׁר יְקַלֵּל אֶת אָבִיו וְאֶת אִמּוֹ מוֹת יוּמָת וְגו': (ויקרא כ, ט)

[G-d instructed Moses to tell the people,] "Any man who curses his father or mother must be [tried and] put to death [by the court]."

Honoring parents – at least to some extent – is the classic example of a type of behavior that seems so logical that we would have behaved that way even had G-d not commanded us to. The reason why G-d nonetheless commands us to observe such rules is that what comes naturally to us, be it good or bad, is limited by human nature. By making otherwise self-understood behavior into Divine commandments, G-d enables us to go beyond our natures. The Torah thus frees us of our human limitations, enabling us to partake of G-d's infinity by revealing our infinite, spiritual essence.[6]

---

6. *Likutei Sichot*, vol. 3, p. 889.

SEVENTH READING
Leviticus 20:23–27

G-d then informed Moses of the corrective punishments for engaging in the relationships that were forbidden at the end of the preceding section of the Torah. After concluding these laws, G-d stated that the Jewish people must observe them because "I am G-d."

Whom to Love

אֲנִי ה' אֱלֹקֵיכֶם אֲשֶׁר הִבְדַּלְתִּי אֶתְכֶם מִן הָעַמִּים: (ויקרא כ, כד)

**[G-d instructed Moses to tell the Jewish people,]
"I am G-d...who has distinguished you from
other peoples [by giving you My laws]."**

Feelings of love toward another person can be very strong. So strong, in fact, that they might cause us to consider defying the Torah's prohibitions or even forsaking G-d altogether if we become attached to someone forbidden to us. G-d therefore reminds us that He, the creator of the world and the source of love, issued these prohibitions, so we should not expect any positive outcome from transgressing them. Should we ask why G-d implanted in us the ability to become so strongly attached to another person that it might compel us to defy Him, the answer is: in order to reward us commensurately for overcoming this challenge; we can be assured that G-d can be relied upon to reward us amply when we comply with His will.[7]

Emor

The Priesthood; The Festivals
Leviticus 21:1–24:23

THE EIGHTH SECTION OF THE BOOK OF LEVITICUS BEGINS AS G-d directs Moses to tell (*Emor*, in Hebrew) the elder priests to educate the younger priests regarding the laws of the priesthood. G-d then teaches Moses these laws, after which He teaches him the laws regarding the cycle of festivals in the Jewish year.

FIRST READING
Leviticus 21:1–15

G-d instructed Moses regarding the prohibition for a priest to render himself ritually defiled by touching a human corpse. The exceptions are his close relatives – his parents, siblings, children, and wife – and a corpse that no one else is available to bury.

Not Shirking Responsibility

וְעַל כָּל נַפְשֹׁת מֵת לֹא יָבֹא: (ויקרא כא, יא)

[G-d told Moses that a high priest] may not ritually defile himself by touching a corpse [unless there is no one else to bury it].

The high priest's obligation to ritually defile himself in order to bury an unattended corpse applies even in the unlikely event that such a situation presents itself while he is performing the sacrificial rites of *Yom Kippur* in the Holy of Holies. If there is no one else who can bury this corpse, the high priest must leave the most sacred part of the Tabernacle on the holiest day of the year in order to do so. This teaches us, firstly, that taking care of our fellow Jews' crucial needs takes precedence over tending to our own spiritual tasks.

Secondly, we sometimes encounter people who may be considered, figuratively speaking, "unattended, lifeless bodies" – i.e., people who pay no attention to the spiritual side of life and who have no one else to guide them in this regard. In such cases, we must seize the opportunity to assist them, reminding ourselves that even the high priest is required to disregard his most exalted responsibilities on the holy day of *Yom Kippur* in order to bury an unattended corpse. We, in contrast, have both the obligation and privilege of not merely attending to a "lifeless" person – but of reviving him![1]

---

1. *Hitva'aduyot 5744*, vol. 3, pp. 1844–1845; *Hitva'aduyot 5745*, vol. 2, p. 1201.

SECOND READING
Leviticus 21:16–22:16

Priests are not allowed to marry certain women. Various bodily blemishes disqualify priests from officiating in the Tabernacle. If priests becomes ritually defiled, they may not eat sacrificial meat or the portions of the harvest that Jewish farmers are required to set aside for them.

The Gentle Way to Educate

וַיְדַבֵּר ה' אֶל מֹשֶׁה לֵּאמֹר: דַּבֵּר אֶל אַהֲרֹן וְגו': (ויקרא כא, טז-יז)

G-d spoke to Moses, saying, "Speak to Aaron."

The Torah mainly uses two Hebrew words for "speaking." The first (*dibur*) is reserved for "hard speech," the straightforward, accurate delivery of the message. The second (*amirah*) is "soft speech," i.e., tailoring the message to its intended recipient in order to ensure that it is indeed received and clearly understood.

The first part of this section of the Torah, which contains the laws regarding the priests' duty to educate their children in the responsibilities of the priesthood, is couched exclusively in "soft speech." It is only when G-d returns to the other laws concerning the priests that He once again uses "hard speech."

This teaches us that we must educate primarily with "soft speech." In order to be effective, educators must relate fully to their students and tailor their style of delivery accordingly.

G-d's imperative regarding how the priests educate their youth applies to us all. Whenever we see in someone a behavior or attitude that is in need of inspiration or correction, we are immediately cast by Divine providence in the role of educator. In all such cases, we must remember G-d's instruction to make exclusive use of "soft speech."[2]

2. *Likutei Sichot*, vol. 27, pp. 158–159; *Hitva'aduyot 5742*, vol. 3, pp. 1421–1424.

THIRD READING
Leviticus 22:17–33

Animals are disqualified from being offered up as sacrifices if they are blemished, and are accepted as sacrifices only if they are at least one week old.

Nurturing Emotions to Maturity

שׁוֹר אוֹ כֶשֶׂב אוֹ עֵז כִּי יִוָּלֵד וְהָיָה שִׁבְעַת יָמִים תַּחַת אִמּוֹ
וּמִיּוֹם הַשְּׁמִינִי וָהָלְאָה יֵרָצֶה לְקָרְבַּן וְגוֹ': (ויקרא כב, כז)

[G-d told Moses,] "When [an animal] is born, it must remain in its mother's care for seven days; it will be accepted as a sacrifice . . . from the eighth day [of its life] onward."

The mystical meaning of this law is as follows:

"Mother" signifies the intellect, since the intellect "gives birth" to the emotions. When the intellect recognizes the virtue of something or someone, it "gives birth" to the emotion of love for it; when it recognizes the undesirability or harmfulness of something or someone, it "gives birth" to the emotion of hatred or fear for it; and so on.

The "animal" signifies the emotions, since animals are driven by their instinctive emotions rather than by intellect.

When an emotion is first "born," it must be matured by the intellect. This process takes place over the course of seven "days," i.e., it is a sevenfold process – one for each of the seven basic emotions. Only after the emotions have been matured are they fit to be "an offering for G-d," i.e., worthy of becoming part of the psyche of a human being dedicated to G-d's service.[3]

---

3. *Hitva'aduyot 5725*, vol. 1, pp. 84–85.

FOURTH READING

Leviticus 23:1–22

G-d then instructed Moses regarding the laws of the festivals of the Jewish year. The first festival is Passover, celebrated in the first month of the Jewish calendar, Nisan.

Maintaining Proper Focus

וּבַחֲמִשָּׁה עָשָׂר יוֹם לַחֹדֶשׁ הַזֶּה חַג הַמַּצּוֹת וְגוֹ': (ויקרא כג, ו)

[G-d told Moses,] "On the 15th day of the month [of Nisan] begins the Festival of Matzos."

Although throughout the Torah, this festival is usually referred to as "the Festival of Matzos," in common usage it is usually called "Passover." (The term "Passover" in the Torah always refers to the sacrifice associated with this holiday rather than to the holiday itself.) According to the Chassidic master Rabbi Levi Yitzchak of Berditchev, the two names reflect two different perspectives on the holiday.

G-d wishes to stress the greatness of the Jewish people; He therefore focuses on the matzah. Matzah recalls how the Jews left Egypt in such haste that they did not have time to let their dough rise, highlighting their implicit faith in G-d and their willingness to follow Him wherever He directed them to go. We, on the other hand, relate to the holiday as an opportunity to praise G-d and thank Him; we therefore refer to it as Passover, recalling G-d's great miracles, particularly when He "passed over" the Jewish homes and brought His plagues only upon the Egyptians.

We should relate similarly to all our worldly accomplishments. Rather than focusing on our exceptional abilities, which enabled us to succeed, we should focus on how G-d's "hand" always miraculously assists us. We should leave it to G-d to focus on our merits![4]

4. *Sichot Kodesh 5741*, vol. 4, pp. 236–237.

FIFTH READING
Leviticus 23:23–32

Passover is followed seven weeks later by the holiday of *Shavu'ot* ("Weeks"). Although the months of the Jewish year are numbered from Nisan, the years are counted as beginning on the first day of Tishrei, the seventh month. The first of Tishrei is thus *Rosh HaShanah*, "the Beginning of the Year." This holiday is marked by the sounding of the shofar, a ram's horn – except[5] when it coincides with the Sabbath.

Spiritual Heights of the Sabbath

בַּחֹדֶשׁ הַשְּׁבִיעִי בְּאֶחָד לַחֹדֶשׁ יִהְיֶה לָכֶם ... זִכְרוֹן תְּרוּעָה וְגוֹ': (ויקרא כג, כד)

[G-d told Moses,] "The first day of the seventh month [Tishrei] will be ... a remembrance of the shofar blast."

The sounding of the shofar on the first day of the year elicits new Divine energy that will sustain all creation, spiritual and physical, for that year. However, when *Rosh HaShanah* coincides with the Sabbath, the shofar is not sounded; we only "remember" it by mentioning it in our prayers.

This is because blowing the shofar on the Sabbath is not only superfluous but pointless. G-d's sovereignty over us is the primary theme of *Rosh HaShanah*. Sounding the shofar at G-d's "coronation" is our declaration of our renewed selfless and voluntary submission to His sovereignty. The need for such a declaration, however, implies that we are conscious of ourselves as independent beings who must submit to G-d intentionally. Such self-awareness characterizes our consciousness on weekdays. On the Sabbath, in contrast, when we are inherently absorbed in our heightened Divine consciousness, such a declaration is redundant.[6]

---

5. By Rabbinic decree (*Rosh HaShanah* 4:1).
6. *Sefer HaSichot 5749*, vol. 2, pp. 705–707.

SIXTH READING

Leviticus 23:33–44

The week beginning with 15 Tishrei is *Sukot* ("Huts"), during which we are commanded to dwell in a temporary hut (*sukah*). We are also required on this holiday to hold together and wave four plant-parts: a citron (*etrog*), palm stalk (*lulav*), three myrtle branches (*hadasim*), and two willow branches (*aravot*).

Rising Above the Physical World

בַּסֻּכֹּת תֵּשְׁבוּ שִׁבְעַת יָמִים וְגוֹ': (ויקרא כג, מב)

[**G-d instructed Moses to tell the Jewish people,**] "**You must live in huts throughout this seven-day period.**"

The *sukah* is unique among the Torah's commandments in that it is the only one that we physically enter; the *sukah* surrounds us on all sides. This property of the *sukah* is a physical manifestation of the Divine energy that the *sukah* embodies: the awareness that G-d exists apart from the world and beyond its limitations.

We are taught that spiritually, the *sukah* derives from the cloud produced when the high priest would burn incense in the Holy of Holies on *Yom Kippur*. Whereas the animal sacrifices focused primarily on refining our human/animal soul, the incense expressed the inner consciousness of our Divine soul. Our Divine soul operates on a higher plane than that of our normal, human/animal consciousness. The Divine soul enables us to transcend the limits imposed on our lives by our human/animal soul, whose intellect and emotions are focused solely on physical things. Thus, our task on the holiday of *Sukot* is firstly to focus on G-d's unlimited Divinity by building the *sukah*, and secondly, to internalize our awareness of this Divinity both by dwelling in the *sukah* and by fulfilling the commandment of holding and waving the four plant-parts.[7]

7. *Sefer HaMa'amarim Melukat*, vol. 1, p. 175.

SEVENTH READING

Leviticus 24:1–23

The Torah next recounts an incident that occurred a month after the Tabernacle was erected. In Egypt, the Jewish people carefully preserved the purity of their family life. The only woman who was violated by an Egyptian taskmaster was named Shelomit. Her son, fathered by this Egyptian, attempted to camp together with his mother Shelomit's tribe of Dan. He was refused on the grounds that tribal membership follows the father's tribal lineage, not the mother's. The case was taken to the court, who ruled against Shelomit's son, upon which he cursed G-d. Thus, this section of the Torah closes with G-d informing Moses of the laws regarding blasphemy and its punishment.

Finding the Positive in the Negative

וְשֵׁם אִמּוֹ שְׁלֹמִית בַּת וְגו': (ויקרא כד, יא)

His mother's nickname was Shelomit bat Dibri.

Although the Torah only mentions this woman's nickname, it still identifies her, thereby apparently shaming her in public. Needless to say, this seems inconsistent with the Torah's rule against shaming people publicly.

In truth, however, the Torah is actually praising her by mentioning her name in connection with this incident. She was singled out by Divine providence to be the one through whom the exemplary character of the rest of the Jewish women was demonstrated.

This, in fact, is one of the ways through which misdeeds can be transformed into merits – by serving as the impetus for proper behavior. The negative example of Shelomit inspired future generations of Jewish women to live up to the example set by the rest of our ancestors in Egypt.[8]

8. *Likutei Sichot*, vol. 37, pp. 67–71.

Behar

The Sabbatical and Jubilee Years
Leviticus 25:1–26:2

THE NINTH SECTION OF THE BOOK OF LEVITICUS OPENS AS
Moses hears G-d's voice in the Tabernacle at the foot of the
mountain (*Behar*, in Hebrew), commanding him to convey to
the Jewish people the laws of the sabbatical and Jubilee years.

FIRST READING

Leviticus 25:1–13

G-d told Moses that the Jewish people must let their fields in the Land of Israel lie fallow for one full year after working them for six years. In order to enable them to do this, G-d said that He would "bless" the produce of the sixth year, making the land yield enough for both years.

G-d Promises; G-d Fulfills

וּבַשָּׁנָה הַשְּׁבִיעִת שַׁבַּת שַׁבָּתוֹן יִהְיֶה לָאָרֶץ....וְצִוִּיתִי
אֶת בִּרְכָתִי לָכֶם בַּשָּׁנָה הַשִּׁשִּׁית וְגו': (ויקרא כה, ד)

[G-d instructed Moses to tell the Jewish people,] "In the seventh year, the land must be given a complete rest.... I will command My blessing for you in the sixth year."

Although leaving the land fallow for a year may indeed improve its fertility, this cannot be the purpose of the sabbatical year. If it were, G-d would have promised to increase the yield of the year *following* the fallow year, not the year *preceding* it. By promising an increased yield in the *sixth* year – which should naturally be the least productive! – G-d shows us that it is specifically and exclusively His blessing that is the source of the increased yield.

The lesson for us is as follows: As Jews, we are required to spend time every day praying and studying the Torah; we must give charity, support Jewish education, and abstain from work on the Sabbath and Jewish holidays. How can we hope to live financially sound lives when our non-Jewish neighbors, who are not "handicapped" by any of these obligations and restrictions, struggle to earn their livelihood?

The sabbatical year teaches us that when we do what G-d desires, He will bless us – not only spiritually, but materially as well.[1]

---

1. *Likutei Sichot* vol. 2, pp. 548–549.

SECOND READING

Leviticus 25:14–18

In addition to the sabbatical year, the land must be given a rest every 50th year. This is known as the Jubilee year. At the beginning of this year, fields purchased during the previous 49 years must be returned to their original owners. Therefore, when a person sells his field, he must reduce the full-value price according to the number of years that have elapsed since the previous Jubilee year.

Drawing Down the Infinite

בְּמִסְפַּר שָׁנִים אַחַר הַיּוֹבֵל תִּקְנֶה מֵאֵת עֲמִיתֶךָ וְגו': (ויקרא כה, טו)

[G-d instructed Moses to tell the Jewish people,] "You must purchase it from your fellow Jew according to the number of years since the [previous Jubilee year]."

The 49-year period of seven sabbatical cycles, followed by the Jubilee year, parallels the annual 49-day period of seven weeks during which we are to count the days from Passover until the holiday of *Shavu'ot*, the annual reliving of the Giving of the Torah.

In the annual count from Passover to *Shavu'ot*, the final, 50th day is observed but not counted. This is because the annual reliving of the Giving of the Torah is a Divine revelation that we cannot attain on our own; it is a Divine gift. Similarly, the Jubilee year is observed but not counted, for the same reason. Nonetheless, the Divine revelations on both *Shavu'ot* and in the Jubilee year occur only in response to our having counted the preceding 49 days or years, respectively, through which we ascend through all the levels of Divine consciousness that we can attain on our own.

Thus, we see that with regard to fulfilling our Divine mission, G-d grants us success beyond whatever we can accomplish ourselves – provided that we invest our maximum efforts to accomplish what we can on our own.[2]

2. *Or HaTorah, Vayikra*, vol. 2, p. 605; *Likutei Sichot*, vol. 3, pp. 976, 996.

THIRD READING
Leviticus 25:19–24

As mentioned above, G-d promises to bless the produce of the sixth year, making the land yield enough for both that year and the following, sabbatical year.

The Strength of the Weak

וְצִוִּיתִי אֶת בִּרְכָתִי לָכֶם בַּשָּׁנָה הַשִּׁשִּׁית וְגוֹ': (ויקרא כה, כא)

[G-d instructed Moses to tell the Jewish people,] "I will command My blessing for you in the sixth year."

When G-d hid His presence after Adam and Eve ate the fruit of the Tree of Knowledge, He limited this concealment to 6,000 years. Although we can usher it in earlier, the Messianic era will commence no later than the beginning of the seventh millennium.

The six years during which agricultural work is permitted correspond to the six millennia of the world's present state of existence. The sabbatical year corresponds to the seventh millennium, when the world will "rest" from its present state. We are now in the latter part of the sixth millennium, i.e., nearing the end of the sixth "year."

In this context, we know that the Divine consciousness and spiritual strength of our generation cannot compare to those of earlier ones. This being the case, we may wonder how it can be that the sixth "year" – the weakest one – will be the one to provide for the seventh. How can our relatively weak spirituality usher in the Redemption, when the superior spirituality of our holy ancestors did not?

To this, G-d replies that in the merit of our simple faith – as expressed in our dedication to our Divine mission despite all obstacles and beyond the constraints of logic – He will increase the yield of the "sixth year," and bring us the Redemption.[3]

---

3. *Likutei Sichot*, vol. 27, p. 190.

FOURTH READING

Leviticus 25:25–28

G-d permitted the Jewish people to sell their fields in the Land of Israel only if they were in dire financial straits. Furthermore, if a relative of the seller has the financial means to buy back ("redeem") the sold field from the buyer, he is allowed to do so. As long as at least two years have elapsed since the sale, the buyer may not refuse to sell the land back.

We are G-d's Partners

וּבָא גֹאֲלוֹ הַקָּרֹב אֵלָיו וְגָאַל אֵת מִמְכַּר אָחִיו: (ויקרא כה, כה)

[**G-d instructed Moses to tell the Jewish people,**]
**"The redeemer [of the field], who is related
to [the seller], may come forth and redeem
that [land] which his relative had sold."**

The laws of redeeming land prior to the Jubilee year are based on the principle given two verses ago (Leviticus 25:23): "The land must not be sold [in such a way as] to sever it [permanently from its original owner], for the land belongs to Me." The prohibition of a permanent sale reminds us that the land ultimately belongs to G-d; we should never consider ourselves its true owners.

The same applies to whatever wealth or property we may accrue during our lifetimes. "The earth and its fullness are G-d's."[4] We should never lose sight of the fact that G-d has given us whatever we possess only as His partners, in order to refine it, elevate it, and transform it into His true home.[5]

4. Psalms 24:1.
5. *Hitva'aduyot 5745*, vol. 4, pp. 2077–2079.

FIFTH READING
Leviticus 25:29–38

G-d then taught Moses the laws of giving charity and the prohibition of charging interest on loans to our compatriots.

The Value of Work

אַל תִּקַּח מֵאִתּוֹ נֶשֶׁךְ וְתַרְבִּית וגו': (ויקרא כה, לו)

[G-d instructed Moses to tell the Jewish people,] "You must not take interest [from your compatriot]."

There is a subtle yet crucial difference between an investor profiting from his investment and a lender profiting from a loan. When we invest in a financial venture, the invested money still belongs to us; thus, our money is "working" for us. We have therefore earned the profit that the venture returns. In contrast, a loan transfers ownership of the principal to the borrower; the money now belongs to the borrower, even though he is obligated to repay it later. Thus, taking interest on a loan is profiting from someone else's effort without having participated in that effort. The lender is collecting interest based only upon the fact that the money used to belong to him.

Taking interest on a loan to a compatriot is therefore opposed to the way G-d wants the world to operate. G-d intended that we refine ourselves by working for our achievements, both spiritual and material. In the words of the sages, "If someone says to you, 'I have toiled without results,' do not believe him. If he says, 'I have not toiled, but have nonetheless seen results,' do not believe him either. Only if he says, 'I have toiled and seen results,' believe him."[6]

---

6. *Megilah* 6b; *Likutei Sichot*, vol. 3, pp. 1007–1012.

SIXTH READING
Leviticus 25:39–46

G-d then taught Moses the laws regarding the employment of Jewish servants. If a Jewish thief is convicted of stealing something and cannot pay back the value of what he has stolen, the court can hire him out as a servant, using the proceeds of this "sale" to pay off his debts. Also, if a Jewish man has no other way of supporting himself, he can hire himself out as a servant. In either case, the "master" is required to treat the servant humanely, properly feeding and clothing him, and is not allowed to give him demoralizing jobs to do.

The Purpose of Reward

לֹא תִרְדֶּה בוֹ בְּפָרֶךְ וְגוֹ': (ויקרא כה, מג)

[G-d instructed Moses to tell the Jewish people, "When someone is your bondman,] you must not work him with backbreaking labor."

Working without purpose is demoralizing and can even drive a person insane, whereas working for a constructive purpose – even if the task requires great effort – is richly rewarding. The satisfaction that results from accomplishment can be greater even than the satisfaction from the actual wages.

The efforts we are required to expend in studying the Torah and fulfilling G-d's commandments may be great, but we have been taught that our efforts here below have profound influence on the cosmic realm above. Keeping this knowledge in mind enables us to study the Torah and fulfill G-d's commandments with enthusiasm, joy, and purpose.[7]

---

7. *Likutei Sichot*, vol. 3, p. 1010.

SEVENTH READING
Leviticus 25:47–26:2

Inasmuch as the Jewish people are meant to teach G-d's ways to the rest of the world, G-d forbade Jews to sell themselves as slaves to non-Jews. If, however, a Jew does this, the sale is valid, but his close relatives are required to buy him back ("redeem" him) at the earliest possible opportunity.

Whose Slaves are We?

כִּי לִי בְנֵי יִשְׂרָאֵל עֲבָדִים עֲבָדַי הֵם אֲשֶׁר הוֹצֵאתִי
אוֹתָם מֵאֶרֶץ מִצְרָיִם וגו': (ויקרא כה, נה)

[G-d instructed Moses to tell the Jewish people "The relatives of the servant must redeem him] because the Israelites are My servants, whom I brought out of Egypt."

Some of us are so absorbed in our work during the six days of the workweek that it seems as if we have become slaves to it. Even on the Sabbath – the weekly "seventh year," on which we are supposed to "go free" – it is hard to free ourselves from the grip in which our work holds us.

The Torah teaches us that this is not the right way to live. We were created to serve G-d: to study His Torah and to fulfill His commandments. Since G-d created us for this purpose, He has surely provided us with the ability to fulfill it. Even when we work during the week, we must not consider ourselves enslaved to our work; rather, we should work in order to use the fruits of our labors for holy purposes. And on the Sabbath, we should rise completely above any association with our mundane lives.

By thus liberating ourselves from our personal enslavement, we hasten the general Redemption, when the whole world will be free to pursue spirituality and Divinity unhindered.[8]

8. *Likutei Sichot*, vol. 11, pp. 97–98.

Bechukotai

Reward and Corrective Punishment; Donations

Leviticus 26:3–27:34

THE 10TH AND FINAL SECTION OF THE BOOK OF LEVITICUS opens as G-d promises the Jewish people that if they follow His rules (*Bechukotai*, in Hebrew), they will be rewarded with material wealth and well-being. The opposite is also true: By neglecting G-d's laws, they will forfeit His blessings. G-d then instructs the Jewish people regarding what, how, and under which circumstances they may donate to the Temple or to the priests.

FIRST READING

Leviticus 26:3–5

G-d's promise of material wealth and prosperity is dependent especially upon the Jewish people's observance of His "rules," i.e., those commandments for which there is no rational explanation.

Experiencing Divine Goodness

אִם בְּחֻקֹּתַי תֵּלֵכוּ וְגוֹ': (ויקרא כו, ג)

[G-d instructed Moses to tell the Jewish people,] "If you advance in My rules."

G-d's "rules" are those commandments that defy rational explanation. The word for "rule" in Hebrew (*chukah*) actually means "engraved." When a letter is *engraved* onto something, the letter becomes a permanent part of it. (This is not the case when a letter is *written* on something, for then the letter remains a separate entity from it). In the same way, it is by observing G-d's rules that we truly unite with Him. The reason for this is because just as letters are engraved in stone by *removing* what was there before, observing G-d's rules requires us to "remove" – i.e., negate – our egos. With our egos out of the way, we can connect to G-d in the fullest way possible.

This is why G-d made His blessings dependent especially on our observance of these types of commandments. When we empty ourselves of our ego, we can view G-d's rewards not as the motivation for complying with His will, but as intrinsic components of our relationship with Him. G-d is absolute goodness, so when we relate to Him without the interference of our egos, we can experience His goodness purely, as His self-revelation to us.[1]

---

1. *Likutei Sichot*, vol. 22, pp. 159–165.

SECOND READING

Leviticus 26:6–9

As part of the reward for observing His rules, G-d instructed Moses to tell the Jewish people that He will protect them from wild beasts by removing these types of animals from their land.

Taming the Wild

וְהִשְׁבַּתִּי חַיָּה רָעָה מִן הָאָרֶץ וְגו': (ויקרא כו, ו)

[G-d instructed Moses to tell the Jewish people,] "I will remove [harmful] wild beasts from the land."

This blessing will come to its fullest fruition in the Messianic era, when "the wolf will lie with the lamb" in peace. There will indeed still be wolves, but they will not be predatory.

Both in order to ready ourselves for the Messianic future and in order to hasten its arrival, we should try to live "Messianic" lives now to the fullest extent possible. Therefore, instead of destroying the wild and untamed elements of ourselves and of our world, we should transform them and use them for goodness.[2]

2. *Likutei Sichot*, vol. 7, p. 188–197.

TUESDAY

THIRD READING

Leviticus 26:10–46

After describing the rewards for fulfilling G-d's will, the Torah describes the consequences of neglecting to fulfill His will.

Blessings in Disguise

וְאִם לֹא תִשְׁמְעוּ לִי וְגו': (ויקרא כו, יד-מג)

[G-d said,] "If you do not listen to Me..."

Jewish mysticism teaches us that G-d, the Torah, and the Jewish people all possess both hidden and revealed dimensions. In the Torah's "revealed" dimension, the corrective punishments described in these verses are indeed curses; but in the Torah's concealed dimension, these punishments are really blessings. This does not mean that they are only figurative blessings – painful experiences we must endure for a greater good. They are real blessings, and not just ordinary blessings, but the greatest, most sublime blessings.

In fact, it is specifically the most sublime blessings that have to be couched (and sometimes experienced) as curses. This is because whenever G-d bestows a blessing upon us, it must first pass through the heavenly "court," where the prospective recipient is judged as to whether he or she is worthy of receiving it. However, when a blessing is "disguised" as a curse, it "bypasses" the court's "prosecuting attorneys" and makes its way straight to us, its recipients.

When we experience what appears to be a Divine curse, it is really His blessing in disguise. This awareness helps transform G-d's hidden blessings into revealed ones.[3]

---

3. *Tanya*, chapter 26; *Igeret HaKodesh* 11, 22; *Likutei Sichot*, vol. 7, p. 233, vol. 19, pp. 136–139.

FOURTH READING
Leviticus 27:1–15

G-d then instructed Moses regarding the various forms of donations that individuals may make to the Temple or to the priests.
One type of donation is when someone pledges the monetary
value of a person or article. In such cases, the priest must first
assess the pledger's ability to pay before he collects the pledge.

Our Infinite Worth

עַל פִּי אֲשֶׁר תַּשִּׂיג יַד הַנֹּדֵר יַעֲרִיכֶנּוּ הַכֹּהֵן: (ויקרא כז, ח)

[G-d instructed Moses to tell the Jewish
people,] "The priest must evaluate [the pledger]
in accordance with how much he can afford."

The pledger's wealth is evaluated based on what he actually possesses, regardless of whether he has chosen to make use of all his
wealth or only of part of it. G-d evaluates us in a similar way. All
Jews received the entire Torah when our souls stood at Mount
Sinai, so the entire Torah is our inheritance and our possession.
Therefore, regardless of how much of the Torah we have studied
or internalized, G-d regards us as spiritually wealthy. G-d's favorable evaluation of our wealth and worth is filtered down into the
consciousness of the non-Jewish nations of the world. This is
why non-Jews – whether or not they are conscious of it – have a
deep-seated high regard for the Jewish people.

Nonetheless, merely possessing inherent spiritual wealth is not
enough; we are meant to make use of the Torah's infinite power
to refine both ourselves and the world by studying all aspects
of it and internalizing it to the best of our ability and beyond.[4]

---

4. *Sefer Ma'amarim Melukat*, vol. 1, pp. 461–462.

FIFTH READING
Leviticus 27:16–21

Under specific circumstances, a person may also donate his field to the Temple or its priests.

Honoring our Children

וְאִם מִשְּׂדֵה אֲחֻזָּתוֹ יַקְדִּישׁ אִישׁ לַה' וְגו': (ויקרא כז, טז)

[G-d instructed Moses to tell the Jewish people,] "**If a man consecrates part of his inherited field to G-d…**"

Why should the Torah allow us to give to the Temple or to its priests possessions that G-d has granted us? Isn't this being ungrateful to G-d, or perhaps shirking the responsibility that He has placed upon us by putting these resources at our disposal? The answer is that all our possessions really belong to G-d. He has just entrusted them to our care during our lifetimes in order that we refine them, and in order that by refining them, we refine ourselves and the world. It follows that we have no inherent rights to what we possess; they are not ours to abuse or waste at our discretion.

If this is true of our external possessions, it is true all the more of our talents and our bodies. We must take proper care of them and direct them toward positive ends; they are not ours to abuse or misuse. And this is true all the more of our children, whom we value even more than ourselves. Our children belong to G-d, who has entrusted them to our care in order for us to raise them to be good and holy. It is our nature as parents to spare no effort in pursuit of what is best for our children. Our highest priority, then, should be to provide them with a Jewish education, based on the Torah's eternal values. This is the best way to ensure their truest, most lasting happiness.[5]

5. *Likutei Sichot*, vol. 22, pp. 166–172; *Sichot Kodesh 5741*, vol. 1, pp. 567–575.

SIXTH READING
Leviticus 27:22–28

G-d then instructed Moses regarding the special laws that apply to firstborn animals and to every tenth animal that is born.

Answering G-d's Call

אַךְ בְּכוֹר אֲשֶׁר יְבֻכַּר לַה' בִּבְהֵמָה לֹא יַקְדִּישׁ אִישׁ אֹתוֹ . . . לַה' הוּא: (ויקרא כז, כו)

[G-d instructed Moses to tell the Jewish people,] "No man may consecrate a firstborn animal [as any other type of sacrifice] . . . since it must be for G-d."

The final two topics in this section of the Torah are what must be done with our firstborn cattle, sheep, and goats; and with one tenth of our cattle, sheep, and goats in general. Firstborn animals must be offered up as sacrifices (the priests are given part of their flesh to eat); tithed animals must be eaten in Jerusalem by their owners. These two commandments reflect the two complementary facets of the institution of sacrifices: sanctifying the world and sanctifying ourselves.

As such, these two commandments form a fitting conclusion to the Book of Leviticus, the book in which we hear G-d calling out to us, challenging us to live life in full awareness of our innate potential as G-d's chosen people. By so doing, we transform ourselves into "a kingdom of priests," sanctifying mundane reality. In this way, we fulfill the purpose of Creation: making the world into G-d's true home.[6]

6. *Likutei Sichot*, vol. 17, pp. 332–339.

SEVENTH READING
Leviticus 27:29–34

Every tenth animal born must be offered up as a sacrifice, its meat eaten by the owner and his family. The owner is not allowed to substitute another animal for the tithed animal, but if he nevertheless does, both animals must be treated as having been tithed.

Protection from Harm

וְאִם הָמֵר יְמִירֶנּוּ וְהָיָה הוּא וּתְמוּרָתוֹ יִהְיֶה קֹּדֶשׁ וְגוֹ': (ויקרא כז, לג)

[G-d instructed Moses to tell the Jewish people,] "If [the tithed animal's owner] does substitute it, then both it and its replacement will be holy."

Sanctifying an animal is a good thing. Why, then, should the Torah forbid the owner to substitute another animal for the original, tithed one, if by doing so both animals become sanctified?

When someone tithed his animals, he was lifted out of his mundane world and drawn into the holy process of having to take the animal to Jerusalem and eat it there with his family. This gave him the opportunity to renew his religious inspiration at the holy Temple. The Torah wants the owner to take advantage of this opportunity and see it through – not to focus on some other, unconsecrated animal.

Normally, we should follow this advice, as well: If we are involved in some holy pursuit, we should stay focused on it. We should not sacrifice our spiritual momentum for some material diversion.

However, when other people are in spiritual danger, we must overlook this prohibition in order to reach out to them. In such cases, the Torah assures us that G-d will protect us. Both we and those whom we elevate to holiness will indeed remain holy.[7]

7. *Likutei Sichot*, vol. 26, pp. 90–92.

NUMBERS

Bemidbar

The Jewish Army
Numbers 1:1–4:20

NUMBERS, THE FOURTH BOOK OF THE TORAH, DESCRIBES THE journey of the Jewish people from the foot of Mount Sinai to the threshold of the Land of Israel. The first section begins as G-d tells Moses to take a census of the adult Jewish males in the desert (*Bemidbar*, in Hebrew). The purpose of the census is to form the adult males into an army, should it be necessary to fight the non-Jewish occupants of the Land of Israel.

FIRST READING
Numbers 1:1–19

On 1 Iyar 2449, G-d told Moses to take a census of the Jewish men in preparation for their conscription into the Jewish army. This census excluded the tribe of Levi, who were exempt from military service in order to serve in the Tabernacle. The men were counted by families, which were then grouped by tribes.

Love and Family

שְׂאוּ אֶת רֹאשׁ כָּל עֲדַת בְּנֵי יִשְׂרָאֵל לְמִשְׁפְּחֹתָם וְגוֹ': (במדבר א, ב)

[G-d told Moses,] "Take a census of all the
congregation of the Israelites by families.

The Torah records only the total number of men, and not the number of families, in each tribe. Nevertheless, G-d had the families counted, in order to stress the centrality of the family in Judaism.

Our individual and national goals are certainly important, but the Torah also demands of us the selflessness necessary to forge the family unit. A husband and wife are two separate people, with their own natures, desires, and even missions in life; yet each must work for and work with the other, completing and complementing each other and merging into one harmonious, loving unit.

The strife and breakdown of communication from which the world suffers stem from selfishness. In contrast, the Torah commands us to love our neighbors as ourselves. The primary setting in which this commandment is fulfilled is that of our families. Inasmuch as loving our fellow Jew is an expression of our love of G-d, loving our fellow Jew enhances our love of G-d. Love of G-d, in turn, brings us to love His Torah and study it – not merely out of our obligation to do so, but out of love. This threefold love of our fellow Jew, of G-d, and of the Torah ripples outward from the family setting and affects the entire world for the better.[1]

1. *Likutei Sichot*, vol. 8, pp. 209–215.

SECOND READING
Numbers 1:20–54

The Torah records the total number of adult males in each tribe. Miraculously, all those counted were fit to go to war; they were all strong, all able-bodied men.

Health and Healing

וַיִּהְיוּ בְנֵי רְאוּבֵן ... כֹּל יֹצֵא צָבָא: (במדבר א, כ)

[The tally] of the tribe of Reuben ... all who were fit to serve in the army.

All the sick and crippled Jews were healed when the Torah was given; thanks to the protective Clouds of Glory, the Jews remained healthy throughout their journey, despite the adverse conditions of the desert.

We see from this that the Jewish people – by virtue of their connection to G-d expressed through studying the Torah and fulfilling its commandments – were not bound by the laws of nature. Furthermore, their ability to override nature was self-evident, expressed not only in spiritual concerns, but in physical health and well-being as well.

This holds true today as it did when the Torah was given on Mount Sinai. To the extent that we live our lives according to the dictates of the Torah, we too will be blessed with spiritual and physical health, despite any obstacles posed by the laws of nature.[2]

2. *Likutei Sichot*, vol. 8, pp. 220–222.

TUESDAY

THIRD READING
Numbers 2:1–34

G-d then instructed Moses to organize the Jewish people into a specific army formation. The Tabernacle was in the middle, surrounded by three tribes on each of its four sides. (For this purpose, the descendants of the two sons of Joseph – Manasseh and Ephraim – were counted as separate tribes; thus, there were 12 non-Levite tribes.)

Guarding our Inner Sanctuary

מִנֶּגֶד סָבִיב לְאֹהֶל מוֹעֵד יַחֲנוּ: (במדבר ב, ב)

[G-d told Moses, "The Israelites] must camp around the Tent of Meeting [i.e., the Tabernacle]."

The people's encampment on all four sides of the Tabernacle symbolized how they protected the holy edifice and the Torah that resided in its innermost chamber. Certainly, the Torah does not need our protection – on the contrary, the Torah and its commandments protect *us*. However, G-d chose to entrust us with the noble mission of protecting the Torah.

Similarly, we must guard our personal, inner sanctuary – within our hearts and within our homes – from all four sides: from cool spiritual indifference on the cold north; from hot, lustful passions on the warm south; from self-gratification over brilliant accomplishments on the morning east; and from dark despair on the evening west.[3]

3. *Hitva'aduyot 5745*, vol. 4, p. 2103; *Reshimot 62* (p. 15); *Or HaTorah, Bemidbar*, vol. 4, pp. 1360–1361, 1396–1397; *Zohar* 2:156a; *Igrot Kodesh*, vol. 6, p. 185.

FOURTH READING

Numbers 3:1–13

G-d then instructed Moses to count the Levites. The Levites were exempt from military service because they were conscripted to serve in the Tabernacle. They guarded the Tabernacle, dismantled it whenever the Jewish people broke camp, reconstructed it whenever they camped, and assisted the priests in the Tabernacle rituals.

Spiritual Aspirations

הַקְרֵב אֶת מַטֵּה לֵוִי וְהַעֲמַדְתָּ אֹתוֹ לִפְנֵי אַהֲרֹן הַכֹּהֵן וְשֵׁרְתוּ אֹתוֹ: (במדבר ג, ו)

[G-d told Moses,] "Bring forth the tribe of Levi and present them before Aaron the priest, that they may serve him."

The Levites were singled out from among the rest of the Jewish people to act as G-d's personal servants. Nevertheless, the medieval Jewish sage Rabbi Moses Maimonides points out that anyone who wishes to dedicate himself to the service of G-d can do so. He or she thereby becomes a "spiritual Levite" – and even a "spiritual priest," or even a "spiritual *high* priest!" – regardless of his actual tribal lineage.[4]

4. *Hitva'aduyot 5745*, vol. 4, pp. 2115–2116.

FIFTH READING
Numbers 3:14–39

The Levites were subdivided into four groups: three clans, each descended from one of the sons of Levi, and the priests. Whereas the other 12 tribes were instructed to camp at a distance of approximately 900 meters (half a mile) from the Tabernacle, the Levites were instructed to encamp right next to it. The priests (Aaron and his sons), together with Moses, encamped to the east of the Tabernacle. The three Levite clans encamped on the other three sides of the Tabernacle.

Avoiding Contention

וְהַחֹנִים לִפְנֵי הַמִּשְׁכָּן קֵדְמָה...מֹשֶׁה וְאַהֲרֹן וּבָנָיו וְגו': (במדבר ג, לח)

Camping in front of the Tabernacle... were Moses, Aaron, and [Aaron's] sons.

The tribes of Judah, Issachar, and Zebulun became great Torah scholars by virtue of having camped near Moses and Aaron. In contrast, the tribe of Reuben camped on the same side of the Tabernacle as the Levite clan to which Moses' cousin Korach belonged. They were therefore caught up in Korach's mutiny against Moses, as the Torah will recount later.

This teaches us that the way to avoid being dragged into a dispute is by studying the Torah and living according to its teachings, and the way to connect to G-d through studying the Torah is by distancing oneself from any form of contention.[5]

---

5. *Likutei Sichot*, vol. 33, p. 16–17.

SIXTH READING
Numbers 3:40–51

Unlike the rest of the Jewish men, who were counted from age 20, the Levites were counted from the age of one month. G-d then told Moses to count all the firstborn male non-Levites who were at least one month old. The Levites were replacing the firstborn as employees of the Tabernacle since the firstborn had forfeited this privilege by participating in the incident of the Golden Calf.

Know Him in All Your Ways

קַח אֶת הַלְוִיִּם תַּחַת כָּל בְּכוֹר בִּבְנֵי יִשְׂרָאֵל וְגוֹ': (במדבר ג, מה)

[G-d told Moses,] "Take the Levites in place of all the Israelite firstborn."

The other tribes were counted only from age twenty – the age at which they were old enough to serve in the army. The Levites' task, however, was to protect the Tabernacle, and any increase in their population – even of newborn infants – helped them in this task. Therefore, they were counted virtually from birth.

We can all join the legions of the Levites in a spiritual sense, by nurturing our intrinsic connection to G-d. This connection is not affected by any variations in time, age, or environment. It therefore enables us to "know Him in all your ways," down to the simplest aspects of life that a mature adult shares with the smallest child.[6]

6. *Likutei Sichot*, vol. 2, pp. 558–559.

SEVENTH READING
Numbers 4:1–20

After Moses counted the tribe of Levi as a whole, G-d told him to count each of the three Levite clans separately, appointing each clan to carry specific components of the Tabernacle when the Jewish people would travel.

The Power of Peace

בְּגֶשֶׁתָּם אֶת קֹדֶשׁ הַקֳּדָשִׁים אַהֲרֹן וּבָנָיו יָבֹאוּ וְשָׂמוּ אוֹתָם אִישׁ אִישׁ עַל עֲבֹדָתוֹ וְאֶל מַשָּׂאוֹ: (במדבר ד, יט)

[G-d told Moses,] "When [the members of the tribe of Levi's son Kehat] approach the holiest of the holy things, Aaron and his sons must [first] come and appoint each man to his task."

It often happens that when we strive to reach our potential in spiritual matters, we encounter forms of opposition. Sometimes other people ridicule us or are hostile to us; sometimes we are assaulted by inner voices of self-doubt. The Torah teaches us here that the proper response to these challenges is not to battle them but to use the power of Aaron, who dedicated his life to being a peacemaker. Our loving-kindness will then either neutralize the negativity or eliminate it altogether. And transforming an adversary into an ally is the most complete and effective victory possible.[7]

Naso

Preparations for the Journey
Numbers 4:21–7:89

IN THE SECOND SECTION OF THE BOOK OF NUMBERS, THE narrative begins as G-d instructs Moses to complete his count (*Naso*, in Hebrew) of the Levite clans. The Torah then records certain laws pertaining to the purification process that the Jews needed to undergo before setting out from Mount Sinai toward the Land of Israel. Finally, the Torah records the offerings that the tribal princes donated on the day the Tabernacle was erected and began to function. Their offerings emphasized how the Jewish people's upcoming journey through the desert – as well as each individual's journey through life, to fulfill his or her Divine mission – must be both an individual and collective experience.

FIRST READING
Numbers 4:21–28

After having told Moses to count the Levite clan of Kehat, G-d instructed Moses to count the Levite clan of Gershon.

Avoiding the Negative; Pursuing the Positive

נָשֹׂא אֶת רֹאשׁ בְּנֵי גֵרְשׁוֹן וְגוֹ': (במדבר ד, כב)

[G-d told Moses,] "Take a census of the clan of Gershon."

There are two steps in preparing one's home for an esteemed guest. First the rooms are scrubbed clean; then they are decorated with beautiful furnishings and works of art. The same two steps apply to how we make our lives and ourselves into a home for G-d. First we rid our lives of what is negative and undesirable and then we do what is good and right.

The clan of Gershon carried the outer coverings of the Tabernacle, which protected it from undesirable elements. This corresponds to our job of avoiding harmful activities and influences. The clan of Kehat, on the other hand carried the furnishings of the Tabernacle, each of which represents a particular positive attribute and activity.

Just as Gershon was born before Kehat, it is necessary to first cleanse oneself of negative behavior in order to be able to properly pursue good. Nonetheless, the clan of Kehat was counted before that of Gershon, since cleansing oneself of negativity is only a preparation for the true work: pursuing good.[1]

1. *Likutei Sichot*, vol. 13, p. 19.

SECOND READING

Numbers 4:29–49

G-d then instructed Moses to count the third and final Levite clan, that of Merari.

The Foundation of Everything

בְּנֵי מְרָרִי ... תִּפְקֹד אֹתָם: (במדבר ד, כט)

[G-d told Moses,] "You must count the clan of Merari."

The clan of Merari carried the "skeletal" part of the Tabernacle – the planks that formed the walls, together with their bases and connecting poles. The walls were the least "functional" of all the components of the Tabernacle, but they made up its essential frame, the environment in which all of the more "glamorous" activities took place.

In our lives, the framework and basis of our relationship with G-d is our selfless devotion to His will. While this is the least glamorous aspect of our relationship with G-d, it is the foundation upon which all the other, more appealing or exciting aspects rest.[2]

2. *Hitva'aduyot 5748*, vol. 3, pp. 457 ff.

THIRD READING
Numbers 5:1–10

G-d then reviewed the laws of theft, in order to encourage the Jewish people to make sure they were not in any way guilty of this sin before setting out on their journey toward the Land of Israel.

Counteracting Negativity

אִישׁ אוֹ אִשָּׁה כִּי יַעֲשׂוּ מִכָּל חַטֹּאת הָאָדָם ...וְאָשְׁמָה הַנֶּפֶשׁ
הַהִוא: וְהִתְוַדּוּ אֶת חַטָּאתָם אֲשֶׁר עָשׂוּ וְגוֹ': (במדבר ה, א-ז)

**[G-d instructed Moses to tell the Jewish people,]
"When a man or woman sins, and feels guilty and
confesses the sin he [or she] committed."**

If we have wronged a fellow human being in some way, we must first ask their forgiveness; then, we must restore the item or pay for any damage we caused. Then, we must "apologize" to G-d, through repentance. Repentance consists of three steps:

- regret for the past,
- positive resolution for the future, and
- verbal confession to G-d of the misdeed.

Every misdeed creates negative energy, which has a "body" and a "soul." The "body" of this energy is the misdeed itself, while its "soul" is the lust that caused the misdeed and the will that accompanied it. Feeling regret for having committed a misdeed destroys the "soul" of the negative energy; confessing verbally – physically using our mouths – destroys the "body" of the negative energy.[3]

---

3. *Derech Mitzvotecha, Vidui* (pp. 38a ff).

FOURTH READING

Numbers 5:11–6:27

G-d then instructed Moses the laws regarding a suspected adulteress. If a husband has grounds to suspect his wife of adultery, he should first raise the issue with her privately; if her actions continue to arouse his suspicions, he may subject her to a test by which G-d would indicate whether she was innocent or guilty. This test only worked if the husband's motives were totally pure, if he himself was not guilty of adultery, and when society as a whole was horrified by adultery. (In consideration of all these factors, this ritual was discontinued some time before the second century CE.)

Who in Their Right Mind?

אִישׁ אִישׁ כִּי תִשְׂטֶה אִשְׁתּוֹ וּמָעֲלָה בוֹ מָעַל: (במדבר ה, יב)

**[G-d instructed Moses to tell the Jewish people,]
"Should a man's wife stray, [causing him to
suspect that] she was unfaithful to him."**

Committing a misdeed is a terrible act because the Jewish people are "married" to G-d. Were adulterers not married, their behavior would not be judged so harshly; the fact that they betrayed a covenant-relationship is what makes them deserve punishment. The same is true of the Jewish people. A misdeed is not merely a technical transgression; it is a personal affront to our beloved Divine Spouse.

As Jews, our connection to G-d is so strong that it is inherently impossible for us to transgress His will. The only way we can commit a misdeed is by deluding ourselves into thinking that it will not jeopardize our connection to G-d. Reminding ourselves that G-d is our "spouse" helps us avoid committing misdeeds.[4]

4. *Likutei Sichot*, vol. 2, pp. 311–314.

FIFTH READING

Numbers 7:1–41

G-d then taught Moses the laws governing a person who vows to abstain from wine for a period of time, and how the priests should bless the people after the daily morning sacrifices. The Torah then returns to the events of the first day that the Tabernacle began functioning officially. The princes of each tribe pledged a set of sacrifices to inaugurate the Altar. Although the sacrifices of all 12 princes were identical, the Torah enumerates them all separately.

Same Act, Different Intentions

וְקָרְבָּנוֹ קַעֲרַת כֶּסֶף אַחַת שְׁלֹשִׁים וּמֵאָה מִשְׁקָלָהּ וְגו': (במדבר ז, יג)

**The offering [of the first prince] consisted of
one silver bowl, weighing 130 [shekels] ...**

The Torah could have simply given the details of one prince's offering and then stated that this same offering was brought by all 12 leaders. The reason that it does not is because each prince initiated the Altar into a different way of elevating the physical world and drew a different type of spiritual energy into the world, corresponding to the spiritual nature of his tribe.

Similarly, we all recite the same words in our prayers and perform more or less the same commandments. Yet, at the same time, we are individuals. We are not only *permitted* to express our own individual feelings and intent in our prayers and in our performance of the commandments – we are *required* to do so.

Furthermore, just as the Torah repeats the same words but each time the inner meaning is different, so are we intended to bring new meaning to the actions and words that we repeat daily. Every day's prayers and deeds should reflect the unique spiritual accomplishments we have made since the last time we prayed or performed them.[5]

5. *Hitva'aduyot 5743*, vol. 1, p. 528.

SIXTH READING
Numbers 7:42–83

The Torah continues to list the offerings of each tribal prince.

The Torah Makes the World Alive

קָרְבָּנוֹ קַעֲרַת כֶּסֶף אַחַת שְׁלֹשִׁים וּמֵאָה מִשְׁקָלָהּ וְגוֹ': (במדבר ז, מג)

**The offering [of the sixth prince] consisted of
one silver bowl, weighing 130 [shekels] ...**

The princes brought two types of offerings: objects (silver and gold vessels, flour, oil, and incense) and animals (bulls, sheep, and goats). The lifeless objects were not consumed by the heavenly fire that descended onto the Altar, whereas the animals were consumed by this fire, either entirely or partially.

The lifeless objects thus symbolize the "lifeless" era before the Giving of the Torah, when physicality could not be infused with Divinity. The consumption of the animals by Divine fire symbolizes our present, post-Sinai era, in which physical objects – and the physical world in general – can be sanctified. Through the Tabernacle and its successor – the holy Temple – and through the sanctuary for G-d that we all construct out of ourselves, our lives, and our sphere of influence, Divine vitality is revealed in the physical world.[6]

6. *Likutei Sichot*, vol. 18, pp. 86–87.

SEVENTH READING

Numbers 7:84–89

After concluding its account of the princes' offerings, the Torah describes how G-d spoke to Moses inside the Tabernacle. Moses would hear G-d's voice as loud as it had been heard on Mount Sinai, but the sound miraculously stopped at the entrance to the Tent of Meeting; thus, no one outside could hear it.

Hearing the Voice

וּבְבֹא מֹשֶׁה אֶל אֹהֶל מוֹעֵד לְדַבֵּר אִתּוֹ וַיִּשְׁמַע אֶת הַקּוֹל וְגוֹ': (במדבר ז, פט)

When Moses would come into the Tent of Meeting so G-d could speak with him, he would hear His voice.

Much as we might wish it, we cannot be allowed to hear G-d's voice everywhere and at all times. If we could, we would be deprived of our freedom of choice. A world in which G-d's voice is constantly heard does not challenge its population. It was G-d's desire to create a world of Divine silence, in which, through our efforts, we can uncover G-d's concealed voice. It is our task to take what we heard during that short period at Mount Sinai and within that small space of the Tabernacle – and each of us has heard G-d's voice somewhere and at some time, however fleetingly – and transmit it to the rest of time and space.[7]

7. *Likutei Sichot*, vol. 13, pp. 22–23.

Beha'alotecha

The Journey Begins
Numbers 8:1–12:16

THE THIRD SECTION OF THE BOOK OF NUMBERS BEGINS AS G-d tells Moses to instruct Aaron how to kindle (*Beha'alotecha*, in Hebrew) the lamps of the Tabernacle's Candelabrum. It continues with the final preparations for the Jewish people's departure from Mount Sinai and the events that occurred at their first stops in the desert.

FIRST READING
Numbers 8:1–14

The tribal princes did not include Aaron when they brought their offerings for the inauguration of the Altar. G-d reassured Aaron by noting that he had inaugurated the Candelabrum, which was just as important – if not more so – than inaugurating the Altar.

Setting the Soul on Fire

בְּהַעֲלֹתְךָ אֶת הַנֵּרֹת וגו': (במדבר ח, ב)

[G-d instructed Moses to tell Aaron,]
"When you kindle the lamps."

G-d instructed Moses to tell Aaron that whenever he would light the lamps of the Candelabrum, he should hold the fire to the wick until it remained burning steadily on its own.

Spiritually, this means that when we "light the flame" of our own soul or the soul of another person, we should not just deliver some quick inspiration and then move on. We should remain near, nurturing the soul's flame until it becomes a steady and self-reliant glow.[1]

---

1. *Likutei Sichot*, vol. 2, p. 316–317.

SECOND READING
Numbers 8:15–26

The Torah now records how the Levites were installed into office. The Levites first had to be purified of any ritual defilement; they then had to offer up, together, certain pre-designated sacrifices. G-d further told Moses that Levites should start training for their service at the age of 25, and actually serve from age 30 to age 50.

Starting Fresh

מִבֶּן חָמֵשׁ וְעֶשְׂרִים שָׁנָה וָמַעְלָה יָבוֹא לִצְבֹא צָבָא וְגו': (במדבר ח, כד)

[G-d told Moses,] "From 25 years old and upwards [the Levites] must enter the service.

The Levites were given the responsibility of carrying the Tabernacle and its vessels through the desert. G-d led the Jews through the desert with the Tabernacle – in which His presence was openly manifest – in order to subdue the forces of evil, which the uninhabited, uncultivated, desolate, and dangerous desert embodied.

Similarly, our own environment can sometimes seem like a spiritual "desert," devoid of G-dliness. In fact, it may sometimes seem to us that we *ourselves* have become a "desert" – i.e., that we have developed habits that are contrary to our task of spreading Divine consciousness. How can we possibly hope to change ourselves (let alone the world around us) when these habits and modes of behavior have already become ingrained within us?

Here, we can learn from the Levites. They did not even begin training for their occupation until they were 25 years old, yet they were nevertheless empowered to begin their holy service at this age. G-d gives us, too, the ability to remake ourselves and begin new directions in life, even though we may feel unqualified, unprepared, or unworthy to carry them out. All we have to do is make use of His assistance.[2]

2. *Likutei Sichot*, vol. 13, pp. 16–19.

THIRD READING
Numbers 9:1–14

On 14 Nisan 2449 – two weeks after the inauguration of the Tabernacle – G-d commanded the Jewish people to observe the holiday of Passover. (Since G-d had previously told the Jews that they would not be required to observe the festivals until entering the Land of Israel, this exceptional case necessitated an explicit command.) However, some of the people were ritually defiled and therefore unable to participate in the festival. They complained about being left out, and in response, G-d informed the people that whoever was unable to perform the Passover rituals on the date of the holiday should perform them a month later, on 14 Iyar.

It's Never Too Late

בַּחֹדֶשׁ הַשֵּׁנִי בְּאַרְבָּעָה עָשָׂר יוֹם...יַעֲשׂוּ אֹתוֹ וְגוֹ': (במדבר ט, יא)

[G-d told Moses,] "[If someone was unable to offer up the Passover sacrifice on 14 Nisan,] he must offer it up in the afternoon of 14 [Iyar,] the second month."

The lesson of the second Passover is that it is never too late to set things right. Even if one is spiritually sullied or has wandered far from the realm of holiness, G-d still gives him a fresh opportunity to rewrite the past and to right all wrongs.[3]

---

3. *HaYom Yom*, 14 Iyar.

FOURTH READING

Numbers 9:15–10:10

The Torah then describes how G-d would signal the Jewish people that it was time to proceed in their travels. When the cloud that always hovered above the Tabernacle would spread over the entire camp, the people began to prepare to travel. When they were ready, this cloud would lead the way through the desert.

The Permanence of Temporary Situations

עַל פִּי ה' יַחֲנוּ וְעַל פִּי ה' יִסָּעוּ וְגו': (במדבר ט, כג)

**At G-d's bidding they encamped, and
at G-d's bidding they traveled.**

The Jewish people never knew in advance how long they would be staying at any given camp – it could have been for a day or for years. Nonetheless, they would set up the Tabernacle in its entirety at each encampment, following G-d's instructions to keep the Tabernacle functioning at all times.

This teaches us two important lessons. First, we should recognize that it is G-d who leads us through all our journeys in life – whether geographical, emotional, mental, or spiritual. We should indeed make our own plans based on our lives' goals, but at the same time, we must realize that G-d knows when it is in our best interest to stay put or to move on to the next station in life, and that He arranges things accordingly.

Second, we should not "put our lives on hold" when we are in temporary situations. Since G-d is beyond time and place, when we connect with Him even for one moment, that moment lasts for all time. Whether a personal journey lasts a day or a decade, we can make it into a sanctuary, imbued with the eternal permanence of G-d's presence.[4]

---

4. *Likutei Sichot*, vol. 2, p. 687.

FIFTH READING
Numbers 10:11–34

On 20 Iyar 2449, G-d gave the signal and the people set out from Mount Sinai. Besides the golden Ark that housed the second set of Tablets and was transported with the rest of the Tabernacle, Moses had constructed a second ark to house the first, shattered set of Tablets. This ark was carried in front of the people, right behind G-d's cloud that led the way.

Following the Ark of the Torah

וַאֲרוֹן בְּרִית ה' נֹסֵעַ לִפְנֵיהֶם וגו': (במדבר י, לג)

The ark of G-d's covenant traveled ahead of them.

In all of their travels in the desert, the Jewish people were preceded by this ark and by the cloud of G-d, which led the way and cleared the path of potentially harmful animals and obstacles. And so has it been in the long history of the Jewish people: Throughout our journeys, whenever we follow the "ark" – i.e., the light of the Torah – we have found spiritual and physical rest. We are protected from the emotional and physical dangers of the world, enabling us to find true meaning in our existence.[5]

---

5. *Likutei Sichot*, vol. 8, p. 288.

SIXTH READING
Numbers 10:35–11:29

The Jewish people miraculously covered a three-days' journey on the first day of their trek through the desert, for G-d was anxious to bring them into the Land of Israel. But once the Jewish people were on their way, some of the former non-Jews who had accompanied them when they left Egypt and had converted to Judaism began to have second thoughts about submitting to G-d's laws. Seeking an excuse for their attitude, these recent converts complained about having to travel so far on the first day.

Rectifying Rebellions

וַיְהִי הָעָם כְּמִתְאֹנְנִים וגו': (במדבר יא, א)

The people sought a pretext [to rebel against G-d].

To be sure, we should not allow ourselves to rebel (or even consider rebelling) against G-d. If this requires us to "force" ourselves to acquire a second, Divine nature – by habituating ourselves to living in accordance with G-ds' will – so be it.

But the more profound way of quelling a rebellion against G-d is by exposing its true nature: our refusal to be satisfied with our present understanding of G-d and our revulsion at the shallowness of our present relationship with Him. Our rebellion articulates our despair: "If this is all there is to the Divine life, I want nothing of it!"

Seen in this positive light, our rebellions – and the rebellions of the Jewish people so soon after having set out on their journeys – are a desperate cry for sincere return to G-d, for reestablishing our relationship with Him on a much deeper level than it ever was before.[6]

6. *Sefer HaSichot 5751*, vol. 2, pp. 598–610.

SEVENTH READING
Numbers 11:30–12:16

G-d appointed 70 elders to assist Moses. Moses' wife remarked to his sister Miriam that these elders would probably separate from their wives, just as Moses had separated from her in order to be ready for prophecy at any moment. Hearing this, Miriam, together with Aaron, disapproved of Moses' behavior. G-d told Miriam and Aaron that Moses had acted correctly, since he had to be ready at all times for Divine communication, which was not the case with other prophets. G-d afflicted Miriam with the skin disease of *tzara'at*, which specifically results from slander. Moses then prayed for Miriam's recovery, and G-d healed her.

True Humility

וְהָאִישׁ מֹשֶׁה עָנָו מְאֹד מִכֹּל הָאָדָם אֲשֶׁר עַל פְּנֵי הָאֲדָמָה: (במדבר יב, ג)

**Moses was exceedingly humble, more so
than any other person on earth.**

Humility is not the result of underestimating one's true worth. Moses understood very well that he was an extraordinary individual, who had been chosen by G-d to lead the Jewish people out of Egypt and to receive the Torah on their behalf. However, Moses also thought that had G-d given his lofty traits to someone else, that person would have been able to reach an even higher level than he had attained.

Humility is often misunderstood as simply the lack of boastfulness: We are "humble" if we feel superior to others so long as we don't boast about it! True humility, however, is learned from Moses. We should be fully aware of whatever greatness we possess, but attribute it to G-d rather than to ourselves. This allows us to respect other people and see them in a positive light, inasmuch as G-d has blessed them with their own unique qualities.[7]

---

7. *Sefer HaMa'amarim 5710*, p. 236.

Shelach

Scouting Out the Land

Numbers 13:1–15:41

THE FOURTH SECTION OF THE BOOK OF NUMBERS RECOUNTS
how G-d told Moses to send (*Shelach*, in Hebrew) scouts to
spy out the Land of Israel in preparation for the Jewish people's
conquest of it.

FIRST READING
Numbers 13:1–20

By 29 Sivan 2449, the Jewish people had reached the border of the Land of Israel. Some of the people asked Moses to send spies to scout out the land. Moses consulted with G-d, and G-d agreed to this plan. Moses chose 12 men, one from each tribe, for this mission. These men were among the most distinguished leaders of the Jewish people. However, all but two of them – Caleb, and Moses' chief disciple Joshua – made the mistake of overstepping the limits of their mission.

The Limits of Reason

שְׁלַח לְךָ אֲנָשִׁים וְיָתֻרוּ אֶת אֶרֶץ כְּנַעַן וגו': (במדבר יג, ב)

[G-d told Moses,] "Send out men, if you wish, who will inspect Canaan."

G-d wants us to understand as clearly as possible the goals of our Divine mission and the methods by which He wants us to carry it out, for this helps us fulfill it more enthusiastically. Moses therefore thought that it was proper to send out scouts to spy out how best to conquer the land. That way, the people would be more enthusiastic about entering and conquering the land.

The spies' error consisted of going beyond the scope of their mission and drawing conclusions. Moses only asked them to see *how* the land should be conquered, not *if* it could.

The lesson we learn from the spies' error is that even when we employ our own understanding in fulfilling our Divine mission, we must keep in mind that we are doing so because G-d wants us to – that we are doing so on *His* behalf. This way, we can be sure that we are using our intellect solely to arrive at the objective truth, rather than to supply ourselves with evidence that bolsters some conscious or subconscious subjective agenda.[1]

1. *Likutei Sichot*, vol. 23, pp. 92–95.

SECOND READING

Numbers 13:21–14:7

After 40 days, the spies returned to the camp and reported their findings. But then – with the exception of Caleb and Joshua – they made their fatal mistake, drawing their own conclusions from the evidence they had gathered, rather than letting Moses interpret it. They concluded that the land could not be conquered.

The Pitfalls of the Spiritual Life

הָאָרֶץ אֲשֶׁר עָבַרְנוּ בָהּ לָתוּר אֹתָהּ אֶרֶץ אֹכֶלֶת יוֹשְׁבֶיהָ הִוא וְגוֹ': (במדבר יג, לב)

[The spies said,] "The land we traveled through to
inspect is a land that consumes its inhabitants."

The spies' heightened but misdirected spiritual orientation led them astray. The spies wanted to experience life and pursue G-dliness unencumbered by the distractions of materiality. In the desert, the Jewish people were protected by the Clouds of Glory, sustained by the manna and the well of Miriam, and all their physical needs were fully attended to. All of their time was spent in the study of the Torah, in meditation, and in prayer. The spies were repulsed by the notion of entering the real world, where we must waste time working for our daily bread.

The vision of a life devoted to expanding our Divine consciousness unburdened by material distractions is of course praiseworthy. This vision has inspired us to yearn throughout history for the Messianic era, when the materiality of the world will no longer distort our spiritual focus.

Nonetheless, this yearning must be balanced with humble submission to G-d's plan. The purpose of life is to live within mundane reality, revealing the G-dliness concealed within it. Only by entering the material world can G-d's essence be found, through fulfilling His commandments on the physical plane.[2]

2. *Likutei Sichot*, vol. 23, pp. 92 ff.; *Sefer HaSichot* 5751, vol. 2, pp. 617 ff.; *Likutei Sichot*, vol. 13, pp. 39–40. ff.

THIRD READING

Numbers 14:8–25

The overwhelming majority of the Jewish people accepted the other spies' conclusions, threatening to kill Caleb and Joshua for differing. Since the people demonstrated that they lacked the faith in G-d necessary to enable them to conquer and live in the Land of Israel, G-d informed Moses that this generation would have to die in the desert. Only the next generation would enter the Promised Land.

To Learn from Miracles

אִם יִרְאוּ אֶת הָאָרֶץ אֲשֶׁר נִשְׁבַּעְתִּי לַאֲבֹתָם וְגוֹ': (במדבר יד, כג)

[G-d told Moses, "All those . . . who did not listen to My voice] will not see the land that I swore to their fathers."

The generation of the Exodus did not work hard enough to learn from the Divine miracles they witnessed. They therefore remained subject to their "slave mentality," the assumption that reality is enslaved to the laws of nature, and that G-d is unwilling or incapable of overriding them whenever He chooses. The spies and their followers therefore forfeited the privilege of entering the Promised Land, for in order to remain true to our Divine mission while leading material lives, we need to believe that this is indeed possible.

We, too, should take care to recognize the implications of all the Divine miracles we have witnessed, both throughout Jewish history and in our own personal lives. Only then will we be capable of fulfilling our Divine mission of making the world into G-d's home. In this merit, we will experience our miraculous return to the Promised Land, led by the Messiah in the final Redemption.[3]

---

3. *Likutei Sichot*, vol. 23, p. 112.

FOURTH READING
Numbers 14:26–15:7

After hearing of G-d's plan to keep them in the desert for 40 years, some of the Jewish people regretted doubting that the Land of Israel could be conquered. They organized their own army and attempted to enter the land on their own. But because they went against G-d's will and lacked Moses' leadership, the nations who lived near the border of the land repulsed them.

Doubting Doubts

הִנֶּנּוּ וְעָלִינוּ אֶל הַמָּקוֹם אֲשֶׁר אָמַר ה' כִּי חָטָאנוּ: (במדבר יד, מ)

[Some of the Jewish people said,] "We are ready to go up to the place that G-d said [He would give us]."

The people had initially refused to proceed toward the Land of Israel because they believed that it was impossible to conquer it, even with G-d's help. What caused them to suddenly abandon their skepticism? After all, Moses did not show them any new miracles, nor did G-d appear and perform some heavenly exhibition of His strength.

Our sages point out that every Jew inherently believes in G-d. Thus, even while the people were voicing their skepticism, they still believed in Him; their belief was just overshadowed temporarily by their emotions. Therefore, as soon as G-d rebuked them and informed them of the severity of the consequences of their lapse of faith, their inherent faith was awakened.

The same is true of many of the doubts from which we occasionally suffer. Our questions are often due to an exaggerated material perspective on life. Deep within our hearts we indeed believe in G-d. In such cases, the way to overcome our doubts is not to attempt to answer them directly but simply to reawaken the pure faith that lies dormant within us.[4]

4. *Tanya,* end of chapter 29 (37b).

THURSDAY

FIFTH READING
Numbers 15:8–16

After the incident of the spies, G-d comforted the Jewish people by reminding them that their children would eventually enter and possess the Land of Israel. He did this by giving them some laws that would only apply once they would enter the land. The first of these laws was that their animal sacrifices would have to be accompanied by offerings of grain, oil, and wine.

Rectifying the Desire to Shirk Responsibility

כְּמִסְפָּר אֲשֶׁר תַּעֲשׂוּ כָּכָה תַּעֲשׂוּ לָאֶחָד כְּמִסְפָּרָם: (במדבר טו, יב)

**[G-d instructed Moses to tell the Jewish people,]
"In accordance with the number [of animals]
you offer up, so must you present [offerings
of grain, wine, and oil] for each one."**

G-d gave the Jewish people specifically these laws because they counter the mistake of the spies. The spies wished to remain in the desert, studying the Torah without the distractions of material life. This one-sided focus on spirituality was similar to animal sacrifices, which *ascended* in smoke. In contrast, the oil and wine were poured *down*.

Thus, by instructing the Jewish people regarding the oil and wine offerings, G-d was telling them that the period of their spiritual "incubation" in the desert would eventually come to an end. Their children's entry into the Land of Israel would mark the Jewish people's descent into the physical world, in order to fulfill the purpose of creation by transforming it into G-d's home.

Similarly, whenever we feel unprepared or reluctant to tackle life's challenges, we should remind ourselves that our lives need to balance the need to rise above the world and the devotion to descend into it in order to refine and elevate it.[5]

5. *Sefer HaSichot 5751*, vol. 2, p. 617, note 9.

SIXTH READING
Numbers 15:17–26

The next law that G-d taught the Jewish people was the requirement to separate a portion of their dough and give it to the priests.

Authority

רֵאשִׁית עֲרֹסֹתֵכֶם חַלָּה תָּרִימוּ תְרוּמָה וְגוֹ': (במדבר טו, כ)

**[G-d instructed Moses to tell the Jewish people,] "[Of]
the first of your dough, donate a loaf [to a priest]."**

The Torah grants the privileges and responsibilities of the priests only to the descendants of Aaron. To be sure, all Jews are of equal inherent value and equally deserve our love and respect. However, when dealing with the question of who can be a religious practitioner or authority – whether a priest or a rabbi – we must realize that G-d has determined who can and who cannot assume these titles. Just as priests can only be descendants of Aaron, rabbis and teachers can only be individuals who have attained the necessary levels of knowledge, who are truly G-d-fearing, who observe *all* the dictates of the Torah, and who have absorbed the traditions transmitted through the generations.

Just as we require strict qualifications for those entrusted with guiding and facilitating our external religious lives, we should equally require strict qualifications for those inner voices that purport to tell us how to behave. We should constantly question our inner voices, in order to be sure that we are being guided only by pure and positive motives.[6]

---

6. *Likutei Sichot*, vol. 2, pp. 584–588.

SEVENTH READING
Numbers 15:27–41

G-d then instructed Moses regarding the laws of three commandments that are deemed equivalent to observing the entire Torah: not worshipping idols, observing the Sabbath, and wearing tassels (*tzitzit*) on the corners of four-cornered garments. The numerical value of the Hebrew word *tzitzit* is 600; when this number is added to the number of half-threads (8) and knots (5) in each tassel, the sum is 613, the number of commandments in the Torah.

Remembering the Source

וּרְאִיתֶם אֹתוֹ וּזְכַרְתֶּם אֶת כָּל מִצְוֹת ה' וַעֲשִׂיתֶם אֹתָם וְגו': (במדבר טו, לט)

[G-d instructed Moses to tell the people,] "When you see [the tassels], you will remember all the commandments of G-d, in order to perform them."

Granted that we need the tassels to remind us of the 613 commandments, but why do we need the garment to which the tassels are attached? Why not just carry the tassels themselves?

The answer lies in the significance of garments. The difference between clothing and food – our two main necessities – is that food becomes a part of us when we eat it, while clothing always remains outside of us. Food therefore alludes to the aspects of the Torah that we can comprehend and "digest," while clothing alludes to that which remains beyond our grasp.

The instruction to attach the tassels to a garment indicates that it is not sufficient simply to remember the commandments. Wearing such a garment helps us remember that the Torah and its commandments originate in G-d's wisdom, which transcends the limitations of human intellect.[7]

---

7. *Likutei Sichot*, vol. 2, pp. 324–325.

Korach

Mutiny

Numbers 16:1–18:32

THE FIFTH SECTION OF THE BOOK OF NUMBERS RECOUNTS
the rebellion of Korach, Moses' first cousin, and its repercussions.

FIRST READING
Numbers 16:1–13

The incident of the spies, recounted in the previous section, underscored the importance of entering the Land of Israel in order to fulfill G-d's commandments in the physical world. Soon afterward, Moses' cousin Korach staged a rebellion against Moses' authority.

The Danger of Either-Or Thinking

וַיָּקֻמוּ לִפְנֵי מֹשֶׁה וגו': (במדבר טז, ב)

[Korach and his supporters] confronted Moses.

Korach mistakenly concluded from the incident of the spies that the study of the Torah is not intrinsically superior to the performance of the commandments. Therefore, he reasoned, a person who works for a living has no need to aspire to moments of "reconnection" to spirituality. As such, he further concluded that there is no need for an elite class of individuals – the tribe of Levi, the priests, and the high priest in particular – who would be devoted exclusively to the spiritual life in order to inspire the rest of us.

Moses responded to Korach's claims by telling him that a clergy devoted exclusively to the service of G-d is indeed necessary, in order to inspire those involved in the mundane world and instruct them as to what is permitted and what is prohibited. Without such inspiration and guidance, it is too easy to lose sight of our ideals and end up as slaves to materiality rather than its masters.[1]

---

1. *Likutei Sichot*, vol. 8, pp. 108 ff.

SECOND READING

Numbers 16:14–19

G-d told Moses to conduct a test that would demonstrate the error of Korach and his supporters. Offering up incense was part of the Tabernacle service that was allowed to be performed only by the priests, and only at specified times. The Jewish people had previously witnessed how Aaron's two elder sons had died on account of having offered up an unauthorized incense offering. Now, G-d had Moses instruct Korach and his company to offer up incense, as would Aaron, also. Whoever's incense was not accepted by G-d would perish.

Holy Rebels

וּקְחוּ אִישׁ מַחְתָּתוֹ וּנְתַתֶּם עֲלֵיהֶם קְטֹרֶת וְהִקְרַבְתֶּם

לִפְנֵי ה' אִישׁ מַחְתָּתוֹ וְגוֹ': (במדבר טז, יז)

Let each man take his censer and place incense upon it, and let each man present his censer before G-d.

Although they knew that unauthorized use of the incense would cause their death, Korach and his followers took up the challenge. They wished to experience the lofty service of the high priest even if it would cost them their lives.

In this sense, their motivations were pure, and we can learn from their example, similarly aspiring to the most uplifting spiritual experiences. Their error, which we must also learn from, was disregarding the absurdity of going against G-d's will in order to get close to Him.[2]

2. *Likutei Sichot*, vol. 18, pp. 190–191.

THIRD READING

Numbers 16:20–17:8

There were 250 people who offered up incense. Besides these, there was a large crowd of people whom Korach had won over to his side, with the help of two members of the tribe of Reuben, the brothers Dathan and Aviram. Moses tried to convince these other rebels to abandon Korach's mutiny.

Never Despair of Anyone

וַיָּקָם מֹשֶׁה וַיֵּלֶךְ אֶל דָּתָן וַאֲבִירָם וגו': (במדבר טז, כה)

Moses arose and went to Dathan and Aviram.

Dathan and Aviram had openly demonstrated their animosity toward Moses, accusing him of being a despot and an impostor. Moreover, G-d Himself had already sealed their punishment, instructing Moses only to save the other rebels from Dathan and Aviram's impending fate. Still, Moses did not give up hope that his "enemies" would repent, doing everything in his power to influence them to reconsider.

We learn from Moses to always do whatever we can to bring our brethren back to G-d and His Torah – even when it seems that all hope is lost. This is true even when they are ignoring their faith intentionally, and all the more so when they are acting out of ignorance.[3]

3. *Likutei Sichot*, vol. 28, pp. 102–103.

FOURTH READING

Numbers 17:9–15

When Korach and his followers refused to back down, G-d sent forth fire to consume the people who had offered up incense; the rest of the rebels were swallowed up in pits that opened up in the ground. The following day, the Jewish people complained about the rebels' fate. They asserted that the incense was an instrument of death. To demonstrate their error and to punish those who still adhered to Korach's mistaken beliefs, G-d unleashed an epidemic, which started killing people instantaneously. He then instructed Aaron to stave off this epidemic by offering up incense, proving that when used in G-d's service, it promotes life and saves from death.

Killing Death

וַיִּתֵּן אֶת הַקְּטֹרֶת וַיְכַפֵּר עַל הָעָם: (במדבר יז, יב)

[Aaron] placed the incense [on the censer] and atoned for the people.

Smell is the most "spiritual" of our five senses; it can transport us to the loftiest levels of consciousness, and it can be used to restore consciousness to people who have fainted. For this reason, the incense in the Tabernacle expressed our inner unity with G-d.

When this lofty experience of oneness with G-d is balanced by humble submission to His will, it is positive; when it outweighs our devotion to G-d's will, it becomes suicidal and therefore negative. Thus, when incense was offered up out of the selfish desire to escape reality and responsibility, it proved fatal.

The antidote to this misguided "suicidal" drive is to channel it positively. By persistently choosing to "give up our lives" – i.e., our selfish involvement with unholy enticements – in favor of studying the Torah with humility, the Torah becomes part of us and will remain with us.[4]

4. *Or HaTorah, Shemot,* vol. 5, p. 1761.

FIFTH READING
Numbers 17:16–24

In order to demonstrate conclusively that the tribe of Levi (the priests and the Levites) had been set apart from the rest of the Jewish people for their respective tasks by G-d Himself, G-d commanded Moses to take the staffs of the princes of each of the 12 tribes and place them next to the Ark in the Holy of Holies, the inner chamber of the Tabernacle. Moses did so, and Aaron's staff miraculously sprouted almonds overnight, whereas the other staffs remained unchanged.

The Need for Speed

וְהִנֵּה פָּרַח מַטֵּה אַהֲרֹן לְבֵית לֵוִי וַיֹּצֵא פֶרַח וַיָּצֵץ
צִיץ וַיִּגְמֹל שְׁקֵדִים: (במדבר יז, כג)

Aaron's staff – for the house of Levi – had blossomed; it gave forth blossoms, sprouted buds, and produced ripe almonds.

Of all fruits, almonds are the quickest to blossom, ripen, and be ready for human consumption. This attribute of speed characterized the priests' function in the Tabernacle in two ways:

- The priests blessed the people every morning. The purpose of their blessings was to enable G-d's goodness to reach the Jewish people speedily and directly.
- The priests performed their duties quickly and with liveliness.

Inasmuch as the Jewish people are "a kingdom of priests and a holy nation," we should learn from the priests' quickness to fulfill their duties. We should not relate to our Divine mission in life halfheartedly or resignedly. Rather, we must respond to every opportunity quickly, energetically, and wholeheartedly. When we do so, we are assured that G-d's blessings and the success of our efforts will not delay in coming.[5]

5. *Likutei Torah* 3:55c- 56b; *Likutei Sichot*, vol. 4, pp. 1318–1320.

SIXTH READING
Numbers 17:25–18:20

The Jewish people finally accepted the Divinely ordained distinction between the priests and the Levites, on the one hand, and the lay people, on the other. However, they then complained that since entering designated areas of the Tabernacle compound was a capital offense for non-Levites, they were constantly exposed to the danger of death. G-d therefore made the priests and Levites responsible for keeping non-Levites from entering off-limit areas.

Ecstatic Love of G-d

עֲבֹדַת מַתָּנָה אֶתֵּן אֶת כְּהֻנַּתְכֶם וגו': (במדבר יח, ז)

[In the course of describing the priests' duties, G-d instructed Moses to tell the priests,] "I have given your priesthood [to you] as a gift of service."

We see here that there is a level of relationship with G-d that we cannot achieve on our own; it can only be given to us by G-d as a gift. This wondrous state is referred to in the Song of Songs (King Solomon's poetic description of the love between G-d and the Jewish people) as "a love of delights,"[6] and is likened by the Talmudic sages to the pleasure of G-dly revelation that awaits us in the afterlife.

This ecstatic love of G-d was felt by the priests regularly, but inasmuch as the entire Jewish people is "a kingdom of priests and a holy nation," we can all aspire to this rapturous love of G-d, at least occasionally.[7]

6. Song of Songs 7:7.
7. *Tanya*, chapter 14.

SEVENTH READING
Numbers 18:21–32

Finally, in order to certify the selection of the priests from the rest of the people as His explicit will, G-d enumerated the entitlements that they were to receive from the Jewish people. These included specific portions of their sacrifices, of their crops, and of their herds and flocks. The Levites also received specified portions of the Jewish people's crops, part of which they, in turn, were to give to the priests.

The Priests' Allotments

כִּי תִקְחוּ מֵאֵת בְּנֵי יִשְׂרָאֵל אֶת הַמַּעֲשֵׂר ...
וַהֲרֵמֹתֶם מִמֶּנּוּ תְּרוּמַת ה' וְגו': (במדבר יח, כו)

[G-d instructed Moses to tell the Levites,] "When you take the tithe from the Israelites ... you must set aside from it a portion for G-d[, which you will give to the priests]."

Although the physical priesthood was reserved for the descendants of Aaron, the spiritual priesthood is accessible to all Jews. G-d calls the entire Jewish people "a kingdom of priests." As Rabbi Moses Maimonides explains, "Any human being whose spirit moves him – and whose intellect has motivated him – to distinguish himself by standing before G-d, serving Him, and knowing Him ... has become sanctified like the Holy of Holies ... and will be granted all of his physical needs, just as they were provided for the priests and Levites."[8]

In other words, when we recognize the purpose of our lives – to serve G-d – and dedicate ourselves to accomplishing it, we are assured of the best of everything, material and spiritual, at all times.[9]

---

8. *Mishneh Torah, Shemitah veYoveil* 13:13.
9. *Likutei Sichot*, vol. 2, pp. 690–691.

Chukat

Final Journeys in the Desert

Numbers 19:1–22:1

THE SIXTH SECTION OF THE BOOK OF NUMBERS OPENS WITH the law (or "rule," *chukat,* in Hebrew) governing the process of purification from the state of ritual defilement that a person contracts through contact with a human corpse. After this, the Torah's narrative advances to the final years of the Jewish people's wanderings in the desert until they arrived at the threshold of the Land of Israel.

FIRST READING
Numbers 19:1–17

On the day the Tabernacle was inaugurated, 1 Nisan 2449, G-d instructed Moses how to purify the Jewish people from ritual defilement contracted by contact with a human corpse. First, a perfectly red-haired cow must be slaughtered and burned to ashes. Then, a liquid solution is compounded out of spring water and the ashes of the cow. The ritually defiled person begins a seven-day count. A priest then sprinkles some of the red-cow ash-solution on the defiled person on the third and seventh days. The defiled person must then immerse himself in a ritual pool (*mikveh*) and wait until nightfall in order to complete the purification process.

Mercy and Selflessness

בַּיּוֹם הַשְּׁלִישִׁי וּבַיּוֹם הַשְּׁבִיעִי יִטְהָר וגו': (במדבר יט, יב)

On the third and seventh days [the defiled person] must purify himself.

In order to purify ourselves from the defilement of death – which in psychological terms means the paralysis caused by depression or deadness toward the spiritual dimension of life – we must invoke the third and seventh emotional attributes of the soul. The third emotion is pity and the seventh emotion is lowliness. When we feel the pain our Divine soul suffers from its constricted consciousness in the material world, we are aroused to rescue it by studying G-d's Torah and performing His commandments. When we are not egocentric, the flow of Divine life-force and vitality that should energize our lives is not blocked by our self-centered interests.[1]

1. *Likutei Torah* 3:61cd.

SECOND READING
Numbers 19:18–20:6

G-d instructed the Jewish people to remain encamped at the border of the Land of Israel for 19 years after Korach's rebellion. They then wandered in the desert for another 19 years, arriving at the border of the kingdom of Edom. On 10 Nisan 2487, Moses' sister Miriam died. The Jewish people's source of water – the miraculous well that had followed them in the desert – disappeared, for it had existed only in Miriam's merit. G-d subsequently restored it to the Jewish people in Moses' merit.

Doing What is Not Our Job

וְלֹא הָיָה מַיִם לָעֵדָה וַיִּקָּהֲלוּ עַל מֹשֶׁה וְעַל אַהֲרֹן: (במדבר כ, ב)

The congregation had no water, so they assembled against Moses and Aaron.

Food nourishes the body, but the body needs water in order to absorb the nutrients in the food. Similarly, the "food" of the soul is the Torah and its "water" is the Torah's ability to influence all facets of our personalities, all types of people, and all aspects of life.

When the Jewish people's existence was threatened in Egypt, Miriam was the one who ensured that there would be a new generation of Jews to carry on G-d's mission. She both encouraged the Jewish people to continue having children and saved their newborns from Pharaoh's decree. On account of her efforts to ensure that the Torah would continue to "flow" into the next generation, the well existed in her merit.

With her passing, Moses had to assume her role. This teaches us that when other Jews are in physical or spiritual danger we should come to their aid, even if offering this type of assistance is not our forte. When we help others, G-d in turn will help us with all our own needs.[2]

---

2. *Likutei Sichot*, vol. 2, p. 335; *Sefer HaArachim Chabad*, vol. 2, cols. 186–187.

THIRD READING
Numbers 20:7–13

G-d instructed Moses to restore the well by speaking to the rock from which the water had previously flowed. However, Moses mistook another rock for the correct one, so when he spoke to it, nothing happened. Moses and Aaron thought that perhaps G-d intended them to strike the rock, as He had when He first provided the people with water. They acted on this conjecture without consulting with G-d. By Divine providence, Moses struck the original rock, and it indeed gave forth water. G-d had intended for the people to learn reverence for Him from Moses' *speaking* to the rock: "If an undiscerning, self-sufficient rock obeys G-d's will, how much more so should we, who can understand why we ought to obey Him and need His assistance." But since Moses struck the rock, this lesson was no longer self-evident. So G-d had to teach the Jewish people the same lesson by punishing Moses and Aaron for their disobedience. He decreed that they would die in the desert, never to enter the Land of Israel.

Implications of Our Deeds

וַיֹּאמֶר ה' אֶל מֹשֶׁה וְאֶל אַהֲרֹן יַעַן לֹא הֶאֱמַנְתֶּם בִּי וגו': (במדבר כ, יב)

G-d told Moses and Aaron, "Since you did not have enough faith in Me..."

Whatever rationalizations may justify their conduct, Jewish leaders must decide how to act based on whether their actions will inspire the public to greater devotion to the Torah and its ways.

Similarly, when interacting with others, we should always consider the potential impact that our words or actions may have on their attitudes toward the Jewish people in general and toward the Torah's message in particular.[3]

3. *Likutei Sichot*, vol. 28, pp. 127–128.

FOURTH READING

Numbers 20:14–21

Moses then asked the king of Edom to allow the Jewish people to pass through his land on the way to the Land of Israel. The Edomites refused, so Moses led the people southward, detouring around their territory.

The Soul is Never in Exile

דֶּרֶךְ הַמֶּלֶךְ נֵלֵךְ לֹא נִטֶּה יָמִין וּשְׂמֹאול עַד אֲשֶׁר נַעֲבֹר גְּבֻלֶךָ: (במדבר כ, יז)

[In his message to the king of Edom, Moses said,] "We will walk along the king's road, turning neither to the right nor to the left until we have passed through your territory."

Moses' message to the Edomite king is the same message that our Divine souls must convey to the material world so long as we are still in exile. "True, we Jews are physically the same as all people; we have physical needs that must be met by working and living in the physical world. Nonetheless, we will not let this fact obscure our true purpose in life: to fulfill our Divine mission of elevating and refining physicality. We will walk along our Divine King's road; we will not deviate from G-d's ways, either to the right or to the left!"

By remaining true to both our inner selves and to our Divine mission, we will merit witnessing the ultimate redemption of the world and its transformation into G-d's true home.[4]

4. *Likutei Sichot*, vol. 18, p. 468.

FIFTH READING
Numbers 20:22–21:9

Moses then asked the kingdom of Moab, which was situated to the east of Edom, for permission to pass through their land, but they too refused. After this, Moses' brother Aaron died, and the nation of Amalek attacked the Jewish people for the second time.

The Two Faces of Cold Indifference

וַיִּלָּחֶם בְּיִשְׂרָאֵל וַיִּשְׁבְּ מִמֶּנּוּ שֶׁבִי: (במדבר כא, א)

[Amalek] waged war against Israel and took [back] a captive from them.

Amalek first attacked the Jewish people when they were on the way to receive the Torah and again as they were preparing to enter the Land of Israel.

Similarly, our inner Amalek first attempts to cool our enthusiasm toward G-d and His Torah. As long as we are fulfilling our religious obligations, this might not seem to pose such a problem. But if we approach our Divine mission without warmth and enthusiasm, we will eventually lose interest in it, seeking diversions that offer more immediate material or spiritual gratification.

If our inner Amalek fails to cool our enthusiasm, it will attempt to take over our life in the "land," i.e., the material life we enter after our daily prayers and studies. It will argue, "Be holy while you're praying and studying the Torah, but when you're earning your living and dealing with the physical world, live by *my* rules."

Although this may sound like the voice of a clever businessman, we must recognize it as the voice of Amalek. Despite its concessions to our spiritual endeavors, its goal is to destroy us. The only proper response to Amalek is to wipe it out – by constantly renewing our enthusiasm for G-d and His Torah, and our desire that G-d be our guide in all aspects of life.[5]

5. *Likutei Sichot*, vol. 1, pp. 208–213.

SIXTH READING
Numbers 21:10–20

The Jewish people traveled around the kingdom of Moab and then turned northward. The Amorites, who lived north of Moab, planned to ambush them as they crossed into their territory, but G-d caused an earthquake, killing the Amorites in their hideouts. The Jewish people were thus able to continue safely through Amorite territory northward.

Living in the Future

מִשָּׁם נָסָעוּ וַיַּחֲנוּ מֵעֵבֶר אַרְנוֹן וְגוֹ': (במדבר כא, יג)

[The Jewish people] journeyed [northward] and encamped on the side of the Arnon River.

G-d originally promised Abraham the territories of ten nations: seven in Canaan and three to the east of the Jordan. The Jewish people were at this point supposed to only conquer Canaan, leaving the land east of the Jordan for the Messianic era. But because Edom and Moab refused them passage, the Jewish people had to enter Canaan by way of the very territories that G-d had promised them would be theirs in the future. Circumstances thus enabled them to conquer large parts of these lands even before entering Canaan. The originally intended order was reversed; they began to consummate the future even before actualizing the present.

The new generation did not ask to send out spies, nor did they question Moses' leadership. Having grown up immersed in G-d's presence and teachings in its desert "academy," it did not subject its connection to G-d to the approval of human intellect.

Similarly, when we inspire ourselves to fulfill our Divine mission unconditionally, optimistically focused on our ultimate goal, G-d grants us the opportunity to make our dreams come true and lead us to the final Redemption.[6]

---

6. *Sefer HaSichot 5750*, vol. 2, pp. 541–550; *Likutei Sichot*, vol. 4, p. 1056.

SEVENTH READING

Numbers 21:21–22:1

Moses then asked Sichon, king of the Amorites, for permission to pass through his land into Canaan. Sichon refused, so Moses led the Jewish people into battle against him, conquering Amorite territory as far north as the Yabok River. The same occurred with Og, king of the Amorites of Bashan: The Jewish people defeated him and thereby conquered the northern Amorite territory as well.

The Need for Leadership

וַיִּשְׁלַח יִשְׂרָאֵל מַלְאָכִים אֶל סִיחֹן מֶלֶךְ הָאֱמֹרִי וגו': (במדבר כא, כא)

Israel sent messengers to Sichon, king of the Amorites.

The medieval sage Rabbi Shlomo Yitzchaki (known universally by his initials as "Rashi") points out that the Torah says that *Moses* sent messengers to Edom but that *Israel* sent messengers to Sichon, even though in both cases Moses sent the messengers on behalf of all the Jewish people. As Rashi notes, this teaches us that Moses and the Jewish people are essentially equivalent. The true Jewish leader does not just represent the people, he is one with them in essence. His affairs are not divided into his private and public lives. He is a public servant to his very core.

The true Jewish leader's total identification with his people and his selfless devotion to them makes him the conduit through which G-d provides all their material and spiritual needs. Therefore, not only is he one with them: they are one with him. As such, they can rise to his perspective on reality and share his Divine consciousness and his inspired life, even if they have not yet refined themselves enough to be worthy of these on their own.[7]

7. *Likutei Sichot*, vol. 33, pp. 131–136.

Balak

Curses into Blessings

Numbers 22:2–25:9

THE SEVENTH SECTION OF THE BOOK OF NUMBERS DESCRIBES the plot of Balak, king of Moab and his hired sorcerer Balaam to curse the Jewish people in order to prevent them from attacking Moab. G-d frustrates their plan and forces Balaam to bless the Jewish people instead.

FIRST READING
Numbers 22:2–12

Balak, the king of Moab, heard how the Jewish people miraculously overcame the Amorite kings Sichon and Og. Even though it was common knowledge that G-d had not promised the Jews the territory of Moab, Balak feared that these victories would embolden them to exact revenge from the Moabites for not having allowed them to pass through their country.

Responsible Leadership

וַיָּגָר מוֹאָב מִפְּנֵי הָעָם מְאֹד וגו': (במדבר כב, ג)

**[Due to Balak's predictions,] Moab became
terrified of the [Jewish] people.**

Balak had no reason to make the Moabites afraid of the Jewish people. He did not ask them to do anything to counter the supposed threat posed by the Jews. But he could not contain himself, and needlessly spread fear among his people.

In contrast, although Moses was afraid of King Og, he did not disclose his fear to the Jewish people. Moses realized that he must refrain from doing anything that would weaken the people's morale, and instead bolstered his own inner morale. Because of his positive attitude and steadfast trust in G-d, he successfully preserved the Jewish people's self-image and pride in their Divine mission. Moses knew that we earn G-d's helpful intervention in our lives by trusting Him to provide it. Moses set the standard of fearless behavior for all Jewish leaders who would succeed him.

We are all leaders, to one degree or another, whether in the context of our jobs, our families, or our circle of friends. We should therefore learn from Moses' example, taking care to foster others' optimism and confidence in their Divine mission, rather than the opposite, as did Balak.[1]

---

1. *Likutei Sichot*, vol. 8, pp. 148–149.

SECOND READING

Numbers 22:13–20

Balak sent for the sorcerer Balaam, proposing that he curse the Jews. Balaam agreed, but informed Balak's messengers that he would only be able to curse the Jews if he could convince G-d to agree.

G-d is in Control

לֹא אוּכַל לַעֲבֹר אֶת פִּי ה' אֱלֹקָי לַעֲשׂוֹת קְטַנָּה אוֹ גְדוֹלָה: (במדבר כב, יח)

[Balaam told Balak's messengers,] "I cannot do anything – small or great – that would transgress the word of G-d."

Evil possesses no autonomy; it is nothing more than a tool that G-d uses to hide Himself from the world, thereby enabling us to choose freely between good and evil. The *Zohar*, the classic work of Jewish mysticism, likens evil to a prostitute hired by a king to entice the prince. Although she makes full use of all her seductive powers to ensnare the prince, she really hopes – as does the king – that the prince will be strong enough to withstand her advances. Similarly, evil tries to confuse us and entice us into misbehaving, but it is in fact only doing its job and would rather we not pay attention to it.

When we are aware of the true nature of evil, it is much easier for us to resist it.[2]

2. *Hitva'aduyot 5743*, vol. 4, p. 1763; *Tanya*, chapter 9 (14b); ibid., chapter 29 (38a); *Zohar* 2:163a.

THIRD READING

Numbers 22:21–38

Balaam hoped to get G-d to agree to curse the Jewish people by "reminding" Him of how quick they had been to rebel against Him repeatedly during their 40 years in the desert.

Love Conquers Hatred

וַיָּקָם בִּלְעָם בַּבֹּקֶר וַיַּחֲבֹשׁ אֶת אֲתֹנוֹ וגו': (במדבר כב, כא)

Balaam arose in the morning and saddled his donkey.

Balaam loathed G-d and His emissaries, the Jewish people, with a passion. By rising early to set out on his mission of evil, he hoped to "remind" G-d how quick the Jews had been to rebel against Him. But G-d informed Balaam that his quickness had been preempted by that of the patriarch Abraham. Abraham had risen early in the morning in order to lovingly and devotedly fulfill G-d's command to sacrifice his son Isaac. The merit of Abraham's love of G-d counterbalanced Balaam's hatred. Abraham's love had been inherited by the Jewish people; their rebellions in the desert had merely been temporary lapses in their inherent, undying devotion to G-d.

Similarly, whenever we find ourselves having to repair the damage we might have caused by having deliberately disregarded G-d's will, the surest way to make amends for such misdeeds is to bolster our love for Him. This love will in turn transform past misdeeds into the motivation for doing good deeds. Just as G-d transformed Balaam's curses into a blessing, we too can always transform "curses" into blessings.[3]

3. *Likutei Sichot*, vol. 28, pp. 163–164.

FOURTH READING

Numbers 22:39–23:12

Balaam arrived in Moab. Balak proceeded to take Balaam to a place he thought would be conducive to cursing the Jews. But G-d forced Balaam to praise and bless the Jews rather than curse them.

Hidden Treasure

מִי מָנָה עֲפַר יַעֲקֹב וְגֹו': (במדבר כג, י)

[Balaam said,] "Who can count the dust of Jacob?"

The Jewish people are here compared (positively) to dust. Just as there are hidden treasures buried in the earth, so are there treasures of pure faith in G-d and deep love and fear of Him hidden in every Jew. These treasures may at times be hard to uncover, just as the treasures buried in the earth are often buried deep below the surface. But they are there, nonetheless, and with sufficient effort they can be revealed.[4]

---

4. *Keter Shem Tov* (ed. Kehot, 2004), addendum 57 (addendum 44 in previous editions).

THURSDAY

FIFTH READING
Numbers 23:13–26

Balak then took Balaam to a second location, thinking that perhaps it would be easier for Balaam to curse the Jewish people from there. But once again, G-d forced Balaam to bless the Jews rather than curse them.

Our Infinite Divine Potential

לֹא הִבִּיט אָוֶן בְּיַעֲקֹב ... ה' אֱלֹקָיו עִמּוֹ וְגוֹ': (במדבר כג, כא)

[Balaam said, "G-d] does not look at the evil in Jacob [i.e., the Jewish people] ... G-d, their G-d, is with them."

The reason G-d does not see any evil in us is because He views us as having already fulfilled our potential to reorient our animalistic sides toward Divinity, i.e., to harness our inner animal's raw power in the pursuit of higher, Divine consciousness. What enables us to perform this transformation is our Divine soul. The spark of Divine consciousness within each of us possesses a spark of G-d's irresistible power, and can therefore overcome our inner animal.

Thus, Balaam said, "*He does not look at the evil in Jacob* – i.e., G-d sees that we can conquer our inner animal, because *G-d is with him* – i.e., within him, referring to the Divine soul, which enables us to transform our inner animal.[5]

---

5. *Hitva'aduyot 5743*, vol. 4, p. 1777.

SIXTH READING
Numbers 23:27–24:13

Balak then took Balaam to a third location, thinking that perhaps it would be easier for Balaam to curse the Jewish people from there. Balaam was about to curse them, but then he saw how the Jewish people were camped: First, they were organized by tribes, which was possible only because they had been faithful in their marriages. Second, they set up camp in such a way that no one could accidentally look into another family's tent. The Jewish people's attention to detail in their modest conduct so impressed Balaam that he decided on his own to bless them rather than curse them.

The Power of Modesty

מַה טֹּבוּ אֹהָלֶיךָ יַעֲקֹב מִשְׁכְּנֹתֶיךָ יִשְׂרָאֵל: (במדבר כד, ה)

[Balaam said,] "How good are your tents, O Jacob, your encampments, O Israel."

The lesson for us here is that we must never think that it is important to be concerned only about the "larger" issues of modesty and intimacy, but that we can be lax about the "smaller," "innocent" details. Even the smaller details are important – important enough to be able to transform a curse into a blessing (or an accursed situation into a blessed one).

Lest we think that this alertness to the details of modesty is only required in our day-to-day behavior but not in temporary situations (such as when we are on vacation), we see here that the tremendous power of even the minor details of modest conduct was demonstrated when our forefathers lived in tents, their temporary homes in the desert.[6]

6. *Likutei Sichot*, vol. 13, p. 84.

SEVENTH READING

Numbers 24:14–25:9

Having blessed the Jewish people three times, Balaam prophesied the fate of Balak's people, as well as that of other nations, in the future. In these prophecies, he also mentioned how the Jewish people's future king – the Messiah – would bring all humanity to serve G-d.

Dreaming G-d's Dreams

וְיֵרְדְ מִיַּעֲקֹב וְגוֹ': (במדבר כד, יט)

[Balaam said,] "A ruler will come out of Jacob."

One might ask: "Once we know what G-d requires of us in the here and now, why do we need to know about our ultimate goal and reward? Why not trust G-d to provide the reward when the time comes instead of being concerned now about what and when?"

The answer is that having a clear vision of what it is we are working toward makes all the difference in the quality of our work and the effort we invest in it. G-d wants us to serve Him in an inspired way; He wants our vision to be His vision, our goals to be His goals. Of course, our relationship to G-d must be based on the absolute, unconditional devotion every creature owes its Creator, but that is only the basis, the beginning. Ideally, G-d wants us to dream about what He dreams about; this is why He shares with us His dream for the Messianic future.

It is therefore vital to study the prophecies and statements of our sages about the Messiah and the imminent Redemption. This will enable us to form a clear picture in our mind of what the world is really meant to be and how we can make this dream a reality.[7]

---

7. *Likutei Sichot*, vol. 21, p. 18; ibid., vol. 22, p. 76; *Sefer HaSichot 5751*, vol. 2, pp. 497–498, 501–503, 747–749, etc.

Pinechas

Preparing for Conquest

Numbers 25:10–30:1

THE EIGHTH SECTION OF THE BOOK OF NUMBERS OPENS WITH the account of how G-d installed Moses' great-nephew Pinechas into the priesthood. It continues with the final census in the desert, the laws of inheritance, the transfer of leadership from Moses to Joshua, and the daily and festival sacrifices.

FIRST READING
Numbers 25:10–26:4

Balaam advised Balak to entice the Jewish people into the sin.
Balak had Midianite and Moabite women seduce the Jewish men
and then entice them into idol worship. G-d unleashed a fatal epidemic against the Jewish people. Moses brought the offenders to
trial, but Zimri, prince of the tribe of Simeon, challenged Moses,
consorting publicly with the Midianite princess Kozbi. Aaron's
grandson Pinechas remembered that such offenders may be
executed without trial, and slew Zimri and Kozbi. Pinechas then
prayed to G-d and G-d halted the epidemic. When G-d declared
that the priesthood would pass to Aaron's sons' future progeny,
Pinechas had already been born. Nonetheless, as a reward for his
zealousness, G-d installed Pinechas into the priesthood.

Avoiding False Modesty

הִנְנִי נֹתֵן לוֹ...בְּרִית כְּהֻנַּת עוֹלָם וגו': (במדבר כה, יב-יג)

**[G-d said regarding Pinechas,] "I hereby give
him...the eternal covenant of priesthood."**

The fact that Pinechas was much younger than Moses did not
prevent him from acting in his presence, once it became clear that
Moses had forgotten what needed to be done. Similarly, we should
not be intimidated when we see that those of greater stature are
not righting some wrong that must be addressed. It could well be,
as in the case of Pinechas, that Divine providence is keeping them
silent in order that a "less qualified" individual seize the moment
and answer destiny's call to greatness. When Divine providence
presents us with an opportunity to right some wrong in the world,
we must pursue it with total self-sacrifice, as did Pinechas, who
risked his life when he slew Zimri.[1]

---

1. *Likutei Sichot*, vol. 2, p. 342.

SECOND READING
Numbers 26:5–51

G-d instructed Moses to take a census of the Jewish people after the deaths caused by the epidemic and the administration of justice. Included in this census were the sons of Korach, the instigator of the mutiny against Moses 38 years earlier.

Thinking of Repentance

וּבְנֵי קֹרַח לֹא מֵתוּ: (במדבר כו, יא)

Korach's sons did not die [in their father's mutiny].

The sons of Korach played a key role in his rebellion, and were therefore swallowed up into the ground along with the other rebels. However, since Korach's sons – unlike the others – repented in their hearts, they were spared the death penalty: G-d allowed them to stay alive in an underground cave until the rest of their generation died out, after which He allowed them to emerge from hiding and resume their lives in the community. Had they acted upon their regret, they would have been spared even this lesser punishment. Their survival shows us the tremendous power of repentance – even when it is not acted upon as it should be.

This insight should quiet any doubts that we may have about the possibility of redemption in our times. Even merely *thinking* about repenting is sufficient to bring about the final Redemption – especially when this is added to the merits we have accrued throughout our long exile: the Torah we have studied, the commandments we have performed, and the martyrdom we have suffered.[2]

2. *Likutei Sichot*, vol. 33, pp. 170 ff.

THIRD READING
Numbers 26:52–27:5

After the census was completed, G-d instructed Moses how to divide up the Land of Israel among the Jewish people.

Our Threefold Relationship with G-d

לְאֵלֶּה תֵּחָלֵק הָאָרֶץ וגו': (במדבר כו, נג)

[G-d told Moses,] "The land will be divided up among these [whom you just counted]."

The Land of Israel was divided among the Jewish people in three ways: (1) by population – i.e., the larger the tribe, the more land it received; (2) by lot, which determined which tribe received which area; and (3) through inheritance, by which the fathers' estates were passed down to their children.

These three methods mirror the three different facets of our relationship with G-d: (1) We are connected to G-d in a service-reward relationship. This mirrors the logical division of the land by population. (2) We were chosen by G-d to be His people, regardless of how well we live up to our side of our contractual relationship with Him. This mirrors the division of the land by lot, which is not dictated by logic. (3) We are connected to G-d because we are part of Him; since we are part of G-d, He does not even need to choose us. This mirrors the division of the land by inheritance, for an heir inherits his parents automatically; he does not have to earn his inheritance, nor does his parent need to choose him as their heir.

All three facets of our relationship with G-d are important, but in the Messianic future our inheritance-relationship with G-d will become paramount. It is this aspect of our relationship that we should try to emphasize now, as we prepare ourselves for the imminent Messianic Redemption.[3]

3. *Likutei Sichot*, vol. 28, pp. 176–181.

FOURTH READING
Numbers 27:6–23

In preparation for Moses' imminent death, G-d instructed him to appoint Joshua as his successor.

Humility in Self-Assertion

וַיֹּאמֶר ה' אֶל מֹשֶׁה קַח לְךָ אֶת יְהוֹשֻׁעַ בֶּן נוּן אִישׁ אֲשֶׁר
רוּחַ בּוֹ וְסָמַכְתָּ אֶת יָדְךָ עָלָיו: (במדבר כז, יח)

**G-d said to Moses, "Take Joshua son of Nun, a
man of spirit, and lay your hand upon him."**

Joshua was chosen as Moses' successor by virtue of his consummate diligence in absorbing Moses' instruction – both from the Torah that Moses taught and through Moses' personal conduct. The difference in their leadership was that Moses' was largely based on miracles whereas Joshua's was conducted naturally. Therefore, it was specifically through Joshua's leadership that the purpose of Creation – to sanctify the natural, mundane world – was fulfilled. But Joshua succeeded only because he was a selfless reflection of Moses; his selflessness enabled the miraculous nature of Moses' leadership to carry over into his own, natural leadership. Thus, Joshua's first conquest, the city of Jericho, occurred miraculously.

From Joshua we learn to be fully committed both to humbly absorbing and transmitting the heritage and lessons of the Torah as they have been handed down to us by our predecessors, and to applying the Torah's teachings to the novel situations of our generation.[4]

4. *Hitva'aduyot 5747*, vol. 3, pp. 191–195.

FIFTH READING
Numbers 28:1–15

G-d then instructed Moses regarding the daily and holiday communal sacrifices that were to be regularly offered up in the Tabernacle.

Nourishing G-d

אֶת קָרְבָּנִי לַחְמִי לְאִשַּׁי . . . תִּשְׁמְרוּ וְגו': (במדבר כח, ב)

[G-d instructed Moses to tell the Jewish people,] "You must guard My offering, My food for My fire-offerings."

G-d calls the sacrifices His daily "food," for just as food sustains the body, so did the sacrifices draw sustaining Divine life-force into the world. Furthermore, the constancy of the daily sacrifices expressed the eternal bond between G-d and the Jewish people.

The daily prayers were instituted to parallel the daily sacrifices and to substitute for them in the absence of the Tabernacle or Temple. Thus, our daily prayers also "sustain" G-d. If we ever doubt how important our prayers can be, we should recall that G-d considers them vital to the world's existence and maintenance. They are as important to Him as our daily bread is to us.[5]

5. *Likutei Sichot*, vol. 13, pp. 103–104.

SIXTH READING
Numbers 28:16–29:11

After detailing the procedures for the daily sacrifices, G-d instructed Moses regarding the weekly Sabbath sacrifices, the sacrifices for the first day of every Jewish month, and the sacrifices for the holidays. In the course of these instructions, G-d referred to *Rosh HaShanah*, the Jewish New Year, as a day for sounding the shofar, or ram's horn.

Renewal

וּבַחֹדֶשׁ הַשְּׁבִיעִי בְּאֶחָד לַחֹדֶשׁ ... יוֹם תְּרוּעָה יִהְיֶה לָכֶם: (במדבר כט, א)

[G-d instructed Moses to tell the Jewish people,]
"The first day of the seventh month...must
be a day of shofar-sounding for you."

Annual renewal is necessary if life is to retain its freshness and novelty. If we merely continue cultivating the same type of Divine consciousness, we will remain locked in its limitations, ultimately making our religious lives seem repetitious and dull. *Rosh HaShanah* is an opportunity for us to make a quantum leap to a new plateau of Divine consciousness that will inspire our lives for the coming year.

To accomplish this, however, we cannot rely on the words of our prayers, because words carry specific meanings for us that are limited by the knowledge and experiences we have accrued in our lives. In order to break out of our limited modes of expression, we use the blasts and wails of the shofar, which transcend the confines of verbal language. In this way, we recapture the innocence and inspiration of a newly born soul and of the Jewish people when they received the Torah at Mount Sinai. This renewed inspiration invigorates our relationship with G-d for the coming year.[6]

---

6. *Sefer HaMa'amarim Melukat*, vol. 1, p. 426.

SHABBAT

SEVENTH READING

Numbers 29:12–30:1

Special communal offerings were sacrificed every day of the seven-day holiday of *Sukot*. But as whereas the number of rams and lambs offered up remained constant throughout the seven days, the number of bulls decreased from 13 on the first day to seven on the seventh day. On the following day, the holiday of *Shemini Atzeret*, only one single bull was offered up.

Weaning Ourselves from Materiality

וְהִקְרַבְתֶּם עֹלָה ... פָּרִים בְּנֵי בָקָר שְׁלֹשָׁה עָשָׂר וְגו': (במדבר כט, יג)

[G-d instructed Moses to tell the Jewish people,]
"You must offer up an ascent-offering [on *Sukot*]
of 13 young bulls [on the first day] ..."

If we indulge the "animal" side of our personalities, always giving in to what it insists are its "needs," it will quickly learn to assert itself and make increasing demands on us. Instead, we should accustom it to make do with the minimum, while we strive for greater and greater fulfillment in spiritual areas. On the other hand, if we try to change our animal side too abruptly, it will simply refuse to comply. We must accustom it gently and gradually, showing it step by step how spiritual fulfillment is even more satisfying than material satisfaction.

Once our material drives have been trained in this way, we can make a quantum leap and wean them entirely of their material orientation, just like the quantum leap from the last day of *Sukot* to *Shemini Atzeret*, when the number of bulls offered up drops from seven to one.[7]

Matot

Facing Challenges
Numbers 30:2–32:42

THE NINTH SECTION OF THE BOOK OF NUMBERS BEGINS AS Moses addresses the heads of the tribes (*Matot,* in Hebrew), teaching them the laws of vows and oaths. It then resumes the historical narrative, recounting the events during the last year of the Jewish people's trek in the desert as they prepare to cross the Jordan River into the Land of Israel.

FIRST READING
Numbers 30:2–17

G-d instructed Moses regarding the laws governing how a person can make vows and oaths to Him.

Sacred Speech

אִישׁ כִּי יִדֹּר נֶדֶר לַה' וְגוֹ': (במדבר ל, ג)

[**G-d instructed Moses to tell the Jewish people,**] **"If someone makes a vow to G-d...he must not violate his word."**

The word for "violate" in Hebrew (*yacheil*) comes from the word for "profane" or "unholy" (*chol*). The inner meaning of this verse is therefore that we should not make our words "unholy"; even our mundane conversation should be imbued with holy intentions and be consistent with the greater purpose of Creation, making a home for G-d in this world.[1]

1. *Likutei Sichot*, vol. 13, p. 108.

SECOND READING

Numbers 31:1–12

Even though the Midianites had no quarrel against the Jews, they had joined the Moabites in enticing the Jewish people into sin. In recompense for their consummately evil behavior, G-d told Moses to send the Jewish army to attack the Midianites.

Baseless Hatred

לָתֵת נִקְמַת ה' בְּמִדְיָן: (במדבר לא, ג)

[**Moses told the Jewish people,**] **"Carry out G-d's revenge against Midian."**

The Midianites had no reason to attack the Jews; they did so out of simple, baseless hatred. The root of baseless hatred is ego. An egocentric person feels threatened by others, for their very existence endangers his inflated sense of self. Therefore, although he may not seek to actively harm others, he will be secretly pleased when they suffer, or at least not be troubled by their suffering. Furthermore, he will be blind to other people's good qualities. Since he is not sincere in his relationship with G-d and the world, he cannot believe that others are.

In contrast, someone who is not egocentric focuses only on other people's good qualities. Their suffering will genuinely trouble him, since he will judge them favorably and find no justification for their pain.

Similarly, rather than viewing differences of opinion as an affront to his selfhood, the selfless person will view them as opportunities to reach higher perspectives on the truth. He will expose his shortcomings to others and seek their guidance, thereby allowing him to solve his problems and progress in his self-refinement.[2]

2. *Likutei Torah* 3:85d ff; *Sefer HaMa'amarim 5659*, p. 53 ff; *Sefer HaMa'amarim 5747*, p. 183 ff.

THIRD READING

Numbers 31:13–24

The Jews attacked Midian and killed all the adult males. Moses instructed the soldiers to purify themselves from the ritual impurity that they contracted from their contact with human corpses. Moses' nephew Eleazar (who had taken over as high priest after his father Aaron's recent death) instructed the soldiers to purge the eating utensils that they had plundered in battle.

Moses is not Enough

וַיֹּאמֶר אֶלְעָזָר הַכֹּהֵן אֶל אַנְשֵׁי הַצָּבָא הַבָּאִים לַמִּלְחָמָה וגו': (במדבר לא, כא)

Eleazar the priest said to the soldiers returning from battle...

Ritual defilement is a spiritual condition that *surrounds* the object, while forbidden food physically penetrates *into* the object. Thus, a vessel that has absorbed forbidden food needs to be purged of it by being immersed in boiling water or heated until white-hot, whereas a vessel that has been ritually defiled needs only to be immersed in a ritual pool (*mikveh*), whose waters merely surround the vessel from without.

Moses looked at reality from the higher, Divine perspective. He felt that an overall change in a person's attitude would affect all aspects of their life, down to the minutest details; therefore, purification from ritual defilement should be sufficient. Eleazar, however, inherited the outlook of his father, Aaron. Looking at reality from the earthly perspective, he knew that sweeping, overall changes are not enough; we must work on the details as well.

Similarly, our inner Moses might tell us that it is enough to correct the past by making sweeping, general resolutions. We must therefore also make sure to listen to our inner Aaron or Eleazar in order to ensure that we take all the necessary steps to purify ourselves of crippling negativity.[3]

3. *Likutei Sichot*, vol. 8, pp. 184–185.

FOURTH READING
Numbers 31:25–41

G-d then instructed Moses to count the people and animals that had been captured from the Midianites. The soldiers were allowed to keep half and the other half was to be given to the rest of the Jewish people. The soldiers then had to give ⅟₅₀₀th of their half to the priests, and the people had to give ⅟₅₀th of their half to the Levites. Moses followed G-d's instructions, counting the captured people and animals and then dividing them up and giving the priests and Levites their portions.

Divine Assistance

וַיְהִי הַמַּלְקוֹחַ וגו': (במדבר לא, לב)

The plunder consisted of....

When the soldiers counted the captured people and animals, they found that miraculously, the totals were all divisible by 50 and by 500. It was thus possible for them to follow G-d's instructions regarding the exact percentages of what they had captured to be given to the priests and Levites. This was all the more remarkable considering all the factors that had to contribute to this miracle – such as the fertility and lifespan of the people and animals – all of which took place long before they were captured in battle.

From this, we learn that we should never be fazed by any seeming obstacle in fulfilling G-d's directives or accomplishing our Divine mission. Rather, we should recall that G-d has arranged matters long in advance to enable us to accomplish our Divine goals in the most optimal manner possible.[4]

4. *Likutei Sichot*, vol. 13, p. 113.

FIFTH READING
Numbers 31:42–54

The officers of the army counted the soldiers in their charge, and found that miraculously, not even one was missing.

The War Against Hatred

וְלֹא נִפְקַד מִמֶּנּוּ אִישׁ: (במדבר לא, מט)

**[The officers said to Moses,] "Not one
man is missing from us."**

The war against Midian was a war against baseless hatred and strife. G-d commands us to wage this war constantly, in order that hatred, discord, and spite be replaced by loving-kindness, concord, and altruism. Besides the obvious benefits for us as individuals and as a society, G-d "benefits" from this struggle as well. As the Talmudic sage Rabbi Akiva said, brotherly love is the foundation of the entire Torah.

G-d assures us that in our ongoing war against hatred – just as was the case with the original war against Midian – we will ultimately not suffer any losses: physical, spiritual, or even financial.[5]

5. *Hitva'aduyot 5744*, vol. 4, pp. 2237–2238.

SIXTH READING
Numbers 32:1–19

Noticing that the territory of Kings Sichon and Og were suited to grazing their large herds and flocks, the tribes of Reuben and Gad asked Moses if they could take possession of these territories and not cross the Jordan River into Canaan. Moses rebuked them for trying to avoid battling the nations then occupying Canaan. The tribes of Reuben and Gad then promised to help the other tribes conquer their territories on the west bank of the Jordan River before settling themselves on its east bank.

Moderating Asceticism

וּמִקְנֶה רַב הָיָה לִבְנֵי רְאוּבֵן וְלִבְנֵי גָד עָצוּם מְאֹד וגו': (במדבר לב, א)

**The descendants of Reuben and Gad
had an abundance of livestock.**

These two tribes wanted to live as shepherds because this occupation is conducive to a meditative lifestyle. Moses initially opposed their proposal, since he knew that until the Messianic Era, it is G‑d's intention that we confront the physical world – and even combat it when necessary – in order to refine it and elevate it. Moses only agreed after stipulating that they first help their brethren conquer the Land of Israel. The experience of confronting the material world would ensure that their subsequent return to shepherding would not be an escape from reality.

Similarly, we should not view the time we are forced to spend in the mundane world, elevating and refining it, as an annoying nuisance. Rather, we should view it firstly as our true Divine mission, and secondly, as the key to ensuring that we study the Torah, pray, and perform G-d's commandments with pure and proper intentions.[6]

6. *Reshimot* 51; *Likutei Sichot*, vol. 33, p. 198.

SEVENTH READING
Numbers 32:20–42

Moses agreed to the proposal of the tribes of Reuben and Gad, and also settled half of the tribe of Manasseh on the east bank of the Jordan River.

Living in the Future

וַיִּתֵּן לָהֶם מֹשֶׁה ... וְלַחֲצִי שֵׁבֶט מְנַשֶּׁה ... וְאֶת
מַמְלֶכֶת עוֹג מֶלֶךְ הַבָּשָׁן וְגוֹ': (במדבר לב, לג)

Moses gave ... half of the tribe of Manasseh ... the [former] kingdom of Og, king of Bashan.

In order to ensure that the tribes of Reuben and Gad would retain the proper perspective when they settled on the east bank of the Jordan River, Moses settled half of the tribe of Manasseh there, as well. The tribe of Manasseh was known for its love of the Land of Israel – i.e., its dedication to refining the material world, which was to be accomplished first and foremost in the Land of Israel. Furthermore, by settling half of this tribe on the west side of the Jordan and half of it on the east side, Moses demonstrated that the tribe was not settling on the east bank of the Jordan in order to shirk its responsibility toward its mission on the west bank. Finally, Joseph had named his son – the original founder of this tribe – Manasseh, after his desire not to forget that living outside the land of Israel is not the Jew's natural habitat.

From all of this, we learn that the way to bring the world to its ideal state – the Messianic future – is by fully embracing the challenge of elevating and refining the world, for this is the ultimate goal of the Redemption.[7]

7. *Likutei Sichot*, vol. 28, pp. 210–215.

Mas'ei

Journeys

Numbers 33:1–36:13

THE TENTH AND LAST SECTION OF THE BOOK OF NUMBERS
begins by reviewing the journeys (*Mas'ei,* in Hebrew) of the Jewish people from Egypt until the threshold of the Land of Israel. It
continues with G-d's instructions regarding the Jews' imminent
entry and conquest of the land.

FIRST READING
Numbers 33:1–49

Having concluded its account of the Jewish people's conquests on the east bank of the Jordan River, the Torah reviews all the stops the people made from when they left Egypt until their final camp in the desert.

Life's Journeys

אֵלֶּה מַסְעֵי וגו': (במדבר לג, א)

These are the journeys....

The founder of Chasidism, Rabbi Yisrael Ba'al Shem Tov, taught that these 42 journeys correspond to the 42 spiritual journeys that we make throughout our lives. We begin from birth, just as the Exodus from Egypt is the Jewish people's national birth. The final journey is to the spiritual Promised Land, the life that awaits us in the afterlife.

Although some of the intervening journeys in the Jewish people's trek through the desert were accompanied by setbacks, all the stations on our spiritual journey through life are meant to be holy and positive. If we choose good over evil, we will indeed live through these phases of life in the way G-d intends. If, like the Jewish people in the desert, we make some wrong choices, we will experience them as temporary setbacks. Although at every step in the journey of life, we strive to make the right choices, we should also recognize that even setbacks can be transformed into positive, growth experiences.[1]

1. *Likutei Sichot*, vol. 4, p. 1083.

SECOND READING
Numbers 33:50–53

G-d then informed the Jewish people that in order to conquer the Land of Israel successfully, they must cross the Jordan River with the intention to drive out the idolatrous nations from the land.

Destroying the Idols Within

וְאִבַּדְתֶּם אֵת כָּל מַשְׂכִּיֹּתָם וְאֵת כָּל צַלְמֵי מַסֵּכֹתָם
תְּאַבֵּדוּ וְאֵת כָּל בָּמוֹתָם תַּשְׁמִידוּ: (במדבר לג, נב)

[G-d instructed Moses to tell the Jewish people:] "You must destroy all [the idolaters'] temples, destroy their molten idols, and demolish their [sacrificial] platforms."

The Hebrew term for "idolatry" (*avodah zarah*) literally means "foreign worship." Thus, any type of worship, any type of servitude that is "foreign" to the Divine side of our personalities is a subtle form of idolatry. The object of our foreign worship can be anything from money, success, control, and celebrity to more "innocent" idols, such as security, wisdom, or health. Any object or goal to which we devote ourselves not intending for it to help us accomplish our Divine mission qualifies as "foreign worship."

For our own good, G-d desires our undivided loyalty. He wants to spare us the pain and trauma of trying to serve multiple masters. When we learn to orient even our most mundane activities toward Divinity, so that every part of our lives becomes part of our Divine mission, we can live free of the inner conflicts that unfortunately take their toll on the spiritual and mental health of too many people. It is therefore crucial that we become spiritual warriors, rooting out and destroying our inner idols, in order to enter the "Promised Land" of wholesome, Divinely-oriented living.[2]

2. *Hitva'aduyot 5719*, vol. 2, pp. 116–117; *Likutei Sichot*, vol. 1, p. 190; ibid., vol. 30, p. 158; etc.

THIRD READING
Numbers 33:54–34:15

Since there are many commandments that are to be observed only within the Land of Israel, G-d then described its exact boundaries.

Seizing the Day

זֹאת הָאָרֶץ אֲשֶׁר תִּפֹּל לָכֶם בְּנַחֲלָה וגו': (במדבר לד, ב)

This is the land that will fall to you [by lot] as an inheritance.

The use of the verb "to fall" (*tipol*) to describe how the Land of Israel becomes ours teaches us an important lesson.

The fact that we are obligated to perform certain commandments only within the Land of Israel alludes to the fact that we can perform G-d's commandments and elevate material reality only during our physical lifetime. We do not have this opportunity before and after our souls are within our bodies, even though our souls are alive before birth and live on after death.

Relative to the idyllic existence that our souls enjoy in their heavenly abode before birth, the difficult and challenging lives we must lead in the physical world can indeed seem to be a "fall" from a former height. But by utilizing all our powers to capitalize on the unique opportunity that is ours only in this world, we help G-d achieve His purpose in Creation, fulfill the purpose of our existence, and also vastly enhance our ability to absorb the Divine revelations that await us in the afterlife.[3]

3. *Likutei Sichot*, vol. 13, pp. 126–127; *Tanya*, chapter 37 (48b).

FOURTH READING

Numbers 34:16–29

G-d then specified the names of the tribal leaders who would assume ownership of their respective territories on behalf of their tribes, and then divide the Land of Israel to their tribes' individual members.

When the Shoe Fits

אֵלֶּה שְׁמוֹת הָאֲנָשִׁים אֲשֶׁר יִנְחֲלוּ לָכֶם אֶת הָאָרֶץ וגו': (במדבר לד, יז)

[G-d instructed Moses to tell the Jewish people,] "These are the names of the men who will inherit the land on your behalf."

We are all leaders, whether in our families, in our circle of friends, or among our work associates. In our roles as leaders, we must follow the example of the tribal leaders of the Jewish people. Just as they assigned every member of their tribe a tract of land appropriate to that individual's needs and abilities, we should make sure that our "followers" are employed in the best way possible, both for themselves and for the group. We also learn *how* to do this from the tribal leaders: Just as they assumed ownership of their respective territories on behalf of their fellow Jews, so should we put ourselves mentally in the place of each and every one of our followers in order to appreciate each one's unique personality and strengths.

The true and ultimate leader, of course, is G-d Himself. It follows that when G-d assigns each of us our task in life, He does so in accordance with our unique strengths, gifts, and talents. Therefore, should we ever wish that our specific challenges in life were different than what they are, we should recall that G-d gave us these challenges, tailoring them precisely to our abilities and in accordance with our best long-term interests.[4]

---

4. *Likutei Sichot*, vol. 33, p. 205.

FIFTH READING
Numbers 35:1–8

G-d then instructed Moses and the Jewish people to set aside 48 cities for the Levites, who would not receive any agricultural territory in the Land of Israel. The Levite cities served also as "cities of refuge." When someone committed an unintentional act of murder, the relatives of the victim were allowed to kill the murderer unless he had fled to one of these specially designated cities.

Ambassadors of Love

וְאֵת הֶעָרִים אֲשֶׁר תִּתְּנוּ לַלְוִיִּם אֵת שֵׁשׁ עָרֵי הַמִּקְלָט וְגוֹ': (במדבר לה, ו)

[G-d instructed Moses,] "The cities you must give the Levites must [include] the six cities of refuge."

The reason why Levite cities served also as cities of refuge was because the Levites' lives were the antithesis of unintentional murder. The murderer's confinement to these cities therefore served to neutralize the effect of his crime.

Unintentional murderers were liable to the death penalty only if the murder was the result of their negligence. Negligence that can result in another person's death is a blatant disregard for other people's welfare. This insensitivity toward other people is diametrically opposed to the ideals of brotherhood exemplified by the Levites. The Levites' role is to connect the Jewish people with G-d – through the Tabernacle (and Temple) service – and to connect them with one another, by teaching them the Torah.

Similarly, all of us can learn from and emulate the Levites. We should all strive to enhance our own connection to our fellow human beings, their connection to each other, and their connection to G-d, so that we always take care to ensure that no physical or spiritual harm come to another person.[5]

5. *Likutei Sichot*, vol. 25, pp. 97–98.

SIXTH READING

Numbers 35:9–34

G-d then instructed Moses and the Jewish people to designate, among the 48 Levite cities, six specific cities of refuge for people who would commit unintentional murder.

Signs From Above

וְהִקְרִיתֶם לָכֶם עָרִים עָרֵי מִקְלָט תִּהְיֶינָה לָכֶם וגו': (במדבר לה, יא)

[G-d instructed Moses to tell the Jewish people,] "You must designate [six] cities for yourselves that will act as cities of refuge."

The roads leading to the cities of refuge had to be kept wide and clear, so that anyone who would need to use them could do so easily. Signs were also posted at every crossroads, in order to clearly mark the way to these cities of refuge.

Similarly, G-d keeps the way to the lifestyle of the Torah (our spiritual "city of refuge") open, accessible, and clear for each of us. In addition, He sends us signs and signals to help us find the right direction in life.

In order to hear G-d's voice more clearly, however, we should help others find the right direction in *their* lives. We should all consider ourselves "signposts," whose job it is to point others in the direction of life and goodness. When G-d sees that we are showing others the way, He will show us our way more clearly.

Ideally, we should try to be more than just inanimate "signposts," helping only those who come to us in search of the right way. We can be *living* signposts, reaching out to our fellow human beings and, if necessary, awakening them to the fact that a holy, Divine life should be their highest pursuit.[6]

6. *Likutei Sichot*, vol. 2, pp. 363 ff.

SEVENTH READING

Numbers 36:1–13

G-d then concluded giving the laws of land inheritance.

No One is Isolated

אִישׁ בְּנַחֲלַת מַטֵּה אֲבֹתָיו יִדְבְּקוּ וְגוֹ': (במדבר לו, ז)

[**G-d told Moses,**] "**Each person . . . will remain attached to the inheritance of his fathers' tribe.**"

The laws of inheritance, although an integral part of the Torah, were only given by G-d after five adult, unmarried and orphaned sisters – the only children of a member of the tribe of Manasseh – claimed that they were entitled to their father's portion of the Land of Israel. Their private petition to Moses led to the revelation of sections of the Torah that subsequently became binding on the Jewish people as a whole.

This teaches us that we should never think that our private lives concern only us or our immediate circles of family or friends, and that therefore we are free to conduct ourselves in these matters however we see fit. Just as these women consulted with Moses regarding what appeared to be a purely personal matter, so should we consult with qualified rabbinic authorities regarding even the most seemingly insignificant aspects of life, for even our private actions have wider implications that we may not immediately foresee.[7]

7. *Hitva'aduyot 5747*, vol. 4, pp. 152–153.

DEUTERONOMY

Devarim

Constructive Rebuke

Deuteronomy 1:1–3:22

THE BOOK OF DEUTERONOMY, THE FIFTH AND FINAL BOOK of the Torah, is devoted chiefly to Moses' farewell addresses, which he delivered to the Jewish people shortly before his death and their entry into the Land of Israel. The first section of the book records his words (*Devarim*, in Hebrew) of rebuke to the Jewish people over various incidents that took place during their 40 years of wandering in the desert, and the lessons they must learn from their mistakes.

FIRST READING

Deuteronomy 1:1–11

Moses waited until he was about to die before admonishing the Jewish people. One reason for this was that he wanted to wait until he had defeated the Amorite kings.

The Gift of Rebuke

אַחֲרֵי הַכֹּתוֹ אֵת סִיחֹן מֶלֶךְ הָאֱמֹרִי . . . וְאֵת עוֹג מֶלֶךְ הַבָּשָׁן וְגוֹ': (דברים א, ד)

[Moses rebuked the Jewish people] after he had smitten Sichon, king of the Amorites ... and Og, king of Bashan.

People accept rebuke more readily after having received some material benefit from the person giving the rebuke. By rebuking someone, we are doing them a spiritual favor, so by preceding this spiritual favor with a material favor, we ensure that both parties relate to the rebuke in the proper light – rather than considering it an act of ill will.

By his example, Moses showed us that this principle applies even when the individual or group is in need of rebuke for a sin as grave as that of making the Golden Calf. From Moses' example, we learn that we should extend others our fullest help – both material and spiritual – in order to put them back on the proper path in life.

By helping others in this way, we earn G-d's help in finding our own proper path in life, as well as His assistance in providing for the material needs of ourselves and our loved ones.[1]

---

1. *Likutei Sichot,* vol. 1, pp. 133–134; *Sichot Kodesh 5737,* vol. 1, pp. 155–161, pp. 367–369.

SECOND READING
Deuteronomy 1:12–21

Moses reminded the Jewish people that when they were at Mount
Sinai, G-d instructed him to share the responsibility of resolving
their lawsuits with a system of judges. The people readily accepted
this plan, but not for the right reasons: they hoped to be able to
influence the rulings of judges of lesser moral caliber than Moses.

The Load Always Fits the Camel

אֵיכָה אֶשָּׂא לְבַדִּי טָרְחֲכֶם וּמַשַּׂאֲכֶם וְרִיבְכֶם: (דברים א, יב)

**[Moses told the Jewish people at Mount
Sinai,] "How can I bear your trouble, your
burden, and your strife all by myself?"**

We are all charged with the same mission as Moses: to educate
and lead ourselves – as well as those over whom we have influence – in the ways of the Torah. If we wonder how we can bear
such a heavy responsibility, we should recall that when Moses
asked G-d the same question, G-d immediately provided him
with a practical solution. Just as G-d gave Moses the means to
fulfill his mission, G-d gives us the means and resources to fulfill
our Divine mission, regardless of how difficult or overwhelming
our responsibilities may appear to be.[2]

2. *Sichot Kodesh 5741*, vol. 4, pp. 325–326.

THIRD READING

Deuteronomy 1:22–38

Moses then reminded the Jewish people how they reacted to the scouts' report after they had spied out the Land of Israel, accusing G-d of exhibiting ill will toward them.

G-d Only Loves

וַתֵּרָגְנוּ בְאָהֳלֵיכֶם וַתֹּאמְרוּ בְּשִׂנְאַת ה' אֹתָנוּ
הוֹצִיאָנוּ מֵאֶרֶץ מִצְרָיִם וְגו': (דברים א, כז)

[**Moses said to the Jewish people,**] "**You slandered G-d in your tents, saying 'G-d took us out of Egypt out of His hatred of us.'**"

Until the Final Redemption, when there will no longer be any obstacles impeding the full revelation of G-d's goodness, opportunities will unfortunately remain to mistake G-d's love for us for cruelty. Our challenge, until the Messianic Era, is to remain fully aware that G-d is at all times manifesting His love for us, even if it occasionally appears exactly the opposite. Remaining conscious of this love will inspire us to reciprocate it by fulfilling His will to our utmost ability. This, in turn, will eliminate the last remaining impediments to the Final Redemption.[3]

---

3. *Likutei Sichot*, vol. 34, p. 23.

FOURTH READING

Deuteronomy 1:39–2:1

Moses then reminded the Jewish people that after they heard of G-d's plan to keep them in the desert for 40 years, some of them organized their own army and attempted to enter the Land of Israel on their own. But because they went against G-d's will and lacked Moses' leadership, the nations who lived near the border of the land repulsed them.

The Path to Redemption

וַתַּמְרוּ אֶת פִּי ה' וַתָּזִדוּ וַתַּעֲלוּ הָהָרָה: (דברים א, מג)

[**Moses told the people,**] "**You rebelled against G-d's command and willfully ascended to the mountain.**"

These Jews had repented from the sin of the spies and now wanted to ascend to the Holy Land. Why was this wrong? We are taught that nothing ever stands in the way of repentance.

The answer is that the Land of Israel could only be conquered with the ark's presence and Moses' leadership. Repentance could erase the sins of the people, but it could not change the procedure necessary to acquire the land. Since these people were unwilling to submit to Moses' leadership and wanted to conquer the land on their own, G-d rejected their initiative.

The same is true in our day. The Torah has prescribed a precise procedure for the Messianic Redemption – as well as for all forms of personal redemption. Any attempt to bypass steps in the redemptive process is doomed to failure. Hastening the Redemption, just like success in any endeavor, is possible only when our approach conforms with G-d's plan. Hence the importance of studying the Torah ourselves (our "ark") and seeking out the guidance of qualified Torah scholars (our "Moses") in all aspects of our lives.[4]

4. *Igrot Kodesh*, vol. 7, p. 280.

FIFTH READING

Deuteronomy 2:2–30

Moses then reminded the Jewish people that when it was time to prepare to conquer the Land of Israel, G-d specified exactly which nations they were allowed to attack and which they were not.

A Taste of the Future

וְנִשְׁמַרְתֶּם מְאֹד: אַל תִּתְגָּרוּ בָם כִּי לֹא אֶתֵּן לָכֶם

מֵאַרְצָם עַד מִדְרַךְ כַּף רָגֶל וגו': (דברים ב, ד-ה)

[G-d instructed Moses,] "Take great care that you not provoke [Edom], for I will not give you any of their land."

Spiritually, the seven Canaanite nations correspond to the seven emotions, while the nations of Edom, Ammon, and Moab – located adjacent to but outside of Canaan – correspond to the three facets of the intellect. The fact that G-d instructed us to conquer the seven Canaanite nations but forbade us to conquer the other three until the Messianic future means that, until then, we can only fully refine our emotions, but not our intellect.

This is because the way to rectify something is by correcting its source. Since our emotions are generally governed by our intellect, we can use our intellect to "teach" ourselves what to love and hate.

Presently, however, no such avenue exists for us to influence our intellect. The intellect is governed by deeply hidden aspects of our personalities that lie beyond the reach of consciousness, and the tools to harness this aspect of ourselves have not yet become completely available to us.

Nonetheless, as we approach the Messianic Era and the light of the future begins to shine, we can "taste" the future through studying the teachings of Chasidism in depth. These teachings tap the higher aspects of our souls; through studying them, we can indeed begin to rectify our intellect as well as our emotions.[5]

---

5. *Ma'amarei Admor HaEmtza'i, Devarim*, vol. 1, p. 1 ff; *Sefer HaSichot 5750*, vol. 2, pp. 547–548; *Sefer HaMa'amarim 5741*, pp.86–90.

SIXTH READING

Deuteronomy 2:31–3:14

Moses then encouraged the Jewish people by reminding them how they delivered a devastating defeat to the two Amorite kings they were allowed to attack.

Unity

לֹא הָיְתָה קִרְיָה אֲשֶׁר שָׂגְבָה מִמֶּנּוּ וְגו': (דברים ב, לו)

[Moses told the Jewish people,] "There was not even one communal city that was too strong for us."

Social unity protects a society from danger. The Amorite kings were aware of this and therefore took steps to unify their subjects against the threat of invasion by the Jewish people.

Nonetheless, a society's ability to achieve unity is limited to the extent to which its members can negate their individual egos in order to submit to a common goal. G-d expects the Jewish people to surrender themselves totally to their Divine mission – and He therefore gives us the ability to do so. Therefore, the unity that the Amorites could achieve could not compare to that of the Jews. As a result, the Jewish people were able to overcome the united front presented by the Amorite cities.

We see here the tremendous power inherent in Jewish unity and the need to foster it to the greatest extent possible – especially since, as we are taught by the sages of the Talmud, our present exile is a result of baseless hatred and disunity among the Jewish people.[6]

6. *Likutei Sichot*, vol. 29, pp. 1–8.

SEVENTH READING

Deuteronomy 3:15–22

Moses then reminded the Jewish people how the tribes of Reuben and Gad had requested the territory that had been conquered on the east bank of the Jordan River. Moses agreed to their request on the provision that they first lead the Jewish troops in the conquest of the Land of Israel to the west of the Jordan River.

The Art of Self-Sacrifice

חֲלוּצִים תַּעַבְרוּ לִפְנֵי אֲחֵיכֶם וגו': (דברים ג, יח)

[Moses told the tribes of Reuben and Gad,] "You must cross over armed before your brothers."

The conquest of the Land of Israel corresponds to our inner conquest of the animalistic side of our personalities in order to ensure that we lead our lives in a G-dly way. The power within us that leads us into this battle – i.e., our inner tribes of Reuben and Gad – is our ability to risk our lives for our principles.

In this battle, it is normally enough for us to recall that we would be willing to lay down our lives for our principles, and that, in essence, any threat to our Divine mission is a direct assault on our principles. Resisting our animal drives then becomes a much simpler matter.

However, when we are confronted with a general challenge to our Jewish lifestyle, we need to summon not only the *recollection* of our willingness to sacrifice everything for our principles, but the willingness *itself*. This is our ability to assert our Jewishness no matter how strong the powers of persuasion, ridicule, or compulsion that opposing forces throw at us. Our inner tribes of Reuben and Gad need to leap forth as a separate "battalion" and wipe out the enemy's threat in one fell swoop.

By utilizing this inner strength, we can hasten the true and final Redemption, both of the Jewish people and of all humanity.[7]

---

7. *Likutei Sichot*, vol. 9, pp. 10–13.

Va'etchanan

The Foundations of Judaism
Deuteronomy 3:23–7:11

THE SECOND SECTION OF THE BOOK OF DEUTERONOMY OPENS
as Moses recalls how he pleaded (*Va'etchanan,* in Hebrew) with
G-d to allow him to enter the Land of Israel. Moses tells the rest of
the Jewish people that they will soon enter the land without him.
Moses then continues to review the Jewish people's 40 years in
the desert, focusing on G-d's giving of the Torah at Mount Sinai.

SUNDAY

FIRST READING
Deuteronomy 3:23–4:4

Moses described G-d's forgiveness of the Jewish people.

True Individuality

וְאַתֶּם הַדְּבֵקִים בַּה' אֱלֹקֵיכֶם חַיִּים כֻּלְּכֶם הַיּוֹם: (דברים ד, ד)

[Moses told the Jewish people that in contrast to the rebels among them, who had died out,] "all of you who are alive today are [lovingly] attached to G-d."

One might think that the more we are devoted to G-d, the more our personal individuality disappears. The Torah teaches us here that the opposite is true: Our true individuality depends directly upon the depth of our attachment to G-d. What we normally mistake for our personality is really our secondary, animalistic side. Since we share the same animal drives with the rest of humanity, the personality born of these drives is, at best, a variation on the common theme by which everyone lives. Thus, the apparent individuality of this aspect of our personality is in fact an illusion.

In contrast, since G-d is infinite, the avenues through which His Divinity can manifest itself through us are also infinite; thus, it is only our Divine personality that makes us truly unique. It follows that the more we allow the animalistic side of our personalities to dissolve as we draw closer to G-d, the more we allow our unique, Divine personalities to shine forth.[1]

1. *Siddur im Dach* 82cd.

SECOND READING

Deuteronomy 4:5–40

Moses then proceeded to describe the revelation of G-d at the Giving of the Torah at Mount Sinai.

Overcoming the Limits of Creation

אַתָּה הָרְאֵתָ לָדַעַת כִּי ה' הוּא הָאֱלֹקִים אֵין עוֹד מִלְבַדּוֹ: (דברים ד, לה)

[**Moses told the Jewish people that at Mount Sinai,**] "**You were shown in order to know that G-d is the only deity. There is nothing other than Him.**"

By revealing His essence, which is beyond Creation, G-d enabled us to transcend the limits of nature, as well. In order to overcome life's challenges and tests, we need only remind ourselves that "there is nothing other than Him," i.e., that nothing can constitute a real obstacle to fulfilling G-d's intentions, since everything, in the final analysis, is part of G-d's essence. Evoking this awareness elevates our Divine consciousness to the level of truly perceiving G-d's essence everywhere. This, in turn, serves to hasten the Messianic Redemption, when "the glory of G-d will be revealed and all flesh will see it together."[2]

2. Isaiah 40:5; *Likutei Sichot*, vol. 24, pp. 36–46.

THIRD READING

Deuteronomy 4:41–49

Moses concluded his first address by reminding the Jewish people that their entry and continued residence in the Land of Israel depends on their loyalty to G-d and His Torah. Moses then designated three cities to the east of the Jordan River as "cities of refuge" for unintentional murderers.

The Torah is our Life

וְנָס אֶל אַחַת מִן הֶעָרִים הָאֵל וָחָי: (דברים ד, מב)

[**Cities of refuge were established so an unintentional murderer**] **might flee to one of these cities in order that he might live.**

Someone who committed murder unintentionally had to remain in his city of refuge. He was not allowed to leave, for by doing so, he would expose himself to the vengeance of his victim's relative, who was legally allowed to kill him. The unintentional murderer was forbidden to leave his city of refuge even to save someone else's life.

Similarly, the Torah is our "city of refuge." Inside the Torah and the lifestyle that G-d prescribes for us, we are spiritually alive; if we venture outside the confines of the Torah's lifestyle, we expose ourselves to the risk of spiritual death.

This is true even if it seems that we can save someone's life by making some compromise in the Torah's directives. The Torah is synonymous with life, so only through loyalty to its principles can we both maintain our own spiritual vitality and preserve or enhance the spiritual vitality of others.[3]

---

3. *Likutei Sichot*, vol. 38, p. 131.

FOURTH READING

Deuteronomy 5:1–18

Moses then reviewed the laws that the Jewish people had received from G-d at Mount Sinai. He began with the Ten Commandments.

Repeating the Ten Commandments

פָּנִים בְּפָנִים דִּבֶּר ה' עִמָּכֶם בָּהָר וגו': (דברים ה, ד)

[Moses told the Jewish people, "When He gave you the Torah,] G-d spoke with you at the mountain face to face."

The first account of the Ten Commandments – in the Book of Exodus – is the "real time" description of how this event occurred. The second account of the Ten Commandments is Moses' description of it, as part of his historical review of the Jewish people's Exodus from Egypt and their trek through the desert.

Reliving the first account of the Giving of the Torah allows us to experience G-d's presence in the Torah as we are studying it. This experience prevents us from forgetting that the study of the Torah is a spiritual encounter between G-d and us and not merely an intellectual pursuit. Hearing the second account of the Ten Commandments, couched as part of Moses' address to the people, enables us to employ our own, human intellect in the study of the Torah, in order to internalize it and absorb its message fully. In this way, the goal of making this world into a home for G-d is achieved.[4]

4. *Sefer HaSichot 5752*, vol. 2, pp. 331–338.

THURSDAY

FIFTH READING
Deuteronomy 5:19–6:3

Moses then described the experience of receiving the Torah on Mount Sinai.

Eternal Revelation

אֶת הַדְּבָרִים הָאֵלֶּה דִּבֶּר ה'... קוֹל גָּדוֹל וְלֹא יָסָף וְגו': (דברים ה, יט)

[Moses told the Jewish people], "G-d spoke these words . . . with a great voice, not pausing [at all]."

One meaning of the expression "not pausing" is that the voice of G-d at Mount Sinai continued – and continues – to be revealed in the prophecies and teachings of the prophets and sages of each generation. The fact that these prophecies and teachings were not explicitly articulated when the Torah was first given is simply because the world and the Jewish people did not yet require them. They were nonetheless implicit in the original revelation of the Torah.[5]

5. *Likutei Sichot,* vol. 4, pp. 1092–1098.

SIXTH READING

Deuteronomy 6:4–25

Moses then told the Jewish people that the proper response to
G-d's self-revelation through the Torah is to fulfill His commandments out of love.

How to Love G-d

וְאָהַבְתָּ אֵת ה' אֱלֹקֶיךָ בְּכָל לְבָבְךָ וְגו': (דברים ו, ה)

**[Moses told the Jewish people that if they
contemplate G-d's presence in their lives,]
"You will love G-d with all your heart."**

If someone loves G-d, he does not need to be told to do so; if
he does not love G-d, telling him to will not change his mind.
Therefore, both the medieval sage Rabbi Moses Maimonides and
the founder of Chasidism, Rabbi Yisrael Ba'al Shem Tov, explain
this verse to be both a commandment and a promise. In the preceding verse – "Hear, Israel: G-d is our G-d; G-d is one" – we are
commanded to contemplate the unity of G-d. If we meditate on
the meaning of this verse deeply enough, we are assured that will
we indeed thereby come to love G-d.[6]

6. *Derech Mitzvotecha* 199b.

SEVENTH READING
Deuteronomy 7:1–11

Moses then encouraged the Jewish people to remain loyal to G-d under all circumstances, even though this would mean that they would have to confront the opposition of nations more numerous and powerful than they were.

Spiritual Atomic Fission

כִּי אַתֶּם הַמְעַט מִכָּל הָעַמִּים: (דברים ז, ז)

[Moses told the Jewish people,] "**For you are the least of all peoples.**"

The Jewish people have almost always been a small minority. This may prompt us to wonder how we can be expected to fulfill our Divine mission. Even if we can survive, how can a tiny minority influence the majority? Moreover, assimilation and war have continued to erode our population, and the demands of modern life leave the rest of us progressively less time for spiritual pursuits and less sensitive to spirituality.

But now that scientists have learned to unleash the power of the atom, the world has learned that size is not always an indication of power. Once we learn how to access its latent energy, even the smallest particle of matter can release incredible force.

The basic process used to release atomic power is nuclear fission, in which the atom is broken down into smaller components. As Jews, this teaches us that the key to releasing our latent, infinite potential is by breaking our egos, thereby allowing our inner, Divine essence to shine through. The better we master this "spiritual technology," the less we need be intimidated by being an apparently insignificant minority or by having only limited time and energy to devote to holy endeavors. Within us lies the power to change the entire world for the good![7]

7. *Hitva'aduyot 5711*, vol. 1, pp. 313–319; *Igrot Kodesh*, vol. 8, p. 168; ibid., vol. 11, p. 422.

Eikev

Appreciation and Love
Deuteronomy 7:12–11:25

IN THE THIRD SECTION OF THE BOOK OF DEUTERONOMY,
Moses continues his second farewell address to the Jewish people. He exhorts them to observe even what appear to be minor
commandments, which a person would be likely to figuratively
trample with his heel (*Eikev*, in Hebrew). He then continues his
review of the events of the Jewish people's 40-year trek in the
desert, emphasizing the lessons they were to learn from them.

FIRST READING
Deuteronomy 7:12–8:10

Moses told the Jewish people that if they would be careful to perform all of G-d's commandments, even the seemingly minor ones, G-d would provide them with all the material means that they would need to fulfill His will.

True Reward

וְהָיָה עֵקֶב תִּשְׁמְעוּן אֵת הַמִּשְׁפָּטִים הָאֵלֶּה
וּשְׁמַרְתֶּם וַעֲשִׂיתֶם אֹתָם וְגוֹ': (דברים ז, יב)

[Moses told the Jewish people,] "If you heed [G-d's] ordinances, safeguard them, and perform them...."

If G-d were to bestow His goodness on us even when we do not deserve it, He would not be doing us any favors. First, we would feel like little children whose parents overlook their infantile behavior because adult behavior cannot be expected of them. Worse yet, it would undermine our belief in Divine justice. We would thus live lives of shame and confusion.

The rewards for observing G-d's commandments are so great that they are out of proportion to the effort required to fulfill them. Nonetheless, for the above-stated reasons, G-d made the bestowal their reward dependent upon our efforts, and the bestowal of their *infinite* reward dependent upon effort that specifically mirrors their infinite, unlimited nature.

Therefore, we must take care to fulfill the seemingly less-important commandments with the same devotion with which we fulfill the seemingly more-important ones. This shows that what matters to us is that G-d wants us to observe these commandments, not our own evaluation of which ones are important. G-d then bestows His goodness upon us beyond the strict dictates of what we have earned.[1]

1. *Likutei Sichot*, vol. 9, pp. 71–75.

SECOND READING

Deuteronomy 8:11–9:3

Moses then warned the Jewish people not to take the goodness that G-d would bestow upon them for granted.

The Source of Our Success

וְאָמַרְתָּ בִּלְבָבֶךָ כֹּחִי וְעֹצֶם יָדִי עָשָׂה לִי אֶת הַחַיִל הַזֶּה: (דברים ח, יז)

[Moses warned the Jewish people, "Take care lest] you say to yourself, 'It is my own strength and the might of my hand that have accumulated this wealth for me.'"

Children often surpass their parents in many ways, even though they inherit their talents and abilities from their parents. The reason that children can manifest capabilities their parents do not seem to possess is because these talents remained dormant in the parents and only became active in their children.

Similarly, G-d calls the Jewish people His "children." He has indeed left it up to us to bring the world to its completion, granting us a measure of power that He has relinquished. Thus, when we accomplish something that helps bring the world closer to its ultimate fulfillment, we might mistakenly ascribe this accomplishment to our own power.

Therefore, the Torah reminds us that just as children owe their superior powers to their parents, from whom they inherited them, so do we owe all our power to accomplish great things in this world exclusively to G-d.[2]

2. *Hitva'aduyot 5743*, vol. 4, pp. 1857–1859.

THIRD READING

Deuteronomy 9:4–29

As an example of G-d's willingness to forgive the Jewish people for their misdeeds, Moses recounted the incident of the Golden Calf.

Assuming the Blame

וָאֶתְפֹּשׂ בִּשְׁנֵי הַלֻּחֹת וָאַשְׁלִכֵם מֵעַל שְׁתֵּי יָדָי וָאֲשַׁבְּרֵם לְעֵינֵיכֶם: (דברים ט, יז)

[**Moses said to the Jewish people, "When I saw that you had made the Golden Calf,**] **I grasped the two tablets and hurled them from my two hands, shattering them before your eyes."**

Moses was already carrying the two tablets, so he had no need to "grasp" them in order to break them. He grasped them as a gesture of ownership; he wanted to acquire them as his own personal property in order to assume the full blame for breaking them.

We see here Moses' selfless devotion to the Jewish people. Not only did he break the tablets in order to "destroy the evidence" of the Jewish people's covenant with G-d that they had just broken. Not only was he willing to give up his life in order that G-d forgive the Jewish people. He even took upon himself the blame for breaking the tablets. And let us recall that Moses had absolutely no part in the incident of the Golden Calf – he was not even "guilty" of not trying to prevent it, since he was not present when it took place!

Moses' example is a lesson for all of us, for we are all leaders. We all are responsible for each other – whether in the circle of the family, of our friends, of our associates, of the Jewish people, or of all humanity. We should be ready and willing to give up whatever necessary – our resources, our reputations, even our lives – in order to ensure the survival of the Jewish people and the furtherance of our Divine mission to transform the world into G-d's true home.[3]

---

3. *Likutei Sichot*, vol. 34, pp. 56–58.

FOURTH READING
Deuteronomy 10:1–11

After Moses shattered the first set of tablets, he pleaded with G-d to forgive the Jewish people. G-d did forgive them, and instructed Moses to prepare two replacement tablets upon which G-d would inscribe the Ten Commandments again.

Living in the Past

וְאֶכְתֹּב עַל הַלֻּחֹת אֶת הַדְּבָרִים אֲשֶׁר הָיוּ עַל הַלֻּחֹת הָרִאשֹׁנִים וגו': (דברים י, ב)

[G-d told Moses,] "I will inscribe on the [second set of] tablets the words that were upon the first tablets...."

Moses shattered the first tablets when he saw that the Jewish people had fashioned the Golden Calf. G-d instructed the Jewish army to keep these shattered tablets in a wooden box and take them with them whenever they went into battle.

Moses broke the tablets when he saw the Golden Calf because at that moment the Torah "flew" out of them and returned to heaven, rendering them two "lifeless" stones. True, they possessed inherent worth due to the fact that G-d Himself had carved them, but they were now nothing compared to what they had become when G-d chiseled the Ten Commandments into them. Thus, the lesson of the shattered tablets is that we should never be satisfied with our inherent worth; we should always strive to fulfill our Divine mission.

The purpose of the Jewish army's battles was to spread Divine consciousness. The shattered tablets that accompanied them into battle reminded them that our inherent spirituality is not enough; we must disseminate Divine consciousness to the world at large.

The same lesson applies today. Rather than being content with our own spiritual achievements, we must continually strive to fulfill our Divine mission to make the world into G-d's home.[4]

4. *Likutei Sichot*, vol. 14, pp. 30–36.

FIFTH READING

Deuteronomy 10:12–11:9

Moses then told the Jewish people that G-d's demands on them are not excessive, and certainly not disproportionate to the great mercy that G-d continues to show them.

Channeling Moses

וְעַתָּה יִשְׂרָאֵל מָה ה' אֱלֹקֶיךָ שֹׁאֵל מֵעִמָּךְ כִּי אִם לְיִרְאָה אֶת ה' אֱלֹקֶיךָ וְגו': (דברים י, יב)

[**Moses said to the Jewish people,**] "**What does G-d demand of you? Only to revere G-d.**"

This "reverence" is the fear that G-d would see us doing something that we would be embarrassed or ashamed to have Him see us do. This constant awareness that we are living in G-d's presence might have been easy for Moses, but how could he assume that it would be easy for the rest of us?

The answer is that indeed, every Jew contains within him a spark of Moses. When we reveal our inner Moses, the fear of G-d does indeed become relatively easy to attain.

The Moses within us is thus our inborn ability to reach profound levels of Divine consciousness. Possessing this inner spark enables us all to contemplate and meditate upon G-d's presence within the world and His being absolutely beyond the world, and thereby awaken ourselves to a profound awareness of His presence. Even though we may not be able to sustain this awareness constantly, the depth of its impression upon us when we contemplate how G-d is both within and beyond the world profoundly makes it relatively "simple" to reawaken this awareness at any time.[5]

5. *Tanya,* chapter 42.

SIXTH READING

Deuteronomy 11:10–21

Moses then told the Jewish people that they should express their love of G-d not only as individuals, but as a community.

Two Ways of Loving G-d

וְהָיָה אִם . . . לְאַהֲבָה אֶת ה' אֱלֹקֵיכֶם וּלְעָבְדוֹ
בְּכָל לְבַבְכֶם וּבְכָל נַפְשְׁכֶם: (דברים יא, יג)

**[Moses told the Jewish people,] "If you love
G-d . . . with all your heart and with all your soul . . ."**

This verse seems to repeat a similar verse in the previous section of the Torah – but in that verse we are told to love G-d "with all your heart, with all your soul, *and with all your might*." Apparently, there are two levels of intensity in loving G-d: one that includes "with all our might" – i.e., constantly rising above what we consider to be rational or even possible – and one that does not.

This is because we are not all the same. Some of us can maintain a constant awareness of G-d's presence in our lives that inspires us to love Him "with all our might," while some of us cannot maintain this awareness constantly.

Nonetheless, even those of us who can serve G-d only "with all our heart and all our soul" on an ongoing basis can still rise to serve Him "with all our might" occasionally. In the Messianic future, we will all be able to sustain this high level of Divine awareness. It is for this reason that both verses – both versions of our love of G-d – have been included in the text of our daily prayers.[6]

6. *Likutei Sichot*, vol. 9, pp. 79–85; *Sefer HaMa'amarim Melukat*, vol. 4, pp. 6–7; ibid., vol. 5, p. 282.

SEVENTH READING

Deuteronomy 11:22–25

Moses promised the Jewish people that if they would keep G-d's commandments, imitate His goodness, and cleave to the sages of the Torah, G-d would enable them to successfully drive out the nations that were occupying the Land of Israel.

Imitating G-d

לָלֶכֶת בְּכָל דְּרָכָיו וְגוֹ': (דברים יא, כב)

[Moses told the Jewish people] to walk in [G-d's] ways.

The sages of the Talmud explain that this phrase means that we are intended to imitate G-d's goodness: "Just as He is merciful, so should you be merciful; just as He performs acts of loving-kindness, so should you perform acts of loving-kindness." But inasmuch as G-d's goodness is infinite, how can we be expected to imitate Him?

The answer is that it is for this very reason that G-d created us in His image. As such, we indeed possess G-d's infinite potential to do good.[7]

7. *Hitva'aduyot 5746*, vol. 2, p. 387.

Re'eih

Devotion to G-d
Deuteronomy 11:26–16:17

THE FOURTH SECTION OF THE BOOK OF DEUTERONOMY CON-
tinues Moses' second farewell address to the Jewish people. Moses
begins by urging the people to see (*Re'eih*, in Hebrew) that G-d
has given them the choice between a life of blessings or one of
curses; the choice is theirs.

FIRST READING
Deuteronomy 11:26–12:10

Moses urged the Jewish people to realize that G-d gives them the choice between good and evil. Their choice will result either in a life of blessings or one of curses.

Seeing and Believing

רְאֵה אָנֹכִי נֹתֵן לִפְנֵיכֶם הַיּוֹם בְּרָכָה וּקְלָלָה: (דברים יא, כו)

[Moses told the Jewish people in G-d's Name,] "See, I set before you today a blessing and a curse."

A Divine curse is actually a blessing that is too great to be revealed within our limited world and must therefore be "disguised" as a curse. Our challenge is to see it in this perspective, rather than falling into the trap of becoming angry with G-d. Thus, pain and negativity exist in order to provide us with free choice. Free choice, in turn, exists in order to enable us to earn the rewards for our choices, so we need not feel unworthy of the blessings that G-d bestows upon us.

When we recognize that evil exists solely to provide us with the free choice to reject it, our struggle with it becomes much easier.[1]

---

1. *Likutei Sichot*, vol. 4, pp. 1339–1342.

SECOND READING

Deuteronomy 12:11–28

Moses instructed the Jewish people to eradicate all traces of idolatry from the Land of Israel. He then instructed them to establish a centralized location for the sacrificial rites (which would eventually become the Temple in the city of Jerusalem). He then informed them that although the blood of the sacrifices is "consumed" by G-d on the Altar, animal blood should not be consumed when they eat meat themselves.

Soul Aspiration

רַק חֲזַק לְבִלְתִּי אֲכֹל הַדָּם וגו': (דברים יב, כג)

[Moses told the Jewish people that when they eat meat, they must] "be resolute not to consume the blood."

Inasmuch as the blood of an animal embodies its vitality, it might seem that consuming blood in order to utilize this vitality for holy purposes would actually be a praiseworthy effort to refine the material world. It is therefore necessary to distinguish between meat and its blood. Meat signifies the material world itself, which we are capable of enjoying in a holy way. Blood, however, signifying the vitality and enthusiasm of life, cannot be *enjoyed* itself, for it is impossible to *enjoy pure enjoyment* in a selfless, holy way.

Thus, blood may be offered up on the Altar as part of a sacrifice, for then it is oriented solely toward holiness. But if it is part of the simple act of eating, oriented merely toward preserving and enhancing the life of the body itself, it must be avoided. We should aspire to become excited and enthusiastic solely about holy matters, rather than about material matters in and of themselves.[2]

2. *Likutei Sichot*, vol. 4, p. 1110; ibid., vol. 14, p. 51.

THIRD READING

Deuteronomy 12:29–13:19

Moses then told the Jewish people that when they are confronted with a challenge to their faith (such as the prosperity of the wicked or of false prophets), they must remember that G-d is testing their loyalty and commitment to Him.

Tests of Faith

כִּי מְנַסֶּה ה' אֱלֹקֵיכֶם אֶתְכֶם לָדַעַת הֲיִשְׁכֶם אֹהֲבִים אֶת
ה' אֱלֹקֵיכֶם בְּכָל לְבַבְכֶם וּבְכָל נַפְשְׁכֶם: (דברים יג, ד)

**[Moses told the Jewish people,] "G-d is testing
you to determine whether you really love G-d
with all your heart and all your soul."**

We are tested when we suffer despite our loyalty to G-d; we assume that if we follow G-d's will, we are entitled to His favor. Voices from both within and without mock our apparently naïve belief.

When G-d's presence is hidden in these situations, it simply means that He wishes to grace us with a closer, more intense relationship with Him. In order to preserve our faith in G-d in the face of situations that test this faith, we have to draw upon deeper levels of commitment than we normally do.

When we pass the test, maintaining our implicit faith in G-d, the suffering disappears, its purpose having been served. Our formerly deep, hidden connection with G-d becomes our new normative consciousness.[3]

3. *Sefer HaMa'amarim 5708*, pp. 94–103; *Likutei Sichot*, vol. 9, pp. 286–287.

FOURTH READING
Deuteronomy 14:1–21

Moses then instructed the Jewish people regarding how they must distinguish themselves from other peoples in order to remain true to their Divine mission. These instructions included the laws regarding bodily mutilation and *kashrut* (i.e., permitted vs. forbidden types of food).

G-d's Only Child

בָּנִים אַתֶּם לַה' אֱלֹקֵיכֶם וְגו': (דברים יד, א)

[Moses told the Jewish people,] "You are the children of G-d."

In the words of Rabbi Yisrael Ba'al Shem Tov, the founder of Chasidism, "Every Jew is as precious to G-d as an only son born to his parents in their old age is to them – and, in fact, even more precious."

G-d created the world for the sake of the Jewish people, having charged them with the mission of transforming it into His home. This challenge is not only the mission of the Jewish people as a whole but of each individual Jew. Therefore, we should all live our lives as if the entire world were created for each of us individually, and awaits our unique contributions to its destiny.[4]

---

4. *Likutei Sichot*, vol. 3, p. 982.

FIFTH READING
Deuteronomy 14:22–29

Moses then taught the Jewish people that after they settle the Land of Israel and begin working the land, G-d has obligated them to bring a tenth of their oil, wine, and grain to the Temple-city and consume it there. This ensured that the people would regularly visit Jerusalem (which was chosen to be the Temple-city) in order to renew their spiritual inspiration.

Charity and Wealth

עַשֵׂר תְּעַשֵׂר אֵת כָּל תְּבוּאַת זַרְעֶךָ הַיֹּצֵא הַשָּׂדֶה שָׁנָה שָׁנָה: (דברים יד, כב)

[Moses told the Jewish people,] "You must tithe all the produce of the seed that the field yields year by year."

This verse includes the instruction to donate a portion of our income to charity. The Talmudic sages pointed out that the similarity of the Hebrew words for "tithe" (*ta'aseir*) and "become rich" (*titasheir*) alludes to the fact that G-d rewards those who give charity with abundant wealth.

Furthermore, when we resolve to give charity beyond our means, G-d grants us the wealth that is required in order for us to give the charity we have resolved to donate.[5]

5. *Igrot Kodesh*, vol. 14, p. 211.

SIXTH READING

Deuteronomy 15:1–18

Moses then taught the Jewish people the law that the sabbatical year cancels loans. He then warned them not to let this fact prevent them from loaning money. Moses then taught the Jewish people that when they dismiss their servants, they must give them a gift. In both cases, they should not worry about the expense, since G-d will provide them with the means to follow His laws.

Work

וּבֵרַכְךָ ה' אֱלֹקֶיךָ בְּכֹל אֲשֶׁר תַּעֲשֶׂה: (דברים טו, יח)

[Moses told the Jewish people,] "G-d will bless you in all that you do."

Although G-d determines how well we will succeed in our efforts to earn a livelihood, we must not rely solely on His providence, but must put forth reasonable efforts to earn our living.

By the same token, however, we must keep in mind that our efforts are not the *direct* cause of our material success; they are only a receptacle to contain G-d's blessing. In this context, our main concern should be with making ourselves worthy of receiving G-d's blessing.[6]

---

6. *Likutei Sichot*, vol. 31, pp. 172–173; *Ma'amarei Admor HaZaken 5565*, vol. 2, pp. 648 ff; *Ma'amarei Admor HaZaken 5568*, vol. 1, pp. 165 ff; *Derech Mitzvotecha* 106a–108a; *Kuntres Umayan* 17 ff; *Sefer HaMa'amarim 5657*, pp. 56 ff.

FRIDAY

SEVENTH READING
Deuteronomy 15:19–16:17

Moses then reviewed with the Jewish people the laws of the three "pilgrim" festivals – Passover, *Shavu'ot*, and *Sukot* – which they were required to celebrate in the Temple-city.

Celebrating Life

וְשָׂמַחְתָּ בְּחַגֶּךָ וְגו': (דברים טז, יד)

[Moses told the Jewish people,] "You must rejoice in your festival."

Rabbi Shneur Zalman of Liadi, the founder of Chabad Chasidism, interpreted this phrase as follows:

"You should internalize the inner message of the festivals. This will infuse joy into your observance of the festivals; they will become your own, personal celebrations."[7]

7. *Sefer HaSichot 5704*, p. 82.

Shofetim

Leaders
Deuteronomy 16:18–21:9

THE FIFTH SECTION OF THE BOOK OF DEUTERONOMY CON-
tinues Moses' second farewell address to the Jewish people. It
opens as Moses instructs the Jewish people to appoint judges
(*Shofetim*, in Hebrew) throughout the Land of Israel to try cases
and uphold the law. It continues with Moses' instructions regarding the other leaders of the Jewish people: the king, the priests,
and the prophets.

FIRST READING

Deuteronomy 16:18–17:13

Moses instructed the Jewish people to appoint judges and sheriffs throughout the Land of Israel to try cases and uphold the law.

Personal Judges and Sheriffs

שֹׁפְטִים וְשֹׁטְרִים תִּתֶּן לְךָ בְּכָל שְׁעָרֶיךָ וְגו': (דברים טז, יח)

[Moses instructed the Jewish people,] **"You must appoint judges and sheriffs for yourself in all your cities."**

The Hebrew word for "cities" used here (*she'arecha*) literally means "gates." The "gates" of our bodies are our ears, eyes, nose, and mouth, through which stimuli from the external world enter our bodies and our personal world. This verse thus requires us to station "judges and sheriffs" to guard these "gates" against the intrusion of any stimuli that could be harmful to our spiritual health. Through studying the Torah, we learn which influences are beneficial (and therefore permitted) and which are harmful (and therefore forbidden). The job of the "sheriff" is to enforce the decisions rendered by the judge. Our inner "sheriffs" are the techniques that each of us needs to cultivate in order to combat the voices within us that oppose the decisions of our inner "judges."

Thus, regarding the Messianic future, G-d only promises to "restore your judges as in former times," but not the sheriffs. In the Messianic future, negativity will not hold sway over us, so there will be no need for protective measures to ensure that we follow G-d's will.[1]

1. *Likutei Sichot*, vol. 34, pp. 104–105, vol. 14, pp. 277–279, vol. 24, pp. 441–442.

SECOND READING

Deuteronomy 17:14–20

In addition to a system of judges and sheriffs, Moses instructed the Jewish people to appoint a king over them.

The Personal King

שׂוֹם תָּשִׂים עָלֶיךָ מֶלֶךְ אֲשֶׁר יִבְחַר ה' אֱלֹקֶיךָ בּוֹ וגו': (דברים יז, טו)

[Moses told the Jewish people,] "You may indeed appoint a king over yourself, whom G-d chooses."

Although the Jewish people have not had a king since the destruction of the first Temple and will not have another until the Messiah himself, we are still enjoined to appoint a higher authority over ourselves, both individually and collectively, wherever relevant. The sages therefore say to each one of us: "Provide yourself with a teacher [of Torah]," with whom we should consult on all matters of spiritual life.

We should not delude ourselves into thinking that we can rely on our own "judges and sheriffs." Nor should we think that there is no one capable of understanding us sufficiently to serve as our "king." The Torah assures us that if we search properly and diligently, we will indeed find the mentors best suited to our spiritual needs.[2]

2. *Likutei Sichot*, vol. 24, pp. 104–106. See below, on 31:11.

THIRD READING

Deuteronomy 18:1–5

Moses then instructed the Jewish people to honor the priests, taking care to give them their allotments from their produce and flocks.

Cultivating the Inner Priest

וְזֶה יִהְיֶה מִשְׁפַּט הַכֹּהֲנִים מֵאֵת הָעָם מֵאֵת זֹבְחֵי הַזֶּבַח אִם שׁוֹר
אִם שֶׂה וְנָתַן לַכֹּהֵן הַזְּרֹעַ וְהַלְּחָיַיִם וְהַקֵּבָה: (דברים יח, ג)

[Moses told the Jewish people,] "The following must
be the priests' entitlement from the [lay] people,
from those who slaughter an ox, a sheep, [or a goat]:
the shoulder, the cheeks, and the stomach."

The priests were allotted these specific parts of our animals in honor of Pinechas, Aaron's grandson. Pinechas used his *cheeks* to pray for G-d's help when he used his *shoulder* to drive his sword through the *stomachs* of those who were defying G-d.

Inasmuch as the Jewish people are all a "kingdom of priests and a holy nation," we are all meant to learn from Pinechas' example. When forces within us or outside us oppose the continued progress of the world toward its Divine goal, we must summon our inner Pinechas in order to overwhelm our own stubbornness or the stubbornness of others with the sheer power of holiness.[3]

---

3. *Sichot Kodesh 5736*, vol. 2, p. 237.

FOURTH READING
Deuteronomy 18:6–13

Moses then encouraged the Jewish people to turn only to G-d for all their needs, and not to seek ways to foretell the future.

Trusting in G-d

תָּמִים תִּהְיֶה עִם ה' אֱלֹקֶיךָ: (דברים יח, יג)

[Moses told the Jewish people, "Rather than trying to divine the future,] be wholehearted with G-d."

When we are connected to G-d, we are not subject to any form of predestination. We should therefore never be concerned with predicting the future, with freeing ourselves from the "spells" of any real or imagined forces, or with dealing with the possible influence of previous incarnations on our lives.

The surest way of ensuring our happiness and success in life is by devoting ourselves wholeheartedly to learning what G-d expects of us (by studying His Torah), by addressing our prayers directly to Him, and by fulfilling His will.[4]

---

4. *Igrot Kodesh*, vol. 18, p. 205.

FIFTH READING

Deuteronomy 18:14–19:13

Moses then warned the Jewish people not to listen to false prophets, and reviewed the laws of Cities of Refuge. When someone commits an accidental murder, this stroke of Divine providence indicates that the accidental murderer needs to be exiled to one of these cities in order to cure himself of some inner defect that would otherwise go unrectified. The victim's close relatives are allowed to kill the accidental murderer unless he has fled to one of these specially designated as asylum cities.

Temporary and Ultimate Refuge

שָׁלוֹשׁ עָרִים תַּבְדִּיל לָךְ וְגוֹ': (דברים יט, ב)

[Moses told the Jewish people,] "You must designate three cities for yourself."

Allegorically, the relative who seeks to avenge the victim's blood is our own evil inclination. It attempts to "kill us," i.e., to trick us into sinning, thereby causing us to suffer some form of spiritual "death," i.e., a loss of vitality in our spiritual life. The Messianic Redemption will be our ultimate refuge from this pursuer, for the evil inclination will be nullified in the Messianic future. Similarly, the future resumption of the Temple service will afford all who need it the opportunity to complete their atonement.

In the meantime, the study of the Torah is our refuge from our evil inclination, for the holiness of the Torah has the power to neutralize the effect of evil on us.[5]

---

5. *Likutei Sichot*, vol. 34, pp. 121–122.

SIXTH READING
Deuteronomy 19:14–20:9

Moses then taught the Jewish people the laws of legal testimony and perjury.

G-d's True Witnesses

עַל פִּי שְׁנֵי עֵדִים אוֹ עַל פִּי שְׁלֹשָׁה עֵדִים יָקוּם דָּבָר: (דברים יט, טו)

[Moses told the Jewish people, "In any court case,] the matter [of a defendant's innocence or guilt] must be confirmed by the testimony of [at least] two witnesses."

It is the Torah's position that creation itself testifies to the *existence* of the Creator, as well as to the fact that His *power* lies beyond our ability to comprehend. However, the notion that G-d's *essence* is not only beyond our ability to understand but beyond our ability to conceive does not follow from examining the world; this truth must be established by "external" witnesses.

The witnesses to the inconceivable nature of G-d's essence are the Jewish people. By studying the Torah and performing G-d's commandments, the Jewish people introduce the world to the ineffability of G-d's *essence*, paradoxically accomplishing the categorically impossible feat of expressing what is by nature inexpressible.[6]

6. *Likutei Sichot*, vol. 19, pp. 188–196.

SHABBAT

Moses then began to instruct the Jewish people regarding how they were to conduct their conquest of the Land of Israel.

Becoming a Fruit-Bearing Tree

כִּי תָצוּר אֶל עִיר . . . לֹא תַשְׁחִית אֶת עֵצָה וְגוֹ': (דברים כ, יט)

[Moses told the Jewish people,] "If you besiege a city … you must not destroy its [fruit] trees."

Our emotions are the measure of our maturity. Many people are gifted with superior intelligence or talent, but truly refined emotions are achieved by shedding childlike self-absorption and by contributing to the world. Similarly, fruit-bearing trees provide us with nourishment and delight at their own expense. In contrast, barren trees merely impress us with their stately presence; they may perhaps offer us shade, but they sacrifice nothing in so doing.

Therefore, when we seek instruction and inspiration, we should turn to people who are not only intelligent and talented, but who consistently utilize their gifts for the world's greater good. And of course, we should emulate the example of the fruit tree ourselves.[7]

---

7. *Likutei Sichot*, vol. 4, pp. 1114–1119; ibid., vol. 24, pp. 115–120.

Teitzei

Expanding Divine Consciousness
Deuteronomy 21:10–25:19

THE SIXTH SECTION OF THE BOOK OF DEUTERONOMY CON-
tinues Moses' second farewell address to the Jewish people. Moses
continues to review many aspects of Jewish law, beginning with
the laws governing the behavior of Jewish soldiers when they go
out (*Teitzei*, in Hebrew) to war.

FIRST READING
Deuteronomy 21:10–21

Moses told the Jewish people that after they conquer the Land of Israel from its occupiers, they would be allowed, if necessary, to attack neighboring countries that posed a threat to their security.

The War Against Evil

כִּי תֵצֵא לַמִּלְחָמָה עַל אֹיְבֶיךָ וּנְתָנוֹ ה' אֱלֹקֶיךָ בְּיָדֶךָ וְשָׁבִיתָ שִׁבְיוֹ: (דברים כא, י)

[Moses told the Jewish people,] "If you go out to war upon your enemies, G-d will deliver [your enemy] into your hands, and you will take [back your enemy's] captives."

When we contend with evil, we are "going *out* to war." We are "going out" of our true selves, for waging war is unnatural. Our soul's native environment is the peaceful, infinite Divine consciousness it experienced before it entered the body.

Since our souls originate in G-d's essence, and evil has no power against G-d's essence, we have the upper hand over evil even before the battle has begun. We are "*upon*" – i.e., above – our enemies. In addition, G-d only created evil in the first place in order for us to vanquish it. For both these reasons, the Torah goes on to assure us that "G-d will deliver [your enemy] into your hands."

The Torah thus teaches us that in order to win the war against evil, we must identify with our Divine soul. We are then backed by the full power of G-d's holiness.[1]

---

1. *Sefer HaSichot 5749*, vol. 2, pp. 677 ff.

SECOND READING
Deuteronomy 21:22–22:7

Moses then reviewed with the Jewish people the laws regarding inheritance, parental responsibility for their children's behavior, returning lost items, helping others, and cross-dressing.

True Gender Equality

לֹא יִהְיֶה כְלִי גֶבֶר עַל אִשָּׁה וְלֹא יִלְבַּשׁ גֶּבֶר שִׂמְלַת אִשָּׁה וְגו': (דברים כב, ה)

[**Moses told the Jewish people,**] "**A man's attire must not be worn by a woman; a man must not wear a women's garment.**"

This directive implies that men should strive to actualize all their G-d-given potential as *men*, and women should strive to actualize all their G-d-given potential as *women*, in accordance with the Torah's guidelines for self-refinement. Although we all comprise male and female qualities, our biological gender clearly indicates which qualities we are meant to chiefly manifest.

Manifesting our G-d-given potential – free of any societal pressure to be something we are not – is true "equal rights." When a woman mistakenly thinks that she must behave like a man and pursue a man's path, she implicitly affirms that women are intrinsically inferior to men. In order to cultivate a sense of self-worth, she must therefore compete with men. The Torah forbids such an affront to the status of women. Instead, it celebrates and values women's femininity, encouraging them to develop their innate female qualities. In this way, women can make their unique and crucial contributions to society, bringing the world to its ultimate, Divine fulfillment.[2]

2. *Hitva'aduyot 5742*, vol. 3, pp. 1660–1661; *Hitva'aduyot 5745*, vol. 1, pp. 128–129.

THIRD READING
Deuteronomy 22:8–23:7

Moses then reviewed with the Jewish people the laws regarding sending away a mother bird before taking her eggs, and the laws requiring them to build railings on the roofs of their homes in order to prevent people from falling.

Building a Jewish Home

כִּי תִבְנֶה בַּיִת חָדָשׁ וְעָשִׂיתָ מַעֲקֶה לְגַגֶּךָ וגו': (דברים כב, ח)

**[Moses told the Jewish people,] "When you build a
new house, you must make a railing for your roof."**

This law can be interpreted to apply to a newlywed couple about to embark on the exciting challenge of building a household. The Torah counsels the couple that they are commencing a new phase in their lives, with new responsibilities and tasks that they have never yet had to face. This new and intensified focus on life in the physical world is a "descent" relative to their previous, single lives, and they are therefore poised to fall from their previous spiritual level unless they take preventative measures.

Therefore, they must "make a railing," i.e., undertake new spiritual safeguards in their observance of the Torah's commandments, not relying on their previous ones alone. Maintaining and enhancing their study of the Torah and observance of its commandments will ensure that the euphoria of the wedding day continue throughout their married life.[3]

---

3. *Likutei Sichot*, vol. 2, pp. 384 ff; vol. 19, pp. 208 ff.

FOURTH READING

Deuteronomy 23:8–24

Moses then reviewed with the Jewish people the laws prohibiting mixing wool and linen in garments, the laws governing cases of suspected unchaste behavior, adultery, rape, prostitution, forbidden marriages, conduct in battle, slavery, paying interest on loans, and keeping promises.

Carrying the Day's First Positive Thought

מוֹצָא שְׂפָתֶיךָ תִּשְׁמֹר וְעָשִׂיתָ וגו': (דברים כג, כד)

[Moses told the Jewish people,] "Observe and do whatever issues from your lips."

According to the Code of Jewish Law (the *Shulchan Aruch*), immediately upon waking up in the morning, our first words should be: "I offer thanks to You, living and eternal King, for You have mercifully restored my soul within me; Your faithfulness is great."

These, our first words each day, are the issuance of our lips that we should observe and preserve throughout the day. In this way, our gratefulness to G-d influences our attitudes and conduct throughout the day, infusing them with joy, and similarly affects all those around us.[4]

4. *Likutei Sichot*, vol. 24, p. 296.

FIFTH READING
Deuteronomy 23:25–24:4

Moses then reviewed with the Jewish people the laws entitling workers in the field or vineyard to partake of the food they are harvesting.

Tasting Rewards

וְאָכַלְתָּ עֲנָבִים כְּנַפְשְׁךָ שָׂבְעֶךָ וגו': (דברים כג, כה)

[Moses told the Jewish people, "If you are a hired worker in a vineyard,] you may eat as many grapes as you desire, until you are sated."

Working the grain field and working the vineyard represent the two aspects of our relationship with G-d. Grain, the basic component of the diet, represents the acceptance of G-d's sovereignty and the observance of His commandments. Grapes, a sweet addition to the normal staples of the diet, represent the expression of our relationship with G-d that goes beyond the letter of the law. When we are spiritually mature enough to feel pleasure and joy in the revelation of G-dliness, we look to bring awareness of G-d into all facets of our lives, not only in the ways expressly required by the Torah.

The Torah entitles the workers of the fields and vineyards to partake of the grain and grapes while they work. This teaches us that whether we are relating to G-d at the basic, "grain" level, or have progressed to relating to Him also on the voluntary, "grape" level, we will be constantly rewarded by receiving further, greater revelations of Divinity and Divine beneficence.[5]

5. *Likutei Sichot*, vol. 34, p. 129.

SIXTH READING
Deuteronomy 24:5–13

Moses then reviewed with the Jewish people the laws regarding divorce, exemptions from military service, conduct when taking collateral on a loan, kidnapping, and the skin disease known as *tzara'at.* This disease afflicts mainly people guilty of improper speech, just as Moses' sister Miriam was struck with it when she voiced her disapproval of Moses' behavior in divorcing his wife Tziporah.

The Power of Words

זָכוֹר אֵת אֲשֶׁר עָשָׂה ה' אֱלֹקֶיךָ לְמִרְיָם וְגוֹ': (דברים כד, ט)

**[Moses told the Jewish people,] "Remember
what G-d did to Miriam."**

It is important to realize that Miriam did not lie or even criticize her brother, Moses. She merely voiced her disapproval of his behavior without bothering to discuss her grievances with him privately first. Nonetheless, Miriam was immediately punished for having spoken against Moses.

This teaches us how careful we must always be when we talk (or write) about other people. Even seemingly harmless discussion can easily slip into gossip or slander. Rather, we should always be careful to speak and write constructively. If someone's behavior seems inappropriate, we should clarify matters with them privately, thereby sparing everyone the grief that inevitably results from misunderstanding.[6]

6. *Likutei Sichot,* vol. 18, pp. 145–146.

SHABBAT

SEVENTH READING

Deuteronomy 24:14–25:19

Moses then reviewed with the Jewish people the laws governing employees' wages, legal justice, consideration for the disadvantaged, resolving disputes, the punishment of lashes, work-animals, the obligation of a brother to marry his childless brother's widow ("levirate" marriage), compensation for embarrassment, honesty in business, and the duty to remember how the nation of Amalek attacked the Jewish people when they left Egypt. As part of the laws governing consideration for the disadvantaged, G-d commands the Jewish people to leave over for converts (who did not own any land to cultivate), orphans, and widows any sheaves of grain that they forget to gather during the harvest.

Our Inner Desire

כִּי תִקְצֹר קְצִירְךָ . . . וְשָׁכַחְתָּ עֹמֶר . . . לֹא תָשׁוּב לְקַחְתּוֹ לַגֵּר לַיָּתוֹם
וְלָאַלְמָנָה יִהְיֶה לְמַעַן יְבָרֶכְךָ ה' אֱלֹקֶיךָ בְּכֹל מַעֲשֵׂה יָדֶיךָ: (דברים כד, יט)

[Moses told the Jewish people,] "When you reap your harvest . . . and forget a sheaf . . . you must not go back to take it. It must be left for the convert, the orphan, and the widow, in order that G-d bless you in all that you do."

The innermost desire of every Jew, no matter what his or her outward level of observance of the Torah, is to perform G-d's will in full. Therefore, even when we perform a commandment unintentionally, or even "mistakenly," it is really the result of our deep-seated desire to do it.

Therefore, if a person loses a coin and a poor person picks it up, G-d rewards the person who lost the coin. How much more so will G-d bless us for intentional acts of charity and kindness![7]

7. *Hitva'aduyot 5751*, vol. 1, p. 189; *Hitva'aduyot 5750*, vol. 4, p. 121.

Tavo

Entering the Covenant

Deuteronomy 26:1–29:8

THE SEVENTH SECTION OF THE BOOK OF DEUTERONOMY concludes Moses' second farewell address to the Jewish people. It contains Moses' completion of his review of the commandments, beginning with one that would become relevant only after the Jewish people would enter (*Tavo*, in Hebrew) the Land of Israel – that of bringing the first fruits of each year's harvest to the holy Temple. It then continues with Moses' review of the covenant between G-d and the Jewish people.

FIRST READING

Deuteronomy 26:1–11

Moses taught the Jewish people that the first specimens of their wheat, barley, grape, fig, pomegranate, olive, and date harvests had to be brought to the Temple and given to the priests. The officiating priest would then present the fruits briefly before the Altar; they then become his to consume personally.

We are One

וְלָקַחְתָּ מֵרֵאשִׁית כָּל פְּרִי הָאֲדָמָה...וְהָלַכְתָּ אֶל הַמָּקוֹם

אֲשֶׁר יִבְחַר ה' אֱלֹקֶיךָ לְשַׁכֵּן שְׁמוֹ שָׁם: (דברים כו, ב)

[Moses told the Jewish people, "When you enter the Land of Israel,] you must take the first of all the fruit of the earth... and go to the place on which G-d will choose to rest His Name [i.e., the holy Temple].

This commandment became operative only after the entire Jewish people were settled in their land. As can be seen in the Book of Joshua, this process took 14 years. Until the conquest and settlement of the land was complete, no one was obligated to bring their first fruits annually to the Temple.

The reason for this is because the ritual of the first fruits expresses our thankfulness for G-d's goodness, and as long as there remained even one Jew who had not yet received his portion in the Land of Israel, the people as a whole could not experience complete joy and thanksgiving.

The same applies to us today: As long as there is even a single Jew who is materially or spiritually deprived, the rest of us cannot experience complete joy. The material or spiritual plight of our fellow Jews – and through them, the plight of all humanity and creation in general – should inspire us to action designed to remedy this situation.[1]

---

1. *Likutei Sichot*, vol. 9, pp. 155–156.

SECOND READING

Deuteronomy 26:12–15

Moses then reviewed with the Jewish people the deadlines for giving the annual tithes of their produce. Twice every seven years, during the holiday of Passover, the Jewish farmer was required to declare that he had fulfilled his obligation to tithe his produce, and to ask G-d to bless the Jewish people in return.

Challenging Ourselves; Challenging G-d

הַשְׁקִיפָה מִמְּעוֹן קָדְשְׁךָ מִן הַשָּׁמַיִם וּבָרֵךְ אֶת
עַמְּךָ אֶת יִשְׂרָאֵל וְגו': (דברים כו, טו)

[The person who gives his agricultural tithes to the Temple says,] "Look down from Your holy dwelling, from the heavens, and bless Your people, Israel."

The person who makes this declaration is testifying that the Jewish people are devoted to G-d passionately, beyond the limits of what would be dictated by logic. In return for this "irrational" devotion, we ask that G-d treat us "irrationally," as well – crowning our efforts with success that surpasses what would rationally be expected.

We should not consider such irrational devotion to G-d to be voluntary or supplementary; G-d *requires* us to constantly challenge ourselves, to prove to Him and to ourselves that our devotion to Him and to our life's mission knows no bounds. In return, He showers us with His unbounded blessings, transforming even dire situations into revealed good.[2]

2. *Likutei Sichot*, vol. 19, p. 120.

THIRD READING
Deuteronomy 26:16–19

Moses then began to encourage the Jewish people to uphold their covenant with G-d that was forged at the Giving of the Torah on Mount Sinai. In return for keeping the covenant, G-d would hold them especially dear, above His love for all other people.

What It Means to be Set Apart

וַיהוָה הֶאֱמִירְךָ הַיּוֹם לִהְיוֹת לוֹ לְעַם סְגֻלָּה וגו': (דברים כו, יח)

[Moses told the Jewish people,] "G-d has set you apart today to be His treasured people."

G-d has "set us apart" from evil and wrongdoing. Our Divine nature and true inner self render us totally above any involvement with evil, and therefore, inherently incapable of wrongdoing.

Therefore, when we do something that distances us from G-d, we can always return to Him. When we are motivated to return to G-d out of passionate love for Him, not only can we forsake negative behavior and habits at any instant (thereby defying the natural forces of inertia and habituation); we can even convert past deliberate wrongdoings into motivations for positive behavior.[3]

3. *Likutei Sichot*, vol. 9, p. 173.

FOURTH READING

Deuteronomy 27:1–10

In order to renew the covenant between G-d and the Jewish people upon their entry into the Land of Israel, G-d instructed the Jewish people to perform an elaborate ritual between Mount Gerizim and Mount Eival.

Daily Renewal

הַיּוֹם הַזֶּה נִהְיֵיתָ לְעָם לַה' אֱלֹקֶיךָ: (דברים כז, ט)

[After describing the covenant-renewal ceremony, Moses told the Jewish people,] "This day you have become a people [bound by covenant] to G-d."

Our desire for novelty is an intrinsic component of our humanity. Moses therefore told the Jewish people that they become G-d's people anew every single day. The covenant between G-d and the Jewish people was made only once, with the Giving of the Torah at Mount Sinai. But G-d renews it with each one of us on a daily basis. We should therefore view the daily personal renewal of our relationship with G-d with as much interest and enthusiasm as if it were the first time – for indeed, it is![4]

4. *Hitva'aduyot 5745*, vol. 5, p. 2929.

FIFTH READING
Deuteronomy 27:11–28:6

Moses then added his own blessings and warnings to those given by G-d at Mount Sinai.

Drawing Down G-d's Blessings

וּבָאוּ עָלֶיךָ כָּל הַבְּרָכוֹת הָאֵלֶּה וְהִשִּׂיגֻךָ וְגוֹ': (דברים כח, ב)

[**Moses promised the Jewish people, "If you remain faithful to G-d's covenant,**] **all the following blessings will pursue you and overtake you."**

We are taught that on the Jewish New Year (*Rosh HaShanah*), G-d decrees our livelihood and health for the coming year. And yet, we pray every day for health, sustenance, and many other Divine blessings. Is this daily prayer necessary, in that all has already been decreed on *Rosh HaShanah*?

This verse provides the answer to this question: G-d's blessings both "pursue" us and "overtake" us. On *Rosh HaShanah*, all the blessings necessary for their respective purposes descend ("pursue" us) to a certain level of reality where they wait in storage to be drawn down further ("overtake" us) into our physical world. The vehicle for bringing blessings down to us is our daily prayer and devotion to G-d.[5]

---

5. *Or HaTorah, Devarim*, vol. 2, p. 1089.

SIXTH READING
Deuteronomy 28:7–69

Included in Moses' blessings was the promise that the Jewish people would not be conquered by their enemies if they remained faithful to their covenant with G-d.

For the Entire World's Sake

בְּדֶרֶךְ אֶחָד יֵצְאוּ אֵלֶיךָ וּבְשִׁבְעָה דְרָכִים יָנוּסוּ לְפָנֶיךָ: (דברים כח, ז)

[**Moses told the Jewish people, "Your enemies**]
will attack you from one direction, but they
will flee from you in seven directions."

Moses did not promise the Jewish people that they would kill their enemies; only that their enemies will be prevented from harming them. From this we see that when the Jewish people follow the Torah's instructions, it elicits Divine blessing not only for us but for the whole world. Even our enemies are allowed to live peacefully and securely in their own land, and are prevented from harming us in any way.[6]

6. *Likutei Sichot*, vol. 29, p. 307.

SEVENTH READING
Deuteronomy 29:1–8

Moses then reassured the Jewish people that despite the threats he had just pronounced, they should be confident in their ability to remain true to G-d's covenant and enjoy His protection.

The Key to Success

לְמַעַן תַּשְׂכִּילוּ אֶת כָּל אֲשֶׁר תַּעֲשׂוּן: (דברים כט, ח)

[Moses told the Jewish people, "You must remain faithful to your covenant with G-d] in order that you succeed in all you do."

The Hebrew word for "succeed" (*taskilu*) also means "comprehend." Thus, this verse implies that by fulfilling G-d's commandments, we will "comprehend all that we should do."

There are many aspects of life in which we struggle to determine how to act in the most spiritually positive manner. By living in accordance with the Torah's instructions, we become sensitive to G-d's will. This, in turn, aids us in comprehending how to act in accordance with G-d's will in the context of those areas of life not directly governed by specific commandments.[7]

7. *Likutei Sichot*, vol. 14, p. 106.

Nitzavim

Sealing the Covenant

Deuteronomy 29:9–30:12

IN THE EIGHTH SECTION OF THE BOOK OF DEUTERONOMY, Moses begins his third and final farewell address to the Jewish people, which he delivered on the day he would die, 7 Adar 2488. He opens his address by telling the people that they are all standing (*Nitzavim*, in Hebrew) before him in order to seal the covenant between them and G-d.

FIRST READING
Deuteronomy 29:9–11

Moses told the Jewish people that in order to merit G-d's unconditional love, they must love one another unconditionally. This
was why he assembled all of them together for the purpose of
sealing G-d's covenant with them.

How to Love Others

אַתֶּם נִצָּבִים הַיּוֹם כֻּלְּכֶם לִפְנֵי ה' אֱלֹקֵיכֶם רָאשֵׁיכֶם שִׁבְטֵיכֶם זִקְנֵיכֶם

וְשֹׁטְרֵיכֶם... מֵחֹטֵב עֵצֶיךָ עַד שֹׁאֵב מֵימֶיךָ: (דברים כט, ט-י)

[Moses said to the Jewish people,] "You are
all standing today before G-d ... the leaders of
your tribes, your elders, your sheriffs ... from
your woodcutters to your water drawers."

How can we truly unite? After all, some of us are "leaders" while
others are "water drawers" and the like. What could Jews of such
a wide spectrum social standing possibly have in common?

The answer to this is threefold: First, who is to say who is
ultimately higher on the ladder of achievement? Appearances
can be deceiving, and we tend to over-evaluate ourselves while
under-evaluating others. Second, even if we have evaluated ourselves correctly, just because we excel in one particular aspect of
life does not mean that there are not other aspects of life in which
others exceed us. Everyone is a leader in some way; therefore, our
collective success depends on every Jew's unique contribution.

Third, the difference between the Creator and any creature
is infinite. Realizing our own puniness relative to G-d's absolute
reality eliminates any feelings of superiority we may have over
other people.

When we consider these three perspectives, we can truly stand
together, united, not only with feelings of love toward each other
but with behavior that testifies to the truth of these feelings.[1]

1. *Likutei Sichot*, vol. 2, pp. 398–400.

SECOND READING
Deuteronomy 29:12–14

Moses told the Jewish people that G-d was sealing His covenant not only with them but with all generations of Jews.

Strength in Numbers

וְאֵת אֲשֶׁר אֵינֶנּוּ פֹּה עִמָּנוּ הַיּוֹם: (דברים כט, יד)

[Moses told the Jewish people that G-d was sealing His covenant not only with them, but also] "with those who are not here with us today."

Even today, affirming our covenant with G-d by resolving to study His Torah and perform His commandments immediately, spontaneously, and automatically unites us with every Jew in the world. It also unites us with every generation of the Jewish people – past, present, and future. We thus benefit from the support of all Jews in all generations in our resolve.

We may be the smallest of nations, but when it comes to issues involving the Torah, the commandments, or fulfilling our broader Divine mission – to transform the world into G-d's home – we need not fear being outnumbered. We stand together with the merits of all the generations of the Jewish people.[2]

2. *Likutei Sichot*, vol. 19, p. 273.

THIRD READING
Deuteronomy 29:15–28

Moses explained why it was necessary to renew and strengthen the covenant that G-d first forged with the Jewish people at Mount Sinai, 40 years prior. Perhaps in the intervening 40 years, some of them began to think that they could avoid G-d's corrective punishment if they would be disloyal to Him.

Why We Wait Impatiently for the Future

לְמַעַן סְפוֹת הָרָוָה אֶת הַצְּמֵאָה: (דברים כט, יח)

[Moses told the Jewish people not to try] "to add the drunken to the thirsty."

We possess two souls: a Divine soul, which seeks to enhance our relationship with G-d, and a human/animal soul, which seeks physical comfort and the pleasures of secular intellectual stimulation.

The pleasures that our human/animal soul craves are readily available in our physical world, so it is "drunk" compared to our Divine soul, which thirsts for G-dliness. Only in the Messianic future, when G-dliness will be openly revealed, will the Divine soul be "drunk" with Divinity.

In the meantime, our human/animal souls attempt to "add the drunken to the thirsty." This side of our personality knows that material pleasures are too shallow to satisfy us in any meaningful or long-lasting way. Yet, it deceptively argues that the spiritual fulfillment that our Divine soul seeks in the study of the Torah, prayer, and the performance of G-d's commandments are more readily available to us in the enticements of this world.

Our challenge in life is not to listen to this voice, but to listen instead to the inner voice of our Divine soul and order our priorities in accordance with both our and G-d's true interests.[3]

3. *Or HaTorah, Devarim*, p. 1193.

FOURTH READING

Deuteronomy 30:1–6

Moses then informed the Jewish people that in the future, they would undergo periods of infidelity to G-d's covenant, and suffer as a result. Nonetheless, even then, the path of return to G-d would always be open.

Rising Above vs. Digging Deeper

וְשַׁבְתָּ עַד ה' אֱלֹקֶיךָ . . . בְּכָל לְבָבְךָ וּבְכָל נַפְשֶׁךָ: (דברים ל, ב)

[Moses told the Jewish people,] "You will return to G-d with all your heart and with all your soul."

Whereas we are here commanded to *return to* G-d with all our heart and soul, we have been commanded previously to *love* G-d not only with all our heart and soul, but with "all our might." What is the reason for this difference?

Loving G-d "with all our might" means being devoted to Him beyond what we consider "normal," i.e., beyond what makes sense logically.

Repentance, on the other hand, requires that we forge a stronger relationship with G-d than our present one. That relationship with G-d, after all, was too weak to keep us from wrongdoing and therefore from needing to repent. We therefore need to deepen our feelings toward G-d, in order for Him to mean more to us than the indulgences that we have learned to rationalize.

Thus, whereas the Torah bids us to love G-d beyond what seems "normal," it bids us to repent by making what used to be "beyond" us into our new "normal." The processes associated with repentance and love are directly opposite, love taking us beyond our innate limitations and repentance bringing transcendence into limited consciousness.[4]

4. *Likutei Sichot*, vol. 14, p. 120, note 9.

FIFTH READING

Deuteronomy 30:7–10

Moses then promised the Jewish people that in the future they would indeed enjoy the fulfillment of all of G-d's blessings.

Listening to G-d's Voice

וְאַתָּה תָשׁוּב וְשָׁמַעְתָּ בְּקוֹל ה' וגו': (דברים ל, ח)

[Moses told the Jewish people that they would enjoy G-d's blessings, for] "You will return [to Him] and listen to His voice."

By "listening to G-d's voice," Moses meant not only that we would obey G-d, but that we would recognize the inner message of His voice. Our belief that G-d is good and that all He does is good enables us to thank Him for everything in life – even what seems to be the opposite of good. In the merit of this belief, G-d will eventually show us how everything He does is truly good.[5]

---

5. *Hitva'aduyot 5746*, vol. 3, pp. 346–348.

SIXTH READING
Deuteronomy 30:11–14

Moses assured the Jewish people that they would always be able to know what G-d expects of them by studying the Torah.

We Can All Study the Torah

כִּי הַמִּצְוָה הַזֹּאת... לֹא נִפְלֵאת הִוא מִמְּךָ וְלֹא רְחֹקָה הִוא... וְלֹא מֵעֵבֶר לַיָּם הִוא... כִּי קָרוֹב אֵלֶיךָ הַדָּבָר מְאֹד וגו': (דברים ל, יא-יד)

[**Moses said to the Jewish people, regarding the study of the Torah,**] **"This commandment is not remote from you; it is not far away... it is not beyond the sea... for this thing is very close to you.**

The Jewish people had been studying the Torah for nearly 40 years when Moses said these words, so they knew firsthand that it was accessible (i.e., not "remote," "far away," or "beyond"). Rather, Moses was telling us that although there are indeed parts of the Torah that are "remote, far away, and beyond," these parts of the Torah are not "remote from, far away from, or beyond" *us.* Inasmuch as we are rooted in G-d's essence, which transcends the Torah, even the most challenging or mystical aspects of the Torah are not beyond us. We are all capable of studying all aspects of the Torah.[6]

---

6. *Sefer HaSichot 5752*, vol. 1, p. 17, note 61.

SEVENTH READING
Deuteronomy 30:15–20

Moses then told the Jewish people that, in the final analysis, G-d is presenting them with the free choice to choose between good and evil.

Free Choice and Reward

רְאֵה נָתַתִּי לְפָנֶיךָ הַיּוֹם אֶת הַחַיִּים וְאֶת הַטּוֹב וְאֶת הַמָּוֶת וְאֶת הָרָע... וּבָחַרְתָּ בַּחַיִּים וגו': (דברים ל, טו-יט)

[Moses told the Jewish people,] "Behold, I have set before you today life and good and death and evil. Choose life!"

It is not always clear that good behavior leads to blessings and life and that bad behavior leads to curses and death. This allows us the free will to *choose* to be good. If it were always clear that good behavior leads to blessing and life, whereas bad behavior leads to the opposite, what choice could we have but to be good? The very fact that being good does not always lead to goodness both forces us and enables us to base our relationship with G-d on a more profound basis.

For this reason, on a deeper level, G-d (through Moses) is here asking us to be good for its own sake, rather than for any expectation of material reward, even when we do see clearly that being good leads to good results.[7]

---

7. *Likutei Sichot*, vol. 28, p. 82.

Vayeilech

Recording and Sealing the Covenant
Deuteronomy 31:1–30

THE NINTH SECTION OF THE BOOK OF DEUTERONOMY CON-
tinues the description of Moses' third and final farewell address
to the Jewish people. It begins with the account of how Moses
went (*Vayeilech*, in Hebrew) and installed Joshua as his successor,
and continues with the account of how Moses wrote down the
Torah and commanded the people to assemble every seven years
to hear it read in the holy Temple.

FIRST READING

Deuteronomy 31:1–3

Moses informed the Jewish people that this day, 7 Adar, was his 120th birthday, and would also be the day that he would die.

Leading a Full Life

וַיֹּאמֶר אֲלֵהֶם בֶּן מֵאָה וְעֶשְׂרִים שָׁנָה אָנֹכִי הַיּוֹם וְגוֹ': (דברים לא, ב)

[Moses] told [the people], "Today I am exactly 120 years old."

G-d ensured that Moses lived his last year to its very end in order to teach us that he lived his life to its fullest, wasting no time and not leaving undone any part of the task with which he was charged.

The fact that Moses' physical life so perfectly mirrored his spiritual life indicated that he successfully overcame the division between the spiritual and the material: his spiritual perfection was mirrored in this manifestation of physical perfection.

Moses' life should inspire us to live our own lives to the fullest, the consciousness of our Divine mission permeating every minute and every item in our lives. When we do so, we dissolve the artificial division of the spiritual and the physical, revealing the innate Divinity underlying all reality.[1]

---

1. *Sefer HaSichot 5752*, vol. 1, pp. 134–137.

SECOND READING
Deuteronomy 31:4–6

Moses reassured the Jewish people that although he was about to die, G-d would still and always be with His people. They therefore had nothing to fear from the nations then occupying the Land of Israel, which they were about to enter and conquer.

Whether We Like it or Not!

לֹא יַרְפְּךָ וְלֹא יַעַזְבֶךָ: (דברים לא, ו)

[**Moses told the Jewish people that they can rely on G-d's assistance;**] **"He will neither fail you nor forsake you."**

Moses informed us with these words that even if it would occur to us that life would be easier if we were free from both G-d's mission and His assistance, such a life is not possible. G-d will never forsake us. We can never completely silence the inner voice that urges us to discard our infatuation with superficial pursuits and assume the mantle of responsible Jewishness.

For this same reason, we should never feel incapable of fulfilling our Divine mission. The same G-d who refuses to leave us alone, always prodding us to join Him in perfecting the world, stands at our side to assist us in our efforts to transform the world into His home.[2]

2. *Sichot Kodesh 5732*, vol. 1, p. 9.

THIRD READING

Deuteronomy 31:7–9

Moses then summoned Joshua and appointed him as his successor in the presence of the entire Jewish people.

How to Seek Inspiration in the Torah

וַיִּקְרָא מֹשֶׁה לִיהוֹשֻׁעַ וַיֹּאמֶר אֵלָיו . . . אַתָּה תָּבוֹא אֶת הָעָם
הַזֶּה אֶל הָאָרֶץ אֲשֶׁר נִשְׁבַּע ה' לַאֲבֹתָם וגו': (דברים לא, ז)

**Moses summoned Joshua and said to him . . . "You
must come with this people into the land
that G-d swore to their forefathers."**

G-d's Torah and His commandments are eternal and unchanging, but the way they must be made relevant and applied in each generation changes as time progresses. In order to ensure that we live life in accordance with G-d's wishes, G-d Himself has authorized the rabbinic leaders of each generation to apply the Torah's teachings to the unique circumstances of their generation.

Therefore, when today's rabbinic authorities apply the Torah's teachings in innovative ways, we cannot try to live in the past, complaining that the leadership of previous generations did not see the need for such innovations. On the contrary: only by reading the Torah through the eyes of our "Joshua" – today's Moses – can we be certain that the Torah will provide us with the inspiration to fulfill our Divine mission and live our lives to the fullest.[3]

3. *Likutei Sichot*, vol. 19, p. 314.

FOURTH READING

Deuteronomy 31:10–13

Moses then conveyed G-d's command to the Jewish people that they assemble once every seven years, during the festival of *Sukot*, in order to hear their king read specific passages from the Torah. Although they were commanded to study the Torah in any case, this ceremony was designed to instill renewed commitment to G-d's covenant with them.

Being a Jewish King

תִּקְרָא אֶת הַתּוֹרָה הַזֹּאת נֶגֶד כָּל יִשְׂרָאֵל בְּאָזְנֵיהֶם: (דברים לא, יא)

[**Moses told Joshua, "At the *Sukot* assembly, as their future 'king,'] you must read this Torah before all Israel."**

The objective of this assembly was to strengthen the foundations of Jewish education and observance. We can thus fulfill this commandment nowadays firstly by "assembling" all the various facets of our personalities in order to imbue them with the knowledge and reverence of G-d. Next, we should assemble our families periodically and strengthen each other in these areas in a spirit of family love and camaraderie. Finally, we should assemble whatever groups of people we can – whether at work, at school, in our synagogues, our extended families, our wider circle of friends, etc. – in order to influence as many people as possible to enhance their commitment to the Torah's values and lifestyle, as based on the love and awe of G-d.

Fulfilling this commandment to the greatest extent possible will elicit G-d's reciprocal response, and He will enable us to finally fulfill it in its optimal fashion, in the rebuilt holy Temple, as we listen to the Torah read to us by the ultimate Jewish king, the Messiah.[4]

4. *Likutei Sichot*, vol. 34, pp. 211–216.

FIFTH READING
Deuteronomy 31:14–19

G-d then summoned Moses to the entrance to the Tabernacle. G-d spoke to him from a pillar of cloud that appeared over the Tabernacle's entrance, informing him that He was going to dictate a poem to him that he should teach the Jewish people. The purpose of the poem was to inspire the Jewish people to remain loyal to G-d throughout any misfortunes that might befall them as a result of their misdeeds.

Interpreting Evil

הֲלֹא עַל כִּי אֵין אֱלֹקַי בְּקִרְבִּי מְצָאוּנִי הָרָעוֹת הָאֵלֶּה: (דברים לא, יז)

[G-d told Moses that the Jews would say during their misfortunes,] "Is it not because our G-d is no longer among us that these evils have befallen us?"

We are naturally disposed to overlook our own faults – or, if we do acknowledge them, to rationalize them. This verse teaches us that in order to show us our own faults, G-d shows them to us in other people. "Because my G-d is not within me" – i.e., "because I am not spiritually mature enough to be sensitive to my own shortcomings" – "this evil has befallen me" – i.e., "I have been forced to see my own evil reflected in my fellow Jew."

Therefore, rather than focusing on others' faults, we should try to focus on their virtues and excuse their shortcomings. This means not only focusing on other's virtues in our own minds, but praising them for their virtues, both directly and to other people. In this way, we foster mutual love and respect.

Just as we are encouraged to inspire those around us to love G-d, so are we encouraged to inspire those around us to love every Jew, for loving our fellow Jew leads us to love G-d.[5]

5. *Sefer HaSichot 5705*, p. 92.

SIXTH READING

Deuteronomy 31:20–24

G-d then addressed Joshua from the cloud at the entrance to the Tabernacle, charging him with the mission of leading the Jewish people into the Land of Israel.

The Purpose of Effort

חֲזַק וֶאֱמָץ כִּי אַתָּה תָּבִיא אֶת בְּנֵי יִשְׂרָאֵל אֶל הָאָרֶץ
אֲשֶׁר נִשְׁבַּעְתִּי לָהֶם וְגו': (דברים לא, כג)

**[G-d told Joshua,] "Be strong and courageous!
For you will bring the Jewish people to the
land that I have sworn [to give] them."**

We are taught that had Moses led the Jewish people into the Land of Israel, its conquest would have been virtually effortless. The intensity of Moses' holiness would have neutralized any opposition. The same would have been true of our "conquest" of the world's materiality: Moses' entry into the Land of Israel would have made our task of elevating and refining the world virtually effortless.

This is the inner reason why G-d did not allow Moses into the Promised Land. G-d wants to shower us with infinite goodness. But were He to do so freely, without requiring us to "earn" it, we would feel ashamed. Thus, His desire to be good to us would backfire. Therefore, G-d made the bestowal of His infinite goodness dependent upon our efforts. When we summon our hidden potential in order to overcome obstacles to the Divine mission of perfecting the world, we earn G-d's infinite goodness.[6]

6. *Hitva'aduyot 5711*, vol. 1, pp. 20–22.

SEVENTH READING
Deuteronomy 31:25–30

Moses then instructed the Levites to place the Torah scroll that he would soon write in the Ark of the Covenant, together with the Tablets of the Covenant that he received at Mount Sinai.

Being United with the Torah

לָקֹחַ אֵת סֵפֶר הַתּוֹרָה הַזֶּה וְשַׂמְתֶּם אֹתוֹ מִצַּד וְגו': (דברים לא, כו)

[Moses told the Levites,] "Take this Torah scroll and place it alongside [the Tablets of Testimony]."

Thus, the Ark in the Tabernacle contained the Torah both engraved in stone and written on parchment. The difference between engraved and written letters is that the engraved letters are part and parcel of the stone, whereas written letters are not part of the parchment but added to it. Thus, engraved letters express our intrinsic connection to the Torah, whereas written letters allude to how we preserve our connection to the Torah even during our mundane lives, when we think of ourselves as being separate from the Torah.

The presence of both the engraved Torah and the inscribed Torah within the Ark indicates that we must first experience our intrinsic connection with the Torah and then carry that experience with us into our mundane lives.[7]

---

7. *Likutei Sichot*, vol. 2, pp. 407–408.

Ha'azinu

The Poem of Testimony

Deuteronomy 32:1–52

THE TENTH SECTION OF THE BOOK OF DEUTERONOMY IS composed almost entirely of the Poem of Testimony that G-d taught Moses and instructed him to teach the Jewish people. In it, Moses bids the Jewish people to hearken (*Ha'azinu*, in Hebrew) to his words as he reviews their history and informs them of the consequences of their future conduct, whether good or bad.

FIRST READING
Deuteronomy 32:1–6

Moses called upon both heaven and earth to bear witness to the message he was about to deliver to the Jewish people.

Heaven on Earth

הַאֲזִינוּ הַשָּׁמַיִם ... וְתִשְׁמַע הָאָרֶץ וְגוֹ': (דברים לב, א)

[**Moses said,**] "**Listen, O heaven ... Hear, O earth.**"

Moses addressed both heaven and earth in order to teach us that we are called upon to harmonize the two. The Torah originates in heaven and consists of G-d's vision for the perfection of the world. By spreading the knowledge of the Torah to ourselves and to others, we are bringing heaven down to earth. By reshaping both our own lives and the lives of others in accordance with the Torah's teachings, we are bringing life on earth up to heaven. When we have made life into "heaven on earth" – reconciling the division between the two – heaven and earth testify how we have fulfilled our mission in life.[1]

---

1. *Likutei Sichot*, vol. 9, pp. 213–214.

SECOND READING
Deuteronomy 32:7–12

G-d told Moses to encourage the Jewish people to remember their history, recalling how G-d chose them to be His people, gave them the Torah, and shepherded them through the desert on the way from Egypt to the Land of Israel.

Maintaining Focus

יְסֹבְבֶנְהוּ וגו': (דברים לב, י)

[Moses said,] "[G-d] made [the Jewish people] surround Him [by commanding them to camp around the Tabernacle]."

By studying the Torah regularly, we construct a "Tabernacle" – i.e., a dwelling for G-d – in our personal lives. By commanding the Jewish people to encamp around the Tabernacle, G-d teaches us that we should center our lives around this inner sanctuary. The innermost point of the Tabernacle was the Ark, which housed the Tablets of the Covenant, i.e., the Torah. When the Torah is the focal point around which our lives revolve, it can positively affect all facets of our lives, as it is meant to. Furthermore, once the Torah is illuminating and influencing our lives as it is meant to, its influence can spread still further outward, enlightening and refining all humanity and the entire world.[2]

2. *Hitva'aduyot 5744*, vol. 4, pp. 2649–2650.

THIRD READING
Deuteronomy 32:13–18

G-d then told Moses to inform the Jewish people how G-d would provide them with material bounty in the Land of Israel. But G-d also cautioned them that should they overindulge in this wealth, it would cause them to rebel against Him.

The Challenge of Wealth

וַיִּשְׁמַן יְשֻׁרוּן וַיִּבְעָט וגו': (דברים לב, טו)

[Moses said,] "The [formerly] upright people became fat and kicked."

There is nothing wrong with wealth per se, as long as we take the necessary steps to ensure that we retain the proper perspective. We should answer the challenge of wealth by striving all the more to refine our human/animal natures, taking care not to indulge in excess mundane gratification – material or cultural. We can then refine the world, as well, by shining the light of the Torah outward,[3] using the blessings of wealth for their intended purposes: to support and further the study of the Torah and the dissemination of Judaism.[4]

If we encounter someone who has "gotten fat and kicked," we should not give up hope, since even the most disinterested Jew remains a Jew at heart, and the light of truth will penetrate even the hardest barrier.[5]

3. *Sefer HaMa'amarim 5700*, p. 158.
4. *Sefer HaSichot 5702*, p. 149.
5. *Sefer HaSichot 5701*, p. 83.

FOURTH READING
Deuteronomy 32:19–28

G-d told Moses to inform the Jewish people that He would punish them for their misdeeds, but would nonetheless never forsake them.

G-d's Children

בָּנִים לֹא אֵמֻן בָּם: (דברים לב, כ)

[Moses said that G-d would say,] "They are children who [act] uneducated."

By referring to us as His "children," G-d let it be known that He would never sever His relationship with us, and that we can never sever our relationship with Him – just as parents can never sever themselves from their children, and children can never sever themselves from their parents. The relationship between parents and their children is so essential, so strong, that no matter how seriously it may be tested, in the final analysis it will always overcome any behavior that might seem to threaten it.

It is therefore pointless to try to hide or flee from this relationship, and senseless to think that it can ever be forfeited. G-d's love for us is infinitely stronger than anything we may have done to weaken it.[6]

---

6. *Sefer HaMa'amarim 5715*, pp. 319–320.

FIFTH READING
Deuteronomy 32:29–39

G-d told Moses to inform the Jewish people that after they would receive their corrective punishment for their lapses in loyalty to G-d's covenant, G-d would comfort them and punish those who had persecuted them.

Healing the World

מָחַצְתִּי וַאֲנִי אֶרְפָּא וגו': (דברים לב, לט)

[G-d said,] "I strike and I heal."

The Hebrew word for "strike" (*machatzti*) is related to the word for "barrier" or "partition" (*mechitzah*). The sickness that the world presently suffers from is the artificial barrier between the spiritual and the material. The difficulty we experience in trying to sense the spiritual in what we do or in trying to apply our inspiration to our daily lives is the true definition of exile. In the Messianic era, G-d will heal this split. The dividing barrier will be transformed into a connecting doorway, enabling the spiritual and the material to once again unite. This is how evil will be eliminated in the future: G-d will be so revealed that evil – the denial of G-d – will simply cease to exist.

It follows that the way to hasten the Messianic era is by taking care to refine even the lowest aspects of our material lives, infusing them with as much spirituality as we can. By living "messianic" lives in this way, we are doing our part to nullify the exile.[7]

---

7. *Sefer HaMa'amarim 5730*, pp. 211–212.

SIXTH READING
Deuteronomy 32:40–43

G-d then told Moses to inform the Jewish people that eventually the non-Jewish nations would appreciate them and praise them for remaining true to their covenant with G-d.

When the Messiah Comes

הַרְנִינוּ גוֹיִם עַמּוֹ וגו': (דברים לב, מג)

[Moses addressed the non-Jews:] "Nations! Praise [G-d] for His people, [the Jews]!"

When the Messianic Redemption occurs, truth will no longer be so easily confused with falsehood. It will become clear to the whole world why G-d chose the Jews to be His people. Our role as the priests and teachers of humanity will finally be universally acknowledged, and our redeeming contributions to human civilization will be fully appreciated. The nations of the world will then do whatever they can to aid the Jews in their Divine mission of bringing the world to its fullest potential.

Educating the world to appreciate not only G-d but G-d's people is therefore an integral part of preparing the world for the Redemption and hastening it.[8]

---

8. *Hitva'aduyot 5748*, vol. 1, p. 41.

SEVENTH READING
Deuteronomy 32:44–52

After Moses finished conveying the Poem of Testimony to the Jewish people, he encouraged them to pay heed to all its lessons, as well as to the Torah in general.

G-d's Guide to Life

כִּי לֹא דָבָר רֵק הוּא מִכֶּם כִּי הוּא חַיֵּיכֶם וְגוֹ': (דברים לב, מז)

[Moses said to the Jewish people,] "For [the Torah] is not an unrewarding pursuit for you; rather, it is your very life."

The Torah contains all the instructions and lessons that every individual needs in order to live his or her life in accordance with G-d's expectations. This is as it should be, for the Torah is the "blueprint" that G-d used when He created the world. If for some reason we are not sure what the Torah requires of us in a specific situation, we are bidden to consult with qualified Torah scholars, who have learned from their own teachers how to correctly apply the Torah's wisdom to our lives.

Thus, the literal meaning of this verse is, "For it is not an empty thing from you," which, the sages of the Talmud tell us, means, "If you find a situation in life that seems empty of – i.e., lacking – the Torah's direction, it is because of you – i.e., your own inability to apply the Torah's wisdom to your life." In such cases, the Torah directs us to seek its application from our teachers and mentors.[9]

9. *Sichot Kodesh 5739*, vol. 1, pp. 129–131.

Vezot Haberachah

The Final Blessing

Deuteronomy 33:1–34:12

THE ELEVENTH AND FINAL SECTION OF THE BOOK OF DEU-
teronomy concludes Moses' third and final farewell address to the
Jewish people. It begins with the blessings (*VeZot HaBerachah*,
in Hebrew) that he pronounced to each of the twelve tribes, and
concludes with his death.

FIRST READING

Deuteronomy 33:1–7

Moses began his blessing by praising the Jewish people for accepting the Torah unconditionally. He contrasted the Jews' acceptance of the Torah with the other nations' refusal to accept it, when G-d offered it to them before giving it to the Jews.

The Noahide Redemption

וַיֹּאמַר ה' מִסִּינַי בָּא וְזָרַח מִשֵּׂעִיר לָמוֹ הוֹפִיעַ מֵהַר פָּארָן וְגו': (דברים לג, ב)

[Moses] said, "G-d came from Sinai [to give the Jews the Torah], shining forth to them from [Mount Sei'ir, after offering the Torah to the Edomites]; He appeared [to the Jews] from Mount Paran [where He had offered the Torah to the Ishmaelites]."

The Edomites and Ishmaelites represent all non-Jewish nations, past and present. By offering the Torah to the non-Jewish nations, G-d rendered them receptive to later accepting their obligation to observe the "Noahide" laws. These are the seven categories of commandments that must be observed by all non-Jews. In order to properly accept this legal code, the non-Jew must acknowledge that G-d gave it to humanity as part of the Torah that He gave at Mount Sinai.

Furthermore, in the Messianic future, the non-Jewish nations will be refined and no longer oppose the lifestyle and world-vision of the Torah. By approaching the nations of the world with the option to accept the entire Torah, G-d implanted within them the receptivity to both their present obligation to accept the Torah's authority over them – obligating them in the Noahide laws – as well as their future acceptance of the Torah's world-vision, transforming them into active participants in the final Redemption.[1]

---

1. *Hitva'aduyot 5742*, vol. 1, pp. 223–224; *Hitva'aduyot 5748*, vol. 1, p. 92.

SECOND READING

Deuteronomy 33:8–12

Moses then blessed each tribe separately, emphasizing each one's unique contribution to the collective mission of the Jewish people. He blessed the tribe of Levi to be worthy of their role as the priests and Levites serving in the holy Temple, and of their charge to teach the Torah to the rest of the Jewish people. He blessed the tribe of Benjamin with the eternal presence of the holy Temple, the main sections of which would forever lie in the territory of the tribe of Benjamin.

Jewish Perpetuity

יוֹרוּ מִשְׁפָּטֶיךָ לְיַעֲקֹב . . . לְבִנְיָמִן אָמַר . . . חֹפֵף עָלָיו כָּל הַיּוֹם וְגוֹ': (דברים לג, י)

[**Moses blessed the tribe of Levi,**] "**They will teach** [**G-d's**] **ordinances to Jacob** [**i.e., the Jewish people**]. . . . [**He blessed the tribe of Benjamin,**] "[**G-d's presence**] **hovers above him all 'day' long** [**i.e., forever**]."

Moses' blessing to the tribe of Levi is meant to inspire all of us to dedicate ourselves to the holy task of promoting Jewish education, to ensuring that every Jew be given the broadest and deepest knowledge of G-d's Torah as possible.

By pronouncing the tribe of Benjamin's blessing immediately after the tribe of Levi's blessing, Moses teaches us that just as Benjamin was blessed with the perpetual presence of the holy Temple, our dedication to Jewish education must be ongoing and perpetual, and that the Jewish education we promote must be of the type that ensures the perpetual dedication of the Jewish people to G-d's Torah and commandments.[2]

THIRD READING
Deuteronomy 33:13–17

Moses blessed the tribe of Joseph that their territory would be abundantly fertile.

The Torah is Sweet

וּלְיוֹסֵף אָמַר מְבֹרֶכֶת ה' אַרְצוֹ מִמֶּגֶד שָׁמַיִם . . . וּמִמֶּגֶד תְּבוּאֹת שָׁמֶשׁ
וּמִמֶּגֶד גֶּרֶשׁ יְרָחִים . . . וּמִמֶּגֶד גִּבְעוֹת עוֹלָם: וּמִמֶּגֶד אֶרֶץ וגו': (דברים לג, יג-טז)

[Moses] said of [the tribe of] Joseph, "May his land be
blessed by G-d with the delicacies of heaven . . . with
the delicacies produced by the sun, with the
delicacies ripened by the moon . . . with the perennial
delicacies of hills, with the delicacies of the land."

Moses blessed the tribe of Joseph not only with their material necessities, but with "delicacies," implying that they will enjoy material abundance. The word "delicacies" is mentioned five times in these verses, corresponding to the five Books of Moses. The Torah is our spiritual food – the nourishment of our souls – so Moses' blessing to the tribe of Joseph was that the study of the Torah should not only nourish the soul but fill it with delight and pleasure.

This teaches us that during the time that we set aside for studying the Torah, we should forget about all our worldly concerns, in order to be able to immerse ourselves in the Torah totally, thereby enjoying our study of it to the fullest. By so doing, we elicit G-d's blessings for material abundance.[3]

3. *Hitva'aduyot 5743*, vol. 1, pp. 196–198.

FOURTH READING

Deuteronomy 33:18–21

The territory of the tribe of Gad guarded the border of the Land of Israel. Moses therefore blessed this tribe with military valor.

Battling Intimidation and Hesitation

וּלְגָד אָמַר ... כְּלָבִיא שָׁכֵן וְטָרַף זְרוֹעַ אַף קָדְקֹד: (דברים לג, כ)

[**Moses**] **said of the tribe of Gad, "May he dwell like a fearsome lion, tearing off the arm and the head** [**of its prey in one blow**].**"

Our physical conquest of the seven nations who occupied the Land of Israel alludes to our spiritual conquest of the seven emotions of the human/animal soul. The two major obstacles to this conquest are the "arm" and the "head."

The "head" is the mental block that results from calculating the odds of success against the dominant material culture. Confronted with the overwhelming resources commanded by materialistic society, the lone Jew is tempted to give up before even beginning the fight. The "arm" is the physical resources we have at our disposal. We have worked hard to earn these resources, and are therefore reluctant to expend them on spiritual pursuits whose material benefits are not at all apparent.

We must therefore deny the validity of both these attitudes together, "in one blow."[4]

4. *Hitva'aduyot 5744*, vol. 4, pp. 2321–2322; *Hitva'aduyot 5749*, vol. 1, pp. 128–129.

FIFTH READING
Deuteronomy 33:22–26

Moses blessed the tribe of Asher with such an abundance of olive orchards that it would seem as if they were always dipping their feet in olive oil. They would share this abundance of oil with their fellow Jews.

The Virtue of Simplicity

וּלְאָשֵׁר אָמַר ... יְהִי רְצוּי אֶחָיו וְטֹבֵל בַּשֶּׁמֶן רַגְלוֹ: (דברים לג, כד)

[Moses] said of [the tribe of] Asher: "He will gratify his brothers, for he will immerse his foot in [olive] oil."

The foot – the lowest part of the body – signifies the simplest aspect of our relation to G-d: submission to His will. In contrast, oil – the source of candlelight – signifies insight (*chochmah*, in Hebrew), the most sublime faculty of the intellect. Thus, immersing the foot in oil signifies our recognition of the virtue of simple submission over intellect.

The fact that the tribe of Asher "gratified his brothers" by supplying them with olive oil indicates that this recognition of the virtue of submission over intellect influenced the other tribes, as well. This deep sense of selflessness enables us to weather even the most difficult challenges to our faith.[5]

5. *Likutei Sichot*, vol. 1, pp. 102, 107–109.

SIXTH READING

Deuteronomy 33:27–29

After blessing each of the tribes individually, Moses blessed the Jewish people collectively, contrasting their role in the world with that of all other nations.

A Light to the Nations

וַיִּשְׁכֹּן יִשְׂרָאֵל בֶּטַח בָּדָד . . . וְיִכָּחֲשׁוּ אֹיְבֶיךָ לָךְ וְאַתָּה
עַל בָּמוֹתֵימוֹ תִדְרֹךְ: (דברים לג, כח-כט)

[Moses said of the Jewish people,] "Israel will dwell safely and individually.... Your enemies will lie to you [pretending to be your friends], but you will tread upon their heights."

Moses here referred prophetically to a non-Jewish nation who pretended to be the Jewish people's ally after witnessing the miraculous fall of Jericho.

These verses encapsulate the attitudes that we, as Jews, should cultivate vis-à-vis our relationship with the rest of humanity. First, we must realize that we have a unique purpose in this world that sets us apart. We are Jews intrinsically, because of the mission that G-d has charged us with – not because of anything that others may say about us or do to us.

With this self-assurance, we can then proceed to help the rest of humanity realize its potential. Respectfully, but firmly, we must help them eliminate any residual negativity or antagonism toward Divinity. Then, we can show them how to join us in bringing the world to its ultimate fulfillment, transforming it into G-d's true home.[6]

6. *Hitva'aduyot 5744*, vol. 1, pp. 200–201.

SEVENTH READING

Deuteronomy 34:1–12

After Moses concluded his farewell address, G-d instructed him to ascend Mount Nebo. G-d showed Moses prophetically the future of the Jewish people. The Torah then concludes with Moses' death, informing us that no other prophet would ever arise equaling his level of prophecy.

Sparks of Moses

וַיַּרְאֵהוּ ה' אֶת כָּל הָאָרֶץ וְגוֹ': (דברים לד, א)

G-d showed [Moses] all [that would befall] the Land [of Israel].

The vision of the Jewish people's future that G-d granted Moses, up to and including the vision of the final, Messianic Redemption, is a fitting conclusion to the Torah. The Torah was given to humanity in order to enable us to make the world into G-d's home. This goal will ultimately be achieved only upon the advent of the final Redemption.

We are taught that a spark of Moses' soul is present in the leaders of every generation, as well as in each of us as individuals. Thus, Moses' blessings – which provide us with the means, the impetus, and the vision to fulfill our Divine mission and our destiny, bringing the world to its fullest completion – are channeled through the spiritual leaders of our generation and then through our own selves, as we look to the Torah as our guide to living life to its fullest, to connecting ourselves with G-d, and to transforming our lives and our world into G-d's true home.[7]

7. *Hitva'aduyot 5724*, vol. 1, pp. 31–33; *Hitva'aduyot 5745*, vol. 1, p. 89; *Hitva'aduyot 5750*, vol. 1, p. 117.

Appendix: The Jewish Calendar

Month	Natural Order	Torah Order	Gregorian Equivalent
Tishrei	1	7	September–October
Marcheshvan	2	8	October–November
Kislev	3	9	November–December
Tevet	4	10	December–January
Shevat	5	11	January–February
Adar	6	12	February–March
Nisan	7	1	March–April
Iyar	8	2	April–May
Sivan	9	3	May–June
Tamuz	10	4	June–July
Menachem-Av	11	5	July–August
Elul	12	6	August–September

ANNUAL TORAH STUDY CALENDAR

As explained in the introduction, it is customary to study a portion of the weekly Torah section each day. The schedule for this study program is given below. This calendar applies to the Diaspora. For the calendar for the Land of Israel, as well as for additional years, see www.chabadhousepublications.org

Section	Pages	2017–2018	2018–2019	2019–2020	2020–2021	2021–2022	2022–2023	2023–2024	2024–2025
GENESIS									
Bereishit	3–10	Oct 12–14 '17*	Oct 2–6 '18*	Oct 22–26 '19*	Oct 11–17 '20*	Sep 29–Oct 2 '21*	Oct 18–22 '22*	Oct 8–14 '23*	Oct 25–26 '24*
Noach	11–18	Oct 15–21	Oct 7–13	Oct 27–Nov 2	Oct 18–24	Oct 3–9	Oct 23–29	Oct 15–21	Oct 27–Nov 2
Lech Lecha	19–26	Oct 22–28	Oct 14–20	Nov 3–9	Oct 25–31	Oct 10–16	Oct 30–Nov 5	Oct 22–28	Nov 3–9
Vayeira	27–34	Oct 29–Nov 4	Oct 21–27	Nov 10–16	Nov 1–7	Oct 17–23	Nov 6–12	Oct 29–Nov 4	Nov 10–16
Chayei Sarah	35–42	Nov 5–11	Oct 28–Nov 3	Nov 17–23	Nov 8–14	Oct 24–30	Nov 13–19	Nov 5–11	Nov 17–23
Toledot	43–50	Nov 12–18	Nov 4–10	Nov 24–30	Nov 15–21	Oct 31–Nov 6	Nov 20–26	Nov 12–18	Nov 24–30
Vayeitzei	51–58	Nov 19–25	Nov 11–17	Dec 1–7	Nov 22–28	Nov 7–13	Nov 27–Dec 3	Nov 19–25	Dec 1–7
Vayishlach	59–66	Nov 26–Dec 2	Nov 18–24	Dec 8–14	Nov 29–Dec 5	Nov 14–20	Dec 4–10	Nov 26–Dec 2	Dec 8–14
Vayeishev	67–74	Dec 3–9	Nov 25–Dec 1	Dec 15–21	Dec 6–12	Nov 21–27	Dec 11–17	Dec 3–9	Dec 15–21
Mikeitz	75–82	Dec 10–16	Dec 2–8	Dec 22–28	Dec 13–19	Nov 28–Dec 4	Dec 18–24	Dec 10–16	Dec 22–28
Vayigash	83–90	Dec 17–23	Dec 9–15	Dec 29–Jan 4 '20	Dec 20–26	Dec 5–11	Dec 25–31	Dec 17–23	Dec 29–Jan 4 '25
Vaichi	91–98	Dec 24–30	Dec 16–22	Jan 5–11	Dec 27–Jan 2 '21	Dec 12–18	Jan 1–7 '23	Dec 24–30	Jan 5–11
EXODUS									
Shemot	101–108	Dec 31–Jan 6 '18	Dec 23–29	Jan 12–18	Jan 3–9	Dec 19–25	Jan 8–14	Dec 31–Jan 6 '24	Jan 12–18
Va'eira	109–116	Jan 7–13	Dec 30–Jan 5 '19	Jan 19–25	Jan 10–16	Dec 26–Jan 1 '22	Jan 15–21	Jan 7–13	Jan 19–25
Bo	117–124	Jan 14–20	Jan 6–12	Jan 26–Feb 1	Jan 17–23	Jan 2–8	Jan 22–28	Jan 14–20	Jan 26–Feb 1
Beshalach	125–132	Jan 21–27	Jan 13–19	Feb 2–8	Jan 24–30	Jan 9–15	Jan 29–Feb 4	Jan 21–27	Feb 2–8
Yitro	133–140	Jan 28–Feb 3	Jan 20–26	Feb 9–15	Jan 31–Feb 8	Jan 16–22	Feb 5–11	Jan 28–Feb 3	Feb 9–15
Mishpatim	141–148	Feb 4–10	Jan 27–Feb 2	Feb 16–22	Feb 9–13	Jan 23–29	Feb 12–18	Feb 4–10	Feb 16–22
Terumah	149–156	Feb 11–17	Feb 3–9	Feb 23–29	Feb 14–20	Jan 30–Feb 5	Feb 19–25	Feb 11–17	Feb 23–Mar 1
Tetzaveh	157–165	Feb 18–24	Feb 10–16	Mar 1–7	Feb 21–27	Feb 6–12	Feb 26–Mar 4	Feb 18–24	Mar 2–8
Tisa	165–172	Feb 25–Mar 3	Feb 17–23	Mar 8–14	Feb 28–Mar 6	Feb 13–19	Mar 5–11	Feb 25–Mar 2	Mar 9–15
Vayakheil	173–180	Mar 4–10**	Feb 24–Mar 2	Mar 15–21**	Mar 7–13**	Feb 20–26	Mar 12–18**	Mar 3–9	Mar 16–22
Pekudei	181–188	Mar 4–10**	Mar 3–9	Mar 15–21**	Mar 7–13**	Feb 27–Mar 5	Mar 12–18**	Mar 10–16	Mar 23–29
LEVITICUS									
Vayikra	191–198	Mar 11–17	Mar 10–16	Mar 22–28	Mar 14–20	Mar 6–12	Mar 19–25	Mar 17–23	Mar 30–Apr 5
Tzav	199–206	Mar 18–24	Mar 17–23	Mar 29–Apr 4	Mar 21–27	Mar 13–19	Mar 26–Apr 1	Mar 24–30	Apr 6–12
Shemini	207–214	Mar 25–Apr 14***	Mar 24–30	Apr 5–18***	Mar 28–Apr 10***	Mar 20–26	Apr 2–15***	Mar 31–Apr 6	Apr 13–26***

Parashah	Pages								
Tazri'a	215–222	Apr 15–21**	Mar 31–Apr 6	Apr 19–25**	Apr 11–17**	Mar 27–Apr 3	Apr 16–22**	Apr 7–13	Apr 27–May 3**
Metzora	223–230	Apr 15–21**	Apr 7–13	Apr 19–25**	Apr 11–17**	Apr 4–9	Apr 16–22**	Apr 14–20	Apr 27–May 3**
Acharei	231–238	Apr 22–28**	Apr 14–May 4***	Apr 26–May 2**	Apr 18–24**	Apr 10–30***	Apr 23–29**	Apr 21–May 4***	May 4–10**
Kedoshim	239–246	Apr 22–28**	May 5–11	Apr 26–May 2**	Apr 18–24**	May 1–7	Apr 23–29**	May 5–11	May 4–10**
Emor	247–254	Apr 29–May 5	May 12–18	May 3–9	Apr 25–May 1	May 8–14	Apr 30–May 6	May 12–18	May 11–17
Behar	255–262	May 6–12**	May 19–25	May 10–16**	May 2–8**	May 15–21	May 7–13**	May 19–25	May 18–24**
Bechukotai	263–270	May 6–12**	May 26–Jun 1	May 10–16**	May 2–8**	May 22–28	May 7–13**	May 26–Jun 1	May 18–24**
NUMBERS									
Bemidbar	273–280	May 13–19	Jun 2–8	May 17–23	May 9–15	May 29–Jun 4	May 14–20	Jun 2–8	May 25–31
Naso	281–288	May 20–26	Jun 9–15	May 24–Jun 6***	May 16–22	Jun 5–11	May 21–Jun 3***	Jun 9–15	Jun 1–7
Beha'alotecha	289–296	May 27–Jun 2	Jun 16–22	Jun 7–13	May 23–29	Jun 12–18	Jun 4–10	Jun 16–22	Jun 8–14
Shelach	297–304	Jun 3–9	Jun 23–29	Jun 14–20	May 30–Jun 5	Jun 19–25	Jun 11–17	Jun 23–29	Jun 15–21
Korach	305–312	Jun 10–16	Jun 30–Jul 6	Jun 21–27	Jun 6–12	Jun 26–Jul 2	Jun 18–24	Jun 30–Jul 6	Jun 22–28
Chukat	313–320	Jun 17–23	Jul 7–13	Jun 28–Jul 4**	Jun 13–19	Jul 3–9	Jun 25–Jul 1*	Jul 7–13	Jun 29–Jul 5
Balak	321–328	Jun 24–30	Jul 14–20	Jun 28–Jul 4**	Jun 20–26	Jul 10–16	Jun 25–Jul 1**	Jul 14–20	Jul 6–12
Pinechas	329–336	Jul 1–7	Jul 21–27	Jul 5–11	Jun 27–Jul 3	Jul 17–23	Jul 2–8	Jul 21–27	Jul 13–19
Matot	337–344	Jul 8–14**	Jul 28–Aug 3**	Jul 12–18**	Jul 4–10**	Jul 24–30**	Jul 9–15*	Jul 28–Aug 3**	Jul 20–26**
Mas'ei	345–352	Jul 8–14**	Jul 28–Aug 3**	Jul 12–18**	Jul 4–10**	Jul 24–30**	Jul 9–15*	Jul 28–Aug 3**	Jul 20–26**
DEUTERONOMY									
Devarim	355–362	Jul 15–21	Aug 4–10	Jul 19–25	Jul 11–17	Jul 31–Aug 6	Jul 16–22	Aug 4–10	Jul 27–Aug 2
Va'etchanan	363–370	Jul 22–28	Aug 11–17	Jul 26–Aug 1	Jul 18–24	Aug 7–13	Jul 23–29	Aug 11–17	Aug 3–9
Eikev	371–378	Jul 29–Aug 4	Aug 18–24	Aug 2–8	Jul 25–31	Aug 14–20	Jul 30–Aug 5	Aug 18–24	Aug 10–16
Re'eih	379–388	Aug 5–11	Aug 25–31	Aug 9–15	Aug 1–7	Aug 21–27	Aug 6–12	Aug 25–31	Aug 17–23
Shofetim	387–394	Aug 12–18	Sep 1–7	Aug 16–22	Aug 8–14	Aug 28–Sep 3	Aug 13–19	Sep 1–7	Aug 24–30
Teitzei	395–402	Aug 19–25	Sep 8–14	Aug 23–29	Aug 15–21	Sep 4–10	Aug 20–26	Sep 8–14	Aug 31–Sep 6
Tavo	403–410	Aug 26–Sep 1	Sep 15–21	Aug 30–Sep 5	Aug 22–28	Sep 11–17	Aug 27–Sep 2	Sep 15–21	Sep 7–13
Nitzavim	411–418	Sep 2–8	Sep 22–28**	Sep 6–12**	Aug 29–Sep 4	Sep 18–24	Sep 3–9**	Sep 22–28**	Sep 14–20
Vayeilech	419–426	Sep 9–15	Sep 29–Oct 5	Sep 6–12**	Sep 5–11	Sep 25–Oct 1	Sep 3–9**	Sep 22–28**	Sep 21–27
Ha'azinu	427–434	Sep 16–22	Oct 6–12	Sep 13–26***	Sep 12–18	Oct 2–8	Sep 10–23***	Sep 29–Oct 5	Sep 28–Oct 4
Vezot Haberachah	435–442	Sep 23–Oct 2*	Oct 13–22*	Sep 27–Oct 11*	Sep 19–29*	Oct 9–18*	Sep 24–Oct 8*	Oct 6–25*	Oct 5–15*

*Vezot Haberachah/Bereishit: On Shemini Atzeret, the remaining portions of the section *Vezot Haberachah* are studied; on Simchat Torah, the section *Bereishit* is studied up to the portion of that day of the week.

**Double section: The first section is studied during the first half of the week and the second during the second half of the week.

***Study of weekly section is repeated due to holiday schedule.

Bibliography

IN ADDITION TO THE STANDARD VOLUMES OF THE BIBLE, Talmud, Midrash, and Kabbalah, the following Chassidic works are cited in the footnotes:

The Rebbe, Rabbi Menachem Mendel Schneerson (1902–1994)
    Likutei Sichot (39 volumes)
    Hitva'aduyot (*Torat Menachem,* cited by year; 94 volumes)
    Igrot Kodesh (30 volumes)
    Reshimot
    Sichot Kodesh (cited by year; 49 volumes)
    Sefer HaMa'amarim Melukat (6 volumes)
    Sefer HaMa'amarim (cited by year; 40 volumes)
    Sefer HaSichot (cited by year; 12 volumes)

Rabbi Yisrael Ba'al Shem Tov (1698–1760)
    Keter Shem Tov
    Tzava'at HaRibash

Rabbi Shneur Zalman of Liadi (1745–1812)
    Tanya (Likutei Amarim)
    Torah Or
    Likutei Torah
    Igeret HaKodesh
    Igeret HaTeshuvah
    Ma'amarei Admur HaZaken (cited by year; 32 volumes)

Rabbi DovBer Shneuri (1773–1827)
    Ma'amarei Admur HaEmtzai (19 volumes)
    Sidur im Dach

Rabbi Menachem Mendel Schneersohn of Lubavitch (1789–1866)
    Derech Mitzvotecha
    Or HaTorah (38 volumes)

Rabbi Shmuel of Lubavitch (1834–1882)
Torat Shmuel (cited by year; 30 volumes)

Rabbi Shalom DovBer Schneersohn of Lubavitch (1860–1920)
BeSha'ah sheHikdimu 5672
Kuntres Umayan
Sefer HaMa'amarim (cited by year; 35 volumes)
Yom Tov shel Rosh HaShanah 5666

Rabbi Yosef Yitzchak Schneersohn of Lubavitch (1880–1950)
HaYom Yom
Igrot Kodesh Mehorayatz (15 volumes)
Likutei Diburim (4 volumes)
Sefer HaMa'amarim (cited by year; 29 volumes)

Index

A

Aaron
    completed revelation begun by
        Moses, 208
    humility of, 209
    perspective of, 212
    symbolizes prayer, 111
Abraham
    G-d's promise to, 25
    greatest test of, 34
    inn of, 33
    not intimidated, 21
    self-surrender of, 28, 29, 39
    three altars of, 22
    tithing spoils of war, 23
    transcended own abilities, 20
Action (in contrast to study), 204
Adam and Eve
    burial site of, 36
    innocence of, 6
Adversity
    as opportunity, 127
    G-d gives us means to
        overcome, 357, 365
    neutralizing through power of
        Aaron, 280
    See also Tests
Almonds, 310
Altar(s)
    alludes to Jewish heart, 200
    inner, 164
    of Abraham, 22
    outer, 180
    sanctification through mere
        touch of, 162
Amalek
    as manifestation of inner
        doubts, 132, 134
    goal of, 318
    response to, 318
Ambition. *See* Aspiration
Ammon (nation), 360
Angels, 31
Animals
    cattle, sheep, and goats, 155
    cruelty towards, 146
    domestic and wild, 96
    male and female, 197
    mammals, foul, and fish, 193
    not predatory in messianic
        era, 265
    symbolic of emotions, 250
Ark (of Noah)
    as study and prayer, 13
    leaving, 15
Ark (of Covenant)
    contained both tablets and
        Torah scroll, 426
    preceded the Jewish people in
        desert, 294
    significance of dimensions
        of, 178
Arm and Head (blow of Gad), 439
Arrogance (warped mental
    attitude), 220
Asceticism, 343
Asher (tribe), 440
Aspiration
    as foundation for relationship
        with G-d, 105
    never ending, 135
Assembly (on seventh year), 423
Assimilation (urgency of dealing
    with), 84
Atomic Energy (spiritual lesson
    of), 370

Authority, 303

B

Balaam (counterbalanced by
    Abraham), 324
Balak, 322
Balance (in life), 30
Benjamin (as Jewish child at
    risk), 84
Bikurim. See First Fruits
Blessing (human effort conduit
    for), 128, 130
Blood
    plague of, 113
    prohibition of consuming, 381
Blood Avenger, 392
Body (education of), 145
Breastplate. *See* High Priest

C

Cain and Abel (lesson of), 7
Canaanites (personify unrectified
    emotions), 171
Candelabrum
    as insight, 179
    as transformation of material
        pursuits, 152
    kindling of, 290
    seven lamps of, 179
Cave of Machpeilah, 36
Challenges. *See* Adversity, Tests
Chaos (world of), 66
Charity (leads to wealth), 384
    See also Tithing, Wealth
Cherubim, 151
Child who knows not how to
    ask, 124
Children, 151
    of G-d, 373, 383, 431
    See also Education
Circumcision
    of Egyptians, 79

spiritual significance of, 26
Cities of Refuge, 350, 351, 392
Commandments
    analogous to clothing, 52
    bringing life to, 236
    fulfilling with joy, 95
    importance of fulfilling
        seemingly minor, 372
    mistaken performance of, 402
    that defy rational
        explanation, 264
Compromise, 107
Confidence
    in G-d hastens redemption, 104
    when tackling mundane
        activities, 53
    See also Trust
Contention (avoiding), 278
Creation (purpose of), 4
Curses (in Torah, are blessings in
    disguise), 266, 380, 416

D

Dathan and Aviram, 308
Daughters of Tzelofchad, 352
Death (purification from
    defilement of), 314
Defilement. *See* Ritual Defilement
Devotion
    accessible to all, 277
    irrational, 405
    unconditional, 148, 319
Dinah (intentions and efforts
    of), 64
Discharge (bodily), 228
Disease. *See* Illness
Discouragement, 47
Divine Providence. *See* Providence
Divine Soul. *See* Soul
Doorpost, 122
Doubt, 132, 301
    See also Amalek

Dust (Jewish people compared positively to), 325

E

Eating (as sacrifice), 194
Ecstasy (management of), 210
Edom (nation), 360
Education
environment of children during, 237
importance of Jewish education, 268, 437
key to successful education of children, 175
using "soft speech" in, 249
See also Children
Effort (reason why necessary), 425
Egypt
as familiar level of Divine consciousness, 121
elevating wealth of, 129
Eleazar (son of Aaron), 340
Eliezer, 37–40
Emotions
are measure of maturity, 394
born from intellect, 250
unrectified, 171
way to rectify, 360
Enoch (holiness of), 9
Enthusiasm (as key to transformation), 138
Envy. *See* Jealousy
Ephod, 183
See also High Priest
Ephraim and Manasseh, 78, 93, 94
Esau
and Jacob, 44–45, 48
rectification of, 62, 63
Evil
as distortion of holiness, 120
exists to provide freedom of choice, 380
how to win war against, 396
is only a tool for G-d's hiding Himself, 323
seen in others is reflection of our own, 17, 424
Exile
compared to dream, 77
façade of, 63
not feeling at home in, 57, 87
prototype of, 103
purpose of, 63, 86, 93–94, 102, 108
two aspects of life in, 78, 85, 92
yearning for end of, 110

F

Faith
internalization of, 108
is inherent to Jews, 301, 421
of patriarchs and matriarchs, 110
Family (primary setting for loving fellow Jew), 274
Festivals (joy on), 386
First Fruits, 404
Fish (as constant Divine consciousness), 193
Flood (Noah)
as exile, 14
as holocaust, 18
as purification, 16
as worldly stress, 13
spiritual sustenance during, 98
Food
and water, 315
of soul is Torah, 315
Foolishness (holy and unholy), 153
Forgiveness (through understanding nature of human evil), 90
Free choice
and reward, 418
purpose of, 380

used by early generations to
ignore G-d, 4

G

Galbanum (incense ingredient), 187
Gender Equality, 397
    See also Male and
        Female, Women
Generosity, 38
Gershon (son of Levi), 282
G-d
    imitation of, 378
    Jew's unseverable relationship
        with, 431
    only loves, 358
    testifying to existence and
        essence of, 393
Golden Calf ("forced" upon the
    nation), 167
Gossip, 219, 401
Grain, 400
Grapes, 400
Gratitude, 399
Greek Letter, 161
Greek Philosophy, 161

H

Hagar, 21
Hail (plague, uniqueness of), 116
Hakheil. See Assembly
Half-Shekel (lesson of), 166
Ham (son of Noah), 17
Hatred
    baseless hatred rooted in
        ego, 339
    war against, 342
Health (by virtue of connection
    with G-d), 275
Heaven and Earth (as
    witnesses), 428
Heresy (of government as sign of
    Messiah's imminent arrival), 217

High Priest
    daily offering of, 201
    garments of, 159, 160, 183,
        184, 233
    obligation of to bury
        unattended corpse, 248
    "spiritual high priest," 277
Holiness
    Divine assistance in
        attaining, 244
    infusing life with, 242
    meaning of, 240
Honesty in Business, 243
Honoring Parents, 245
Houses of Study (positive
    influence of), 33
Hospitality, 81
Humility, 296

I

Idolatry (as any violation of G-d's
    will), 201, 347
Illness (physical and spiritual), 142
Incarnation (rectifying
    previous), 144
Incense (service)
    as inclusiveness, 187
    as private service, 164
    dangers of, 309
Indifference, 113, 318
Individuality
    as expression of Divine
        personality, 364
    expressed in prayer, 286
Inheritance (laws of), 352
Inspiration (must be followed by
    self-refinement), 46
Instinct (development of through
    Torah study), 214, 410
Intellect
    holy vs. secular, 161
    using in study of Torah, 367

Intention, 286
Interest (prohibition of), 260
Intimidation (by the "world"), 21,
   341, 439
Isaac, 45–49
Ishmael
   as "fallen" love, 42
   repentance of, 41
Israel (name), 61

J

Jacob
   and Esau, 44–45
   two names of, 61
Japheth (son of Noah), 17
Jealousy
   cure for, 139
   proper use of, 54
Jethro, 133–136
Joseph
   beauty of, 72
   dreams of, 68, 76
   meaning of name, 55, 126
   repaying brothers with
      kindness, 69, 90
   sensitivity of, 74
   silver goblet of, 82
   temptation of, 73
Joshua, 333
Joy
   in fulfilling the
      commandments, 95
   on festivals, 386
Jubilee Year, 257
Judges and sheriffs, 388

K

Kehat (son of Levi), 282
King (as higher authority), 389
Knowledge
   knowing G-d, 278
   of good and evil, 6

Korach
   error of, 306, 307
   sons of, 331
Kosher animals (significance of
   signs of), 213

L

Laban, 56–58
Land of Israel
   conquest of, 362
   inheritance of every Jew, 25
   three ways of portioning, 332
Leadership
   for each generation, 422
   involves weighing impact of
      actions, 316
   qualifications for, 48, 209, 320,
      349, 374
Lemech, 8
Lending money, 144
Leprosy. *See Tzara'at*
Letters (engraved and written), 426
Levi (sons of), 282, 283
Levites
   corrective role of, 350
   spiritual, 277, 279
Lice (plague), 114
Light to the Nations, 441
Lineage, 277
Locusts (plague), 118
Lot (nephew of Abraham), 23, 31
Love
   forbidden, 246
   G-d loves us at all times, 358
   of fellow and love of G-d, 140,
      274, 424
   of G-d has two levels, 377
   of G-d in contrast with
      repentance, 415
   of G-d, "love of delights," 311
   of G-d, attaining, 369

M

Ma'akeh. See Railing

Male and Female
  complementary relationship, 8
  harmony between, 232
  See also Gender
    Equality, Women

Malki-tzedek, 23

Manasseh (half tribe of), 344

Manna, 130, 131

Marriage
  analogous to Jew's relationship
    with G-d, 37
  of physical and spiritual, 39

Material World
  ideal relationship to, 58
  infusing with Divinity, 156, 242
  importance of, 348

Menorah. *See* Candelabrum

Menstruation (inner meaning
  of), 229

Mentors, 389, 434

Merari, 283

Messiah (seemingly scandalous
  entry of), 71

Messianic Era
  nature of, 202, 432, 433
  need to study subject of, 328
  sharing G-d's dream of, 328
  "taste" of through Chasidic
    teachings, 360
  ways to hasten, 202, 265, 328,
    359, 365, 432, 433
  See also Redemption

Midianites, 339, 342

Miracles
  need to learn from, 300
  human effort as conduit for, 128

Miriam, 315

Misdeeds
  correction of, 284, 406

may serve as impetus for proper
  conduct, 254
surest way to make amends
  for, 324
transcendence of on *Yom
  Kippur,* 234
unintentional misdeeds reveal
  "subconscious" self, 196
way to avoid committing, 285
See also Repentance

Misfortune
  positive aspects of, 227, 346
  transformation of, 416

Mitzvot. See Commandments

Moab, 360

Modesty
  as means of regaining innate
    innocence, 6
  tremendous power of, 327

Moses
  attitude towards rebels, 308
  every Jew contains a spark
    of, 376
  lived life to the fullest, 420
  message to Edomite king, 317
  need for, 185
  perspective of, 212, 340
  reason for shining face of, 172
  reason why didn't enter Land
    of Israel, 425
  selfless devotion to Jewish
    people, 374
  spark of Moses in leaders and
    individuals, 442
  symbolizing Torah, 111

N

Nadav and Avihu, 210

Nature
  laws of, 147, 300
  transcendence of, 211

Negativity (can always be overcome), 228
    See also Confidence
Noah, 11–17
Noahide Laws, 436
Non-Jews
    have deep-seated high regard for Jews, 267
    significance of G-d's offering Torah to, 436

O

Omer (fiftieth day of counting of), 257
Ownership, 259

P

Passover (festival, names of and their meaning), 251
Pharaoh
    as distorted expression of G-d's power, 120
    dreams of, 76
    talking to, 112
Pinechas, 330
Pit (law of), 143
Plagues (ten), 113–121
Prayer
    as "food" of G-d, 334
    selfless, 60
    when favorable outcome seems natural, 80
Precautions, 238
Pride. *See* Arrogance
Priest
    "inner priest," 158, 203, 390
    parts of animals given to, 390
    purpose of, 203
    quickness of, 310
    spiritual priesthood accessible to all Jews, 312
    See also High Priest

Promised Land. *See* Land of Israel
Providence (understanding indirectly), 169

R

Rachel, 54–55
    devotion of, 65
Railing (*mitzvah* to put on roof, as instruction for newlyweds), 398
Rebecca, 38–41
Rebellion (as cry for deeper relationship), 295
Rebuke (gift of), 356
Rectification (world of), 66
Redemption
    backsliding during, 121
    of those opposed to redemption, 119
    promise of, 106
    See also Messianic Era
Renewal
    of covenant every day, 407
    possibility of, 291
    through shofar, 335
Repentance
    as returning "robbed" spiritual goods, 198
    constant possibility of, 12, 118
    elevates Divine spark in misdeed, 170
    in contrast to Love of G-d, 415
    male and female varieties of, 197
    past misdeeds as opportunity for, 167
    power of, 230, 331, 406
    See also Misdeeds
Reuben and Gad (tribes of), 343
Revelation (ongoing), 368
Reward
    and free choice, 418

as intrinsic component of
relationship with G-d, 264
as satisfaction of
accomplishment, 261
importance of knowing
about, 328
infinite, 372
supernatural reward
for fulfilling G-d's
directives, 163
See also Free Choice
Ritual Defilement, 340
Rosh HaShanah, 335
need for prayer despite decree
of livelihood on, 408

S

Sabbath
liberation from personal
enslavement on, 262
purpose of, 131
significance of rest on, 174
Sabbatical Year
corresponds to seventh
millennium, 258
lesson of, 256
Sacrifice (Temple)
and respect for animal life, 235
as drawing close to G-d, 192, 235
as renunciation of animalistic
orientation, 155
during Messianic era, 202
elevation of all creation
through, 194, 287
message of oil and wine
offering, 302
reason fish not used for, 193
sanctifying world and ourselves
through, 269
significance of male and female
animals for, 197

significance of sacrificial
procedures, 205
substituted by prayer, 334
Sanctuary
as way of overcoming spiritual
handicaps, 182
furnishings of, 154
making our lives into, 206, 429
protection of, 276
significance of gold, silver, and
copper in, 176
significance of tapestry
materials in, 177
three kinds of, 150
Sarah
positive influence on
Ishmael, 41
superior spiritual insight of, 32
Second Passover, 292
Secular Society (relationship
to), 115
Self
authentic, 20
inflated sense of, 339
surrender of, 28
transcendence of, 29
Self-Sacrifice
inner strength of, 362
of Moses, 168, 374
Sensuality
and self-centeredness, 6
as "fallen" version of love of
G-d, 42
elevation of, 186
Setbacks. *See* Misfortune
Shabbat. See Sabbath
Shem (son of Noah), 17
Shelomit bat Dibri, 254
Shemini Atzeret, 336
Shemitah Year. *See* Sabbatical Year
Shofar

breaks confines of language, 335
when *Rosh HaShanah* coincides
with Sabbath, 252
Silence (of G-d), 288
Simplicity (virtue of), 440
Sin. *See* Misdeeds
Slave Mentality (is assumption
about laws of nature), 300
Slavery (as one's work), 262
Sodom (wickedness of), 30
Soul
Divine, 5, 326
Divine in contrast to animating,
44, 414
transformation of animating,
326, 336
Speech
power of, 10, 401
refined and delicate, 50
should be imbued with holy
intentions, 338
Spies
error of, 298, 299
misdirected spiritual
orientation of, 299, 302
Splitting of Sea (as immersion in
holiness), 134
Stars (metaphor for Jewish
People), 24
Substitution (sacrifice), 270
Supernatural (as "second
nature"), 147
Superstition, 391
Speech
power of, 241
soft and hard, 249
Stubbornness (positive and
negative), 184
Sukah (spiritual significance
of), 253

Synagogues (positive influence
of), 33

T

Tabernacle. *See* Sanctuary
Tablets
breaking of, 374, 375
difference between first and
second, 172
Tassels, 304
Temurah. See Substitution
Ten Commandments (reason for
repetition of), 367
Tests (of faith, purpose of), 34, 382
See also Adversity
Thought
carrying first positive thought
of the day, 399
power of, 241, 331
Tikun. See Rectification
Tithing, 23
See also Charity, Wealth
Tohu. See Chaos
Torah
accessible to every Jew, 417
analogous to bread, 52
as antidote to destructive
notions, 70
as refuge from evil
inclination, 392
attaining instinct through, 214
engraved and inscribed, 426
enthusiasm for, 113
focal point of life, 429
immersion in study of, 438
inner dimension of, 95
purpose of, 102
receiving each day, 134
revelation of G-d through, 188
study of brings harmony to
world, 226
study of vs. action, 204

study with pure and humble
heart, 225

sweetness of, 438

tool for purpose of humanity, 4

universal relevance of, 136

vocation of, 89

Tower of Babel, 18

Transience, 293

Trees (fruit bearing vs. barren), 394

Trials. *See* Tests

Trickery, 49

Trust (in G-d), 391

See also Confidence

Tumah. See Ritual Defilement

Tzara'at

as call for character
refinement, 216

as degeneration of holy
energy, 219

as spiritual blockage, 218

negative energy of neutralized
by Torah study, 224

on head, 220

priest judges cases of, 222

progressive symptoms of, 221

Tzitzit. See Tassels

U

Unity

in community, 97, 404

necessity for Jewish unity, 160

of Jacob's sons, 183

power of, 361

symbolism of half-shekel, 166

three ways of attaining, 412

through focusing on G-d,
137, 413

W

War (against evil), 396, 439

Wealth

and tithing, 23

challenge of, 430

purpose of, 45

spiritual, 56, 267

See also Charity, Tithing

Wild Beasts (plague), 115

Women

commandments entrusted
to, 88

depersonalization of, 8

higher spiritual insight of, 32

innate deep-seated faith of, 123

unique ability of Jewish women
and girls, 40

See also Gender Equality, Male
and Female

Work

enslavement to, 262

for constructive purpose, 261

is receptacle for G-d's
blessing, 385

value of, 260

World. *See* Material World

Y

Yom Kippur

as renewal of our relationship
with G-d, 232

transcendence of misdeeds
on, 234

RABBI MENACHEM MENDEL SCHNEERSON (1902–1994), one of the great Jewish leaders of the 20th century, changed the map of world Judaism and deeply affected both Jews and non-Jews throughout the world. His written works span over 200 volumes, many of which are still being published. His students continue to disseminate his teachings in many varied forms, while his global network of emissaries continues to spread his message of goodness and kindness, a message that informs every page of *Daily Wisdom*.

CHABAD HOUSE
PUBLICATIONS